Pearson BTEC National

Applied Psychology
Book 1
Certificate Units

Revised Edition

Cara Flanagan • Rob Liddle
Advisor: Mark Walsh

Illuminate Publishing

Acknowledgements

The team who manage and produce this book are simply the best.

Illuminate Publishing, with the psychology list headed by the unique Rick Jackman, and assisted by Clare Jackman, Peter Burton, Saskia Burton and Vikki Mann, represent the best in educational publishing – always looking out for their authors and also for the people who buy the books.

Nic Watson, our editor, puts nothing short of love into ensuring our final product is as perfect as can be. We couldn't do it without her.

The third part of our team is design, fitting the text and pictures on each page. The initial ideas came from the gloriously talented Nigel Harriss and then Sarah Clifford of Kamae Design had the job of implementing this and has done a fabulous job of it.

Finally Cara, the lead author, owes much to Rob for the huge amount of work he has done (and always with such grace) and to the invaluable advice from Mark.

A very special thank you to all of you.

Endorsement Statement

In order to ensure that this resource offers high-quality support for the associated Pearson qualification, it has been through a review process by the awarding body. This process confirms that this resource fully covers the teaching and learning content of the specification or part of a specification at which it is aimed. It also confirms that it demonstrates an appropriate balance between the development of subject skills, knowledge and understanding, in addition to preparation for assessment.

Endorsement does not cover any guidance on assessment activities or processes (e.g. practice questions or advice on how to answer assessment questions), included in the resource nor does it prescribe any particular approach to the teaching or delivery of a related course.

While the publishers have made every attempt to ensure that advice on the qualification and its assessment is accurate, the official specification and associated assessment guidance materials are the only authoritative source of information and should always be referred to for definitive guidance.

Pearson examiners have not contributed to any sections in this resource relevant to examination papers for which they have responsibility.

Examiners will not use endorsed resources as a source of material for any assessment set by Pearson. Endorsement of a resource does not mean that the resource is required to achieve this Pearson qualification, nor does it mean that it is the only suitable material available to support the qualification, and any resource lists produced by the awarding body shall include this and other appropriate resources.

The authors

Cara has written many books for A Level Psychology, and she speaks at and organises student conferences. In addition to books, she is senior editor of *Psychology Review*. In a previous life she was a teacher probably for more years than you have been alive and also an examiner for an equally long time. Her spare time (what there is of it) involves travelling with her husband and/or children (all now 25+). She lives in the Highlands of Scotland (despite being American by birth) and loves a long walk in the mountains and night in a bothy.

Rob was an A Level Psychology teacher for more than 20 years, before turning to writing. He ventured back into teaching again recently and would like to give a big shout out to his ex-colleagues at Winstanley College. In his spare moments, Rob likes nothing better than to pluck away skill-lessly at his guitar. He is enthusiastically looking forward to *Frozen 2* coming out, even though his granddaughters couldn't care less.

Mark is a teacher, writer and mental health worker when he's not baking bread or playing football. He currently works with students in further and higher education teaching sociological psychology and providing mental health support. He has written many textbooks, course specifications and exam papers over the last 25 years, usually whilst listening to long, slow albums of electronic music.

Published in 2022 by Illuminate Publishing Limited, an imprint of Hodder Education, an Hachette UK Company, Carmelite House, 50 Victoria Embankment, London EC4Y 0DZ

Orders: please contact Hachette UK Distribution, Hely Hutchinson Centre, Milton Road, Didcot, Oxfordshire, OX11 7HH. Telephone: +44 (0)1235 827827. Email: education@hachette.co.uk. Lines are open from 9 a.m. to 5 p.m., Monday to Friday. You can also order through our website: www.hoddereducation.co.uk

© Cara Flanagan, Rob Liddle, Mark Walsh 2022

The moral rights of the authors have been asserted.

All rights reserved. No part of this book may be reprinted, reproduced or utilised in any form or by any electronic, mechanical, or other means, now known or hereafter invented, including photocopying and recording, or in any information storage and retrieval system, without permission in writing from the publishers.

British Library Cataloguing in Publication Data

A catalogue record for this book is available from the British Library

ISBN 978-1-913963-38-5

Printed by Ashford Colour Press Ltd

Impression 2

Year 2023

The publisher's policy is to use papers that are natural, renewable and recyclable products made from wood grown in well-managed forests and other controlled sources. The logging and manufacturing processes are expected to conform to the environmental regulations of the country of origin.

Every effort has been made to contact copyright holders of material produced in this book. Great care has been taken by the authors and publisher to ensure that either formal permission has been granted for the use of copyright material reproduced, or that copyright material has been used under the provision of fairdealing guidelines in the UK – specifically that it has been used sparingly, solely for the purpose of criticism and review, and has been properly acknowledged. If notified, the publisher will be pleased to rectify any errors or omissions at the earliest opportunity.

We have made every effort to ensure that website addresses are correct at the time of printing, and links are provided for information only. Illuminate Publishing cannot be held responsible for the content of any website listed or detailed in this book.

Editor: Nic Watson
Design: Nigel Harriss
Layout: Kamae Design

Contents

Introduction
How to use this book   4
What is psychology?   6

Unit 1   Psychological approaches and applications   8

Content area A: Key psychological approaches, their assumptions and concepts   10
   Revision summary   52
   Multiple-choice questions   54
   Assessment and revision guidance, Practice questions, answers and feedback   58–63

Content area B: Application of psychological approaches   64
   Revision summary   88
   Multiple-choice questions   90
   Assessment and revision guidance, Practice questions, answers and feedback   92–95

Unit 2   Conducting psychological research   96

Learning aim A: Understand research methods and their importance in psychological inquiry   98
   Assessment guidance   116

Learning aim B: Plan research to investigate psychological questions   118
   Assessment guidance   132

Learning aim C: Carry out a pilot study to explore current issues in psychology   134
Learning aim D: Review implications of research into psychological inquiry   142
   Assessment guidance   144

Index with glossary   146

References
A full set of references is available for download from the Illuminate Publishing website.
Please visit www.illuminatepublishing.com/btecpsychreferences1_revised_edition

National Certificate in Applied Psychology BTEC Level 3

Structure of the qualification

Unit	Unit title	Type	How assessed	GLH Guided learning hours	TQT Total qualification time (an estimate of the total amount of time to complete and show achievement for the qualification)
1	Psychological approaches and applications	Mandatory	External exam 1.5 hours 72 marks	90	235 hours This means: Unit 1: 90 GLH + about 25 hours revising and taking the exam. Unit 2: 90 GLH + about 30 hours writing three reports and conducting the pilot study.
2	Conducting psychological research	Mandatory and synoptic	Internal	90	

How to use this book

Unit 1 and Unit 2 both open with a spread which has:
- A set of questions to start you thinking about the content to come.
- A detailed table of contents.

Content areas or learning aims?
Unit 1 is divided into *content areas* A and B (because it is externally assessed).

Unit 2 is divided into *learning aims* A, B, C and D (because it is internally assessed).

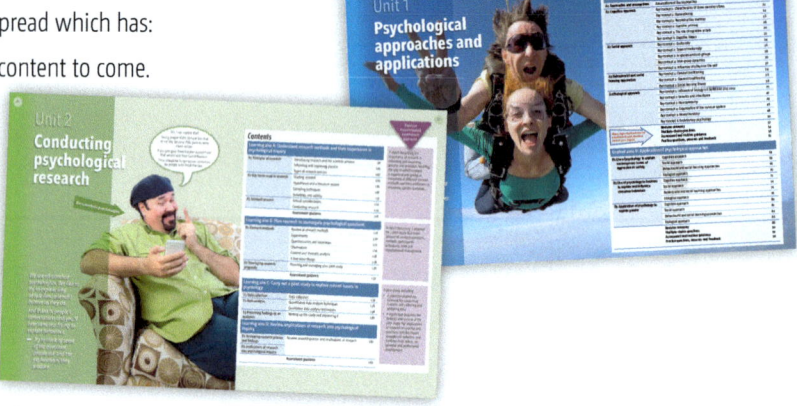

Main spreads
The specification content is covered on spreads such as the one on the facing page.
They all contain a similar pattern of boxes.

Extra material

Unit 1
Content areas A and B end with:

Summaries to revise from.

Multiple-choice questions to test yourself.

Assessment guidance to help supply the right material in your exam answers.

Revision guidance.

Practice questions, answers and feedback to see how answers are marked.

Unit 2
Learning aims A, B, C+D end with:

Assessment guidance to help you to write your internally assessed report.

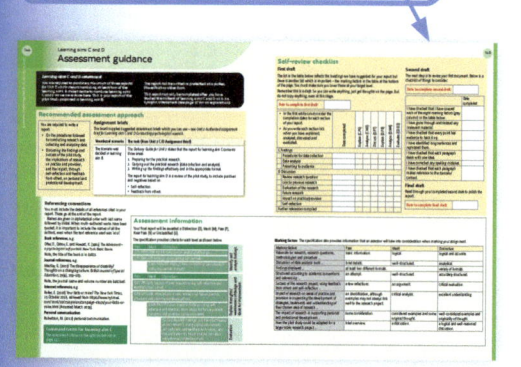

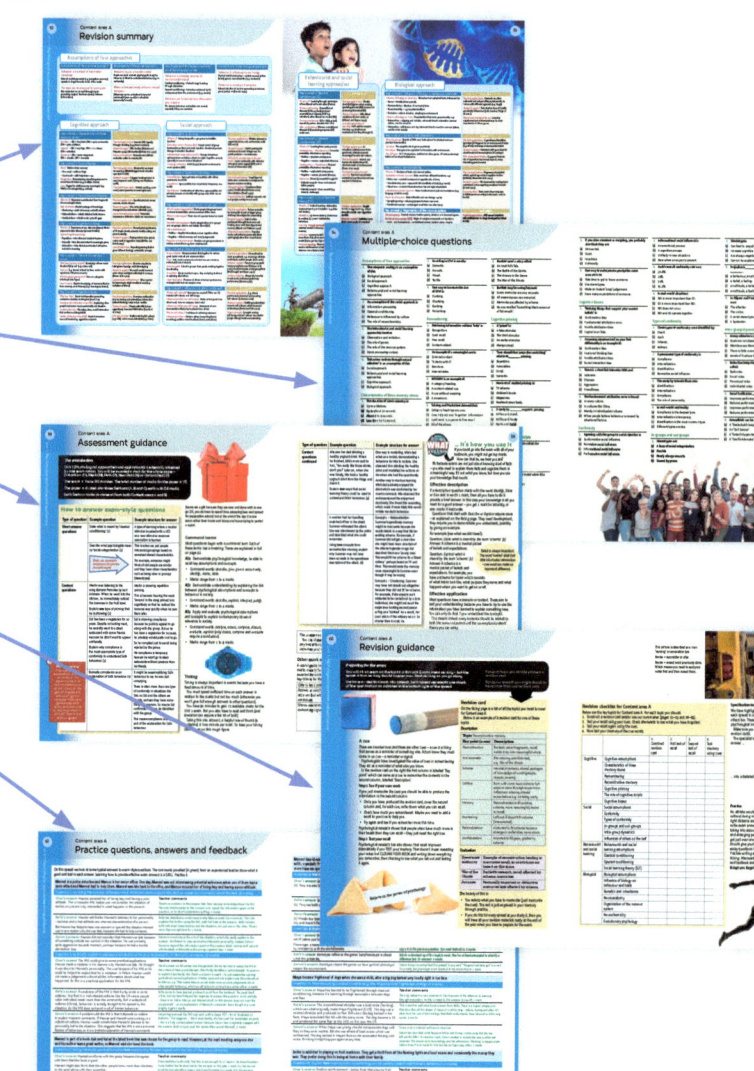

A beginning
Each spread begins with something we hope will grab your interest – it represents the nub of the topic to be studied on the spread.

Description
Assessment objective 1 (AO1) is concerned with your ability to report *detailed* descriptions of psychological knowledge and demonstrate your *understanding* of this knowledge.

We have generally presented the AO1 material just on the left-hand side of each spread, though sometimes it is on both sides.

Evaluation
Assessment objective 3 (AO3) is concerned with your ability to *evaluate* (*assess*, *analyse*, etc.) the assumptions and concepts you have learned about.

On most spreads in this book we have presented some AO3 material on the right-hand side. Some topics don't require evaluation so there isn't any on the spread.

Special note
Each evaluation point is divided into three **PET** paragraphs because this is a great way to ensure you explain your point well:
1. **Point** State the Point simply.
2. **Elaboration** The point is now Explained, using Evidence and/or Examples.
3. **This/Therefore** ... Finish with a conclusion often beginning 'This suggests' or 'This shows' or 'Therefore ...'.

That's your PET-friendly evaluation.

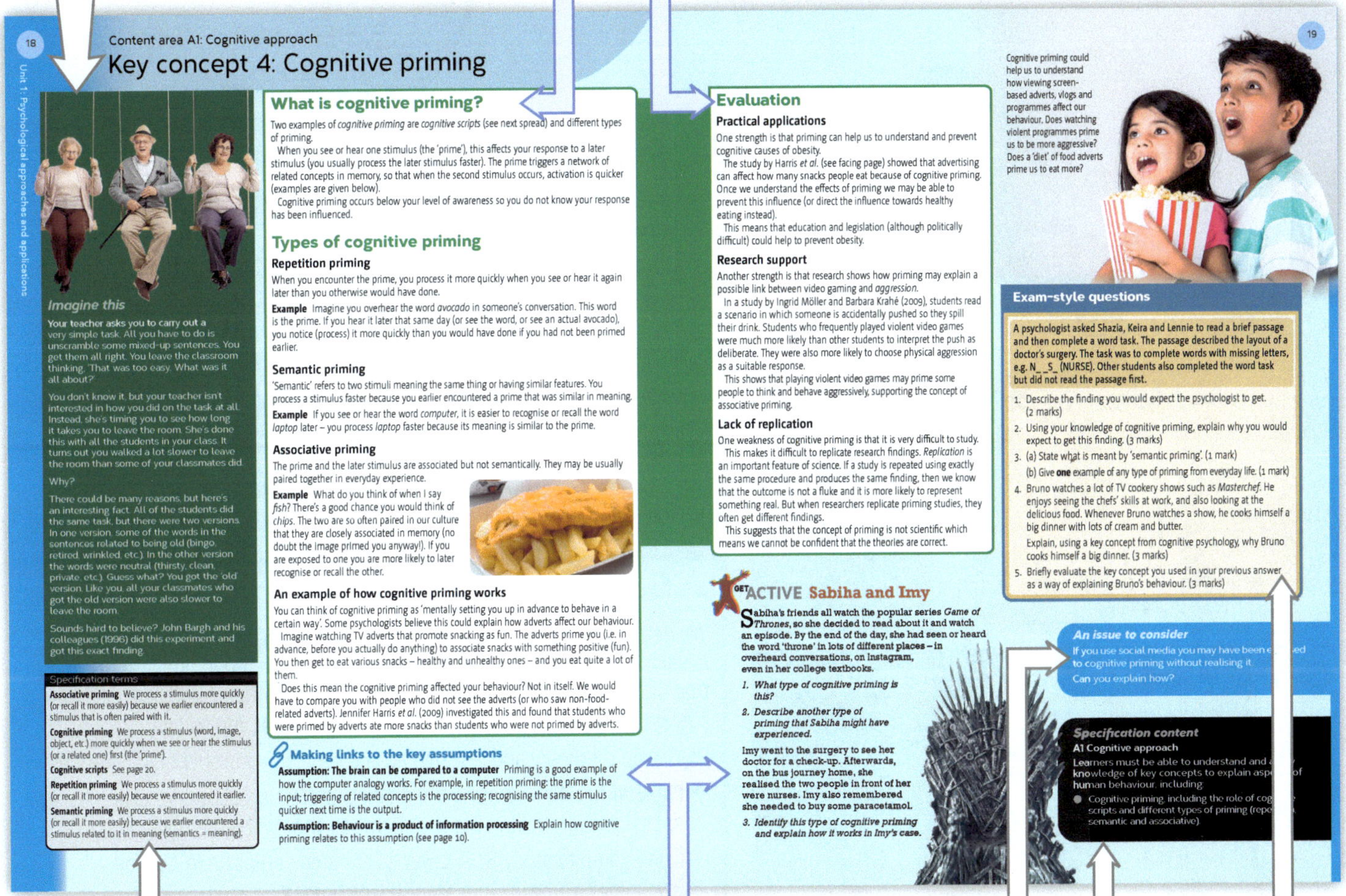

Specification terms
We have defined the terms in the specification box for this spread. Other terms are defined in the index/glossary starting on page 146.

What are assessment objectives?
At the end of your studies you hope to have gained a qualification – this means someone has to assess your work.

To assist this process there are three assessment objectives (AOs): AO1, AO2 and AO3.

The course is designed so you can include all these AOs in what you learn. Each involves different skills:
- AO1 involves reporting the knowledge coherently and including key terminology (details).
- AO2 involves application skills (see right).
- AO3 involves using PET skills (see top of page).

Application
Assessment objective 2 (AO2) is concerned with being able to *apply* your psychological knowledge and understanding.

Many of the topics you study are applied and therefore involve AO2.

On each spread there is a '**Get active**' which gives you a chance to practise this AO2 skill of application.

'**Making links to the key assumptions**' helps you to understand how the key concepts relate to the assumptions for each approach.

An issue to consider
An opportunity to reflect on the issues discussed on the spread.

Specification content
Tells you what you are required to study on this topic.

Exam-style questions
Questions similar to those in the exam provide some exam practice.

In Unit 2 these boxes are called **Assessment practice**, and aim to help you practise skills for writing your internally-assessed reports.

What is psychology?

Psychologists study everything about people – and what could be more interesting than people? Just look in any newspaper or on social media – full of stories about people's behaviour.

These stories tell us about what people are doing and try to explain why they do the things they do – for example, reporting that someone has been married for 60 years, and offering an explanation about why their marriage is so successful. Or reporting that a person has committed a terrorist act and trying to explain that.

But psychology is more than just everyday interest in people...

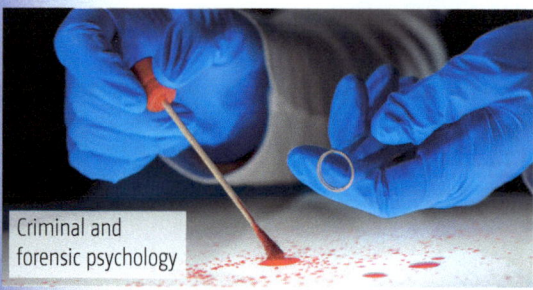

Studying people (and animals).

Health psychology

Criminal and forensic psychology

Child psychology

Sport psychology

... Psychology is a science

This means it is a systematic investigation of what people do and why. This systematic investigation involves two things:

1. Developing theories to explain why people do things. In Unit 1 you will be studying the main approaches (theories) in psychology.
2. Conducting research studies to collect evidence of what people actually do. In Unit 2 you will be studying the research process.

Science is not perfect. Science takes small steps towards gradually getting at the 'truth'. This is where evaluation comes in – at all times scientists must question and retest their ideas.

But science is more than knowledge and evaluation...

... Science is applied

We depend on science to govern our world. Without science we could not develop safe and effective methods to treat disease, build bridges or buildings that don't fall down, try to forecast dangerous weather conditions, develop successful methods to deal with criminal behaviour and so on.

Psychological theory and research have a very large number of applications.

→ **Physical health** – advising the medical profession about, for example, how to best explain treatments to patients so they will remember what to do.

If you go on to study BTEC Level 3 Extended Certificate in Applied Psychology, you will study **Health psychology**.

→ **Mental health** – developing treatments for depression or anorexia and so on. This involves testing both psychological therapies and physical treatments such as drugs.

If you go on to study the BTEC Level 3 Extended Certificate you may have the chance to study **Psychopathology** which is concerned with mental health.

The following three branches of psychology are also options for the Extended Certificate.

→ **Criminal and forensic psychology** Theories and approaches in psychology are applied to explain why some people become criminals. Psychological approaches are also used to develop successful methods to reduce reoffending and to research strategies to help the police solve crimes.

→ **Child psychology** is concerned with explaining how and why people change as they develop from birth through to adolescence.

→ **Sport psychology** Any sportsperson will tell you that winning is all in the mind. Yes, you do have to have certain skills but in the end it is the winning mindset that makes the difference between success and failure.

Professions using psychology

The BTEC course is a vocational one – which means it is concerned with the world of work. Therefore, a focus of the course is how the academic study of psychology is applied to the world of work. Someone who is a professional psychologist is likely to have a degree in psychology and then has gone on to do a postgraduate degree.

On the left we have mentioned some of these vocational areas, such as **criminal and forensic psychology** and **sport psychology**, but there are jobs in these fields (and the ones further down this page) that don't require a degree in psychology or even a degree, but do benefit from knowledge of psychology, such as the ones below:

- Healthcare practitioner (nurse, radiographer, dietician, paramedic, physiotherapist, social care worker).
- Social worker.
- Teacher (understanding cognitive development).
- Counsellor (bereavement, drugs).
- Chaplain.
- Town planner.
- Police (dealing with people, not just crime).
- Crime scene investigator.
- Working with animals (zoo keeper, veterinarian, trainer).
- Law (solicitor, judge, court clerk).
- Military psychologist.
- Sports coach.
- Advertising and marketing.

Any job involving people involves psychology – even **mind reading**. But psychology does not teach you to actually read minds, it teaches you about what people are likely to think and do.

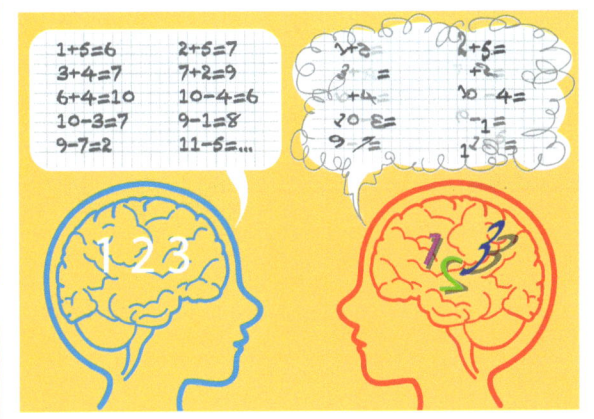

Dyscalculia – trouble with numbers. Perhaps a psychologist can help.

Specialist branches of psychology

Clinical psychology
People often confuse psychologists with psychiatrists – a psychiatrist is first of all qualified as a medical doctor and then specialises in psychiatry. Psychiatrists study psychological disorders, diagnose patients and provide treatments.

Clinical psychologists, counselling psychologists and other therapists are concerned with health issues – both physical and mental (psychopathology). Like psychiatrists, they may research, diagnose and treat clients. However, only a psychiatrist can prescribe medicine.

Educational psychology
Educational psychologists may be involved in designing, implementing and evaluating educational programmes for autistic or dyslexic children. They may also advise on how to deal with problem behaviour and may work directly with children who challenge the educational system. They are often involved in using psychological tests, such as intelligence tests, to help diagnose educational or behavioural issues.

Organisational psychology
Also sometimes called industrial psychology, occupational psychology or business psychology – using psychological theory and research in the world of commerce, addressing the needs of employers, employees and consumers. An organisational psychologist might help human resources departments to interview applicants and find the best person–organisation fit. An organisational psychologist might also advise on strategies to improve sales by addressing customer needs or how to assess consumer satisfaction. The 'organisation' does not have to be commercial – the focus of the organisational psychologist is on how any organisation functions.

Environmental psychology
Environmental psychology studies the interaction between people and their environment, i.e. their surroundings. The physical and human environment affects our behaviour, feelings, health and performance. Environmental psychologists might advise on the design of cities or buildings or office work spaces, including schools and hospitals as well as businesses. They are also concerned with ways to encourage people to care more for the environment.

Research psychology
Many psychologists work in universities, teaching students but also pursuing their own research interests.

What are the ethical issues of using psychology to boost sales or win more votes? All practising psychologists must be registered with the British Psychological Society (BPS) and must show respect, competence, responsibility and integrity. So they can use psychology to make more money as long as they behave ethically in doing so.

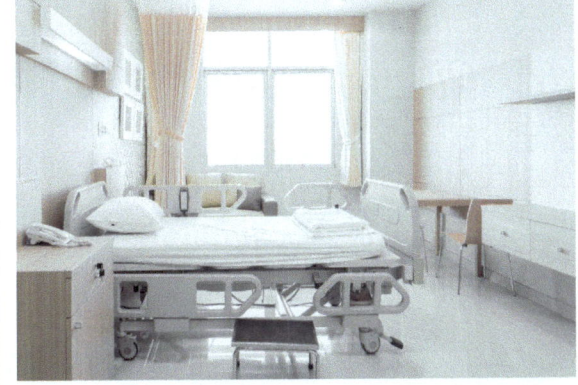

Designed by a psychologist? Research shows people recover more quickly if they have a nice view from their hospital room (Ulrich 1984).

Unit 1
Psychological approaches and applications

What is happening in these people's heads?

What is going on in their bodies?

How is their behaviour affecting each other?

How have their past experiences affected them?

There are so many different ways of explaining the same behaviour – what is the best approach to take?

Contents

Content area A: Key psychological approaches, their assumptions and concepts

A1 Approaches and assumptions	Assumptions of four approaches	10
A1 Cognitive approach	Key concept 1: Characteristics of three memory stores	12
	Key concept 2: Remembering	14
	Key concept 3: Reconstructive memory	16
	Key concept 4: Cognitive priming	18
	Key concept 5: The role of cognitive scripts	20
	Key concept 6: Cognitive biases	22
A2 Social approach	Key concept 1: Conformity	24
	Key concept 2: Types of conformity	26
	Key concept 3: In-groups and out-groups	28
	Key concept 4: Intra-group dynamics	30
	Key concept 5: Influences of others on the self	32
A3 Behaviourist and social learning approaches	Key concept 1: Classical conditioning	34
	Key concept 2: Operant conditioning	36
	Key concept 3: Social learning theory	38
A4 Biological approach	Key concept 1: Influence of biology on behaviour and traits	40
	Key concept 2: Genetics and inheritance	42
	Key concept 3: Neuroanatomy	44
	Key concept 4: Organisation of the nervous system	46
	Key concept 5: Neurochemistry	48
	Key concept 6: Evolutionary psychology	50
Read important advice on assessment and revision before you begin!	**Revision summary**	52
	Multiple-choice questions	54
	Assessment and revision guidance	58
	Practice questions, answers and feedback	62

Content area B: Application of psychological approaches

B1 Use of psychology to explain contemporary issues of aggression in society	Cognitive approach	64
	Social approach	66
	Behaviourist and social learning approaches	68
	Biological approach	70
B2 Use of psychology in business to explain and influence consumer behaviour	Cognitive approach	72
	Social approach	74
	Behaviourist and social learning approaches	76
	Biological approach	78
B3 Application of psychology to explain gender	Cognitive approach	80
	Social approach	82
	Behaviourist and social learning approaches	84
	Biological approach	86
	Revision summary	88
	Multiple-choice questions	90
	Assessment and revision guidance	92
	Practice questions, answers and feedback	94

Content area A1: Approaches and assumptions

Assumptions of four approaches

Some people call this addiction

Why do people become addicted? This is a question that psychologists would very much like to answer. There are lots of theories and lots of disagreement. Addiction is a behaviour and, like all behaviours, it can be explained from different points of view (or approaches, as we call them in this Unit).

The people in the image above may well be addicted to their phones (are you?). Think about these questions:

- Is it possible to *think* in an 'addicted' way? How?
- Is there a *social* aspect to being addicted? What is it?
- Can you *learn* to be addicted? How?
- Is addiction *biological*? Is there something happening in the brain?

Specification terms

Central nervous system (CNS) Consists of the brain and the spinal cord and is the origin of all complex commands and decisions.

Computer analogy The human brain can be compared to a computer with input, processing and output stages.

Culture Ideas, customs and social behaviour of a particular group of people or society.

Evolution The changes in inherited characteristics in a biological population over successive generations.

Genes Inherited DNA with instructions for building physical and psychological characteristics that influence behaviour. (See also page 42.)

Imitation Occurs when a learner copies the behaviour they observed being carried out by a model. It is more likely to occur when the observer identifies with the model. (See also page 38.)

Information processing Behaviour can be understood in terms of information flowing through the cognitive (mental) system in a series of stages.

Learned response A behaviour acquired through conditioning, either association (classical) or rewards/punishments (operant).

Neurochemistry Relating to chemicals in the nervous system that regulate psychological functioning. (See also page 48.)

Observation Actively attending to and watching (or listening to) the behaviour of others (models).

Social context Influences from other people, either individually or in groups.

Assumptions of the cognitive approach

Behaviour is a product of information processing

The word *cognitive* means mental processes. The cognitive approach views humans as processors of information – we take in information and blend it with stored knowledge to come up with new thoughts. Our minds use internal mental processes such as reasoning and remembering, which work together to enable us to make sense of the world and respond to it.

Information from the environment passes through a series of stages as it is processed by the cognitive system. At each stage 'something happens' to the information (i.e. it is processed). These processes occur together and work cooperatively. For example, when you see a dog, you notice it (perception), you focus on it to the exclusion of other things (attention), you recognise it (memory) and you can even name it (language).

The brain can be compared to a computer

A computer processes information, so we might understand the brain better by comparing it to a computer. Computers and humans process information through three basic stages. Information goes into the system (input), it is changed and/or stored (processed) and then it is used to respond to the environment (output).

Cognitive psychology uses several concepts borrowed from computing. The brain is our central processing unit (the 'hardware') and it codes information to change it from one format to another (the 'software'). This approach to understanding the brain and behaviour has helped to develop artificial intelligence (AI).

Assumptions of the social approach

Behaviour occurs in a social context

The word 'social' means other members of your species. Humans are 'social animals', so social psychologists believe behaviour is best understood by considering the influence of other people. For example, have you ever 'gone along' with a group of friends just because you didn't want to be the odd one out? Perhaps you had a different view from everyone else, but still outwardly agreed with them. *Conformity* is one way in which *social context* affects our behaviour.

This pressure can be so powerful that other people do not even have to be physically present – we just have to think about how others behave. Many social psychologists believe that social situations are the biggest influence on behaviour rather than an individual's disposition (their personality).

Wider culture and society influence people's behaviour

Behaviour can also be understood and explained in terms of wider society or *culture*. Some psychologists believe there are two broad types of culture: *individualist* and *collectivist* (Hofstede 2001).

In individualist cultures (e.g. the UK and USA), the main priority is the needs of the individual person. So what really matters is that we can achieve our potential and goals in life. For example, two people who want to share their lives together are expected to be 'in love' – the important thing is their individual happiness.

In collectivist cultures (e.g. China and India), people prefer to prioritise their family and community before their own needs and wants. In such cultures, people tend to seek partners approved by their family, so being 'in love' is less important (Bejanyan *et al.* 2015).

GET ACTIVE Fishing reels

Norman Triplett (1898) found that children would wind fishing reels much faster when competing against each other than when they did it alone (even when they were told to wind as quickly as they could). However, some of the children consistently performed worse against a partner than when alone.

Choose **one** assumption from the cognitive approach and **one** from the social approach. Explain how these assumptions relate to this scenario.

Assumptions of the behaviourist and social learning approaches

Behaviour is a learned response to environmental stimuli
Things in the environment bring about learning. If you touch a frying pan that has just been on the hob, you get hurt and you learn not to do that again. If you smile when you ask a favour you may find you are more likely to get what you want, so you learn to do that again.

Classical conditioning The word *conditioning* means 'learning'. *Classical conditioning* is learning through association. Ivan Pavlov (1927) noticed that his laboratory dogs salivated when they heard a door opening because they learned to associate that noise with the arrival of food.

Operant conditioning Burrhus Frederic Skinner (1938) demonstrated that when a behaviour produces a pleasurable consequence from the environment (e.g. a reward) it is likely to be repeated in future. The environment reinforces (strengthens) the behaviour, so this is called *reinforcement*.

Behaviour can be learned from observation and imitation
Albert Bandura (1977) argued that learning occurs through *observation* and *imitation* of other people's behaviour. As children, we observe the behaviour of other people (e.g. parents) who may become *role models*. We are likely to imitate role models if we observe their behaviour being rewarded (e.g. with praise, fame, money). This is *vicarious reinforcement*. It is not the child's behaviour that is reinforced, but the behaviour of the *model* they are observing.

Assumptions of the biological approach

Behaviour is influenced by our biology
This approach believes that everything that is psychological is firstly biological – our behaviours, thoughts and feelings have a physical basis.

The central nervous system (CNS) is your brain and spinal cord. This is the control centre of your body. Different areas and regions of the brain perform different functions (e.g. language, aggression, vision, emotions). Damage to the brain/CNS can seriously affect these functions.

Genes are biological 'units' of DNA inherited from our parents. These interact with environmental influences. Genes involved in many behaviours are in part passed on from one generation to the next.

Neurochemistry refers to chemicals called *neurotransmitters* (e.g. *serotonin*, *dopamine*) that are active in the brain and affect behaviour. For example, a low level of serotonin is thought to be involved in depression.

Behaviour is a product of evolution
According to Charles Darwin (1859), genetically-determined behaviours continue into future generations (i.e. they are inherited). The behaviours that continue are those that are *naturally selected* because they enhance the individual's chances of survival and particularly reproduction.

For example, an individual who has good hunting skills is more likely to survive because they have food to eat. If they are well fed they are more likely to reproduce successfully and then their hunting skills (e.g. fast reactions) are passed on to their offspring.

GET ACTIVE Running in the family – but why?

An educational psychologist is working with a 14-year-old boy who behaves aggressively in and out of school. He grew up in a violent household and witnessed his father assault his mother. His mother also has a conviction for assault. When the psychologist asked the boy why he was aggressive, he replied, 'Because it helps me get what I want'. Last year his older sister, who has been in prison for violence, had a serious brain injury in an accident and is now a very placid and calm person.

Explain how the assumptions of the two approaches on this page can help us understand the behaviour in this scenario.

The giraffe's long neck gives it an advantage in reaching food that is not available to shorter-necked rivals.

This shows how an animal has adapted physically in response to its environment. But what psychologists are really interested in is the evolution of *behaviour*, i.e. how some behaviours are *adaptive* (give an individual a special advantage).

Identify some behaviours in humans and/or animals and suggest what their adaptive advantages might be.

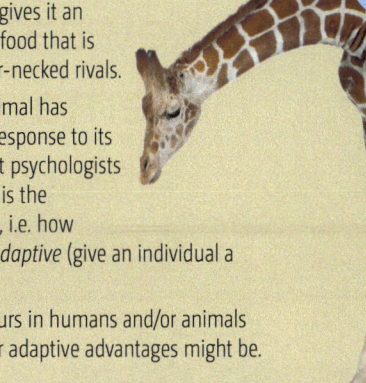

Exam-style questions

Fen and Park are sister and brother. When they were very young they loved pointing at objects and naming them ('digger!', 'horsey!'). Their mum played rugby, and Fen followed in her footsteps when she was old enough. In their teens, Fen and Park had strong friendship groups. They both dressed like their friends and followed the same influencers on TikTok. Sadly, when he was 18, Park had an accident which damaged part of his brain so he had problems reading and speaking.

1. Give **one** key assumption of the cognitive approach and identify **one** aspect of the scenario that illustrates this assumption. (2 marks)
2. Some psychologists believe behaviour is best understood in terms of how other people influence us. State the approach for which this is a key assumption and identify **one** example of the assumption in the scenario. (2 marks)
3. Give **one** key assumption of the behaviourist/social learning approaches and identify **one** aspect of the scenario that illustrates this assumption. (2 marks)
4. Using an example from the scenario, briefly explain **one** key assumption of the biological approach. (3 marks)

Specification content
Learners must be able to understand and apply knowledge of key assumptions as used to explain aspects of human behaviour.

A1 Cognitive approach:
- Behaviour is a product of information processing.
- The brain can be compared to a computer (computer analogy) – input, processing and output.

A2 Social approach:
- Behaviour occurs in a social context (influenced by people around us).
- Wider culture and society influence people's behaviour.

A3 Behaviourist and social learning approaches:
- Behaviour is a learned response to environmental stimuli.
- Behaviour can be learned from observation and imitation.

A4 Biological approach:
- Behaviour is influenced by central nervous system (CNS), genes and neurochemistry.
- Behaviour is a product of evolution.

Content area A1: Cognitive approach

Key concept 1: Characteristics of three memory stores

Persistence of vision (and hearing)

Who doesn't love a sparkler?

You light one, it eventually catches, and you start waving it around with glee, just like you did when you were six. It's great fun because you can trace letters and words in the air – your name, 'Hello' and other less polite words perhaps. As a six-year-old maybe you accepted this air-writing without question.

But of course, a lit sparkler can't really leave words in the air (unless it's a magic sparkler, obviously).

You can 'see' the words because your eyes have a memory. An after-image persists on your retinas for about 1/25th of a second after the sparkler has moved on. This is called *persistence of vision* and is an example of sensory memory.

Your ears have a 'memory' too. Has a teacher or parent ever said to you, 'What did I just say?' when they spotted you daydreaming? If you surprised them (and yourself) by repeating their last few words back to them, that's another example of your sensory memory in action.

Specification terms

Capacity Amount of material that can be kept in a memory store.

Duration Length of time material can be kept in a memory store.

Encoding The process of converting information from one form ('code') to another so it can be stored in the various memory stores and passed between them.

Long-term memory (LTM) Permanent memory store with practically unlimited capacity, storing memories for up to a lifetime. Encoding is mainly semantic (meaning).

Sensory memory (SM) Memory stores for each of our five senses, e.g. vision (iconic store) and hearing (echoic store). Encoding in the iconic store is visual and in the echoic store is acoustic. Capacity is huge but duration is very brief.

Short-term memory (STM) Limited-capacity memory store. Encoding is mainly acoustic (sounds), capacity is between 5 and 9 items, duration is up to 30 seconds without rehearsal.

Duration

Sensory memory (SM) The first part of the memory system – all stimuli from the environment pass into it. SM is actually five stores, one for each of our senses. *Duration* of SM is very brief.

For example, information in the visual store (called iconic memory) lasts for less than half a second. Information in the auditory (sound) store (called echoic memory) lasts for about 2–4 seconds.

Short-term memory (STM) A temporary store. Information lasts up to 30 seconds before it disappears (Peterson and Peterson 1959). Material stays in STM for longer if we repeat it over and over (maintenance rehearsal). If we do this for long enough, the material may pass into long-term memory.

Long-term memory (LTM) The potentially permanent memory store for information that has been rehearsed for a prolonged time. Material in LTM may last up to a lifetime. Harry Bahrick *et al.* (1975) found that many people could recognise the names and faces of school classmates after almost 50 years.

Capacity

Sensory memory *Capacity* is very high. For instance, there are over one hundred million cells in the retina of each eye and each of these cells stores sensory data.

Short-term memory A limited-capacity store because it can only contain a certain number of 'things' before forgetting occurs. George Miller (1956) noted that this capacity is between five and nine items of information. He called this 'the magic number 7 plus or minus 2'.

Long-term memory Capacity is practically unlimited. We store everything we have learned in it. When you forget information in LTM, it may still be there but you just can't access it because you don't have the right cues (discussed on the next spread).

Encoding

Sensory memory *Encoding* involves converting information from the environment (sights, sounds, smells, etc.) into a form in which it can be stored in memory. Encoding in each SM store depends on the sense.

For example, in the iconic store it is visual (information received by the eyes). Encoding in the echoic store is acoustic (sound information received by the ears).

Short-term memory Encoding is mainly acoustic (based on sounds, e.g. of words). Alan Baddeley (1966a) found that when people recall words from a list immediately after hearing them, any mistakes they make are acoustic, such as substituting a word with another that *sounds* the same (e.g. recalling 'cat' instead of 'cap').

Long-term memory Encoding is mainly semantic (based on meaning). Baddeley (1966b) found that mistakes in recalling words from LTM tended to involve substituting a word that *means* the same thing (e.g. recalling 'big' instead of 'large').

Making links to the key assumptions

Assumption: Behaviour is a product of information processing The three memory stores are different but connected. Information from the environment goes into SM first, then some of it is passed on to STM. Most of this is forgotten but some of it is passed to LTM. Some processing of the information takes place in each memory store (e.g. rehearsal in STM).

Assumption: The brain can be compared to a computer How do you think the concept on this spread illustrates the 'computer analogy' assumption (see page 10)?

Evaluation

Practical applications

One strength is that knowledge of memory stores has practical applications.

For example, the limited capacity of STM can be increased through 'chunking'. There are 15 letters in this list: C A R D O G L I T P E N B U Y. This is more than double the average capacity of STM. But the letters are organised: CAR DOG LIT PEN BUY. Putting the letters into bigger 'chunks' (words) means the number of items to be stored is five, well within most people's STM capacity. This 'chunking approach' is applied to vehicle registrations, post codes and phone numbers.

This shows how understanding the characteristics of memory stores can help to improve memory.

Research support

Another strength is evidence showing there are three memory stores with different characteristics.

The studies on the facing page demonstrate this clearly in terms of duration. STM lasts up to about 30 seconds (Peterson and Peterson 1959) but LTM is up to a lifetime (Bahrick *et al.* 1975). A study by George Sperling (1960) found that information in the iconic sensory store (vision) lasts for about 50 milliseconds. There are also many studies showing differences in capacity and encoding.

Therefore, SM, STM and LTM are separate memory stores because they differ so much in their characteristics.

Issues with research

One weakness is that a lot of research is not typical of everyday memory.

For example, the participants in one study had to remember consonant syllables such as 'YCG', which have no meaning (Peterson and Peterson 1959). Other studies have used letters and digits. But in everyday life we form memories related to many useful things (faces, facts, places, etc.), which is more meaningful to us than the materials used in many studies.

This means that the different characteristics of the memory stores may not be so clear when we use our memories in everyday life.

Less is more

Each of our spreads includes three evaluation points. One is usually about practical applications, one usually covers support from research and the third is a weakness of the key concept. This gives you a good range to choose from.

You need to choose because you don't need all of these points for Content area A. LESS IS MORE – it is always better for you to describe ONE of these points in MORE detail than just to list all three.

GET ACTIVE Digit span in STM

Here are four digits: 4 5 2 9

Close your eyes and try to repeat them in the same order. Was that easy? Now repeat the process with the following lists:

5 digits: 7 2 8 6 3

6 digits: 2 6 1 8 3 4

7 digits: 8 6 9 2 5 6 1

8 digits: 5 2 7 9 6 4 2 7

9 digits: 3 6 2 5 9 7 1 8 2

10 digits: 4 8 1 7 3 9 1 5 2 7

1. How many digits was the last list which you got completely right?
2. How does this relate to capacity of STM?

Cara says, 'Here is my own yearbook photo (taken and scribbled over some 50+ years ago when I was an American schoolgirl). Good old Karen, excelled at everything, Betsy not so much.'

KAREN FITZPATRICK "Fitzy"
Pet peeve: Braces
Hobby: Sports
Activities: Chorus, Cheerleading, Hall Monitor, Hockey, Basketball

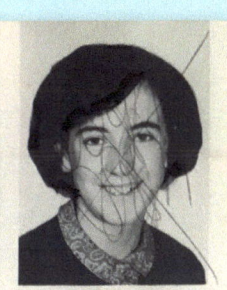

CARA FLANAGAN "Clara-Belle"
Pet peeve: Riding bike to school on cold mornings
Hobby: Sports
Activities: Hockey, Basketball, Journalism, Junior Red Cross

ELIZABETH FOGLESONG "Betsy"
Pet peeve: School lunches
Hobby: Talking on the telephone
Activities: Hockey, Yearbook, Cafeteria monitor, Chorus, Swimming

Exam-style questions

When Jo was revising for a psychology exam, they started by trying to learn a list of ten key concepts, but forgot some of them. However, they kept trying and in the exam two months later Jo was able to remember nearly all of the concepts.

1. Identify **one** characteristic of long-term memory that could be a reason for Jo's exam performance. (1 mark)
2. Describe how capacity of short-term memory may explain what happened when Jo first started revising. (2 marks)
3. Describe **two** characteristics of sensory memory. (4 marks)
4. State what is meant by 'encoding' in relation to memory. (1 mark)
5. Describe what psychologists mean by 'duration' in relation to memory. (2 marks)
6. During revision, Jo learned some psychological theories by trying to apply them to their own life and found that they could remember these theories better in the exam.

    Describe how encoding in long-term memory could be a reason for this. (3 marks)
7. Briefly evaluate **one** characteristic of Jo's short-term or long-term memory. (3 marks)

An issue to consider

List some examples of short-term and long-term memories you have recalled today.

Aside from duration, can you identify any differences between these short-term and long-term memories?

What conclusions can you draw about STM and LTM?

Specification content

A1 Cognitive approach

Learners must be able to understand and apply knowledge of key concepts to explain aspects of human behaviour, including:

- Characteristics of sensory, short-term, and long-term memory (encoding, capacity, duration).

Content area A1: Cognitive approach

Key concept 2: Remembering

What is remembering?
Every time we retrieve some information from a memory store, we are *remembering*. There are two main forms of remembering – *recall* and *recognition*.

Recall

Free recall
We recall a piece of information when we retrieve it from a memory store (e.g. STM) without any 'assistance'. This is known as *free recall*. For example, if an exam question asks you to write down a definition of 'remembering', you have to generate the answer from memory. In a research study, participants might read a list of words, put the list away and then try to recall the words from memory.

Cued recall
Sometimes we can only recall something if we get assistance from a *cue* (see below). For instance, you might struggle to recall a word but find it easier if someone says, 'It starts with F'. The letter F is a cue that triggers recall – this is called *cued recall*. You still have to retrieve the rest of the material.

Cued recall shows we have more in our memory than we can usually access. Often, when we can't recall something, we assume we've forgotten it. But when the right cue appears we remember the information, which shows it must have been stored all along.

Recognition
We often remember something because we have encountered it before. For example, we might not be able to recall the name of someone we went to school with 30 years ago but we would probably recognise it if we heard it.

Another example is a multiple-choice exam question such as, 'Which is the best definition of remembering?', followed by four alternative answers. You are given the entire answer (not just the first letter), so hopefully you recognise the correct one.

Like cued recall, recognition demonstrates that we store more in LTM than we can immediately retrieve.

Cues
Cues are important in remembering because they contribute to superior retrieval. Cues can be meaningful or not meaningful.

Meaningful cues
Consider a cue such as 'STM'. You learn this cue at the same time as you learn other material about short-term memory. The cue contains the letter 'S', which triggers retrieval of 'short'. This triggers retrieval of other stored knowledge about STM, e.g. it has short duration and limited capacity.

Cues without meaning
Cues without meaning are also learned at the same time as you learn about or experience something. For example, when you read this page there might be a thunderstorm outside. The next time you are in a thunderstorm this may cue you to remember some things about STM, or the next time you think about STM you may recall the thunderstorm.

Emotions can also act as cues. For example, when people are feeling happy they tend to recall other happy events, and when they are feeling sad they think of sad experiences – which in turn may then lower their mood further. The emotion acts as a cue to remember times when the person experienced similar emotions.

The memory palaces of champions
The World Memory Championship is held each year. Competitors have to memorise long lists of hundreds of numbers and words. You would think this is impossible but champions have a trick up their sleeve – the *method of loci*.

It's also called the *memory palace* (the fictional detective Sherlock Holmes used it). You turn words (e.g. a big shopping list) into images and mentally place them around an environment you know well – your school/college, your journey to college, your house, or simply your bedroom.

The weirder the links the better. Who could forget the sight of a river of batteries rushing towards you down the stairs?

You remember the items by taking a mental walkabout and retrieving them – the locations trigger your memory and you can even recall the items in order. It takes practice but if you put in the time it's a powerful method, very useful for remembering facts in exams.

You can see some demonstrations of this technique on YouTube, e.g. tinyurl.com/d4kfatj4

Specification terms
Cue A 'trigger' that allows us to access material in memory. Cues can be meaningfully linked to the material (e.g. mnemonics) or can be indirectly linked by being encoded at the time of learning (e.g. external context and internal state).

Recall In free recall the individual generates information without a cue. In cued recall, a cue assists retrieval of information.

Recognition A form of memory retrieval where you identify something based on previous experience.

Remembering The activity of retrieving information from a memory store.

GET ACTIVE Mars bars

I (Rob) am of the generation that grew up on the advertising slogan for Mars bars: 'A Mars a day helps you work, rest and play'. Even now when I hear that slogan, I really want a Mars bar!

There are several slogan generators available online (search 'free slogan-maker'). Generate a slogan and repeat it over and over while you think about (or eat!) your favourite chocolate bar. Wait a day or two and repeat the slogan to yourself. You'll most probably find it conjures up a lovely image of your favourite chocolate bar.

Can you explain this in terms of cues?

Evaluation

Practical applications

One strength is practical applications of retrieval cues.

Mnemonics are a method of improving memory based on cues. For instance, you might be familiar with the mnemonic BIDMAS (each letter stands for one maths operation and reminds you of the order of maths operations) and 'Richard Of York Gave Battle In Vain' (each initial letter represents a colour of the rainbow). These are cues that trigger retrieval of information stored in LTM.

This shows how understanding the role of cues can help us to improve memory.

Research support

Another strength is support for cues from many studies.

For example, participants in one study had to learn and remember lists of words (Tulving and Pearlstone 1966). The words came from distinct categories, such as animals and clothing. When they recalled the lists, some participants were given the category headings as cues whereas other participants were not given the cues. The cued-recall participants remembered significantly more words than the non-cued participants.

This finding shows that cues are important in retrieving memories that would otherwise be 'forgotten', and also that cued recall is superior to free recall.

Cues are not always useful

One weakness is that some cues are not very important in everyday remembering.

For instance, the idea of a context-related cue is that the environment in which you learn acts as a cue to retrieve information. However, context-related cues are not as powerful as meaningful cues (e.g. BIDMAS) because it is rare that two contexts are very similar. If you learn material in your classroom and then take an exam in that classroom, then there may be some context effects. But usually you sit an exam in a different room.

Therefore, not all cues are equally important and some are relatively useless in everyday situations.

Making links to the key assumptions

Assumption: The brain can be compared to a computer When we remember something, it first has to be inputted (learned or registered) and then processed in some way before we get the output (retrieval of the memory). This is also how a computer works. But note that the analogy is very limited, e.g. a computer's retrieval doesn't depend on whether or not a cue is present.

Assumption: Behaviour is a product of information processing
Explain how the concept of remembering relates to this assumption (see page 10).

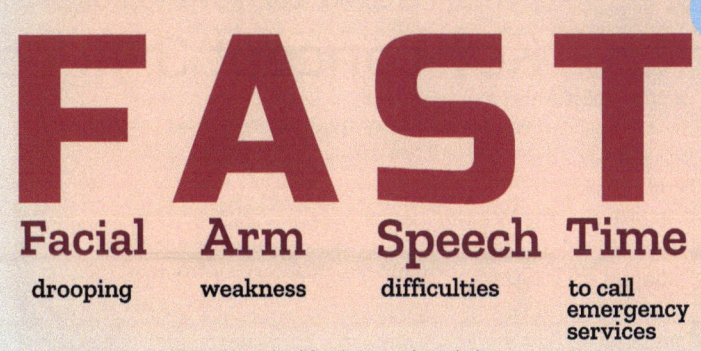

Not that kind of cue. Except, if you think about it, it IS that kind of cue.

FAST

Facial drooping **Arm** weakness **Speech** difficulties **Time** to call emergency services

Mnemonics can be useful in everyday life. The one above helps you to identify the signs of a stroke.

Throughout this book, we have used the names of researchers and the dates of their studies because this is the correct academic convention. But don't worry – you don't need to memorise researchers' names (and definitely not the dates). The important thing is to understand why a research study supports (or sometimes doesn't support) a concept or theory.

Exam-style questions

Torrey is taking her driving theory test. She finds the multiple-choice questions quite easy compared with the questions she had to answer when she was doing her BTEC exams.

1. State what is meant by 'recognition' and give **one** example of recognition from this scenario. (2 marks)
2. With reference to the scenario, explain **one** difference between recall and recognition. (2 marks)
3. Torrey is a stand-up comedian. She has to remember jokes, funny stories, observations and the order in which to tell them. In her early days, Torrey could not remember much. But now she learns her material by imagining a room, which she mentally goes round putting jokes in various places. During the gig, she takes a mental tour of the room and 'finds' the material.

   Explain Torrey's success in remembering her material. Use **one** concept from the cognitive approach in your answer. (3 marks)
4. Bish is a big fan of Torrey and has been to several of her gigs. Bish can never remember any of Torrey's jokes, but he always notices when Torrey reuses some of her older material.

   Explain the reason for this in terms of recognition and recall. (3 marks)
5. Bish tells his children to use cues to help them in their exam revision. Briefly evaluate Bish's advice in terms of how people remember. (3 marks)

An issue to consider

TV ads often plant cues in the minds of viewers which later remind the viewer to use the advertised product. Can you think of an example of this? Do you think this is unethical?

Specification content

A1 Cognitive approach

Learners must be able to understand and apply knowledge of key concepts to explain aspects of human behaviour, including:

- Remembering (recognition, recall and the importance of cues).

Content area A1: Cognitive approach
Key concept 3: Reconstructive memory

The War of the Ghosts

Would you like to hear a story?

One night two young men from Egulac went down to the river to hunt seals, and while they were there it became foggy and calm. Then they heard war cries, and they thought, 'Maybe this is a war party'. They escaped to the shore and hid behind a log. Now canoes came up, and they heard the noise of paddles, and saw one canoe coming up to them. There were five men in the canoe, and they said:

'What do you think? We wish to take you along. We are going up the river to make war on the people.'

One of the young men said, 'I have no arrows.'

'Arrows are in the canoe,' they said.

'I will not go along. I might be killed. My relatives do not know where I have gone. But you,' he said, turning to the other, 'may go with them.'

So one of the young men went, but the other returned home.

And the warriors went on up the river to a town on the other side of Kalama. The people came down to the water, and they began to fight, and many were killed. But the young man heard one of the warriors say, 'Quick, let us go home; that Indian has been hit.' Now he thought, 'Oh, they are ghosts.' He did not feel sick, but they said he had been shot.

So the canoes went back to Egulac, and the young man went ashore to his house and made a fire. And he told everybody and said, 'Behold, I accompanied the ghosts, and we went to fight. Many of our fellows were killed, and many of those who attacked us were killed. They said I was hit, and I did not feel sick.'

He told it all and then he became quiet. When the sun rose, he fell down. Something black came out of his mouth. His face became contorted. The people jumped up and cried.

He was dead.

If you're wondering what that was about, read on!

Source: Bartlett (1932) *Remembering: A Study in Experimental and Social Psychology*, reproduced with permission of Cambridge University Press through PLSclear.

Specification terms

Confabulation When details are added to a memory to fill in the 'gaps', to make recall meaningful.

Rationalisation When parts of a memory are distorted to fit your schema, to make the memory meaningful.

Reconstructive memory Pieces of stored information are reassembled during recall. The process is guided by our schema so that we produce a 'memory' that makes sense (even if it is inaccurate).

Schema Mental frameworks of beliefs and expectations that influence cognitive processing. They are developed from experience.

Shortening When part of a memory is left out, so what remains is shorter.

What is reconstructive memory?

Sir Frederic Charles Bartlett (1932) argued that memories are *reconstructions* (constructing the memory again). We don't record events in memory and then reproduce them later like a video recorder would.

Instead, we store fragments of information. When we recall something, we build (reconstruct) these fragments into a meaningful whole. The result is that memory is not a totally accurate record of what happened.

Role of schema in memory

A *schema* is a mental structure or 'package' containing our stored knowledge of an aspect of the world. We have a schema for mother, teacher, birthday party, firework, etc. – for people, objects, events.

Schema are based on past personal experiences and also on shared cultural experiences. For example, most people in a culture have similar expectations about birthday parties – they usually involve food, presents and fun.

Bartlett believed our schema affect memory by influencing what we store and later recall. He used the story on the left to investigate this.

As an Inuit folk tale, the War of the Ghosts has ideas that are unfamiliar to you because they're not part of your experience. When you try to recall the story, it changes to become more familiar. The memory is reconstructed to fit your existing schema. This makes the memory more meaningful to you and easier to recall. Schema can reconstruct memories in three main ways:

Shortening Parts of a memory that don't fit in with your schema are left out (e.g. unfamiliar details) so what you remember is shorter.

For instance, in Barlett's research, the supernatural elements of the story were very unfamiliar to the participants. So they were unable to recall them.

Rationalisation Parts of a memory are recalled but in a distorted way that fits your schema. So your memory of an event changed because it didn't match relevant schema (but now it does). This happens so that strange or unfamiliar memories make more sense.

In Bartlett's research, people replaced unfamiliar words with familiar ones (e.g. 'arrows are in the canoe' became 'guns are in the boat').

Confabulation Parts of a memory are invented to fill in 'gaps'. This isn't deliberate (it's not 'lying') and it doesn't happen randomly. It is guided by your schema to (again) make better sense of the memory.

Some participants in Bartlett's research recalled details that were not in the story because they made it more meaningful (e.g. 'They stopped the boat and tried to lift him out').

Making links to the key assumptions

Assumption: Behaviour is a product of information processing
Reconstructive memory shows one way that information processing operates. To reconstruct a memory, the 'fragments' of memory have to be mentally processed to make sense of them. This processing depends on schema, so the memory does not stay the same but changes in some way.

Assumption: The brain can be compared to a computer Explain how reconstructive memory links to this assumption [HINT: it doesn't have to support the assumption. Perhaps reconstructive memory challenges the idea that the brain is like a computer – you decide] (see page 10).

Evaluation

Practical applications

One strength is that reconstructive memory can help explain problems with eyewitness testimony (EWT).

EWT is often used in court trials to establish what happened when a crime was committed. The eyewitness swears on oath that they will tell the truth about what they saw. But their recollection of what they saw may be affected by their schema. For example, they might have seen a person with a gun and expected it to be a man. Memory can be affected by schema (including expectations of what 'should' happen), so people do not always recall events accurately.

This means evidence in court is never based on EWT alone as it can be inaccurate – a very important application of this research.

Research support

One strength is evidence for reconstructive memory from Bartlett's research.

As you read on the facing page, Bartlett showed that recall of an unfamiliar story was affected in a number of ways. His participants did not recall too many details but instead tried to make more sense of what they heard before storing it in memory. So the story changed significantly – there was evidence of shortening, rationalisation and confabulation.

This shows that we reconstruct memories from elements that are influenced by our schema, often making recall inaccurate.

Some memories are accurate

One weakness of reconstructive memory is that not all memories are affected by schema.

Recall can be very accurate. For example, in situations that are personally important or distinctive or unusual, we can remember a lot of accurate detail. In Bartlett's study, participants often recalled the phrase, 'Something black came out of his mouth', because it was quite unusual.

This shows that people may not always reconstruct memories, and some memories can be relatively unaffected by schema.

Witnesses very rarely lie. But they do sometimes get it wrong. They take an oath to tell 'the truth, the whole truth and nothing but the truth', so they try their hardest to remember things accurately. But memory is often reconstructive, so piecing together memories of what they saw is likely to be affected by schema. This is why witnesses to the same crime can often have different memories of it.

GET ACTIVE The telephone game

The method of recall that Bartlett used in his research is a bit like the game 'Telephone'. You and four or five friends could have a go at it. Start with a brief unfamiliar piece of text, something like this:

'One day I met my doppelgänger. We look very similar but we had never met before. We went to the same college, we both married men called Henry, we both work in IT and we both play the ukulele.

Read this to yourself, then phone a friend and repeat what you can remember to them. They listen to you, then they phone someone else and repeat what they can remember, and so on five or six times. The last person writes down what they can recall.

1. Compare the last recalled version with the original – how has it changed?
2. How do schema affect this activity?
3. What would happen to recall if the material was even more unfamiliar? Why?

Exam-style questions

Bob and Sue are friends who together witnessed a street robbery and gave statements to the police. They discussed afterwards what they had said in their statements. Bob remembered seeing a knife but Sue didn't. Bob thought the robber was wearing a hoodie, but Sue recalled it was a baseball cap. Bob thought the robber was a teenager, but Sue said he was in his twenties.

1. Using the concept of schema, explain why Bob's and Sue's statements were different. (3 marks)
2. (a) In the context of reconstructive memory, state the meaning of 'confabulation'. (1 mark)
   (b) Give **one** example of possible confabulation from the scenario. (1 mark)
3. Write down a sentence that could illustrate rationalisation in the scenario. (1 mark)
4. State what is meant by the term 'reconstructive memory'. (1 mark)
5. Explain **one** way reconstructive memory could be used to understand Bob's or Sue's recall of the robbery. (2 marks)
6. Briefly evaluate the view that memory is reconstructive, using Bob and/or Sue as examples. (3 marks)

An issue to consider

Can we rely on memory if it is reconstructive? Can you think of any real-life examples where inaccurate recall could have serious consequences?

Specification content

A1 Cognitive approach

Learners must be able to understand and apply knowledge of key concepts to explain aspects of human behaviour, including:
- Reconstructive memory, including the role of schema (shortening, rationalisation and confabulation).

Content area A1: Cognitive approach

Key concept 4: Cognitive priming

Imagine this

Your teacher asks you to carry out a very simple task. All you have to do is unscramble some mixed-up sentences. You get them all right. You leave the classroom thinking, 'That was too easy. What was it all about?'

You don't know it, but your teacher isn't interested in how you did on the task at all. Instead, she's timing you to see how long it takes you to leave the room. She's done this with all the students in your class. It turns out you walked a lot slower to leave the room than some of your classmates did.

Why?

There could be many reasons, but here's an interesting fact. All of the students did the same task, but there were two versions. In one version, some of the words in the sentences related to being old (bingo, retired, wrinkled, etc.). In the other version the words were neutral (thirsty, clean, private, etc.). Guess what? You got the 'old' version. Like you, all your classmates who got the old version were also slower to leave the room.

Sounds hard to believe? John Bargh and his colleagues (1996) did this experiment and got this exact finding.

Specification terms

Associative priming We process a stimulus more quickly (or recall it more easily) because we earlier encountered a stimulus that is often paired with it.

Cognitive priming We process a stimulus (word, image, object, etc.) more quickly when we see or hear the stimulus (or a related one) first (the 'prime').

Cognitive scripts See page 20.

Repetition priming We process a stimulus more quickly (or recall it more easily) because we encountered it earlier.

Semantic priming We process a stimulus more quickly (or recall it more easily) because we earlier encountered a stimulus related to it in meaning (semantics = meaning).

What is cognitive priming?

Two examples of *cognitive priming* are *cognitive scripts* (see next spread) and different types of priming.

When you see or hear one stimulus (the 'prime'), this affects your response to a later stimulus (you usually process the later stimulus faster). The prime triggers a network of related concepts in memory, so that when the second stimulus occurs, activation is quicker (examples are given below).

Cognitive priming occurs below your level of awareness so you do not know your response has been influenced.

Types of cognitive priming

Repetition priming

When you encounter the prime, you process it more quickly when you see or hear it again later than you otherwise would have done.

Example Imagine you overhear the word *avocado* in someone's conversation. This word is the prime. If you hear it later that same day (or see the word, or see an actual avocado), you notice (process) it more quickly than you would have done if you had not been primed earlier.

Semantic priming

'Semantic' refers to two stimuli meaning the same thing or having similar features. You process a stimulus faster because you earlier encountered a prime that was similar in meaning.

Example If you see or hear the word *computer*, it is easier to recognise or recall the word *laptop* later – you process *laptop* faster because its meaning is similar to the prime.

Associative priming

The prime and the later stimulus are associated but not semantically. They may be usually paired together in everyday experience.

Example What do you think of when I say *fish*? There's a good chance you would think of *chips*. The two are so often paired in our culture that they are closely associated in memory (no doubt the image primed you anyway!). If you are exposed to one you are more likely to later recognise or recall the other.

An example of how cognitive priming works

You can think of cognitive priming as 'mentally setting you up in advance to behave in a certain way'. Some psychologists believe this could explain how adverts affect our behaviour.

Imagine watching TV adverts that promote snacking as fun. The adverts prime you (i.e. in advance, before you actually do anything) to associate snacks with something positive (fun). You then get to eat various snacks – healthy and unhealthy ones – and you eat quite a lot of them.

Does this mean the cognitive priming affected your behaviour? Not in itself. We would have to compare you with people who did not see the adverts (or who saw non-food-related adverts). Jennifer Harris *et al.* (2009) investigated this and found that students who were primed by adverts ate more snacks than students who were not primed by adverts.

Making links to the key assumptions

Assumption: The brain can be compared to a computer Priming is a good example of how the computer analogy works. For example, in repetition priming: the prime is the input; triggering of related concepts is the processing; recognising the same stimulus quicker next time is the output.

Assumption: Behaviour is a product of information processing Explain how cognitive priming relates to this assumption (see page 10).

Evaluation

Practical applications

One strength is that priming can help us to understand and prevent cognitive causes of obesity.

The study by Harris *et al.* (see facing page) showed that advertising can affect how many snacks people eat because of cognitive priming. Once we understand the effects of priming we may be able to prevent this influence (or direct the influence towards healthy eating instead).

This means that education and legislation (although politically difficult) could help to prevent obesity.

Research support

Another strength is that research shows how priming may explain a possible link between video gaming and *aggression*.

In a study by Ingrid Möller and Barbara Krahé (2009), students read a scenario in which someone is accidentally pushed so they spill their drink. Students who frequently played violent video games were much more likely than other students to interpret the push as deliberate. They were also more likely to choose physical aggression as a suitable response.

This shows that playing violent video games may prime some people to think and behave aggressively, supporting the concept of associative priming.

Lack of replication

One weakness of cognitive priming is that it is very difficult to study.

This makes it difficult to replicate research findings. *Replication* is an important feature of science. If a study is repeated using exactly the same procedure and produces the same finding, then we know that the outcome is not a fluke and it is more likely to represent something real. But when researchers replicate priming studies, they often get different findings.

This suggests that the concept of priming is not scientific which means we cannot be confident that the theories are correct.

Cognitive priming could help us to understand how viewing screen-based adverts, vlogs and programmes affect our behaviour. Does watching violent programmes prime us to be more aggressive? Does a 'diet' of food adverts prime us to eat more?

Exam-style questions

A psychologist asked Shazia, Keira and Lennie to read a brief passage and then complete a word task. The passage described the layout of a doctor's surgery. The task was to complete words with missing letters, e.g. N_ _S_ (NURSE). Other students also completed the word task but did not read the passage first.

1. Describe the finding you would expect the psychologist to get. (2 marks)
2. Using your knowledge of cognitive priming, explain why you would expect to get this finding. (3 marks)
3. (a) State what is meant by 'semantic priming'. (1 mark)
   (b) Give **one** example of any type of priming from everyday life. (1 mark)
4. Bruno watches a lot of TV cookery shows such as *Masterchef*. He enjoys seeing the chefs' skills at work, and also looking at the delicious food. Whenever Bruno watches a show, he cooks himself a big dinner with lots of cream and butter.

   Explain, using a key concept from cognitive psychology, why Bruno cooks himself a big dinner. (3 marks)
5. Briefly evaluate the key concept you used in your previous answer as a way of explaining Bruno's behaviour. (3 marks)

GET ACTIVE Sabiha and Imy

Sabiha's friends all watch the popular series *Game of Thrones*, so she decided to read about it and watch an episode. By the end of the day, she had seen or heard the word 'throne' in lots of different places – in overheard conversations, on Instagram, even in her college textbooks.

1. What type of cognitive priming is this?
2. Describe another type of priming that Sabiha might have experienced.

Imy went to the surgery to see her doctor for a check-up. Afterwards, on the bus journey home, she realised the two people in front of her were nurses. Imy also remembered she needed to buy some paracetamol.

3. Identify this type of cognitive priming and explain how it works in Imy's case.

An issue to consider

If you use social media you may have been exposed to cognitive priming without realising it.

Can you explain how?

Specification content

A1 Cognitive approach

Learners must be able to understand and apply knowledge of key concepts to explain aspects of human behaviour, including:

- Cognitive priming, including the role of cognitive scripts and different types of priming (repetition, semantic and associative).

Content area A1: Cognitive approach
Key concept 5: The role of cognitive scripts

Your first day

Do you remember your first day at college or your school sixth form? Or in a part-time job?

Were you a bit anxious beforehand? Maybe you were worried you wouldn't know what you were doing or where you were meant to be, especially if you went to a new place altogether.

On the other hand, perhaps you did have a bit of an idea about what to expect. After all, you've often been in situations 'for the first time' and some of them were probably similar to your first day at college/sixth form. You remembered some of these experiences and they helped to prepare you.

You might not have known which classroom to go to, but you knew how to behave like a student when you got there. You didn't know when your psychology lessons would be, but you knew what a timetable is and what it's for.

It's almost as if you knew the script for a play called 'My First Day'.

Specification terms

Cognitive scripts Information stored in memory that describes the behaviours typical in a given situation. They are automatically retrieved to guide our behaviour. They are also known as memory scripts.

Memory scripts See above.

Person perception Information stored in memory about which personality characteristics often go together, which guides our impressions of other people.

OK, he's friendly. But what else is he? Kind, helpful, clever, shy?

Memory scripts

Psychologists often use the terms *cognitive scripts* and *memory scripts* interchangeably – they are basically referring to the same thing.

What is a memory script?

A memory script contains knowledge of how a social situation 'plays out'. It includes what we can usually expect to happen in a situation, how we should behave and what the consequences could be.

The classic example is the restaurant script (Schank and Abelson 1977). This memory script includes our knowledge and expectations of the setting (the restaurant itself), props (menus, tables, etc.) and actors (waiting staff, customers, chefs and so on).

Features of memory scripts

Using the example of a restaurant script, here are some of the main features of memory scripts:

- They are broken down into scenes ordered by time. For example, you enter the restaurant first, then sit at a table, then you order, eat and finally pay the bill.
- They concern multiple goals, e.g. to satisfy hunger, to enjoy the occasion, to impress a partner, etc.
- They are dynamic and evolve with experience (including from TV and other media) – the more often you visit restaurants, the more refined and detailed your restaurant script becomes.
- They are influenced by culture, which is not surprising because they reflect our experiences – for example, in most restaurants in China, customers find a table themselves.
- They influence memory – we remember events that are consistent with a script (because that is what we expect), but we may also remember those events that are inconsistent (because they stand out).

Person perception

What is person perception?

When we meet someone new, we do not view ('perceive') them as an individual person with their own unique combination of traits. Instead, we quickly categorise them – that is, we mentally place them into a group or 'type' of people (often just on the basis of what the person looks or sounds like).

How person perception works

Making assumptions There are gaps in our knowledge of someone new to us. But once we have categorised the person, we fill in the gaps with information from memory about that category, even if the information is wrong.

Our memories contain our knowledge of other people's personalities, especially which characteristics typically go together. For example, if you view someone as 'outgoing', you probably assume they have a few other attributes as well, such as being impulsive and loud.

Stereotyping and bias This knowledge can be wrong because it is partly based on stereotypes (see page 28). In other words, we assume the person in front of us is representative of a group – they are 'this *type* of person'.

Therefore, *person perception* is not objectively accurate, but is affected by our own cognitive biases (see next spread). A danger of this process is that we may later recall information about the person that matches the category we put them in.

GET ACTIVE A very familiar script

An example of a script that is highly relevant to students is 'sitting an exam'. As you have a lot of experience of this, your script will be detailed – you are an expert on sitting exams.

1. Make a list of the behaviours that form your 'sitting an exam' script and put them in time order.
2. Does this script share any elements with other scripts such as 'attending a class' or 'going to a concert'?
3. How has your 'sitting an exam' script evolved over the years?
4. What are the differences between the script of an expert and a novice?

This image will probably cue a strong memory script you have built up over many years.

Evaluation

Practical applications

One strength is that we may be able to make person perception more accurate and objective.

When we meet someone new, we find it easy to make inaccurate judgements about their personality. Sometimes these are based on stereotypes, i.e. what we expect someone 'should' be like. This is undesirable because stereotypes are often negative. Instead, we can make sure we take the time to properly know someone without making instant 'snap' judgements about them.

Therefore, by knowing how person perception works, we can resist the tendency to negatively stereotype others.

Research support

Another strength is evidence to support the role of memory scripts.

When people are presented with routine events where the steps are in the wrong order, they tend to recall them in the correct order. For instance, a 'getting ready for college' script might be presented as: 'get dressed, get out of bed, wake up', but is recalled as: 'wake up, get out of bed, get dressed' (Bower *et al.* 1979). The correct order is familiar and consistent with the script stored in memory.

This finding supports the argument that cognitive scripts strongly influence how we remember everyday events.

Cannot explain all behaviour

One weakness is that we may assume a script is guiding behaviour when it is not.

When someone behaves in a script-consistent way, how do we know it is because they are following a cognitive script? For instance, someone eating a meal in a restaurant might be imitating those around them and thus following external cues rather than an internal memory script. The same issue arises with person perception. On meeting a stranger, my impressions of them may be guided more by how others respond than by information stored in memory.

Therefore, scripts and internal processes are not always important influences on behaviour.

Making links to the key assumptions

Assumption: Behaviour is a product of information processing
We perceive a new person's traits ('they are friendly, talkative, sociable'). We focus our attention on (process) central traits that really stand out ('friendly'). We retrieve knowledge from memory (more processing) to fill in what we don't know ('they're probably also enthusiastic').

Assumption: The brain can be compared to a computer Explain how the concept of cognitive scripts relates to this assumption (see page 10).

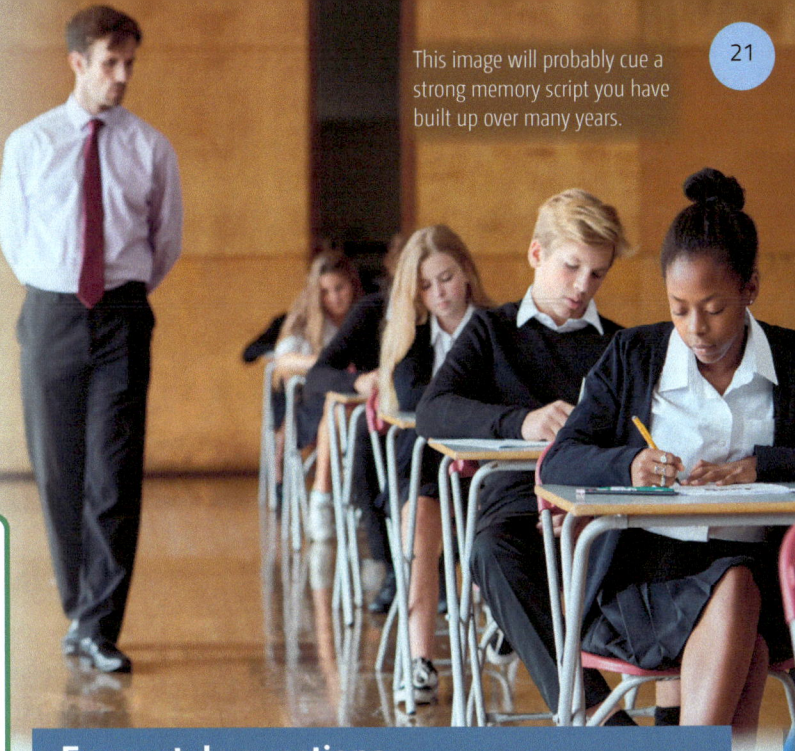

Exam-style questions

Pearl pops into a supermarket, taking a couple of carrier bags with her and picking up a basket from inside the door. This is only Pearl's third trip to this shop, but she knows she will get to the fruit and veg first and she will have to go to the other end of the shop for the drinks. Once Pearl has everything she wants to buy, she gets out her loyalty card and bank card and heads for the checkouts.

1. Give **two** examples from the scenario above that could be part of Pearl's cognitive script for 'shopping in a supermarket'. (2 marks)
2. Give **one** example of a behaviour that is part of a cognitive script from any everyday scenario other than the one above. (1 mark)
3. Explain what psychologists mean by 'memory scripts'. (2 marks)
4. When Pearl gets to the checkout she has a conversation with the assistant called Dean who she has never met before. Pearl feels that Dean comes across as very friendly and thinks to herself, 'I bet Dean is clever and knows lots of people. I reckon he's definitely interested in travelling!'

   Explain why Pearl thinks this about Dean. Use **one** key concept from the cognitive approach in your answer. (3 marks)
5. Briefly assess the key concept you used in your previous answer as a way of explaining Pearl's behaviour. (3 marks)

An issue to consider

It could be said that person perception is a bit like following a memory script. Can you explain how? [HINT: we expect some personality characteristics to go together – why is this?]

Specification content

A1 Cognitive approach

Learners must be able to understand and apply knowledge of key concepts to explain aspects of human behaviour, including:

- The role of cognitive scripts (memory scripts, person perception).

Content area A1: Cognitive approach

Key concept 6: Cognitive biases

What are cognitive biases?

A 'bias' refers to leaning in one direction or prejudging a situation. A *cognitive bias* refers to how our thinking can 'lean' in one direction.

Negative effects Cognitive biases are automatic and affect what we notice, what we remember, how we make decisions and how we interpret other people's behaviour. So how we process information becomes flawed, and our ability to make rational choices is undermined.

Positive effects However, on the plus side, cognitive biases simplify how we view the world and allow us to make decisions quickly (they are 'shortcuts' that help us process information).

Fundamental attribution error (FAE)

We can understand the FAE by looking at the individual words in the term.

Attribution This is about how we try to explain the reasons for other people's behaviour. For example, why was your friend late? You might attribute lateness to their personal characteristics (maybe they were late because they don't think it's important to be on time) or to situations (perhaps the bus broke down).

Fundamental error Most people overemphasise personal characteristics and downplay situations. This is a bias towards one explanation, which psychologists call the *fundamental attribution error* because it is the most basic (fundamental) error.

For example, if a student is late handing in an essay, the teacher might believe it's because the student is lazy (a personal characteristic). But there could be many situational causes (e.g. the dog ate it).

Confirmation bias

We favour information that confirms beliefs we already hold – we show a *confirmation bias*. For example, if you support a football team you are more sensitive to information that confirms your existing view of the team (see also the example of filter bubbles on the left).

We notice confirmatory information quickly and we store and recall it easily. But we ignore, downplay or reject examples that challenge our beliefs, and eventually we don't even look for contradictory information.

Hostile attribution bias (HAB)

Hostile attribution bias is a special form of bias in explaining the reasons for other people's behaviour. Someone with a HAB:

- Wrongly believes somebody else's behaviour is threatening (hostile) when it is actually neutral, e.g. interpreting an accidental bump in a crowded pub as deliberately aggressive.
- Believes the other person is being hostile because that is what the other person is like (a personal characteristic). However, this ignores the role of the situation (the crowded pub).

Do you live in a filter bubble?

You might well do if you get your news from social media. Algorithms detect your preferences and tailor what the news feeds serve up to you. You see only items that match your preferences and these reinforce your current opinions. You rarely get to see information that contradicts or challenges what you already believe.

Such filter bubbles are sometimes called 'echo chambers' because all you ever read or hear are your own views reflected back at you.

Some people argue that filter bubbles are a threat to democracy because other viewpoints and opinions are excluded from social media feeds. If you want to read other views you have to work harder to find them. Many people can't be bothered to spend the time or effort doing that extra work.

Specification terms

Cognitive biases Errors in how we process information, which affect our attention, memory and decision-making.

Confirmation bias We pay more attention to (and recall more easily) information that supports our existing beliefs. We may seek it out and ignore contradictory information.

Fundamental attribution error In explaining the reasons for other people's behaviour, we focus on their personal characteristics and overlook the role of the situation.

Hostile attribution bias A tendency to assume that someone else's behaviour has an aggressive or antagonistic motive when it is actually neutral.

'Ever since I learnt about confirmation bias I've started seeing it everywhere' (Jon Ronson).

🔗 Making links to the key assumptions

Assumption: Behaviour is a product of information processing When we meet other people, we often have to make quick decisions ('Are they friendly?', 'Should I cooperate with them?'). So we process information quickly (our survival might depend on it). But this comes at a cost because the processing may be biased. For instance, we wrongly perceive the other person as hostile, so we behave aggressively towards them.

Assumption: The brain can be compared to a computer Explain how the concept of cognitive biases relates to this assumption (see page 10).

Evaluation

Practical applications

One strength of cognitive biases is that they can be applied to real-world behaviour.

For example, we can work to overcome confirmation bias by deliberately seeking out information that contradicts our existing views about political parties or football teams or whatever (e.g. by reading a variety of news sources and applying critical thinking skills).

This is useful because, by understanding cognitive biases, we can improve our decision-making and reduce negative effects on behaviour.

Research support

Another strength is evidence of the link between hostile attribution bias and aggression.

People with a strong HAB often behave aggressively. When they are behaving aggressively, they may experience a temporary increase in their hostile attributions (which are already at a high level). This makes further aggression even more likely – a vicious circle (Tuente *et al.* 2019).

This shows the central role of a HAB in aggressive behaviour, and also a potential way of tackling it (by turning hostile attributions into neutral ones).

The FAE is not universal

One weakness is that the fundamental attribution error (FAE) only exists in some cultures.

In *individualist* cultures (e.g. USA), people tend to value individual needs above the needs of the wider community. Behaviour is usually attributed to individual characteristics – that is how behaviour is understood in such cultures. However, in *collectivist* cultures (e.g. China) the group/community is prioritised over individual needs, so people more often attribute behaviour to situational factors rather than to personality.

This suggests the FAE may not be a 'fundamental' feature of human information processing after all.

GET ACTIVE A wrong diagnosis

This real case was described by Caroline Wellbery (2011). A woman visited her doctor with two major symptoms – a rash under her arms and pain in her joints. The patient was obese and had Type 2 diabetes. The doctor diagnosed *intertrigo*, which is inflammation caused by folds of skin rubbing together. He prescribed ointment for the rash and ibuprofen for the pain.

Unhappy with this outcome, the patient sought a second opinion. The second doctor ordered a blood test to be carried out and diagnosed Lyme disease. This is a bacterial infection usually caused by a bite from a tick (for example when walking in the countryside).

1. How did confirmation bias contribute to the wrong diagnosis and treatment? Identify at least **two** specific examples from the case to support your explanation.
2. Explain how the fundamental attribution error and hostile attribution bias might also have contributed to the wrong diagnosis.

'Did you spill my pint?' Some aggression can be explained by the hostile attribution bias. Spilling someone's drink is not usually deliberate but someone with this cognitive bias might think it is.

Exam-style questions

Maneet is a police detective and Marcus is her senior officer. One day, Maneet was out interviewing potential witnesses when one of them had a panic attack and had to receive medical help. Maneet was late back to the office, so Marcus accused her of being lazy and having a poor attitude.

1. Using **one** concept from the cognitive approach, explain Marcus's comments about Maneet. (3 marks)
2. Maneet politely explained why she was late. Marcus said he did not like Maneet's angry tone and warned her she could go on report.

   Identify the type of cognitive bias shown by Marcus and explain why it could be a reason for his behaviour. (3 marks)
3. Briefly evaluate the use of cognitive biases to explain Marcus's behaviour. (3 marks)
4. State what is meant by 'cognitive biases'. (1 mark)
5. (a) State the meaning of 'confirmation bias'. (1 mark)

   (b) Explain **one** way that confirmation bias could affect behaviour in everyday life. (2 marks)
6. Describe **one** example of the fundamental attribution error in everyday life. (2 marks)

An issue to consider

Think back over what you have done today. What attributions have you made about the people around you (i.e. what explanations have you given for someone's behaviour)? List some of them.

Now tick the ones which might be biased.

Specification content

A1 Cognitive approach

Learners must be able to understand and apply knowledge of key concepts to explain aspects of human behaviour, including:

- Cognitive biases, including fundamental attribution error, confirmation bias and hostile attribution bias.

Content area A2: Social approach

Key concept 1: Conformity

Cavewoman speaks!

A woman is visiting a museum and has to pass through a metal detector on the way in. There is a queue. While she queues she watches as someone dressed as a 'cavewoman' is encouraged by the tour guide to grunt very loudly at the visitors, as if trying to communicate with them. The tour guide (who is 'fluent in Neanderthal, Caveman and Geordie') asks the visitors to join in.

Without questioning what is going on, the woman begins grunting along with the others, with the tour guide 'interpreting' for her. All the other visitors behave as if this is the most natural thing in the world.

Of course the whole situation was a set-up, for the BBC programme *Michael McIntyre's Big Show*. But have you ever 'gone along' with what everyone else was doing, even if you thought it a bit strange?

Specification terms

Conformity When a person changes their opinion/behaviour because they are pressured (or believe they are pressured) by another person or a group.

Informational social influence (ISI) We agree with the behaviour of others because we believe it is correct. We accept it because we want to be correct.

Normative social influence (NSI) We agree with the behaviour of others because we want to be accepted and liked, and to avoid rejection.

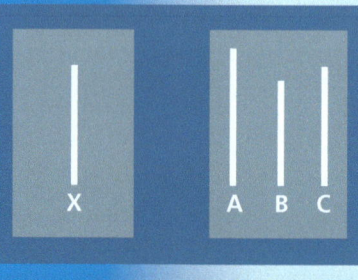

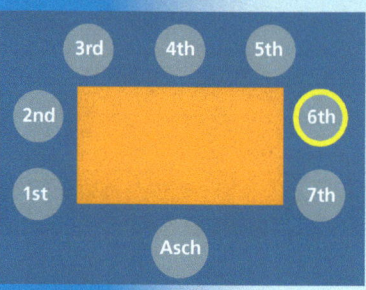

Asch's study

The line X on the left-hand card is the standard line. The lines A, B and C are the three comparison lines. The participants had to say which of the comparison lines was the same length as the standard line (the answer was always obvious – here it is C).

The naïve (genuine) participant was always seated either last or (as here) next-to-last in the group. Participants gave their answers out loud, one at a time, beginning with the first person.

What is conformity?

When we are part of a group, we may choose to 'go along' with other people by agreeing with their opinions or behaving as they do. This is *conformity*. The other people do not tell us how to behave or what opinions to have. Conformity is the result of 'invisible' pressure from others.

Morton Deutsch and Harold Gerard (1955) argued there are two main processes that explain why people conform.

1. Normative social influence (NSI)

Group norms NSI is about group norms. In any group of people there are behaviours and beliefs that are considered to be 'normal' or typical. Norms guide the behaviour of the individuals in the group and are part of what glues the group together, which is why we pay attention to them. We accept the norms of a group (i.e. we conform) because we want to be liked by the other group members and to avoid being rejected by them.

Emotional process NSI is an *emotional* process because it is about how you *feel*. It may be stronger in stressful situations where people have a greater need for social support.

2. Informational social influence (ISI)

Information ISI is about who has the better information, you or others. Often we are unsure about what behaviours/beliefs are right or wrong. For example, you may not know the answer to a question in class. But if most students agree on one answer, you accept it because you think they are probably right. So we may conform to their views because we want to be right.

Cognitive process ISI is a *cognitive* process because it is about what you *think*. It is most likely to happen in situations that are new to you (so you don't know what is right) or situations where it isn't clear what is right (ambiguous). It also occurs when one person is regarded as being more of an expert.

Studying conformity

Solomon Asch (1951) demonstrated conformity in a famous study.

In groups of about six or seven, students were asked in turn to identify which line out of three was the same length as another line (see diagram bottom left). Only one student was a genuine participant ('naïve') who did not know what the task was really about. The others ('confederates') were told to sometimes give the same (obviously) wrong answer.

The naïve participants agreed with the wrong answers (i.e. they conformed) 36.8% of the time. 75% of the participants conformed at least once.

The task is very obvious (unambiguous), so ISI does not explain the conformity in the study (because the naïve participants knew the others were wrong). Instead, Asch believed the students conformed in order to avoid rejection by the group (which is NSI).

Making links to the key assumptions

Assumption: Behaviour occurs in a social context (influenced by people around us) It is impossible to understand conformity without considering the social context in which it occurs, i.e. group pressure. You can probably think of many things that you have agreed to do as a result of group pressure. Even when a group is not physically present it still exerts pressure, e.g. posting on social media only because you saw other posts first. However, it's also true that some people are more able to resist group pressures than others (as in Asch's research).

Assumption: Wider culture and society influence people's behaviour Explain how the concept of conformity relates to this assumption (see page 10).

Evaluation

Practical applications

One strength is that understanding conformity can have useful practical applications in workplaces.

For example, 'whistle-blowers' are people who risk their jobs to highlight wrongdoing in organisations, even when everyone else accepts it. They are anti-conformists because they choose *not* to go along with the group. They are prepared to be rejected by colleagues and to 'rock the boat' (resisting NSI), and/or they do not think other people automatically know better than them (resisting ISI).

Therefore, having an understanding of NSI and ISI means we can take steps to counteract and resist mindless conformity.

Research support

Another strength is that Asch provided evidence of NSI in his study on conformity.

He discovered that many of his participants went along with a clearly wrong answer just because other people did. When he asked them why, some said they felt self-conscious giving the correct answer and were afraid of disapproval. So Asch repeated his study but asked the naïve participants to write down their answers instead of saying them out loud. In this study, the conformity rate fell to just 12.5%.

This suggests that we sometimes conform in order to avoid rejection by the majority. When this pressure is removed because you don't have to disagree publicly, then conformity is less likely.

NSI and ISI are less clear in the real world

One weakness is that the two processes (NSI or ISI) are interdependent.

You are less likely to conform if there is another person present ('dissenter') who disagrees with the group. But it is difficult to know why this is the case. The dissenter may reduce the power of NSI (because they provide social support). Or they may reduce the power of ISI (because there is an alternative source of information).

This shows that we can't always be sure whether NSI or ISI is responsible for conformity. It is most likely that both are operating, especially in real-life situations.

Sometimes giving up our independence and pulling in the same direction makes us feel part of a group. Then we can achieve things we wouldn't be able to on our own.

GET ACTIVE True stories of conformity

A man is lying on the pavement in a busy street, not moving. People are walking round him and ignoring him. No one stops to see if there is anything wrong with the man. One woman finally kneels on the ground to speak to him. She looks like she knows what she is doing. Several other people stop to help now as well.

Twelve members of a jury are discussing the trial they have been involved in. Most of the jury members have been convinced by the evidence and the comments of other jurors, so they believe the defendant is guilty. One jury member is sure the defendant is not guilty. But he suddenly changes his mind and votes 'guilty'.

1. Why do you think the people in these cases conformed – NSI or ISI, or another reason? Explain your answer.
2. Are there any real-life examples of conformity that you have been involved in (remember, in conformity, no one tells you to agree)? Why do you think conformity happened in these cases?

Exam-style questions

Alex is part of a book club and hated the latest book that was chosen for the group to read. However, at the next meeting Alex said they loved it along with everyone else.

1. Using **one** concept from the social approach, explain why Alex agreed with the rest of the group. (3 marks)
2. State what is meant by the term 'conformity'. (1 mark)
3. Using an example from everyday life, explain what is meant by 'informational social influence'. (2 marks)
4. A team of nurses is meeting to discuss a patient's treatment plan. All are agreed that the plan should continue. However, Amos disagrees but doesn't say so publicly. So he goes along with the plan even though he thinks it is not the best option.
   (a) Outline how the social approach might explain Amos's behaviour. Use the concepts of normative social influence and informational social influence in your answer. (4 marks)
   (b) Briefly assess the explanation of Amos's behaviour you gave in your answer to question 4(a). (3 marks)
5. Briefly explain **one** example of normative social influence from everyday life. (2 marks)

An issue to consider

Conformity is often seen as a bad thing in individualist cultures because it undermines a person's independence.

Is conformity a good or bad thing?

Specification content

A2 Social approach

Learners must be able to understand and apply knowledge of key concepts to explain aspects of human behaviour, including:

- Conformity (normative social influence and informational social influence).

Content area A2: Social approach
Key concept 2: Types of conformity

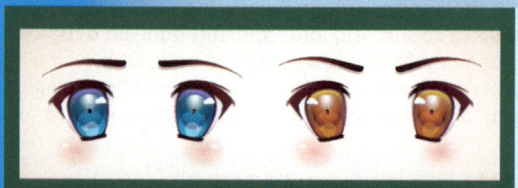

Are brown eyes better?

Did you know that people with brown eyes are superior to their blue-eyed minions? They are more intelligent, they have greater capacity to learn, are cleaner and better behaved.

This is what Jane Elliott, a teacher, told her class of primary-aged children in 1968. With their agreement, she divided them into 'brownies' and 'blueys'. She gave the brownies privileges and helped them with their work. She gave the blue-eyed children collars to wear round their necks to mark them out as inferior.

According to Elliott (2016), within an hour the children began to behave in ways that matched their status. The brownies became more confident and worked harder, but also acted with contempt towards their blue-eyed classmates. The blueys became demotivated and their work suffered.

But there's a twist in this tale. On the next school day, the roles were reversed, and the blueys were deemed superior. Everyone's behaviour changed with the new situation.

The children all conformed to the roles they were given in a process called *identification*.

Specification terms

Compliance The individual privately disagrees with the group but goes along with it anyway, usually because they do not want to be rejected.

Identification The individual temporarily goes along with the norms and roles of the group because they see membership as part of their identity.

Internalisation The individual goes along with the group opinion because they genuinely believe it is correct, so private views are changed.

'OK, I'll go along with you all but I won't enjoy it!'

Psychologists believe that there are different types of conformity. Herbert Kelman (1958) argued for three types.

1. Internalisation

Sometimes we genuinely agree with the view of the group, so we publicly change our view and behave like the rest of the group. The group's opinion becomes part of how we think (we internalise it). *Internalisation* is a deep and permanent type of conformity. We continue to conform with the group even when other members are not physically present.

Internalisation is most likely to occur because of *informational social influence* (ISI) – we think the group view is right.

Example When Jess was a student, she lived with other students who were vegans. They became good friends and eventually Jess internalised her friends' values and became a vegan herself ('it was the right thing to do'). Jess sees herself as 'being a vegan' – it is a complete lifestyle, not just a type of diet. She continues to be a vegan years after leaving university.

Asch's research There was no evidence of internalisation because the group wasn't together long and there were no meaningful opinions or values for the participants to internalise.

2. Compliance

Sometimes we just 'go along' with the group, but privately we do not change our opinion/ behaviour. This is a shallow and temporary type of conformity because agreement with the group ends when it is no longer present.

Compliance is most likely to occur because of *normative social influence* (NSI) – we want the group to accept us.

Example You might agree with your friends' choice of holiday destination, film or nightclub because you don't want to 'rock the boat' or risk being excluded. But really, you don't like hot weather, horror films or sweaty clubs.

Asch's research It is most likely the participants were complying with the rest of the group. In other words, they knew the answers the others gave were wrong, but they chose to go along with the group anyway – they publicly agreed but privately disagreed.

3. Identification

Identification combines elements of the other two types. We conform because we identify with the members of the group (look up to them, want to be like them, etc.). This is stronger than compliance because we privately change some of our views (as well as publicly). It is weaker than internalisation because we conform only as long as we are part of the group.

Example Rowan is a professional psychologist. He has to follow a code of conduct which guides how psychologists are expected to behave. Rowan conforms to the code because he identifies with his role as a psychologist. But if he were to change career, Rowan would identify with a new role and conform to a different set of behaviours.

Asch's research It is possible that some participants identified with the other people in the group because they thought they were all in the same boat (they were mistaken). It's unlikely though because there was nothing particularly attractive or admirable about the group (no one even spoke except to identify the comparison lines).

Making links to the key assumptions

Assumption: Wider culture and society influence people's behaviour Compliance may be more common in collectivist cultures than in individualist ones. Going along with the wishes of the group – even when you privately prefer not to – contributes to group cohesion and the happiness of the wider community. Perhaps identification is more common in collectivist cultures as well – it is easier to put the needs of the group before your own when you share the group's values.

Assumption: Behaviour occurs in a social context (influenced by people around us) Explain how different types of conformity relate to this assumption (see page 10).

Evaluation

Practical applications

One strength is that we can apply knowledge of conformity types to the workplace.

Some conformity is necessary for society and workplaces to function. But some conformity is destructive because it can lead to the wrong decisions being made. For example, compliance means everyone in a workplace agrees with each other for the sake of a 'quiet life'. On the other hand, a group can identify with each other so strongly that outside voices are silenced. In both cases, wrong decisions can be made because the group does not consider alternative courses of action.

Therefore, by understanding the different types, we can target destructive conformity to improve decision-making in the workplace.

Research support

Another strength is that research has found evidence for all three types of conformity.

Many of Asch's participants gave answers they knew were wrong, to avoid disapproval (compliance). A study by Norma Jean Orlando (1973, see 'Get active' below) strongly demonstrated identification. Participants in other research have conformed with the answers of people they believed had more expertise than they did, showing internalisation (Sherif 1935).

These supporting studies show that Kelman was right to suggest there is more than one type of conformity.

Oversimplification

One weakness is that our understanding of how conformity operates in the real world may be inaccurate.

This is partly because research does not resemble real-world situations. For instance, the task in Asch's research (identifying line lengths) was extremely artificial, and the group of participants was not a 'real' group in any meaningful sense. Also, identification combines features of compliance and internalisation, so it is sometimes hard to separate identification from the others in real-world situations.

Therefore, conformity is oversimplified in research and may be more complex in the real world because the different types overlap.

GET ACTIVE Conformity and role-playing

Norma Jean Orlando (1973) investigated how conformity can influence people to behave in extreme ways.

She selected staff at a psychiatric hospital to play the roles of patients on a ward for one week. After two days, several of these mock patients experienced symptoms of psychological disturbance, some cried uncontrollably and others became extremely withdrawn. Some tried to escape. Most of the participants became more anxious and depressed with time, and felt very strongly that they were trapped and isolated. The study had to be ended early to avoid more psychological damage.

1. Which type of conformity operated in this study? How does this type of conformity explain what happened?
2. Choose an everyday situation. With other students, act out roles in which one person conforms because of identification. Repeat with internalisation and then compliance as the reasons. Discuss the differences.

'Yes, we agree with each other about everything! Isn't that great?!' Conformity in the workplace – whether through compliance, internalisation or identification – is potentially risky because no one challenges bad decisions.

Exam-style questions

Vik's friends decide to go to a steak restaurant for a meal. Vik doesn't eat steak but he tags along with the group anyway. Vik has been a vegan for 20 years, since his university days when he lived with some students who were vegans.

1. Identify **two** types of conformity that Vik is showing in the scenario. (2 marks)
2. Use these **two** types of conformity to explain why Vik goes to the restaurant and why he became a vegan. (4 marks)
3. State what is meant by the term 'identification' in the context of conformity. (1 mark)
4. Vik is a carer in a nursing home. He wears a uniform and has to carry out certain tasks every day. He is very popular with the residents and staff because he is always helpful and cheerful towards everybody as he believes that is an important part of his job.
   (a) What type of conformity is Vik showing? Explain your answer. (3 marks)
   (b) Briefly assess your explanation of Vik's behaviour in your answer to question 4(a). (3 marks)
5. Briefly explain **one** example of internalisation from everyday life. (2 marks)

An issue to consider

Psychologists disagree over whether unthinking conformity is due to the pressure of the situation or to the personalities of individuals.

What do you think? When people conform (at work, with friends or strangers, etc.), is it because they are the 'conforming type' or do you think it more likely that the situation is responsible? How could you find out?

Specification content

A2 Social approach

Learners must be able to understand and apply knowledge of key concepts to explain aspects of human behaviour, including:
- Types of conformity, including internalisation, identification, compliance.

Content area A2: Social approach

Key concept 3: In-groups and out-groups

PSYCHO

This word is often used to describe people with mental health problems. The musician and activist Professor Green faced such language on Twitter after speaking about his own mental health. That's one reason he joined the YMCA's #IAMWHOLE campaign to encourage young people to challenge this language.

A survey found that two thirds of young people have heard this word (and worse) used to refer to people with mental health issues – such words are commonplace on social media (YMCA 2017).

This is bad news because words like this create negative stereotypes of people with mental health issues. These words are harmful because their use makes it harder for people with difficulties to seek help.

Imagine how hard it must be to admit to your friends that you are depressed, when you know that they think a depressed person is a 'psycho'. The reaction you might get could be enough to put you off.

Specification terms

Discrimination Harmful behaviour directed at groups or individuals because they share characteristics (e.g. ethnicity).

In-groups and out-groups Social groups we perceive ourselves to be members of (in-groups) and not members of (out-groups).

Prejudice A negative attitude towards a group or an individual because they are a member of that group.

Social categorisation Putting people into social groupings based on their shared characteristics (e.g. ethnicity).

Stereotypes Fixed views of other people based on their perceived membership of a social category.

Some older and younger people, smashing some stereotypes.

Social categorisation

We divide people into social groups (categories) depending on their shared characteristics, often based merely on appearance (e.g. gender, ethnicity, age). We perceive people in a category as similar, e.g. we think all young people are the same. At the same time, we perceive the people in one category to be very different from the people in another, e.g. all young people are completely different from old people (Tajfel 1979).

In-groups and out-groups

Most humans have a strong desire to belong, so it is easy for us to think of ourselves as a member of a category – this is an *in-group* ('us'). As we draw strict boundaries between categories, if you are part of one group, there will usually be another group you are not part of – the *out-group* ('them').

We identify with the in-group (e.g. its norms and values), which brings us a sense of belonging, self-esteem and status. We increase these by exaggerating differences and minimising similarities with the out-group. This means we stereotype members of the out-group.

Stereotypes

A *stereotype* is a fixed view we hold of a person based on our placing them into a social category (e.g. 'old people are slow', 'feminists hate men', etc.). We assume the person represents the social category. The danger of this is that our assumptions may be wrong and unfair.

Formation of stereotypes

Social categorisation One way stereotypes are formed is explained above – *social categorisation* and increasing the psychological distance between the in-group and out-group.

Social learning theory (see page 38) This argues that we learn stereotypes by observing sources of social information (parents, peers, media). For example, if a child hears a parent telling a racist joke, they may enjoy the reaction (e.g. laughter) the parent receives (*vicarious reinforcement*). This makes the child more likely to repeat the stereotype (*imitate* the behaviour).

Effect of stereotypes

Positive effects Stereotypes simplify our interactions with other people in a complex social world. We assume the individuals we meet share the stereotyped characteristics of a social category, which saves time and cognitive processing effort.

Negative effects Stereotypes influence our behaviour because they are self-fulfilling. We end up behaving towards other people in line with our stereotypes of them. Stereotypes also affect our memories. We tend to remember positive information about the in-group and negative information about out-groups (Iacozza *et al.* 2019). Perhaps the most dangerous effect of stereotypes is that they distort and bias our social judgements, which can lead to *prejudice* and ultimately *discrimination*.

Prejudice and discrimination

Prejudice Often the result of stereotyping the out-group because it becomes easier to form negative attitudes about its members. We perceive out-group members as inferior, which makes us feel good about our in-group and ourselves. So prejudice is a way of increasing in-group members' self-esteem.

Discrimination Often (but not always) the outcome of prejudice towards an out-group. People are excluded (e.g. from employment and housing) just because they share a characteristic such as skin colour, gender, sexuality, etc. Discrimination is also faced by people in less obvious 'everyday' ways (e.g. 'microaggressions' such as disrespectful comments).

Making links to the key assumptions

Assumption: Behaviour occurs in a social context (influenced by people around us) The troubling thing about stereotyping other people is that you may behave towards them in line with your stereotype. This could eventually lead to discriminating against them in ways big and small. Other people influence stereotypes without even being physically present – you just have to think about them.

Assumption: Wider culture and society influence people's behaviour Explain how the concepts on this spread relate to this assumption (see page 10).

Evaluation

Practical applications

One strength of understanding in-groups and out-groups is that we can take steps to reduce prejudice.

One way is to encourage people to perceive themselves as part of a bigger social category (e.g. 'human beings') instead of a smaller one (e.g. a specific religion, gender, social class, etc.). This emphasises similarities and lessens psychological distance between in-group and out-group, reducing the influence of stereotypes. Another way is to challenge stereotypes by creating opportunities for in-group and out-group members to meet, mix and cooperate towards shared goals.

Therefore, there are several ways we can counteract the negative effects of social categorisation and stereotyping to reduce prejudice.

Research support

Another strength is there is psychological research showing the effects of stereotypes on memory.

Gordon Allport and Leo Postman (1947) showed participants a drawing that reversed a well-known harmful stereotype (see right). The image was viewed by a participant, who described it to another, and so on for six or seven participants. This procedure was carried out many times. In 50% of these sequences, participants wrongly recalled the razor was held by the black man.

This shows that a racist stereotype (the black man was the attacker) can bias memory in a way that supports the stereotype (at least in a substantial proportion of people).

Alternative explanations

One weakness is that the social approach may not give the best explanation of stereotyping and prejudice.

There is evidence that some people are prejudiced because of their personality and not just because of social factors. Some people develop an 'authoritarian personality', the result of a very harsh upbringing (Adorno et al. 1950). These people blame out-groups for their own perceived failings and are therefore more likely than most to be open to stereotyping and strong prejudices.

This means that prejudice cannot always be explained by social factors alone and may not be reduced without also considering personality factors.

GET ACTIVE Measure your in-group membership

One effect of belonging to an in-group is increased self-esteem when you compare your group to an out-group. The *Collective Self-Esteem Scale* (Luhtanen and Crocker 1992) is one way of measuring this effect.

You can find the scale here: tinyurl.com/2p933s6n and instructions on how to find your score are here: tinyurl.com/5ysv9e74

Remember that completing the scale is a way of helping you to understand the concept of in-groups and out-groups a bit better. It is not meant to reveal anything deep and meaningful about you personally.

1. Think about your score. Do you think it truly reflects how you think about your in-groups?
2. From your own experience, would you say that if you identify strongly with an in-group you are bound to stereotype an out-group?
3. Do stereotypes always lead to prejudice? Explain your answer.

In this drawing (based on the one from Allport and Postman's 1947 study), a white man is holding a razor and is confronting a black man with it. This reverses a commonly-held harmful stereotype of the time (still held by some people today) that a black man is more likely to be the attacker.

Exam-style questions

Leon has cerebral palsy and learning difficulties. At school, there is one small group of students who spend most of their time together. They call Leon hurtful names focusing on his disability. Other students are supportive, but they still sometimes assume that Leon cannot do anything for himself.

1. Give **one** example of social categorisation from this scenario. (1 mark)
2. Explain how the scenario illustrates the concepts of in-groups and out-groups. (2 marks)
3. Explain **one** way in which students may stereotype Leon. (2 marks)
4. Explain **one** effect that this stereotyping may have on Leon. (2 marks)
5. Leon uses a wheelchair, but around town there are shops he can't get into. He sometimes finds people ignore him but he can hear them making rude comments.
   State what is meant by 'discrimination'. (1 mark)
6. Give **one** difference between prejudice and discrimination. (1 mark)
7. Identify **one** example of prejudice from the scenario. (1 mark)
8. Briefly analyse the social approach to understanding Leon's experience. (3 marks)

An issue to consider

In the past, TV programmes used to cast white men in the roles of doctors, judges, detectives, etc. But now we are likely to see a woman or a person from an ethnic minority group in such roles.

Do you think this has helped change attitudes?

Specification content

A2 Social approach

Learners must be able to understand and apply knowledge of key concepts to explain aspects of human behaviour, including:

- In and out groups – social categorisation (formation and effect of stereotypes, prejudice and discrimination).

Content area A2: Social approach
Key concept 4: Intra-group dynamics

'How could we have been so stupid?'

In April 1961, the United States government of President John F. Kennedy tried to remove by force the communist dictator of nearby Cuba, Fidel Castro. With the support of the US military, 1,400 Cuban exiles invaded Cuba at the Bay of Pigs. But it was a disaster, one of the most embarrassing foreign policy mistakes ever made.

The decision to invade was made by a group of experts. As Kennedy himself said, 'There were 50 or so of us, presumably the most experienced and smartest people we could get... How could we have been so stupid?'

Irving Janis was a psychologist at Yale University who asked himself the same question. He believed the answer was to do with how some groups work, a process he called 'groupthink'.

Janis's teenage daughter challenged him to prove this because she didn't believe social psychological processes could explain such a catastrophic failure (Forsyth 1986).

Janis researched numerous other such failures (e.g. the US not pulling out of the Vietnam War). He concluded that groupthink is a feature of cohesive groups whose members value their 'groupiness'. Their desire to agree with each other is stronger than their motivation to realistically consider alternative courses of action.

Specification terms

Common goals The outcomes of group activity that all members share and work towards.

Group cohesion The extent to which group members are psychologically bonded and 'pull in the same direction'.

Groupthink The tendency of cohesive groups to strive for agreement, which overrides the need to analyse decisions realistically and to consider criticisms and alternatives.

Intra-group dynamics The psychological processes that take place in any group.

Roles The functions that individuals perform within a group – task, social, procedural or individualist roles.

Social facilitation The tendency for individuals to perform better on a task when other people are present.

Group cohesion

In cohesive groups, members stick together to pursue *common goals* – they enjoy being in the group, look forward to meeting, communicate willingly and work together efficiently.

Group cohesion is greater when group members perceive themselves to be similar, in both external characteristics (e.g. age) and internal characteristics (e.g. attitudes). This creates trust and communication which leads to more cohesion, which in turn produces greater trust and communication (a virtuous circle).

But despite these benefits, cohesive groups are especially susceptible to *groupthink* (see left and below) because no one wants to 'rock the boat'.

Roles

There are three categories of *roles* that increase group cohesion (Benne and Sheats 1948):

- **Task roles** focus on getting work done, e.g. 'Task leaders' coordinate the group's work, 'Energisers' challenge the group to move forward.
- **Social roles** focus on creating harmony in group relationships, e.g. 'Encouragers' support and praise others, 'Compromisers' back down for the good of the group.
- **Procedural roles** involve keeping the group 'on task', e.g. 'Gatekeepers' ensure everyone has a say, 'Recorders' keep track of the group's activities.

However, there is also a category of roles that weaken group cohesion:

- **Individualist roles** seek to undermine the group, e.g. 'Blockers' resist every idea but offer nothing themselves, 'Jokesters' make light of the group's work and distract others.

Common goals

Well-functioning groups share goals. This is another dynamic that makes the group more cohesive, increasing members' sense of 'working together'.

Goals are beneficial because they motivate group members to increase their efforts, provide direction and focus and give meaning to tasks. For example, common goals can help individuals understand their place in what may seem a large and impersonal organisation.

Goals also provide a standard against which to measure progress, evaluate performance and resolve conflicts.

Groupthink

Irving Janis (1982) investigated decision-making in cohesive groups. He found there is a strong need for members to agree with each other, regardless of whether decisions are correct or not. Members quickly stop analysing decisions and, instead of looking for weaknesses, they convince themselves the reasons for the decision are sound. They refuse to listen to alternatives and actively discourage opposing views.

Groupthink is more likely in situations of stress and when the decision is very important. It is also more likely when the group is cohesive because members wish to maintain their cohesiveness, are like-minded and isolated from external influences that might challenge them.

Social facilitation

When group members work together on relatively simple tasks, the presence of others can enhance an individual's performance. This is called *social facilitation* (the opposite is true for complex tasks, called social inhibition).

According to Robert Zajonc (1965), if we believe other people are observing our task performance, we become physiologically and psychologically aroused (e.g. our heart rate increases and we become more alert). Arousal is even greater when we believe our performance is being evaluated by others in the group.

This state of arousal enhances our performance of simple, well-learned responses, but is unhelpful in complex tasks.

Evaluation

Practical applications

One strength is that each concept has produced practical applications in various real-world situations.

For instance, Janis (1982) suggested ways to avoid groupthink such as encouraging criticism, involving people from outside the group and breaking the group into smaller (preferably competing) subgroups. Also, greater cohesion in therapy groups can reduce the symptoms of depression (Crowe and Grenyer 2008).

These findings show that improving *intra-group dynamics* can have benefits for individuals, groups and organisations.

Research support

Another strength is evidence to support some of the intra-group dynamics on this spread.

For example, Lukas Thürmer et al. (2017) found that when group members believe their contribution to shared goals is recognised by others, the group performs better. This is because members focus on the group's goals rather than their own personal goals. Also, groupthink can be partly avoided by assigning a group member the role of 'Devil's Advocate', so they can challenge the group consensus by asking awkward questions and offering alternative viewpoints (MacDougall and Baum 1997).

Therefore there is strong evidence that intra-group dynamics have a real impact on the functioning of many groups.

Contrary evidence

One weakness is evidence that challenges intra-group dynamics.

For example, group roles are rarely clear-cut. They can be vague and overlap significantly between members, who may not fully understand their roles in the group, so their performance suffers. In terms of goals, Charles Gowen (1985) found that group performance on a task improved by 12% when members worked towards group goals. But when they were allowed to work towards both group *and* individual goals, there was a 31% improvement.

These findings show that the links between intra-group dynamics and performance are complex and not yet fully understood.

Making links to the key assumptions

Assumption: Behaviour occurs in a social context (influenced by people around us)
A jury is a good example of how this assumption relates to intra-group dynamics. Jury members play different roles – some speak a lot, others almost not at all, some are passionate and persuasive, others are not much bothered. By the time they get to a verdict, members feel they've been working towards the same goal.

Assumption: Wider culture and society influence people's behaviour
Explain how the concepts on this spread relate to this assumption (see page 10).

GET ACTIVE Testing social facilitation

Have a go at this experiment with some other students. Each student should perform a simple task (e.g. completing an online Tetris game). They should do this twice – once in front of an audience and once on their own.

You could repeat the same procedure with a more complex task (e.g. tinyurl.com/yknhpyk3).

1. How can you carry this out without introducing extraneous variables (see page 105), e.g. ensuring the experience is the same for everyone?
2. What can you do about practice effects (see counterbalancing on page 120)?
3. Did the presence of an audience affect performance?
4. If you also tried a complex task, did the type of task make any difference to your results?
5. How can you explain your results in terms of social facilitation?

Work groups should include someone willing to play the role of 'Devil's Advocate' and argue against everyone else.

Exam-style questions

A group of eight college students meets together every week to discuss ways of improving the college environment. They are very enthusiastic about the task and are all committed to making the college a better place. The group members quickly realise that they like each other and enjoy their meetings.

1. Name **two** intra-group dynamics and give an example of each from the scenario above. (4 marks)
2. Explain **one** example of intra-group dynamics from any everyday scenario other than the one above. (2 marks)
3. Pieter is very supportive of the other students in the group. Ursula is always urging the group to come up with more ideas. Ayla is the group leader.

   Describe **one** example of roles within this student group. (2 marks)
4. Explain what is meant by 'groupthink'. (2 marks)
5. The group members always support each other's ideas. They feel there is no need to expand the group because everyone is already doing a great job.

   Briefly describe how the group's behaviour illustrates the concept of groupthink. (3 marks)
6. Briefly evaluate the intra-group dynamics of the student group. (3 marks)

An issue to consider

Which is the best type of group – a highly cohesive one or one with no cohesion at all? Or is there another type? What would be the features of such a group?

Specification content

A2 Social approach

Learners must be able to understand and apply knowledge of key concepts to explain aspects of human behaviour, including:

- Intra group dynamics including group cohesion, roles, common goals, groupthink and social facilitation.

Content area A2: Social approach
Key concept 5: Influences of others on the self

Who do you think you are?

This spread is about your sense of self – who you think you are. Psychologists call this your self-concept.

There is a deceptively simple way to find out who you think you are. It's called the *Twenty Statements Test* (Kuhn and McPartland 1954). All you have to do is complete this statement:

I am _____.

You can put anything you want, with as many words as you like. But you should do it 20 times (with a different response each time). OK, you don't have to do it 20 times, but as many as you can. Don't worry about logic or anything sensible like that.

Did you find out anything about yourself?

Specification terms

Self-concept How a person perceives and thinks about themselves (self-image) and values themselves and their attributes (self-esteem).

Self-efficacy A person's confidence in their ability to achieve success.

Self-esteem How a person values themselves and the extent to which they accept and like themselves.

Self-image A person's awareness of their mental and physical characteristics, based on positive and negative beliefs about themselves.

Smug self-concept.

Self-concept

Your *self-concept* is about how you see yourself. It's the answer to the question, 'Who am I?'. For example, you might see yourself as a friendly person.

Your self-concept is strongly influenced by other people, especially by how they evaluate you and the feedback they provide. In this sense other people are 'mirrors' in which we perceive their judgements of ourselves (the 'looking-glass self', Cooley 1902).

There are two key components to your self-concept: *self-esteem* and *self-image*.

Influences of others on self-esteem

Self-esteem concerns the extent to which we accept and like ourselves. People with high self-esteem have a positive self-image (see below), they accept themselves and have confidence in their own abilities (see section on self-efficacy below). High self-esteem has been strongly linked with psychological wellbeing.

According to Michael Argyle (1973), a key source of self-esteem is our interactions with others:

- **Others react to us** We develop high self-esteem if others respond to us in ways that make us feel good, for instance they agree with us, make positive comments, etc.
- **We compare ourselves to others** Our self-esteem rises when we compare ourselves with people whose qualities we believe are less desirable than our own (e.g. less successful, attractive or clever than ourselves).
- **We play social roles** Some social roles are widely admired (e.g. nurse, parent), leading to high self-esteem. Other roles carry social stigma (e.g. ex-prisoner, drug user) and are linked with low self-esteem.

Influences of others on self-image

Self-image is your awareness of your mental and physical characteristics. It is based on your beliefs about yourself acquired from life experiences, e.g. how others respond to your successes and failures. Someone with a positive self-image may be satisfied with their body shape/size and perceive themselves as helpful and kind.

Your self-image is also based on feedback from other people, especially important people such as parents, teachers and peers. A positive self-image tends to develop from positive feedback. However, self-image is more complex than this because people do not always interpret feedback accurately. For instance, someone may reassure you that you are successful or likeable, but you interpret this as 'they're only being polite'.

Self-efficacy

Self-efficacy is the extent to which we are confident we can achieve a successful outcome (e.g. in performing a task). It is linked to self-image and self-esteem. For example, someone with high self-efficacy is confident they have the ability and skills to get a high grade in an exam or score a goal in a football match. They feel better about themselves (self-esteem) and have a more positive view of themselves (self-image).

Influences of others on self-efficacy

Albert Bandura (1997) suggests two main ways other people influence self-efficacy:

- **Social modelling** When you observe another person achieving success on a task, it increases your belief that you are capable of doing the same (especially if you perceive them to be similar to yourself). These other people are called *role models* (see page 38).
- **Social persuasion** Using positive verbal feedback (encouragement) can increase a person's self-efficacy. This overcomes self-doubt and persuades a person that they are capable of achieving success, e.g. telling a student they are capable of achieving a top grade because they have great skills (of course, discouragement lowers self-efficacy).

Evaluation

Practical applications
One strength is that understanding the self-concept can lead to positive practical outcomes.

Denis Lawrence (2006) ran workshops with children who were underperforming at school. He found the best way to improve academic achievement and reduce behavioural issues was to increase self-esteem. Children who had only counselling or class teaching didn't show the same improvements as those with self-esteem enhancement.

This suggests that self-esteem is an important factor in wellbeing and academic achievement.

Research support
Another strength is research evidence that other people influence our self-esteem.

A review of 52 studies concluded that our self-esteem is increased when our relationships with others are fulfilling and supportive (Harris and Orth 2020). Our high self-esteem in turn improves the quality of our relationships, and so on in a positive feedback loop (poor relationships lower self-esteem and create a negative feedback loop). This is true across all ages, genders and ethnic groups.

This shows that there is a reciprocal (two-way) link in which self-esteem and other people influence each other.

Vague concepts
One weakness is that the different aspects of self explored on this spread are poorly defined.

Some psychologists define self-concept as 'beliefs' about the self, but others include 'feelings' (i.e. the value you put on your self-concept). Many concepts overlap, e.g. self-image and self-esteem are so closely correlated that they may be more or less the same thing. This is a good example of the *jangle fallacy*, the assumption that two identical things are different just because we have given them different names.

This vagueness limits our understanding of ideas such as self-concept and the practical benefits we can derive from them.

Homer Simpson, the master of creating low self-efficacy: 'Bart, you tried your best and you failed miserably. The lesson is, never try.'

Making links to the key assumptions

Assumption: Wider culture and society influence people's behaviour This assumption is illustrated by responses to the *Twenty Statements Test*. People from *individualist* cultures most often describe their own personal characteristics ('I am independent', 'I am happy'). People from *collectivist* cultures are more likely to describe their place in the wider community ('I am a caring parent', 'I am a strong friend').

Assumption: Behaviour occurs in a social context (influenced by people around us) Explain how self-concept relates to this assumption (see page 10).

GET ACTIVE Measuring your self-concept

There are lots of ways to measure the concepts on this spread – understandably they are all based on self-report. After all, the most direct way to understand someone's self-concept is to ask them about it.

You may have had a go at the *Twenty Statements Test* described on the facing page. A different kind of self-report measure is the *Rosenberg Self-Esteem Scale* (Rosenberg 1965), which you can find here: tinyurl.com/3ebsbns5

1. What do you think of the test? Did it reveal anything that surprised you?
2. Can you think of any limitations of the test as a measure of self-concept?
3. What are the advantages and disadvantages of measuring the self in this way as opposed to using the Twenty Statements Test?

Exam-style questions

We all have a self-concept that is influenced by other people. Self-esteem and self-image are both important aspects of self-concept.

1. Explain what is meant by 'self-esteem'. Refer to the influence of others in your answer. (2 marks)
2. Ling and Mei are twins. Ling is confident in most situations, happy with how she looks and doesn't care much what other people think of her. Mei is not very confident, hates her own body and is really anxious about other people's opinions of her.

   Referring to Ling and/or Mei, give **one** example that could illustrate the influence of others on self-esteem. (1 mark)
3. Describe **one** example from the scenario in question 2 that could illustrate the influence of others on self-image. (2 marks)
4. Explain what is meant by 'self-concept'. Refer to the influence of others in your answer. (2 marks)
5. Ling started revising four months before her first exam after watching someone on a YouTube video making a detailed plan. She's confident she'll do well. Mei only started revising two weeks before her first exam because her teachers were nagging her to get on with it. But she still thinks she'll do badly.

   Briefly describe how the behaviour of Ling and/or Mei illustrates self-efficacy. (3 marks)
6. Give **one** possible reason for the difference in Ling and Mei's behaviour. (2 marks)
7. Briefly analyse self-concept as an explanation of Ling and/or Mei's behaviour. (3 marks)

An issue to consider
Which of the 'self' concepts on this spread do you think is most important? Explain your choice.

Specification content
A2 Social approach

Learners must be able to understand and apply knowledge of key concepts to explain aspects of human behaviour, including:

- Influences of others on self-concept (self-esteem, self-image); self-efficacy.

Content area A3: Behaviourist and social learning approaches
Key concept 1: Classical conditioning

What is classical conditioning?

Classical conditioning is a form of learning first scientifically studied by Ivan Pavlov. It is learning through *association*. It takes place when we associate two stimuli with each other.

An *unconditioned (unlearned) stimulus* (UCS) is repeatedly paired with a *neutral stimulus* (NS). Initially, the NS produces no response but eventually it produces the same response as the one produced by the UCS (see diagram below).

Before conditioning

The UCS triggers an unlearned response. The smell of food is a good example of a UCS because it makes us (and dogs) salivate automatically. We do not have to learn to salivate so it is an *unconditioned response* (UCR). Any other stimulus that does not produce the target response (e.g. salivation) is an NS. For example, the sound of a bell or of your name being spoken, a tap on the wrist, none of these will produce salivation.

During conditioning

The individual repeatedly experiences the UCS and NS close together in time ('pairing'). The NS is no longer 'neutral' once the individual eventually learns to associate it with the UCS. Pairing has the strongest effect on conditioning when the NS occurs just before the UCS. It usually has to happen several times for conditioning to take place.

After conditioning

After enough pairings, the NS (on its own) produces the same response as the UCS. The NS is now a *conditioned stimulus* (CS) and the response it produces is called a *conditioned response* (CR).

Making links to the key assumptions

Assumption: Behaviour is a learned response to environmental stimuli The UCS and NS are the environmental stimuli. There are examples on this spread – food, loud noises, white rats, dog bites, Altoids. When the NS produces a response on its own (and therefore becomes a CS), this shows that classical conditioning has taken place – a new behaviour has been learned!

Assumption: Behaviour can be learned from observation and imitation This assumption does not apply here but will wait until page 38.

BOGOF

Everyone likes a special offer – but why do shops and brands do them? Surely these kinds of offers reduce profits?

The answer is that special offers are good in the longer term because they encourage loyalty and repeat business. They do this by making us feel good about the brand.

When a chocolate bar or bottle of wine is 30% cheaper in a shop it makes you feel good to think you've grabbed yourself a bargain. You associate this good feeling with the product, so that next time you see it you'll feel good about it again even if it is full price. You might even feel good about the shop as well and decide to go there again.

Retailers use lots of ways to make us learn to love their products. This spread will help you to understand the psychological principles behind this.

Specification terms

Classical conditioning A form of learning where a neutral stimulus (NS) is paired with an unconditioned stimulus (UCS), taking on its properties so that a new stimulus–response association is learned.

Conditioned response (CR) The response produced by the conditioned stimulus (CS) on its own. A new association has been formed so that the neutral stimulus (NS) now produces the unconditioned response (UCR) (which is now called the conditioned response, CR).

Conditioned stimulus (CS) A stimulus that only produces the desired response after pairing with the unconditioned stimulus (UCS).

Neutral stimulus (NS) Any stimulus that does not produce the desired response. It becomes a conditioned stimulus (CS) after being paired with the unconditioned stimulus (UCS).

Unconditioned response (UCR) An unlearned response to an unconditioned stimulus (UCS).

Unconditioned stimulus (UCS) Any stimulus that produces a response without learning taking place.

The Russian Nobel Prize-winning physiologist Ivan Pavlov kept dogs in his laboratory for experiments. He noticed that the dogs started salivating when they saw the research assistant coming to feed them. Pavlov investigated whether his dogs could learn an association between food and a new stimulus, in this case the sound of a bell.

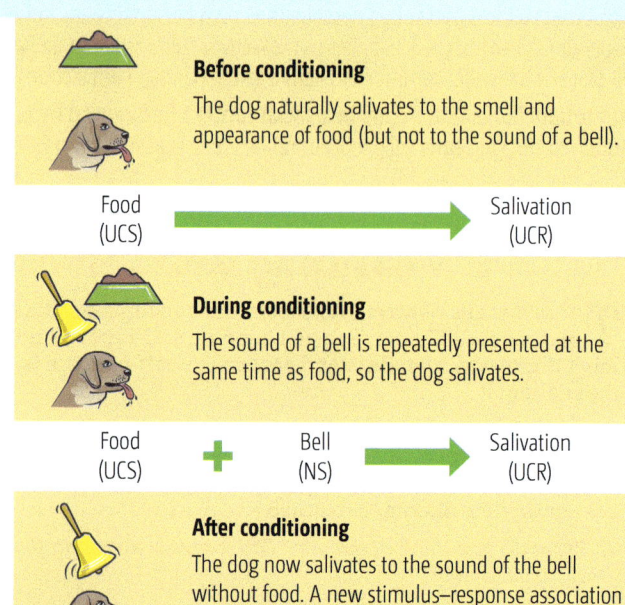

Before conditioning
The dog naturally salivates to the smell and appearance of food (but not to the sound of a bell).

Food (UCS) → Salivation (UCR)

During conditioning
The sound of a bell is repeatedly presented at the same time as food, so the dog salivates.

Food (UCS) + Bell (NS) → Salivation (UCR)

After conditioning
The dog now salivates to the sound of the bell without food. A new stimulus–response association has formed (classically conditioned).

Bell (CS) → Salivation (CR)

Evaluation

Practical applications

One strength is that classical conditioning is the basis of a therapy used to treat some psychological disorders, including gambling addiction.

In *aversion therapy*, an addicted gambler is given a painful electric shock (UCS) when they read gambling-related phrases on cards (NS). The shock produces an unconditioned response (UCR) of discomfort/anxiety. After several pairings, the NS becomes a CS and produces the same discomfort (now a CR).

This shows that classical conditioning has useful applications that can reduce psychological suffering and improve quality of life.

Research support

Another strength is evidence that learning in humans can take place through classical conditioning.

John Watson and Rosalie Rayner (1920) conditioned a fear response in a baby now known to us as 'Little Albert'. Albert initially showed no fear when he played with a white rat. But Watson and Rayner paired the rat with something Albert *was* afraid of – a very loud noise. After several pairings, Albert cried and crawled away from the rat, even when there was no loud noise.

This shows that classically conditioning a fear response to a neutral stimulus is relatively straightforward, at least in very young children.

Limited explanation of learning

One weakness is that classical conditioning can only explain learning of a limited range of behaviours (e.g. simple reflex behaviours).

More complex behaviours involve other learning processes (see the next two spreads). For example, classical conditioning can explain how a phobia of dogs is acquired (i.e. pairing of a dog with loud barking or a painful bite). But it cannot explain how that phobia then continues over time (e.g. how we learn to avoid dogs).

This means classical conditioning is just a partial explanation of learning with limited applications.

A useful application of classical conditioning is for treating gambling addiction. It works on the basis that if a behaviour can be learned through conditioning, then it can be unlearned through counterconditioning. For example, each time a person reads a gambling-related phrase they are given an electric shock so that they learn to associate gambling with pain rather than pleasure.

Exam-style questions

Kit is explaining to their friends how they developed a phobia of dogs. 'It's because I was bitten by a dog when I was a kid. It hurt a lot and made me cry. I'm still frightened of dogs to this day.'

1. Describe, using classical conditioning, how Kit became frightened of dogs. (3 marks)
2. Ran is a smoker. The first time he had a cigarette he enjoyed the pleasurable sensations of the first draw. Now every time Ran looks at his lighter he gets a bit of a buzz.
   Identify the UCR, the CS and the CR in this scenario. (3 marks)
3. Freya is a solicitor who works in a big law firm. Every time Freya's boss asks her to come into her office, Freya feels anxious. Her heart rate increases, she sweats and her hands shake.
   (a) Explain Freya's behaviour using classical conditioning. (3 marks)
   (b) Briefly discuss the explanation of Freya's behaviour that you gave in your answer to question 3(a). (3 marks)
4. State what is meant by the term 'classical conditioning'. (1 mark)
5. Describe **one** example of classical conditioning from everyday life. (3 marks)

An issue to consider

Recent research has found that plants can be classically conditioned.

How would that work and why would this be an advantage for plants?

Specification content

A3 Behaviourist and social learning approaches

Learners must be able to understand and apply knowledge of key concepts to explain aspects of human behaviour, including:

- Classical conditioning – learning by association, to include the role of the unconditioned stimulus, unconditioned response, neutral stimulus, conditioned stimulus and conditioned response.

GET ACTIVE Say cheese!

Laila is a professional photographer. She often takes photos of people indoors using a flash. The camera also makes a 'whirring' noise when the picture is taken. Laila has noticed that most people blink the first couple of times the flash goes off. If she then takes a picture without the flash, they still blink.

1. Draw a diagram of the classical conditioning process in this scenario. Include 'before', 'during' and 'after' stages. Identify the UCS, UCR, NS, CS and CR at the various stages.
2. What do you think might happen to the CR if Laila continued to take pictures without the flash?
3. Watch this clip from 'The Office': tinyurl.com/49r3a6yr. Draw a diagram showing how Dwight was classically conditioned.
4. Think of another scenario that involves learning through association and pairing of two stimuli. Draw a diagram to show the classical conditioning process.

Content area A3: Behaviourist and social learning approaches
Key concept 2: Operant conditioning

Put down your guns

Up until 2010 the city of Richmond in California had a serious problem with gun violence. It was the ninth most dangerous city in the whole of the US. The police knew that 17 young men were responsible for 70% of shootings.

DeVone Boggan was the head of Richmond's Office of Neighborhood Safety and he had a plan to tackle the violence. Prison, fines and other punishments had failed to make a difference. So Boggan began in 2007 by employing streetwise people to build relationships with these young men. In 2010 Boggan invited the men to a meeting and made them an offer – he would pay them not to fire their guns. They could earn up to $1000 every month for nine months as long as they stuck to a mentoring programme and didn't use their guns.

In other words, instead of punishing bad behaviour, Boggan was going to reward (reinforce) good behaviour.

Did it work? In the first year, gun crime in the city reduced by half. By 2014 the reduction was 76%. Drug use also declined, and school and job attendance went up. For most, the positive results continued even after the cash stopped.

Specification terms

Extrinsic rewards Pleasurable consequences of a behaviour that come from the external environment, e.g. praise, money.

Intrinsic rewards Pleasurable consequences of a behaviour that come from within the individual, e.g. feeling of achievement, interest.

Motivation The drive to behave in a way that achieves a goal or satisfies a need.

Negative reinforcement The reinforcer is the removal of an unpleasant stimulus, which makes the behaviour more likely to be repeated.

Operant conditioning A form of learning in which behaviour is shaped and maintained by its consequences – reinforcement (positive or negative) or punishment (positive or negative).

Positive reinforcement The reinforcer is a pleasant consequence of the behaviour, making the behaviour more likely to be repeated.

Punishment The consequence of a behaviour is unpleasant, making the behaviour less likely to be repeated.

Reinforcement A behaviour is followed by a consequence that increases the probability of the behaviour being repeated.

What is operant conditioning?

We form a link between a behaviour (the operant) and its consequence (the result that follows it). This is learning by consequences rather than by association (which is *classical conditioning*, see previous spread).

Depending on the consequence, the probability of the behaviour being repeated increases or decreases. There are two consequences:

Consequence 1 – Reinforcement

This consequence *increases* the probability of a behaviour being repeated. Any consequence that does this is said to *reinforce* the behaviour (it is reinforcing, it is a reinforcer). There are two main types:

- **Positive reinforcement** occurs when a behaviour is followed by a pleasant consequence. The consequence could be something tangible (e.g. food, money) or intangible (e.g. a smile or nice comment). The consequence reinforces the behaviour, making it more likely to happen again.
- **Negative reinforcement** occurs when a behaviour is followed by the removal of an unpleasant stimulus. For example, the removal of pain negatively reinforces the behaviour it follows and makes it more likely the behaviour will be repeated.

Consequence 2 – Punishment

This consequence *reduces* the probability of a behaviour being repeated. Any such consequence is said to *punish* the behaviour (it is punishing, it is a punisher). Again, there are two main types:

- **Positive punishment** is when a behaviour is followed by an unpleasant consequence (e.g. a slap or harsh words).
- **Negative punishment** occurs when a behaviour is followed by the removal of something pleasant (e.g. being fined or grounded, because there has been *removal* of money or freedom).

Motivation

Our behaviour is motivated by the desire to achieve our goals or satisfy our needs. *Motivation* is driven by rewards through operant conditioning. The source of rewards can be external (*extrinsic*) or internal (*intrinsic*).

Extrinsic rewards These come from our environment, usually other people such as parents, teachers and friends. Gaining a reward or avoiding a punishment motivates us to behave in a certain way, e.g. writing an essay to gain a high grade (reward) or to avoid being told off (punishment).

Intrinsic rewards These originate from within yourself, such as your own enjoyment, pleasure, interest, sense of challenge, etc. You do something for its own sake rather than in response to extrinsic rewards, so the activity is rewarding in itself. Some examples include: pursuing a hobby for the challenge, volunteering for a charity because you believe in the cause, doing a certain degree because you find it interesting.

Intrinsic motivation is highly desirable because achieving goals without external rewards is more fulfilling and raises self-esteem.

Making links to the key assumptions

Assumption: Behaviour is a learned response to environmental stimuli Here is just one example. If you smile when you ask someone for a favour, their response will probably be rewarding for you – you get what you want. This is a pleasurable consequence originating from your environment, which reinforces your smiling behaviour so you learn to do it again next time.

Assumption: Behaviour can be learned from observation and imitation This assumption does not apply here but will wait until page 38.

Evaluation

Practical applications
One strength is that there are many practical applications of operant conditioning in education.

Reinforcement is often used in settings such as schools and nurseries. For example, good work and behaviour are reinforced by extrinsic rewards such as praise or gold stars. Intrinsic rewards are encouraged to raise students' self-esteem (e.g. setting their own targets). Punishment is often used in schools and by parents to eliminate undesirable behaviour (e.g. isolation, 'naughty step').

This shows that operant conditioning has wide uses in the real world as well as theoretical importance.

Research support
Another strength is that operant conditioning is supported by both human and animal studies.

Many lab studies have shown how operant conditioning works in various animal species (e.g. rats and pigeons). The findings reliably demonstrate how behaviour is influenced by reinforcement and punishment. Human studies have even discovered brain areas and structures that are linked with reinforcement of behaviour (e.g. Chase *et al.* 2015).

Therefore, research supports the view that operant conditioning is a key form of learning in many animal and human behaviours.

Incomplete explanation of learning
One weakness is that operant conditioning is not a full explanation of some learning.

On the plus side, operant conditioning can explain some complex behaviours where classical conditioning cannot. For example, it can explain how a phobia is maintained over time (through negatively-reinforcing avoidance). However, this only explains how the existing behaviour is strengthened or weakened. It does not explain how the phobia first appears (but classical conditioning does).

This means operant conditioning is an incomplete theory that does not account for all behaviours.

GET ACTIVE Measure your motivation

It takes a great deal of motivation to persist with a two-year BTEC course (or a three-year degree). Lessons, deadlines, assignments, homework, mock exams, actual exams... The list goes on. How do you think you're doing so far? Psychologists have devised various ways to measure motivation, so it would be interesting to have a go at one of these to see what it reveals about you.

You can find a questionnaire here: tinyurl.com/4x75s7ve

1. Think about the individual items on the questionnaire. Were you surprised at any of your responses? Identify **one** of these and try to explain what surprised you.
2. Can you think of any ways you could use what you have learned to improve your intrinsic motivation?

Exam-style questions

Anika works in a call centre selling insurance policies to customers. Every time someone sells a policy, the manager plays a fanfare and praises them. When this happened to Anika, she worked even harder and made more calls.

1. Describe, using operant conditioning, why Anika worked harder. (3 marks)
2. Kammy is addicted to playing on fruit machines. She gets a thrill from all the flashing lights and loud noises and occasionally the money she wins. She prefers doing this to being at home with Anika and their children.
   (a) Explain **two** ways operant conditioning can be used to explain Kammy's behaviour. (4 marks)
   (b) Briefly assess the explanation you gave for Kammy's behaviour in your answer to question 2(a). (3 marks)
3. Larry is Anika and Kammy's five-year-old son. When Larry helped tidy the living room, Anika gave him a sweet. The next day he tidied his bedroom. But when Larry bit his sister he had to go and sit on the naughty step.
   (a) Give **one** example of positive reinforcement and **one** example of punishment from the above scenario. (2 marks)
   (b) Explain how Anika and Kammy could use negative reinforcement to encourage Larry not to bite his sister. (2 marks)
4. Elis is a healthcare assistant working in a nursing home. He gets paid 150% of his hourly rate for any overtime he does and he will get a higher rate if he gains an advanced qualification. Elis enjoys his job because he meets all sorts of people, is interested in healthcare and wants to learn more about it.
   Explain how this scenario indicates that Elis may be motivated by (a) extrinsic rewards and (b) intrinsic rewards. (4 marks)

A person's obsession with their mobile phone can be explained by operant conditioning. There are lots of features of phones that most people find very rewarding.

An issue to consider
Do you think that operant conditioning is a realistic way of changing other people's behaviour (as described in the box on the facing page ('Put down your guns')?

Do you think there are ethical issues with controlling people's behaviour like this?

Specification content
A3 Behaviourist and social learning approaches

Learners must be able to understand and apply knowledge of key concepts to explain aspects of human behaviour, including:

- Operant conditioning – learning by consequences, to include the role of positive reinforcement, negative reinforcement and punishment, motivation (extrinsic and intrinsic rewards).

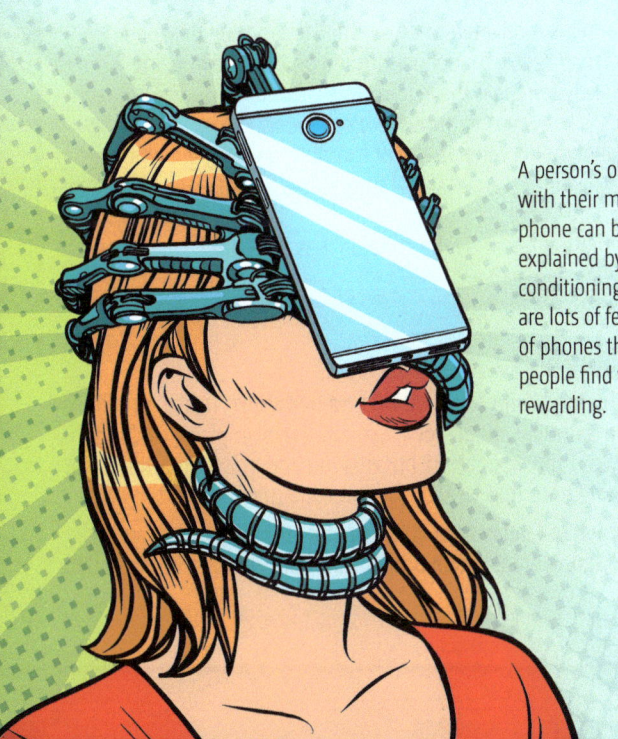

Content area A3: Behaviourist and social learning approaches
Key concept 3: Social learning theory

Are criminals born or made?

The idea that some people are 'born bad' is a popular one. But even bad people have to learn how to behave like criminals. Take Pablo Escobar for instance. He rose from obscurity to control the trade in cocaine between Colombia and the USA, and in the process became one of the wealthiest and most feared people in the world.

But he started his criminal career selling stolen gravestones before moving on to selling stolen cigarettes. He learned his trade from other more experienced criminals. He accompanied them on 'jobs' and observed what was involved in criminal behaviour.

Escobar was highly motivated. He aimed to be a millionaire before he was 22, so he wanted to learn. He was a bodyguard for a local drug kingpin which gave him the opportunity to observe at first-hand exactly what was involved in successful drug smuggling. He was surrounded by people with greater status than him, who were well-off and respected in their world.

This was Escobar's 'training ground'. He used it as the foundation of a criminal career that brought him unimaginable wealth and cost thousands of people their lives before he was killed in a shootout in 1993, aged 44.

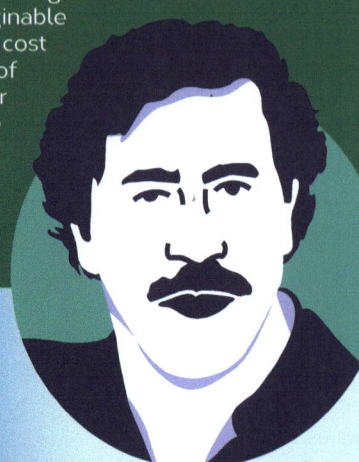

Specification terms

Imitation Occurs when a learner copies the behaviour they observed being carried out by a model. It is more likely to occur when the observer identifies with the model.

Modelling Either an observer imitates the behaviour of a model, or a model demonstrates a behaviour that may be imitated by an observer.

Observation Actively attending to and watching (or listening to) the behaviour of others (models).

Social learning A form of learning in which behaviours are acquired through observation, modelling, imitation and vicarious reinforcement. Cognitive factors play a key role.

Vicarious learning Occurs when a learner observes a model's behaviour being reinforced (hence also vicarious reinforcement).

What is social learning theory (SLT)?

Albert Bandura (1962) proposed *social learning theory* (SLT) to explain how learning often occurs without *direct* reinforcement. Instead, a behaviour can be learned *indirectly* by *observing* and *imitating* another individual whose behaviour has been reinforced.

Bandura and his colleagues demonstrated these processes in a series of famous studies known as the 'Bobo doll studies'.

Modelling

Modelling can mean two things. The first meaning refers to when a behaviour is demonstrated to another person (usually not deliberately). The person who performs the behaviour is the *model*. The other meaning refers to when a person imitates a model's behaviour. In both cases, the individuals involved are modelling a behaviour.

In Bandura *et al.*'s research (1961, 1965), an adult model behaved aggressively towards an inflatable Bobo doll (e.g. punching, kicking, shouting, etc.).

Learning through observation

The observer actively focuses their attention on the model's behaviour and watches how it is performed. The model's actions have to be retained in the observer's memory before they can be repeated.

Children observed the adult model being aggressive in Bandura *et al.*'s studies.

Imitation

The observer may copy the model's behaviour. This is more likely if the observer identifies with the model. This happens for two main reasons:

Similarity The observer perceives the model to be similar to themselves (e.g. same age, gender, etc.).

Value The observer values and/or admires the model (e.g. because they have social status, wealth, fame, intelligence, etc.).

When the children in the Bobo doll studies played with the doll, they behaved aggressively, often imitating exactly some of the aggressive behaviours of the adult model. In some cases, imitation was more likely when the model was the same gender as the child.

Vicarious learning

A behaviour is imitated if the learner is motivated to do so. This depends on observing positive consequences. If the observer sees a model performing an action and being reinforced, the observer is more likely to repeat the action. This is *vicarious* (seeing someone else do it) and reinforcing (so this is known as *vicarious reinforcement*).

This could explain the influence of media celebrities. For example, a young girl who sees a very thin celebrity having her behaviour rewarded with fame, status and attention might be more inclined to imitate the celebrity's 'look'.

The Bobo doll studies showed that imitation by the children was more likely when the adult model was rewarded for being aggressive.

Making links to the key assumptions

Assumption: Behaviour can be learned from observation and imitation This assumption is easy to apply – it's what this spread is all about. Look again at the examples given and try to think of some more of your own. Think about how observation and imitation can lead to learning in these cases and the difference that vicarious reinforcement makes.

Assumption: Behaviour is a learned response to environmental stimuli Social learning theory does not exclude classical and operant conditioning. How does this assumption relate to the key concept (see page 11)?

Evaluation

Practical applications
One strength is that SLT can help us understand how aggressive behaviour in children can be reduced.

SLT explains the effects of observing aggression in the family, in peers and in the media. So children learn to imitate aggressive models, especially when they see them rewarded. SLT suggests several targets for interventions, such as: reducing the rewards available for aggression, limiting access to violent media and providing non-aggressive role models for children to identify with and imitate.

Therefore, SLT is beneficial because it offers practical ways of both reducing undesirable behaviours and increasing desirable ones.

Research support
Another strength is support for SLT from research into a variety of behaviours.

Bandura *et al.*'s research showed that children will imitate an aggressive adult model, and this is more likely when they observe the model's behaviour being reinforced (i.e. rewarded). Also, some phobias may develop in children because they observe fearful and anxious behaviour by adults around them (Askew and Field 2007).

This supports the SLT view that behaviours are learned through observation and imitation, and that vicarious reinforcement plays a key role in imitation.

Alternative explanation
One weakness is that social learning has relatively little influence on many behaviours.

Some behaviours are better explained by alternative theories. For example, research shows that the occurrence of phobia is greater in identical twins than in non-identical twins (Kendler *et al.* 2001). The same pattern is true for depression (Kendall *et al.* 2021). Due to the fact that identical twins are more closely genetically related than non-identical twins, this shows that genes play a greater role than social learning in many behaviours, such as phobias and depression.

This suggests that SLT is not a complete explanation of learning, and a full account can only be produced by considering other factors.

Don't forget to make AO3 PET-friendly: Point, Evidence/Explanation, T-word ('Therefore', 'This shows...' etc.), just like on this and every other spread.

The word 'bobo' is Spanish for 'clown'.
The word 'doll' is English for 'doll'.

GET ACTIVE Guitar lessons

Hari is learning to play the guitar. His favourite musicians are guitarists and he really enjoys listening to guitar-based bands. Hari is getting lessons from Nisha. She shows him how to play the chords, where to place his fingers and how to strum. Hari copies and Nisha praises him when he gets it right. Hari likes the way Nisha really seems to enjoy playing the guitar as well.

How can Hari's learning be explained in terms of:
(a) classical conditioning
(b) operant conditioning
(c) social learning?

Exam-style questions

Ava and Livvy are playing football when Ava flicks the ball up and volleys it into the back of the net. Livvy is impressed and Ava explains that she watched her brother doing the same trick. When he got it right he ran around the garden shouting with joy.

1. Identify from the scenario **one** example each of: (a) observation, (b) imitation and (c) vicarious learning. (3 marks)
2. Use social learning theory to explain Ava's behaviour. (3 marks)
3. Assess how social learning can help us understand Ava's behaviour. (3 marks)
4. State what is meant by the term 'vicarious learning'. (1 mark)
5. Barney is in the canteen at his primary school, watching closely as his teacher has a yoghurt drink. The teacher finishes the drink, smiles and says, 'Mmmmm, delicious'. As soon as he gets home from school, Barney goes straight to the fridge, takes out a yoghurt drink and drinks it.

    Identify in this scenario: (a) modelling and (b) vicarious learning. (2 marks)

An issue to consider
Can you think of any things you do which could not be explained by direct or indirect conditioning?

Specification content
A3 Behaviourist and social learning approaches

Learners must be able to understand and apply knowledge of key concepts to explain aspects of human behaviour, including:
- Social learning theory – learning through observation, imitation, modelling and vicarious learning.

Content area A4: Biological approach

Key concept 1: Influence of biology on behaviour and traits

The Knowledge

On this spread we look at the many ways in which our biology affects our behaviour. But what is perhaps more surprising is that our behaviour can influence our biology.

Drivers of famous 'black cabs' in London don't use satnavs. Instead, they have to pass a very difficult exam before they start the job. The test, called 'The Knowledge', assesses drivers' recall of all the streets and landmarks in London and the routes connecting them. Passing The Knowledge takes huge commitment and many hours of study – it's said to be one of the hardest tests you can take.

A study by Eleanor Maguire *et al.* (2000) compared men who had completed The Knowledge with a matched control group of men who were not taxi drivers. Incredibly, the special learning by the taxi drivers affected the structure of an important part of their brains. Brain scans showed that the hippocampus, which is involved in memory, was on average significantly bigger in the taxi drivers.

So, the relationship between biology and behaviour is sometimes a two-way street!

Specification terms

Extraversion One end of a personality dimension with introversion at the other end. Extraversion includes such traits as being outgoing, sociable, sensation-seeking.

Introversion One end of a personality dimension with extraversion at the other end. Introversion includes such traits as shyness, being withdrawn, avoiding new experiences.

Traits Distinct characteristics that make up personality, e.g. friendliness, warmth, sociability, shyness, moodiness, etc.

This is just the sort of thing extraverts enjoy.

Influence of biology on behaviour

Biological psychologists argue that, as the mind basically 'lives' in the brain, our thoughts, feelings and behaviour have a physical basis (everything psychological is first biological).
We will look on the next few spreads at four ways in which biology influences behaviour:

- *Genes* are made up of strands of DNA inherited from parents. DNA provides chemical instructions to manufacture proteins in the body, which influence our characteristics, e.g. height and personality.
- *Neuroanatomy* refers to the structure of the nervous system, including the brain. Different parts of the brain have different functions, e.g. one area controls what we see (visual area) and another area controls movement (motor area).
- *Neurochemistry* concerns messages sent around the brain and body via *neurons* (nerve cells) and *neurotransmitters* (chemical messengers), e.g. levels of some neurotransmitters affect mood.
- *Evolution* concerns the way organisms change over millions of years. Many behaviours evolved through natural selection, as our ancestors adapted to the environment in order to survive.

Influence of biology on traits

What are traits?

Traits are characteristics that make up a personality. When we ask the question, 'What's her personality like?', we usually answer with a list of traits: 'She's cheerful, friendly, intelligent, kind...'. Traits do not change much from one situation to another (they are stable), or within a situation (they are consistent) or as we get older (they are enduring).

Extraversion and introversion

Extraversion and *introversion* are two aspects of personality that feature in a theory by Hans Eysenck (1947):

- Extraverts are outgoing, sociable, loud, friendly and they constantly seek new experiences and sensations.
- Introverts are mostly the opposite – withdrawn, shy, quiet and uncomfortable with new sensations.

Most people are not pure extraverts or pure introverts. Extraversion–introversion (E–I) is a dimension of personality and each of us lies somewhere between extreme extraversion and extreme introversion.

Biological influences on extraversion/introversion

Eysenck argued that there are two main biological influences on E–I: genes and neurochemistry. Genes inherited from your parents determine your degree of E–I. They do this by influencing the activity of your nervous system (i.e. your neurochemistry):

- Extraverts inherit an underactive nervous system, so in order to arouse it they have to experience constant excitement, e.g. by engaging in risky behaviours.
- Introverts inherit an overactive nervous system, so they avoid the discomfort of arousing it any further by withdrawing and keeping away from exciting activities.

Making links to the key assumptions

Assumption: Behaviour is influenced by the central nervous system (CNS), genes and neurochemistry You can see on this spread how all three main biological influences operate together. Genes affect the activity of neurotransmitters (neurochemistry) in the nervous system, which in turn influences your personality and behaviour (through arousal of the central nervous system).

Assumption: Behaviour is a product of evolution How does this assumption relate to extraversion and introversion (see page 11)?

Evaluation

Practical applications

One strength of understanding the influence of biology is improved approaches to reducing criminal behaviour.

Criminals are often extraverts – they are sensation-seekers who crave the excitement provided by new experiences and taking risks, such as committing crimes. Extraverts tend not to learn through rewards and punishments, so they are not deterred from antisocial behaviour by being punished (e.g. with imprisonment).

Therefore, perhaps some criminal behaviour may be better dealt with using biological methods, e.g. drugs to increase the activity of the nervous system.

Research support

Another strength is research into the genetics of personality traits.

Researchers have compared identical and non-identical twins to calculate a 'heritability estimate' – a figure indicating the degree to which a physical or psychological characteristic is genetically inherited. The figure for extraversion–introversion may be as high as 57% (Sanchez-Roige et al. 2018).

This evidence supports the view that being an extravert or introvert is fairly strongly influenced by genes (i.e. mostly inherited).

Role of non-biological factors

One weakness of biological influences is that they are often less important than other factors.

For instance, genes may make it more likely that a person will become an extravert or introvert. But this is not inevitable. Non-biological factors such as learning experiences may be more important, such as the influences from the social environment in which a person is raised. Alternative theories may be more useful explanations of behaviour.

Therefore, there is a risk of exaggerating biological influences and gaining an oversimplified view of the causes of behaviour.

What's the alternative?

A good way to evaluate a theory/concept is to compare it to another theory/concept. But do it properly – don't just describe another theory. So instead of asking yourself, 'What's the alternative?', you should ask, 'Why is the alternative better?'.

GET ACTIVE What are you?

You can complete a questionnaire to measure your degree of extraversion–introversion here: tinyurl.com/44zyahrd. This works best if you try to avoid giving answers 'in the middle' as much as possible.

This questionnaire measures two other personality dimensions that Eysenck considered important: neuroticism–emotional stability and psychoticism–socialisation. There are explanations on the webpage.

Bear in mind that this is just a bit of fun and not a serious analysis of your personality.

1. How does your score match up with your own opinion of yourself? Are you like your parents in any of these ways?
2. What do you think of the questionnaire itself? Do the questions really measure what they are supposed to?

Exam-style questions

Frankie became a paramedic because they wanted a job working with people and helping them. Frankie finds being a paramedic is exciting, telling their friends on a night out, 'You never know what's going to happen next.' Frankie's mum is a firefighter and their dad is a hospital nurse.

1. Identify **two** of Frankie's traits that indicate they are an extravert. (2 marks)
2. Explain **one** way in which biology may have influenced Frankie's traits. (2 marks)
3. Explain what is meant by 'introversion'. (2 marks)
4. Krystof is a landscape architect and runs a garden design business with his partner. He loves working on his own, designing and drawing, and likes the fact that their day-to-day work is quite predictable. As he feels uncomfortable dealing with clients, he leaves his partner to discuss and present their plans to the clients.

   Identify **two** of Krystof's traits that indicate he is an introvert. (2 marks)
5. Explain **one** way in which biology may have influenced Krystof's traits. (2 marks)
6. Describe **one** example of introversion from any everyday scenario other than the one in question 4. (2 marks)
7. Briefly analyse the view that biology is an influence on Krystof's behaviour and/or traits. (3 marks)

An issue to consider

How much do you think your personality is affected by biology compared with social, cultural and psychological factors?

Specification content

A4 Biological approach

Learners must be able to understand and apply knowledge of key concepts to explain aspects of human behaviour, including:

- The influence of biology on behaviour and traits, including introversion and extraversion.

The intensity and excitement of a paramedic's work may not suit an introvert.

Content area A4: Biological approach

Key concept 2: Genetics and inheritance

How identical is identical?

Psychologists call twins identical because they have exactly the same genes. Most people use the word in everyday language to mean that twins look identical. But do they really? Look more closely and you will see that even the most 'identical' of twins look a bit different.

Things get even more interesting when you consider behaviour. Even identical twins who have been brought up together in the same home do not behave identically. For instance one might be gay and the other straight. One becomes a scientist, the other an artist.

What this tells us is that, even if you had an identical twin, there will never be someone exactly like you. Your experiences and your environment will affect you in different ways to make you the person you are. It's not 'all in the genes'.

Specification terms

Genes Inherited DNA with instructions for building physical and psychological characteristics that influence behaviour.

Genotype An individual's total set of genes.

Phenotype The observable characteristics which result from the interaction between an individual's genotype and environmental factors.

SRY gene Sex-determining region Y gene which triggers the appearance of testes in an embryo and the development of that individual into a biological male.

The chromosome on the left is an X chromosome and on the right is a Y chromosome. They are called X and Y because they resemble the shape of these letters. This photograph was taken using a very high-powered microscope.

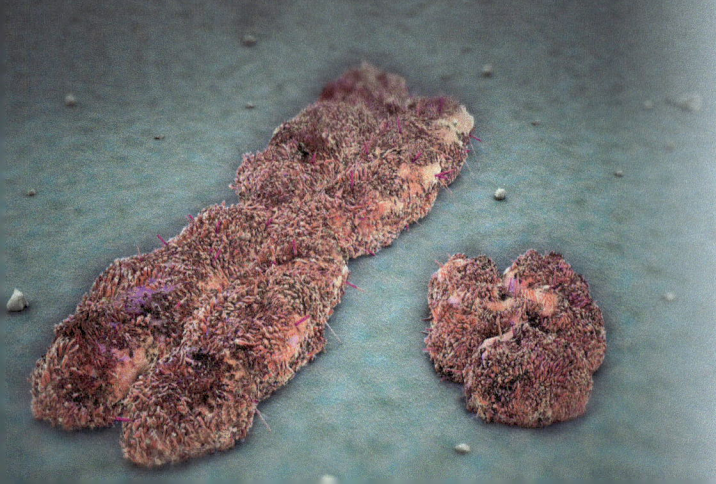

What are genes?

Genes are located on chromosomes and humans usually have 46 chromosomes (23 pairs). Each gene is made up of strands of DNA (deoxyribonucleic acid). Genes carry 'instructions' relating to the physical and non-physical characteristics of living organisms, such as the colour of your hair and whether you have a calm temperament.

Each individual typically inherits two copies (called *alleles*) of each gene, one from each parent.

Genotype and phenotype

Genotype

Genotype refers to an individual's actual genetic make-up. It is the collection of genes you inherit from your parents.

However, your genotype doesn't determine your physical and non-physical characteristics directly because genes are expressed through an interaction with your 'environment'. Even within your body the environment has an influence, for example the food you eat affects your body's internal environment.

Phenotype

Phenotype refers to how an individual's genes are actually expressed in their observable characteristics (brown hair, calm temperament, etc.). So the phenotype is the result of an interaction between genotype and environmental influences.

Example: identical twins

Identical twins have different phenotypes even though they have the same genotype (they inherit exactly the same genes). The different phenotypes are the result of each individual twin experiencing different environmental influences.

For example, twins may look physically different because one goes to the gym and the other doesn't and therefore one twin develops bigger muscles. The other twin might develop bigger muscles too – but only if their environment changed.

The distinction between genotype and phenotype strongly suggests that most human behaviours are due to an interaction of inherited (nature) and environmental (nurture) factors.

The *SRY* gene

One pair of chromosomes determines biological sex – XX for female, XY for male. The so-called Y chromosome is in reality just a stunted X chromosome, missing some of the genetic material.

Located on the Y chromosome is a gene called the sex-determining region Y gene (*SRY gene*). In typical development before birth (at about seven weeks), the *SRY* gene switches on other genes causing an XY embryo to develop testes.

In adult males the testes produce sperm, but during development the testes produce male *sex hormones* (e.g. testosterone). These hormones cause the embryo to become biologically male. Without the *SRY* gene, other genes remain switched off so the embryo develops into a female.

Making links to the key assumptions

Assumption: Behaviour is influenced by the central nervous system (CNS), genes and neurochemistry Genes often influence behaviour by affecting the structure and functioning of the CNS and its neurochemistry. But as this spread shows, genes are not the whole story. The distinction between genotype and phenotype emphasises the importance of environmental influences as well.

Assumption: Behaviour is a product of evolution How does this assumption relate to the concepts on this spread (see page 11)?

Evaluation

Practical applications
One strength is that there are practical benefits in distinguishing between genotype and phenotype.

For instance, depression (phenotype) is the result of a genetic predisposition (genotype) that is triggered by an environmental influence. Without the trigger the individual will not become depressed even though they have a relevant genotype. A good example of an environmental trigger is stress, which can be reduced in various ways (e.g. therapy) so it does not interact with the genotype.

Therefore, although genes cannot be changed, environmental factors can be, which reduces the risk of a negative outcome.

Research support
Another strength is evidence of the role of the *SRY* gene in development.

Very rarely, the process of 'copying' the *SRY* gene goes wrong, producing a variant (mutation) of the gene. In these cases the *SRY* gene cannot perform its usual function of 'switching on' testicular development in XY embryos. So the individual is genetically male but develops female-typical reproductive organs (e.g. uterus and vagina).

This evidence shows that the usual role of the *SRY* gene is to initiate male biological sex development in genetically male embryos.

Risk of oversimplification
One weakness is that the influence of genes is often oversimplified.

For instance, the phrase 'a gene *for* depression' is an inaccurate view of how genes operate. Genes may increase the risk of developing depression but do not cause it. Human behaviours generally are not caused by single genes. Instead, many genes (sometimes hundreds or thousands) make small but important contributions in complex interactions with each other.

Therefore, oversimplified explanations of how genes work exaggerate the role of inheritance (nature) and present a misleading view of the causes of behaviour.

A gene is actually just a stretch of chemicals located on a strand of DNA. For example, the area highlighted in yellow could represent one gene on a long twisted strand. These strands are further coiled and make up chromosomes. Chromosomes typically come in pairs (one from your mother and one from your father) and are shaped vaguely like an X.

Exam-style questions

Wanda and Maya are identical twins. Wanda has always been a 'people person'. She has lots of friends she often goes out with, especially from the local rugby club she plays for. Maya prefers to 'keep herself to herself'. She has always been quiet and shy, spending more time studying and caring for her pet snake than socialising.

1. Identify from this scenario evidence that Wanda and Maya:
   (a) Share the same genotype. (1 mark)
   (b) Have different phenotypes. (1 mark)
2. Explain **one** difference between genotype and phenotype. (2 marks)
3. Wanda is pregnant and having her second ultrasound scan (at 20 weeks). She wants to know the biological sex of the baby. 'It's a boy,' the doctor tells her.
   Explain how the biological approach accounts for the biological sex of Wanda's baby. Use the concept of genes in your answer. (3 marks)
4. Wanda is worried about her baby developing phenylketonuria (PKU). This is a rare genetic disorder that can cause severe learning difficulties, seizures and behavioural problems. However, a baby with PKU placed on a low-protein diet is very likely to develop normally and never experience symptoms.
   Explain how this scenario illustrates the difference between genotype and phenotype. (3 marks)
5. Briefly assess the role of genetics in human behaviour. (3 marks)

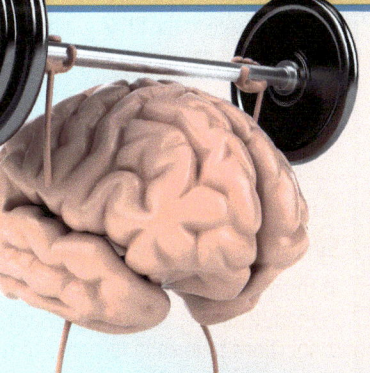

According to biological psychologists, everything that is psychological is first biological, most notably the brain. Our thoughts, feelings and behaviours are all controlled from this mighty organ. The brain itself is created from the instructions encoded in genes.

GET ACTIVE Taste the difference

We have seen that genetically identical twins are not identical in their behaviour or even their appearance (even their fingerprints are different). This is why we make a very important distinction between genotype and phenotype.

For example, the ability to taste phenylthiocarbamide (PTC, a bitter-tasting chemical) in food is genetically controlled by a single gene. But even people in whom the gene is 'switched on' will not always taste it.

1. *How can the concepts of genotype and phenotype explain this?*
2. *What environmental factors could influence the genotype?*

An issue to consider
Given what you have read on this spread, how do you think psychologists use genes in their explanations of behaviour?

Specification content
A4 Biological approach
Learners must be able to understand and apply knowledge of key concepts to explain aspects of human behaviour, including:
- Genetics and inheritance, including genes, genotype, phenotype and the SRY gene.

Content area A4: Biological approach
Key concept 3: Neuroanatomy

Poking around in the brain

If you open up a person's skull you could poke different areas of a person's brain – it wouldn't hurt as there aren't pain receptors in the brain.

The interesting thing is that if you poke some areas (well, electrically stimulate them), the person being poked may suddenly experience a particular memory. If you were then to poke a different area, the person might experience a different memory, hear music, report sensations on their skin or they might move a part of their body.

The brain surgeon who famously did this for the first time in the 1950s was Wilder Penfield. He was treating people with epilepsy and tried to relieve their seizures by destroying small areas of their brains.

This is obviously a drastic method because it is not reversible. Also, Wilder knew that every person's brain is slightly different. So he first of all had to work out which areas to destroy and which to avoid. He didn't want to risk damaging important brain functions and potentially making his patients worse off.

Penfield's poking around allowed him (and others) to draw a map of the brain and the functions of its different areas. Some of the brain areas Penfield stimulated are described on this spread.

Specification terms

Lateralisation of function The two brain hemispheres are specialised to perform different functions. Some functions are mainly controlled by one hemisphere rather than the other (e.g. language).

Localisation of function Specific brain areas control and regulate specific physical and psychological activities.

Neuroanatomy Structure of the brain and other parts of the nervous system.

Plasticity The brain is 'flexible' enough to change and adapt as a result of experience and new learning. This generally involves the growth of new connections (synapses).

What is neuroanatomy?

Neuroanatomy refers to the structure of the brain and nervous system. The most basic neuroanatomical feature of the brain is that it is divided into two (connected) halves, called the left hemisphere (LH) and the right hemisphere (RH).

Localisation of brain function

Psychologists generally accept the view that different brain areas perform certain specific functions. This is *localisation*. If a specific brain area is damaged, the function associated with that area is affected (impaired).

The brain's outer layer is called the *cortex*. It is a very thin and highly folded layer that covers the inner structures of the brain (like an orange peel). This part of the brain is highly developed in humans and the source of higher localised functions. These three major areas are found in both hemispheres (see diagram on facing page):

Motor area This controls the voluntary movements of the opposite side of the body (this is called *contralateral control*). Damage can cause a loss of control over fine movements.

Somatosensory area Sensory information (e.g. heat, touch) from the skin on the opposite side of the body is represented here in proportion to the sensitivity of the body part (e.g. the regions for the face and hands account for over half of the somatosensory area). Damage causes sensory problems such as numbness and tingling.

Visual area Each eye sends information from the right 'half' of the visual field to the left visual area, and from the left 'half' of the visual field to the right visual area. This is why damage to one visual area can cause partial blindness in both eyes.

Lateralisation of brain function

Although most brain functions are localised in both hemispheres, there are some that are found in just one hemisphere (either the LH or RH). These functions are said to be *lateralised* (i.e. 'one side'). This means that the two hemispheres are functionally different – one or the other is specialised ('dominant') for some functions.

Language For most people, the main areas of the brain involved in language are in the LH only. This is why damage to the RH (e.g. a burst blood vessel, called a 'stroke') does not usually cause language problems, but damage to specific areas in the LH does (e.g. difficulty speaking).

Plasticity of the brain

The brain is *plastic* in the sense that it is flexible and can change throughout life. Two examples of plasticity are synaptic pruning and functional recovery.

Synaptic pruning

At three years old, our brains have about 15,000 connections (synapses) per neuron, twice as many as in the adult brain. As we develop, synapses are 'pruned' (cut back) to allow new connections to form in response to new demands on the brain.

Functional recovery

When areas of the brain are damaged, unaffected areas can often adapt and 'take over' their functions. New synaptic connections are formed close to the damaged area (a kind of 'rewiring') or a corresponding area in the opposite hemisphere takes over. The recovery process can be supported by rehabilitation therapy (e.g. speech and language therapy).

Making links to the key assumptions

Assumption: Behaviour is a product of evolution Characteristics evolved because they increased our ancestors' chances of survival by helping them adapt to their environments. Therefore, brain localisation helped survival because damage to one area of the brain would only affect one function (the same applies to plasticity).

Assumption: Behaviour is influenced by the central nervous system (CNS), genes and neurochemistry How does this assumption relate to the concepts on this spread (see page 11)?

Evaluation

Practical applications
One strength of neuroanatomy is its real-world applications to help patients.

For example, programmes have been developed to help protect elderly people against age-related cognitive decline. One programme uses 200 hours of device-based game-type activities targeting attention, memory, coordination, etc. (Merzenich et al. 2014). This approach is based on knowledge of brain plasticity. The activities help support neurotransmitter-producing neurons that would otherwise decline with age.

This shows that understanding neuroanatomy can lead to interventions that benefit a range of conditions where brain injury or degeneration are involved.

Research support
Another strength is research evidence to support brain lateralisation.

For example, some studies suggest that our ability to make emotional facial expressions is controlled by the right hemisphere. This hemisphere is also dominant in recognising emotions in other people's facial expressions (vision) and even in identifying emotions in music (hearing). There is evidence that damage to parts of the right hemisphere disrupts these abilities (Lindell 2013).

This shows there are some significant functions that are lateralised in the human brain, with one hemisphere or the other specialised for each function.

Not so localised
One weakness is that brain functions may be less localised and lateralised than often thought.

An example is language. As brain scans become more advanced, researchers can study brain activity with more clarity than ever. Language seems to be distributed quite widely in the brain rather than being completely localised. Some language processing may even take place in the right hemisphere as well as the left.

This suggests that localisation and lateralisation theories do not fully explain the organisation of language in the brain, and the same may be true of other functions.

GET ACTIVE Phineas Gage

Phineas Gage was working on the railroad in the USA in 1848 when an explosion forced an iron bar through his head. Incredibly, he survived and, apart from his physical injury, seemed normal. But over time his personality changed so much that he could not get his job back. Phineas had gone from someone who was calm, shy and hardworking to somebody who was rude and aggressive. He now swore a lot and was 'a child in his intellectual capacity'. In the words of his friends, he was 'no longer Gage'. Phineas died twelve-and-a-half years after the accident at the age of 36.

Watch this video and answer the questions below: tinyurl.com/35z7v46x

1. What does the case of Phineas Gage tell us about brain localisation?
2. There is some evidence that Phineas's personality change was only temporary and he was back to his normal self within two or three years. How can you link this to the idea of brain plasticity?

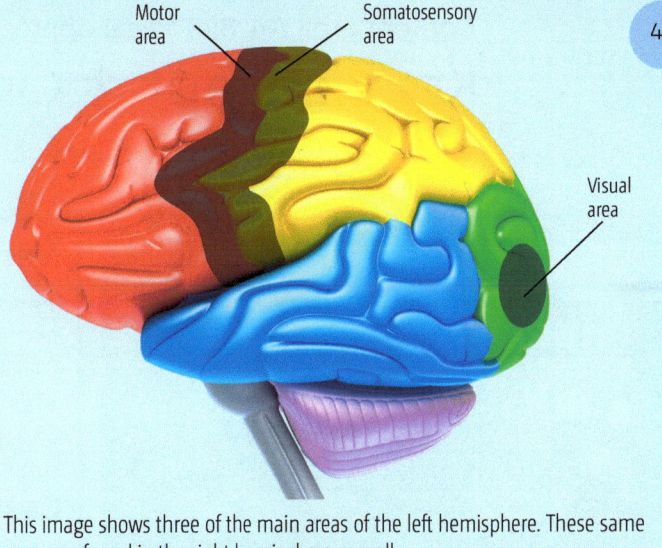

This image shows three of the main areas of the left hemisphere. These same areas are found in the right hemisphere as well.

Exam-style questions

Reg had a stroke which affected his speech. He found it hard to find the right words and spoke very slowly. But he understood everything the doctors and nurses said to him. Reg's right arm was paralysed but his left arm was unaffected.

1. (a) Identify evidence from this scenario that demonstrates localisation of brain function. (1 mark)
   (b) Explain how the evidence you have identified demonstrates localisation of brain function. (2 marks)
2. State what is meant by the term 'lateralisation'. (1 mark)
3. Explain how Reg's experience demonstrates lateralisation. (2 marks)
4. State what is meant by the term 'neuroanatomy'. (1 mark)
5. Family members were worried that Reg would not be able to speak properly again or use his right arm. However, the psychologist explained that Reg would probably improve because of brain plasticity.

   State what is meant by the term 'plasticity' and explain why the psychologist believed that it would help Reg to improve. (3 marks)
6. Briefly discuss neuroanatomy as an explanation of Reg's experiences. (3 marks)

An issue to consider
It's true that the brain is plastic and can compensate if an area is damaged. But this process is helped a lot by rehabilitation therapy.

What does this tell us about the relationship between biological and environmental factors?

Specification content
A4 Biological approach

Learners must be able to understand and apply knowledge of key concepts to explain aspects of human behaviour, including:

- Neuroanatomy, including basic localisation of function, lateralisation and plasticity of the brain.

Content area A4: Biological approach

Key concept 4: Organisation of the nervous system

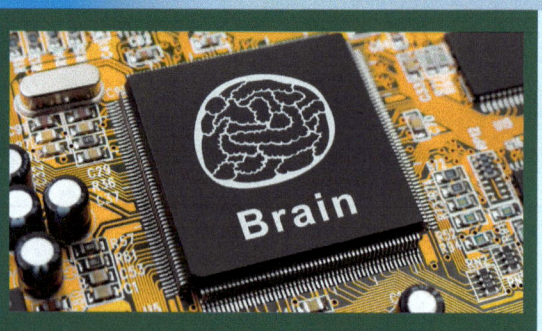

Your own personal internet

What's the most complicated 'system' in the world? Is it the internet perhaps? There are certainly some mind-blowing statistics involved. In a typical minute in 2020:

- 212 million emails were sent worldwide.
- 175 thousand apps were downloaded.
- 210 thousand people participated in Zoom meetings.
- 3 million Facebook videos were viewed.

That's pretty impressive. But perhaps even more impressive is what's going on in your own nervous system. It is made up of nerve cells called *neurons* which send messages around your body at up to 7 kilometres a second!

There are about 100 billion neurons in your brain alone, each connecting to about 1000 other neurons – that's 100 trillion connections. Each neuron fires (or sends a message) at around 200 times a second. That's 20 million billion bits of information sent around your brain every second.

And all this activity is controlled by the nervous system – your body's own version of the internet which works on super, super, superfast broadband!

The autonomic nervous system (ANS) is actually part of a broader system called the peripheral nervous system (not on the specification). This is made up of nerves that connect the brain and spinal cord (CNS) to the rest of the body.

Specification terms

Autonomic nervous system (ANS) Communicates signals between the spinal cord and internal body organs. It is 'autonomic' as the system operates involuntarily (i.e. automatically). It has two main divisions: sympathetic and parasympathetic.

Central nervous system (CNS) Consists of the brain and the spinal cord and is the origin of all complex commands and decisions.

Parasympathetic division The part of the ANS responsible for reducing physiological (body) arousal, e.g. the rest and digest response.

Sympathetic division The part of the ANS responsible for increasing physiological (body) arousal, e.g. the fight or flight response.

Nervous system

The nervous system is a complex network of cells in the human body. It is our main internal communication system and uses both electrical and chemical signals. The two main functions of the nervous system are to:

- Collect, process and respond to information in the environment.
- Coordinate the working of different organs and cells in the body.

Central nervous system (CNS)

The *central nervous system* (CNS) is made up of the brain and the spinal cord.

The brain

The brain is the centre of our conscious awareness and where decision-making takes place. It is divided into two halves called *hemispheres*. The right hemisphere controls the left side of the body and the left hemisphere controls the right side. This is called *contralateral control*. The two hemispheres are connected by several structures (e.g. the corpus callosum).

As we saw on page 44, the brain is covered by an outer layer called the *cerebral cortex* (or just *cortex*). This is about 3 mm thick and highly developed in humans. It is where 'higher' mental processes such as problem-solving and thinking take place.

At the base of the brain is the *brain stem*, which controls basic functions such as sleep and breathing. The brain stem connects the brain with the spinal cord.

The spinal cord

The spinal cord is a tube-like extension of the brain (like a cable) which runs down the middle of the spine. It controls reflex actions such as pulling your hand away from a hot plate. It also passes signals back and forth between the brain and the rest of the body via the *autonomic nervous system*.

Autonomic nervous system (ANS)

The autonomic nervous system (ANS) is a collection of nerves that send and receive signals between the spinal cord and body organs. It is 'autonomic' because it operates involuntarily (i.e. automatically). It controls functions that are vital for survival and do not require our conscious attention, such as breathing and heart rate. It plays a key role in the body's response to stress.

The ANS has two parts, which work in opposition to keep the body in balance – the *sympathetic* and *parasympathetic divisions*.

Sympathetic division

This activates physiological (body) arousal, e.g. increases heart rate, prepares the body for *fight or flight* to cope with stress.

Parasympathetic division

This activates the *rest and digest* response to bring the body back to its normal resting state after stress has passed, e.g. reduces heart and breathing rates.

Making links to the key assumptions

Assumption: Behaviour is influenced by the central nervous system (CNS), genes and neurochemistry There are several examples on this spread of how the CNS influences behaviour. The brain in particular is involved in many behaviours, e.g. thinking and problem-solving take place in the cerebral cortex. But the spinal cord is also part of the CNS and is involved in reflex behaviours.

Assumption: Behaviour is a product of evolution How does this assumption relate to the concepts on this spread (see page 11)?

Evaluation

Practical applications

One strength is that understanding the organisation of the nervous system has some useful real-world applications.

For example, musicians and actors often have problems with anxiety before performing. It is the ANS that causes this – the sympathetic division of the ANS is activated, creating physiological arousal that interferes with performance, e.g. a violinist's hand shaking or a singer's voice trembling. The arousal can be lowered by drugs which reduce activity of the sympathetic division.

This shows that understanding the organisation of the nervous system has led to effective treatments to help reduce anxiety and stress.

Research support

Another strength is that the organisation of the nervous system is supported by research.

Researchers study people who have experienced damage to parts of their nervous system. For example, damage to the spinal cord often results in body paralysis. Damage to the ANS can cause different problems, such as difficulties in responding to stress. Researchers also investigate the nervous systems of non-human animals, e.g. removing or destroying a part of an animal's nervous system to see what effect it has on its behaviour.

Therefore, researchers over time have built up a 'map' of the nervous system, how it is organised and the functions of the various components.

Other systems are involved

One weakness is that the nervous system does not operate on its own.

In many behaviours, the nervous system works in tandem with the *endocrine system*. This is the collection of glands in the body that produce hormones (see page 48). The fight or flight response is a good example of this joint cooperation. The response begins in the brain (nervous system) with the perception of danger. A signal is then sent to the endocrine system which produces several hormones, including adrenaline.

This means that our understanding of the role of the nervous system is incomplete without considering the endocrine system.

Brain (outer layer = cortex)

The central nervous system is physically central in the body but also central in what it does.

Brain stem

Spinal cord

Some of the nerves to and from the spinal cord are part of the autonomic nervous system.

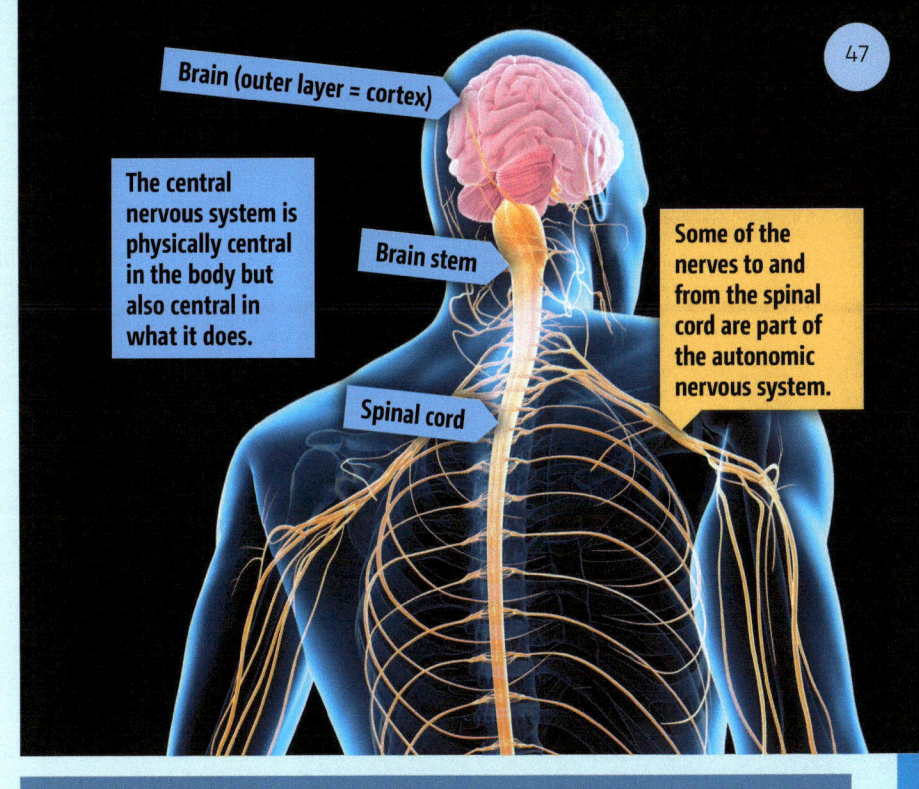

Exam-style questions

Lachlan and Jameela are watching a horror film on TV. It is very tense because the characters are walking around very carefully and the background music is saying 'be frightened'. Lachlan is expecting something scary to happen at any moment. Suddenly, without warning, Jameela leans over and shouts, 'Boo!'

1. Identify the part of the nervous system that controls what happens next to Lachlan. (1 mark)
2. Lachlan is so annoyed he turns the TV off, but after a short while he calms down and is back to normal.
   Explain how the nervous system controls Lachlan's response. (2 marks)
3. Briefly assess the organisation of the nervous system in Lachlan's response. (3 marks)
4. Outline the organisation of the autonomic nervous system. (3 marks)
5. Explain **one** difference between the sympathetic division and the parasympathetic division of the autonomic nervous system. (2 marks)
6. Jameela is a lawyer. One day at work she thinks about whether she has time to make a cup of tea. She decides she does. When she accidentally touches the boiling kettle, Jameela pulls her hand away very quickly.
   Describe how the organisation of Jameela's central nervous system explains her behaviour. (3 marks)

GET ACTIVE Sympathetic or parasympathetic?

Find out more about the two divisions of the ANS. Use your favourite search engine to answer the questions below.

1. *What are the main signs of physiological arousal in the fight or flight response? Here's one example: pupils dilate. Try to identify four or five other examples. Make a table to summarise what you find out.*
2. *Search for this mnemonic: SLUDD. What does it mean and what is the role of the parasympathetic division? Again, summarise your findings in a table.*

An issue to consider

Some of our knowledge of how the nervous system is organised has come from studies of animals. What are the practical and ethical issues involved in such research studies?

Specification content

A4 Biological approach

Learners must be able to understand and apply knowledge of key concepts to explain aspects of human behaviour, including:

- Organisation of the nervous system, including the central nervous system and autonomic nervous system (parasympathetic and sympathetic divisions).

Content area A4: Biological approach
Key concept 5: Neurochemistry

An adrenaline lift!
Does anyone remember the Incredible Hulk? When he got stressed, he developed superhuman strength. He also turned green.

Every now and again, you hear in the news about feats of superhuman strength carried out by ordinary people during extremely stressful events.

These are examples of what is sometimes called 'hysterical strength', such as the time in 1982 when Angela Cavallo lifted a car (a big American one) so her trapped son could escape from underneath.

That's a lift of 1300 kilos for five minutes! How does that work?

It's mostly down to adrenaline, released into the bloodstream in huge amounts. This means more oxygen gets to the muscles, which can work with much more force than usual.

Some scientists think we all have the potential to be superhuman in the right circumstances. Might be a bit sore afterwards though, but at least you won't turn green.

Specification terms
Adrenaline A hormone produced by the adrenal glands as part of the body's immediate stress response (fight or flight). Adrenaline strongly stimulates heart rate and contracts blood vessels.

Cortisol A hormone produced by the adrenal glands as part of the body's longer-term stress response. Cortisol controls how the body uses energy, but it also suppresses the immune system.

Hormones Chemical substances that circulate in the bloodstream and affect target organs. They are produced in large quantities, disappear quickly but have powerful effects.

Neurochemistry Relating to substances in the nervous system that regulate psychological functioning.

Neurotransmitters Chemicals (e.g. serotonin) in the nervous system that transmit signals from one neuron to another across synapses.

Stress response Physiological changes in the body when a stressor occurs. There is an immediate response (fight or flight) regulated by adrenaline, and a longer-term response involving cortisol.

What is neurochemistry?
Neurochemistry concerns the activity of chemical substances in the nervous system. Psychologists are interested in how these substances affect the functioning of the brain and how this in turn influences our thinking, emotions and behaviour.

Hormones and the stress response
What is a hormone?
A *hormone* is a 'chemical messenger', produced within structures called glands. Several glands form a network called the endocrine system. An example of an endocrine gland is the adrenal gland (we have two of these lying above our kidneys). The adrenal glands secrete the hormone *adrenaline* into the bloodstream. It travels around the body, affecting any cells that have adrenaline receptors.

Stress hormones
Some hormones (including adrenaline) are called stress hormones because they help to regulate and control the body's response to stress. This *stress response* is in two phases – immediate (acute) and longer term (chronic). These phases involve different hormones.

Adrenaline Anything that causes stress is called a stressor. When a stressor occurs, the body responds immediately with the fight or flight response. The sympathetic division of the ANS is activated (see previous spread) and stimulates adrenaline to be released from the adrenal glands.

Adrenaline in the bloodstream triggers physiological changes in the body which indicate arousal. Examples include increased heart and breathing rates, greater muscular tension, pupil dilation, inhibited digestion and a feeling of anxiety.

Cortisol If the stressor continues, the body switches to a longer-term stress response involving a different hormone called *cortisol*, also produced by the adrenal glands.

Some functions of cortisol help the body to cope with a stressor. For instance, it mobilises and restores energy supplies (from the liver) to keep the stress response going. However, cortisol has other effects that damage the body. For example, it suppresses the immune system which is why people often become ill during periods of chronic stress.

Neurotransmitters
What is a neurotransmitter?
Neurotransmitters allow communication between nerve cells (called *neurons*) in the brain and nervous system. Neurons are tiny cells not physically connected to each other but separated by gaps called *synapses* (see diagram on facing page). Neurons use electrical signals but, at the synapses, chemical substances (neurotransmitters) pass the signal on.

Serotonin This is one of the main neurotransmitters in the nervous system. It has been linked to a number of behaviours (e.g. sleep) and disorders including depression. It is thought that depressive symptoms are associated with abnormally low levels of serotonin. Because neurotransmitters are chemicals their activity can be altered by drugs. Some drugs that treat depression (antidepressants) work by increasing the levels of serotonin in the synapses between neurons.

📎 Making links to the key assumptions
Assumption: Behaviour is influenced by the central nervous system (CNS), genes and neurochemistry There are several examples on this spread of how neurochemistry influences behaviour. Neurotransmitters work directly on the CNS, especially the brain (e.g. low serotonin and mood). Hormones target other organs in the body, for example the heart and blood vessels in the stress response.

Assumption: Behaviour is a product of evolution How does this assumption relate to the concepts on this spread (see page 11)?

The picture on the right illustrates the gap between two neurons, known as a *synapse*. Molecules of the neurotransmitter (in purple) are released from one neuron into the synapse. They drift across the synapse and attach to special receptors on the next neuron, rather like a key fits into a lock. Depending on the neurotransmitter, this process will either activate (excite) or deactivate (inhibit) the next neuron.

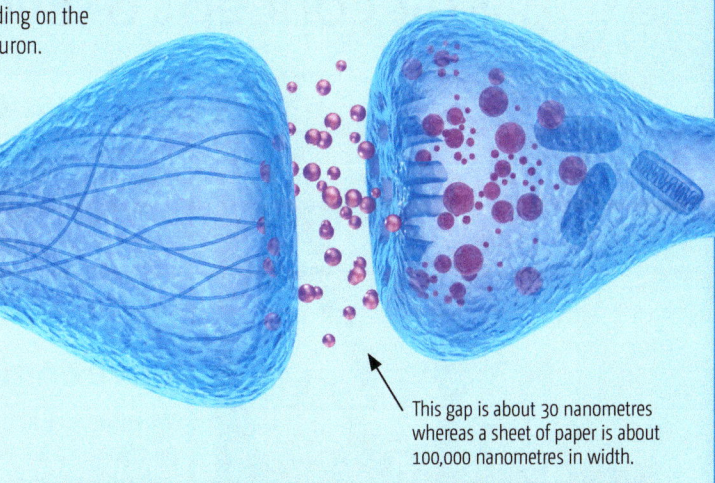

Evaluation

Practical applications

One strength is that our understanding of stress hormones has practical value.

For example, people with Addison's disease cannot produce cortisol, so their bodies cannot mobilise energy to deal with a chronic stressor. The lack of cortisol can trigger a life-threatening Addisonian crisis (mental confusion, abnormal heart rhythm, drop in blood pressure) when a stressor occurs. But there is an effective treatment – individuals can self-administer daily cortisol replacement therapy (hydrocortisone). They should also be aware of stressful situations when they might need an 'extra' injection of hydrocortisone.

This shows that a better understanding of the stress response has improved the lives of many people.

Research support

Another strength is research showing the importance of neurotransmitters and hormones.

For example, serotonin plays an important role in stabilising our mood, with low levels linked to depression (McNeal and Cimbolic 1986). Also, there is strong evidence in humans and animals that cortisol levels remain high during long-term stress and eventually cause damage and disorders such as heart disease (Russell and Lightman 2019).

Therefore, research suggests that neurochemistry plays a key role in regulating many of our behaviours.

Incomplete explanation

One weakness is that neurochemistry does not take psychological factors into account.

For instance, two people can experience the same stressor (e.g. an exam) but their physiological responses differ. One person remains calm, but the other experiences an acute stress response, i.e. fight or flight. The difference occurs because the two people think about the stressor differently. One views the exam as an opportunity to show what they have learned. The other views it as a 'disaster waiting to happen'.

This shows that neurochemistry is not a complete explanation of the stress response because it neglects cognitive factors.

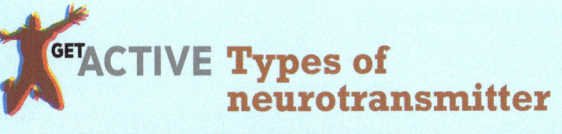

This gap is about 30 nanometres whereas a sheet of paper is about 100,000 nanometres in width.

Exam-style questions

Rolando was chopping vegetables to cook for tea when the very sharp knife slipped and narrowly missed his finger. Rolando's heart raced and he felt sick. His mouth went dry and he started to sweat. But he felt OK soon after.

1. Outline the role of adrenaline in Rolando's response to his near-accident. (3 marks)
2. Despite being only 16, Rolando is his mum's main carer. It is a lot of responsibility and he finds it very hard to balance caring with his studies. For several months Rolando has felt a high level of anxiety. He gets a lot of coughs and colds.
   (a) Identify **one** hormone that could be involved in Rolando's behaviour. (1 mark)
   (b) Outline the role of this hormone in Rolando's behaviour. (2 marks)
3. Rolando has also been feeling depressed for several weeks. He feels down most of the time and finds it hard to motivate himself or get interested in anything.
   (a) State what is meant by 'neurochemistry'. (1 mark)
   (b) Explain how neurotransmitters may affect Rolando. (2 marks)
4. Briefly assess the role of neurochemistry in any of Rolando's behaviours. (3 marks)

Excited.

GET ACTIVE Types of neurotransmitter

Some neurotransmitters are called *inhibitory* because their main effect is to reduce (inhibit) the electrical activity of nerve cells (neurons). An example is serotonin. At normal levels serotonin dampens and calms brain activity, which stabilises our mood.

Other neurotransmitters are *excitatory* because they stimulate (excite) neurons and make them active. An example is *noradrenaline*.

Some neurotransmitters are inhibitory in some parts of the brain and excitatory in others. A very important example of this type is *dopamine*.

1. Find out what effects noradrenaline and dopamine have on behaviour.
2. Like serotonin, noradrenaline and dopamine are thought to play a role in depression. Find out what they do and how they relate to each other and to serotonin.

An issue to consider

The research discussed on this spread suggests that we are controlled by our hormones.

What are the implications of this for a criminal's behaviour?

Specification content

A4 Biological approach

Learners must be able to understand and apply knowledge of key concepts to explain aspects of human behaviour, including:

- Neurochemistry, including the role of hormones in the stress response (adrenaline and cortisol), neurotransmitters.

Content area A4: Biological approach
Key concept 6: Evolutionary psychology

Survival of the fittest

The word *evolution* means change. The form and behaviour of all living things change over time through the process of *natural selection*. When life was hard for our ancestors, those who possessed characteristics that helped them to stay alive (and reproduce) were the ones who passed their *genes* on to the next generation. In this way the genes were 'selected'.

This idea, proposed by Charles Darwin (1859), is often called the *survival of the fittest*. Fittest in this context refers to the characteristics that best match ('fit') the demands of the environment.

Environment of evolutionary adaptation (EEA)

When we look at the living things around us today we see the outcomes of natural selection – all organisms are what they are because their characteristics enabled them to survive in a particular environment.

The vast majority of human evolution took place during the Pleistocene era which ended about 10,000 years ago. Our ancestors lived on the African savannah (warm grasslands) as hunter-gatherers. They changed from apes moving around on four legs to upright hairless animals who could use tools and language. Behaviour and minds changed to ensure survival in that habitat.

Therefore, what we are today is largely based on the evolutionary pressures in that environment, the EEA.

Genome lag

Our minds are still adapted to the EEA. It takes thousands of years for evolutionary pressures to change the human genome (collection of genes). But the world around us changes much more quickly than that. Most of the population no longer lives in small groups but in vast cities alongside countless others – but we still have a 'small group' mentality. Another example of *genome lag* is our stress response – see the panel on the left.

Fight, flight, freeze response

We have already seen that 'fight or flight' is an animal's immediate response to a stressor (see pages 46 and 47). There is a third behaviour which is part of the same response – 'freeze'.

Once a threat is perceived, the sympathetic division of the ANS is activated. This creates physiological arousal in the body that prepares the individual to either confront the threat (fight), run away (flight) or stay still to avoid attention (freeze). The changes are automatic and rapid (e.g. greater blood flow to the muscles) and increase the individual's speed and strength.

The *fight, flight, freeze response* helped our ancestors to cope with threats (e.g. predators). Those who responded in these ways had an advantage – they were more likely to survive and reproduce, so the genes involved were passed on (i.e. natural selection).

Sexual selection

Evolutionary pressures also act on reproductive success. Darwin noted that some characteristics continue to exist even when they threaten an organism's survival. He realised that such characteristics must confer an advantage, which was that they make the individual attractive to potential mates.

An example is the peacock's tail. It is hard for the male bird to carry around (and a big target for predators), but it is attractive to females. So possessing a burdensome tail actually increases the male bird's chances of reproducing and passing on the genes that led to his success.

Stressed out

Modern life can be stressful. So many things to do, so little time. Homework, part-time job, Instagram updates... Today you may have to cope with any or all of these. But I can (almost) guarantee that running away from an attacking lion will not be something you have to worry about.

It wasn't always like this. Our evolutionary ancestors were much more concerned about attacking lions than they were about dealing with their overdrafts. The problem is, the body's stress response is still stuck in those days (referred to as the *environment of evolutionary adaptation*).

Our bodies are great at helping us cope with short-term emergency situations that are over (one way or another) almost as soon as they've begun. But long-term, drawn-out stress, of the type so common in modern life, is much more damaging. We have not evolved to deal with that kind of stress.

Specification terms

Environment of evolutionary adaptation (EEA) The habitat in which a species evolved its most recent adaptations. In humans this ended about 10,000 years ago.

Fight, flight, freeze response The body is physiologically aroused to either confront a threat, flee from it, or stay still to avoid it.

Genome lag Changes to the environment occur much more rapidly than changes to our genes.

Sexual selection Attributes or behaviours that increase reproductive success are more likely to be passed on and may become exaggerated over succeeding generations of offspring.

Survival of the fittest Natural selection selects the genes that give rise to characteristics promoting survival and reproduction, so they are retained in the population.

Making links to the key assumptions

Assumption: Behaviour is a product of evolution The whole of this spread relates to this assumption. Take an example of a behaviour not on this spread – smiling. Use the concepts here to explain how smiling is a product of evolution.

Assumption: Behaviour is influenced by the central nervous system (CNS), genes and neurochemistry How does this assumption relate to the concepts on this spread (see page 11)?

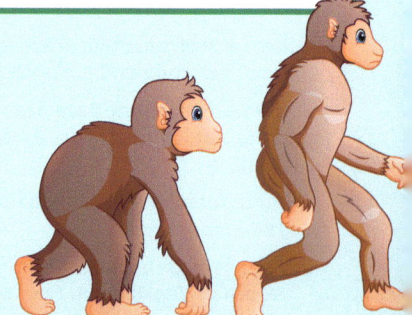

Evaluation

Research support
One strength is support for evolutionary psychology from research into partner preferences.

Our preferences have changed hugely over the last 100 years. Women have a greater role in the workplace and are less dependent on men to provide for them (despite ongoing inequalities in earning power). So women's partner preferences are now less dictated by resource considerations.

This supports genome lag because it shows that a behaviour important to survival – choosing a mate – has been influenced by cultural changes while the genome has hardly changed at all.

Problems with the EEA concept
One weakness is that the EEA concept implies that significant evolution of human characteristics stopped about 10,000 years ago.

However, some evolved changes suggest this is not the case. For example, most humans are lactose intolerant but some are not. The gene that allows us to digest milk was selected and passed on because it conferred a survival advantage. But this happened less than 10,000 years ago. Other changes are occurring now.

Therefore, some human characteristics may be the outcomes of evolutionary pressures operating much more recently than the EEA, which undermines the importance of this concept.

Gender bias
Another weakness is that there is evidence of gender bias in evolutionary psychology.

For instance, fight, flight, freeze may explain men's response to threat but not women's. Such a response would have been disadvantageous for an ancestor woman because it would have been harder for her to protect her offspring. Shelley Taylor *et al.* (2000) suggest a more adaptive response for women is 'tend and befriend' – a focus on nurturing offspring rather than confrontation, and seeking support from social networks.

Therefore, evolutionary psychology's explanation of how we respond to threat may well be biased towards men's behaviour.

GET ACTIVE Phobias

As we have seen on this spread, evolutionary psychologists argue that we try to cope with the stresses of the modern world with a mind that is better suited (or adapted) to the pressures of the EEA.

Perhaps this explains the existence of some psychological disorders. An example is phobia, usually defined as an extreme or irrational fear of an object, situation or event. Many people from all sorts of cultures are afraid of snakes and spiders. A lot of these people are afraid of such creatures even though they have never personally encountered one.

How do you think evolutionary psychology explains the existence of such fears?

Exam-style questions

Josef is feeling very stressed because he has a college deadline to meet on top of his part-time job. 'I don't think humans are cut out for this kind of lifestyle,' he says to his friend.

1. (a) Outline **one** way in which Josef might respond to the stress of the deadline, according to evolutionary psychology. (2 marks)

    (b) Explain the concept of genome lag with reference to Josef's comment. (2 marks)

2. Jameela and Josef are visiting the zoo. They see a peacock unfurl his magnificent tail. Jameela says, 'I don't know how he manages to get around carrying that.'

    With reference to Jameela's comment, explain how the peacock's tail supports the concept of sexual selection. (3 marks)

3. State what is meant by the term 'survival of the fittest'. (1 mark)

4. Humans adapted to live in a very different environment from the ones we live in now. Many behaviours that evolved a long time ago are still helping us to survive today.

    Explain what is meant by the 'environment of evolutionary adaptation'. (2 marks)

5. Briefly analyse the view that evolutionary psychology can explain human behaviour. (3 marks)

We evolved to function in a very different environment from the ones most of us live in today. Perhaps we overeat, become anxious and depressed because we are trying to cope using a mind better-suited to a much earlier time.

An issue to consider
Evolutionary medicine is an application of evolutionary principles to the treatment of modern health and disease. It suggests that genetically-based physical and psychological disorders must have some selective advantages otherwise they would not continue in the gene pool.

If depression is inherited, what might be the selective advantage?

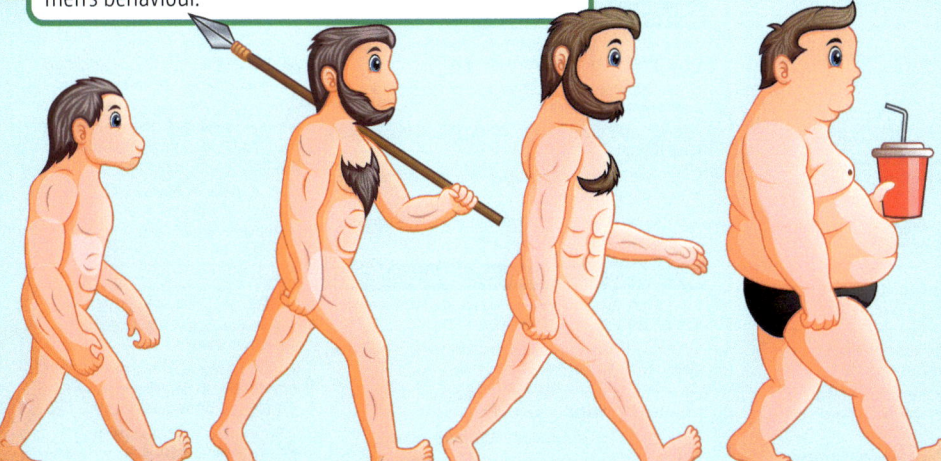

Specification content
A4 Biological approach
Learners must be able to understand and apply knowledge of key concepts to explain aspects of human behaviour, including:
- Evolutionary psychology, including the environment of evolutionary adaptation, survival of the fittest, the fight, flight, freeze response, sexual selection and genome lag.

Content area A
Revision summary

Assumptions of four approaches

Assumptions of the cognitive approach
Behaviour is a product of information processing Internal mental processes (e.g. perception, memory) operate in stages to make sense of the world.

The brain can be compared to a computer Like computers we process through input-processing-output. Hardware (brain), software (information).

Assumptions of the social approach
Behaviour occurs in a social context People are social animals, psychologists study the influence of others to understand behaviour (e.g. in conformity).

Wider culture and society influence people's behaviour Differences can be understood in terms of individualist (own needs) vs. collectivist (community's needs).

Assumptions of the behaviourist and social learning approaches
Behaviour is a learned response to environmental stimuli Classical conditioning – Pavlov's dogs, learning through association. Operant conditioning – behaviour reinforced by its consequences from the environment (e.g. reward).

Behaviour can be learned from observation and imitation We observe behaviour and imitate role models, especially if they are rewarded.

Assumptions of the biological approach
Behaviour is influenced by our biology Physical basis to behaviour – central nervous system (brain), genes, neurochemistry (e.g. serotonin).

Behaviour is a product of evolution Natural selection of survival-promoting behaviours, genes passed on (Darwin 1859).

Cognitive approach

Key concept 1: Characteristics of three memory stores
Duration – SM = Very brief. STM = up to 30 seconds. LTM = up to a lifetime.
Capacity – SM = very high. STM = 7 ± 2 items. LTM = unlimited.
Encoding – SM = sense-dependent. STM = acoustic. LTM = semantic.

Evaluation
Practical applications Increase STM capacity through chunking (e.g. phone numbers).
Research support STM duration (Peterson and Peterson 1959), LTM duration (Bahrick et al. 1975).
Issues with research Research uses artificial materials, unlike in everyday life.

Key concept 2: Remembering
Recall Retrieve from memory:
- Free recall – with no 'help'.
- Cued recall – with help from a cue.

Recognition Remembering something when we've encountered it before (e.g. multiple choice).
Cues Triggers to assist memory, meaningful (e.g. 'STM') or meaningless (e.g. context).

Evaluation
Practical applications Mnemonics are based on cues (e.g. BIDMAS triggers recall of maths operators in LTM).
Research support Category headings acted as cues, improved recall (Tulving and Pearlstone 1966).
Cues not always useful Context cues (e.g. exam room) not as powerful as meaningful cues.

Key concept 3: Reconstructive memory
What is it? Memories reconstructed from fragments into meaningful whole.
Role of schema Mental package of knowledge:
- Shortening – parts of memory cut to fit schema.
- Rationalisation – details distorted to fit schema.
- Confabulation – details made up to fill gaps.

Evaluation
Practical applications Eyewitnesses not always accurate, due to schema.
Research support War of the Ghosts story changed in line with schema (Bartlett 1932).
Some memories are accurate Personally important or distinctive details are remembered.

Key concept 4: Cognitive priming
What is it? Experience of one stimulus (prime) affects response to later stimulus (process it faster).
Types of cognitive priming:
- Repetition – later stimulus identical to prime.
- Semantic – later stimulus related in meaning to prime.
- Associative – later stimulus associated with prime but not in meaning.

Evaluation
Practical applications Prevent priming influence of TV snack adverts, promote healthy eating and prevent obesity.
Research support Playing violent video games, easier recall of aggressive scripts (Möller and Krahé 2009).
Lack of replication Repeating priming studies gives different findings, unscientific concept.

Key concept 5: The role of cognitive scripts
What are memory scripts? Knowledge of how social situations 'play out' (e.g. restaurant).
Features E.g. scenes ordered by time, evolve with experience, influence memory.
What is person perception? How we categorise individuals into 'types'.
How it works Gaps in knowledge of someone filled in from memory, even if wrong (e.g. stereotypes, biases).

Evaluation
Practical applications Be more accurate by taking time to judge, resist stereotyping.
Research support We recall events in correct order when consistent with script in memory (Bower et al. 1979).
Cannot explain all behaviour Other reasons for behaving in script-consistent ways (e.g. imitation of others).

Key concept 6: Cognitive biases
What are they? Errors in information processing, undermine decision-making but speed it up.
Fundamental attribution error (FAE) Explaining other people's behaviour due to personality not situation.
Confirmation bias We notice, store, recall information that confirms existing beliefs.
Hostile attribution bias (HAB) Neutral behaviour seen as threatening, aggressive response.

Evaluation
Practical applications Overcome confirmation bias by seeking out contradictory information (critical thinking), helps reduce conflict.
Research support People with HAB behave aggressively, increases HAB further (Tuente et al. 2019).
FAE not universal Mostly individualist cultures (e.g. USA), not so much collectivist (e.g. China).

Social approach

Key concept 1: Conformity
What is it? Going along with a group due to invisible 'pressure'.
Normative social influence (NSI) Accept norms of group (conform) to be liked and avoid rejection. Emotional process, stronger in stressful situations.
Informational social influence (ISI) Change behaviour/opinions when we believe others are right. Cognitive process, especially in new or unclear situations.
Studying conformity Asch's (1951) students conformed to avoid rejection (NSI).

Evaluation
Practical applications Whistle-blowers in organisations are anti-conformists, resist NSI and ISI.
Research support Asch's participants conformed to avoid disapproval. No public pressure = no conformity.
NSI and ISI are less clear in the real world Lower conformity with dissenter who gives social support (NSI) and is source of information (ISI).

Key concept 2: Types of conformity
Internalisation Agree privately and publicly with others, permanent, due to ISI.
Compliance Agree publicly but not privately, temporary, due to NSI.
Identification Combination of other two, agree publicly and privately because we identify with group, only while we are members.

Evaluation
Practical applications Target types of destructive conformity in workplaces to improve decision-making.
Research support Compliance (Asch 1951), identification (Orlando 1973), internalisation (Sherif 1935).
Oversimplification Artificial research, not real groups, overlap in real world.

Key concept 3: In-groups and out-groups
What is social categorisation? Divide people into groups based on shared characteristics, assume members all the same.
What is a stereotype? Fixed view of a person based on social category.
Formation of stereotypes Social categorisation of in-groups and out-groups, observe and imitate others (SLT).
Effect of stereotypes
- Positive – simplify interactions, reduce cognitive effort.
- Negative – distort memory and social judgements.

Prejudice and discrimination Perceive out-group members as inferior, exclude them e.g. from employment.

Evaluation
Practical application Reduce prejudice by seeing self as part of bigger group, challenge stereotypes by cooperating.
Research support Half of white participants thought black man was holding razor, racist stereotype biased memory (Allport and Postman 1947).
Alternative explanations Prejudice due to authoritarian personality (from upbringing) rather than social factors.

Key concept 4: Intra-group dynamics
Group cohesion Group members stick together to achieve goals, based on trust and communication.
Roles Task, social and procedural roles increase cohesion, individualist roles reduce it.
Common goals Cohesive groups share goals, working together is motivating.
Groupthink Group members agree, stop analysing decisions or exploring alternatives.
Social facilitation Presence of others enhances performance on simple tasks but not complex ones.

Evaluation
Practical applications Use methods to avoid groupthink, e.g. encourage criticism and include outside people (Janis 1982).
Research support Focus on group goals improves performance (Thürmer et al. 2017), Devil's Advocate avoids groupthink (MacDougall and Baum 1997).
Contrary evidence Group roles overlap in real world, individual goals help performance (Gowen 1985).

Key concept 5: Influences of others on the self
What is self-concept? How you see yourself ('Who am I?'), includes self-esteem and self-image.
Influences of others on self-esteem Make us feel good: how others react, how we compare, social roles.
Influences of others on self-image Awareness of own characteristics affected by feedback from others.
What is self-efficacy? Confidence in achieving outcomes.
Influences of others Observe others succeeding (social modelling), positive verbal feedback (social persuasion).

Evaluation
Practical applications E.g. school performance improved by increasing self-esteem (Lawrence 2006).
Research support Fulfilling relationships increase self-esteem, which improves relationships (Harris and Orth 2020).
Vague concepts Concepts overlap, self-image and self-esteem very similar (jangle fallacy), limits understanding.

Behaviourist and social learning approaches

Key concept 1: Classical conditioning (CC)

What is it? Learning through association of two stimuli with each other (Pavlov).
Before conditioning Unconditioned stimulus (UCS e.g. food) produces unconditioned response (UCR e.g. salivation), other stimuli are neutral (NS).
During conditioning UCS + NS (e.g. bell) repeatedly paired, associate NS + UCS.
After conditioning NS now a conditioned stimulus (CS) producing response (CR) on its own.

Evaluation
Practical applications Electric shock (UCS) given when reading gambling phrases (NS), become CS producing discomfort (CR).
Research support Little Albert conditioned to fear white rat (Watson and Rayner 1920).
Limited explanation of learning Can't explain complex learning, e.g. phobias not maintained over time through CC.

Key concept 2: Operant conditioning (OC)

What is it? Learning from consequences.
Consequence 1 – Reinforcement Increases probability of behaviour repeating.
- Positive – pleasant consequence.
- Negative – remove unpleasant stimulus.

Consequence 2 – Punishment Reduces probability of behaviour repeating.
- Positive – unpleasant consequence.
- Negative – remove pleasant stimulus.

Motivation Driven by rewards through OC:
- Extrinsic rewards – from environment (other people).
- Intrinsic rewards – from yourself (e.g. interest, challenge).

Evaluation
Practical applications In education, extrinsic rewards for good work, intrinsic rewards encouraged to raise self-esteem.
Research support Animal and human lab studies show OC, also brain basis of reinforcement (Chase et al. 2015).
Incomplete explanation of learning Explains how phobias maintained over time but not how acquired in first place.

Key concept 3: Social learning theory (SLT)

What is it? Indirect learning: observation, vicarious learning and imitation (e.g. Bobo doll studies).
Modelling (1) demonstrating a behaviour to another, (2) person imitates the behaviour.
Learning through observation Observer watches model's behaviour, retains in memory.
Imitation Copying model's behaviour, more likely if observer identifies with model (same gender, high status, etc.).
Vicarious learning Observing the model receive reinforcement of behaviour makes observer more likely to imitate.

Evaluation
Practical applications Targets to reduce aggression e.g. reduce rewards, provide non-aggressive models.
Research support Imitation more likely when model is rewarded (Bandura 1965). Children develop phobias from observing fearful behaviour in adults (Askew and Field 2007).
Alternative explanation Phobia occurrence greater in identical than non-identical twins (Kendler et al 2001), SLT cannot explain role of genetics.

Biological approach

Key concept 1: Influence of biology on behaviour and traits

Influence of biology on behaviour Behaviour has a physical basis, influenced by:
- Genes – inherited from parents.
- Neuroanatomy – structure of nervous system.
- Neurochemistry – e.g. neurotransmitters.
- Evolution – natural selection, adapting to environment.

Influence of biology on traits Characteristics that make up personality, e.g.:
- Extraversion – outgoing and sociable, extraverts inherit underactive nervous system, need to arouse it.
- Introversion – withdrawn and shy, introverts inherit overactive nervous system, need to avoid arousal.

Evaluation
Practical applications Criminals are often extraverts and not put off by punishments, so reduce with different approach (e.g. drugs).
Research support Twin studies show E-I partly genetically determined (57%, Sanchez-Roige et al. 2018).
Role of non-biological factors Learning experiences and environment may be more important in E-I than genes.

Key concept 2: Genetics and inheritance

What are genes? Strands of DNA carry 'instructions' for physical and non-physical characteristics.
Genotype The complete set of genes you inherit.
Phenotype How genes are expressed in interaction with environment.
The SRY gene On Y chromosome, switches on other genes, XY embryo develops testes and produces testosterone.

Evaluation
Practical applications A genetic predisposition (genotype) is triggered by an environmental factor (e.g. stress), so change environmental factors.
Research support Variants in SRY gene show its usual function is to masculinise XY embryos.
Risk of oversimplification E.g. genes increase risk of depression but do not cause it, many interacting genes needed.

Key concept 3: Neuroanatomy

What is it? Structure of brain and nervous system.
Localisation of brain function Brain areas have different functions, e.g.:
- Motor area – controls movement of opposite side of body.
- Somatosensory area – represents skin sensitivity of body (e.g. hands).
- Visual area – receives information from left and right visual fields.

Lateralisation of brain function Some functions are in just one hemisphere (e.g. language in left for most).
Plasticity of the brain Brain is flexible and can change, e.g. by:
- Synaptic pruning – reducing synapses to form new ones.
- Functional recovery – undamaged areas take over after injury.

Evaluation
Practical applications Programmes to protect elderly against age-related cognitive decline (plasticity, Merzenich et al. 2014).
Research support RH dominant for making facial expressions and recognising emotions in music (Lindell 2013).
Not so localised Brain scans show language is distributed more widely in the brain, even in the RH.

Key concept 4: Organisation of the nervous system

Nervous system Internal communication system, electrical and chemical signals.
Central nervous system (CNS) Origin of complex commands and decisions.
- Brain – two hemispheres = contralateral control; cerebral cortex = higher mental processes.
- Spinal cord – controls reflex actions and communication with body.

Autonomic nervous system (ANS) Controls automatic functions without conscious awareness.
- Sympathetic division – activates arousal (fight or flight).
- Parasympathetic division – activates resting state (rest and digest).

Evaluation
Practical applications ANS arousal interferes with performance, so drugs developed to reduce anxiety.
Research support Damage to human nervous system has specific effects, also studying effects on animal behaviour.
Other systems are involved Endocrine system (hormones) important in fight or flight, not just NS on its own.

Key concept 5: Neurochemistry

What is it? How activity of substances in nervous system affects brain and behaviour.
Hormones and the stress response Stress hormones ('chemical messengers') regulate body's response to stress.
- Adrenaline – stimulated by ANS in fight or flight, acute arousal e.g. heart rate.
- Cortisol – chronic response, mobilises energy but suppresses immune system.

Neurotransmitters Allow communication between neurons across synapses, e.g. serotonin (low levels linked to depression, activity changed by drugs).

Evaluation
Practical applications Addison's disease means body cannot cope with stress but treatment is daily cortisol replacement.
Research support Serotonin helps stabilise mood (McNeal and Cimbolic 1986), high cortisol causes body damage (Russell and Lightman 2019).
Incomplete explanation Ignores psychological factors, e.g. two people perceive same stressor differently (e.g. exam).

Key concept 6: Evolutionary psychology

Survival of the fittest Darwin (1859) explained natural selection – when resources are scarce, genes that produce characteristics helping survival (and reproduction) are selected and passed on.
Environment of evolutionary adaptation (EEA) Human minds and behaviour evolved to adapt to life on the African savannah.
Genome lag The gap between changes in our environment and adaptive changes to genome.
Fight, flight, freeze response An animal's immediate response to a stressor (confront, flee, stay still), sympathetic division of ANS.
Sexual selection Characteristics that threaten survival continue because attractive to potential mates.

Evaluation
Research support Cultural changes in last 100 years (e.g. women less dependent), but not genome change.
Problems with the EEA concept Human evolution continued after EEA (e.g. digest lactose), some characteristics evolved recently.
Gender bias Towards men, e.g. women's response to stress is 'tend and befriend', not 'fight, flight, freeze' (Taylor 2000).

Content area A
Multiple-choice questions

Assumptions of four approaches

1. **The computer analogy is an assumption of the:**
   - (a) Biological approach.
   - (b) Social approach.
   - (c) Cognitive approach.
   - (d) Behaviourist and social learning approaches.

2. **An assumption of the social approach is:**
   - (a) Information processing.
   - (b) Classical conditioning.
   - (c) Behaviour is influenced by culture.
   - (d) The role of neurochemistry.

3. **The behaviourist and social learning approaches involve:**
   - (a) Observation and imitation.
   - (b) The role of genes.
   - (c) The role of the nervous system.
   - (d) Input-processing-output.

4. **'Behaviour evolves through natural selection' is an assumption of the:**
   - (a) Social approach.
   - (b) Behaviourist and social learning approaches.
   - (c) Cognitive approach.
   - (d) Biological approach.

Characteristics of three memory stores

1. **The duration of iconic memory is:**
   - (a) Up to a lifetime.
   - (b) Up to about 30 seconds.
   - (c) About 2 to 4 seconds.
   - (d) Less than half a second.

2. **The capacity of STM is:**
   - (a) Between 2 and 7 items.
   - (b) 7 ± 2 items.
   - (c) Practically unlimited.
   - (d) A few seconds.

3. **Encoding in LTM is mostly:**
   - (a) Semantic.
   - (b) Acoustic.
   - (c) Visual.
   - (d) Tactile.

4. **One way to increase the size of STM is:**
   - (a) Dunking.
   - (b) Chunking.
   - (c) Bunking.
   - (d) Perlunking.

Remembering

1. **Retrieving information without 'help' is:**
   - (a) Recognition.
   - (b) Cued recall.
   - (c) Free recall.
   - (d) Context-related.

2. **An example of a meaningful cue is:**
   - (a) External context.
   - (b) 'It starts with S'.
   - (c) Emotions.
   - (d) Internal state.

3. **ROYGBIV is an example of:**
   - (a) A category heading.
   - (b) A context-related cue.
   - (c) A cue without meaning.
   - (d) A mnemonic.

4. **Tulving and Pearlstone showed that:**
   - (a) Category headings are cues.
   - (b) Cues help retrieve 'forgotten' information.
   - (c) Cued recall is superior to free recall.
   - (d) All of the above.

Reconstructive memory

1. **A schema is:**
   - (a) An accurate memory.
   - (b) A package of stored knowledge.
   - (c) A physical part of the brain.
   - (d) An inaccurate memory.

2. **Inventing details of a memory is:**
   - (a) Shortening.
   - (b) Rationalisation.
   - (c) Fragmenting.
   - (d) Confabulation.

3. **Bartlett used a story called:**
   - (a) An Inuit Folk Tale.
   - (b) The Battle of the Spirits.
   - (c) The Arrows in the Canoe.
   - (d) The War of the Ghosts.

4. **Bartlett may be wrong because:**
   - (a) Some memories are very accurate.
   - (b) All memories are reconstructed.
   - (c) Memories are affected by schema.
   - (d) No one recalled 'Something black came out of his mouth'.

Cognitive priming

1. **A 'prime' is:**
   - (a) A later stimulus.
   - (b) The third stimulus.
   - (c) An earlier stimulus.
   - (d) Always visual.

2. **'Two stimuli that mean the same thing' relates to _____ priming.**
   - (a) Repetition.
   - (b) Associative.
   - (c) Script.
   - (d) Semantic.

3. **Harris et al. studied priming in:**
   - (a) TV adverts.
   - (b) Children's books.
   - (c) Magazines.
   - (d) Facebook news feeds.

4. **A study by _____ supports priming.**
   - (a) Möller and Krahé.
   - (b) Möller and Harris.
   - (c) Harris and Krahé.
   - (d) Morris and Krahé.

The role of cognitive scripts

1. **Schank and Abelson described the _____ script.**
   - (a) Theatre.
   - (b) Football match.
   - (c) Restaurant.
   - (d) Office.

2. **We may remember an event when it is:**
   - (a) Different from a script.
   - (b) Consistent with a script.
   - (c) What we expected.
   - (d) All of the above.

3. **If you view someone as outgoing, you probably also think they are:**
   (a) Introverted.
   (b) Quiet.
   (c) Impulsive.
   (d) Unfriendly.

4. **One way to make person perception more accurate is to:**
   (a) Take time to get to know someone.
   (b) Use stereotypes.
   (c) Make an instant 'snap' judgement.
   (d) Have many expectations of someone.

Cognitive biases

1. **'Noticing things that support your current beliefs' is:**
   (a) Confirmation bias.
   (b) Fundamental attribution error.
   (c) Hostile attribution bias.
   (d) Logical error bias.

2. **Assuming someone trod on your foot deliberately is an example of:**
   (a) Confirmation bias.
   (b) Irrational thinking bias.
   (c) Hostile attribution bias.
   (d) Social interaction bias.

3. **There is a close link between HAB and:**
   (a) Lateness.
   (b) Shyness.
   (c) Aggression.
   (d) Friendliness.

4. **The fundamental attribution error is found:**
   (a) In every culture.
   (b) In cultures like China.
   (c) Mainly in individualist cultures.
   (d) When people believe behaviour is caused by situational factors.

Conformity

1. **Agreeing with the group to avoid rejection is:**
   (a) Conformative social influence.
   (b) Normative social influence.
   (c) Informational social influence.
   (d) Performative social influence.

2. **Informational social influence is:**
   (a) An emotional process.
   (b) A cognitive process.
   (c) Unlikely in new situations.
   (d) Rare when an expert is present.

3. **Asch's overall conformity rate was:**
   (a) 36.8%.
   (b) 25%.
   (c) 75%.
   (d) 63.2%.

4. **In real-world situations:**
   (a) NSI is more important than ISI.
   (b) ISI is more important than NSI.
   (c) NSI does not occur.
   (d) NSI and ISI operate together.

Types of conformity

1. **Three types of conformity were identified by:**
   (a) Sherif.
   (b) Asch.
   (c) Orlando.
   (d) Kelman.

2. **A permanent type of conformity is:**
   (a) Compliance.
   (b) Internalisation.
   (c) Identification.
   (d) Normative social influence.

3. **The study by Orlando illustrates:**
   (a) Identification.
   (b) Internalisation.
   (c) Compliance.
   (d) The role of personality.

4. **In real-world conformity:**
   (a) Compliance is the deepest type.
   (b) Internalisation is temporary.
   (c) Identification is the most common type.
   (d) Different types overlap.

In-groups and out-groups

1. **Stereotypes are:**
   (a) A form of social categorisation.
   (b) Flexible.
   (c) Nearly always accurate.
   (d) Caused by genes.

2. **Stereotypes:**
   (a) Can lead to prejudice.
   (b) Increase cognitive processing effort.
   (c) Are always negative.
   (d) Cannot be explained by social learning theory.

3. **Prejudice is _____ and discrimination is _____ .**
   (a) a behaviour, an attitude.
   (b) a belief, a feeling.
   (c) an attitude, a behaviour.
   (d) an attitude, a feeling.

4. **In Allport and Postman's study, the black man was:**
   (a) The attacker.
   (b) The victim.
   (c) A racist stereotype.
   (d) A bystander.

Intra-group dynamics

1. **Group cohesion is greater when:**
   (a) Goals are not shared.
   (b) Members see themselves as similar.
   (c) There is little communication.
   (d) Levels of trust are low.

2. **Roles that keep the group moving forward are called:**
   (a) Task roles.
   (b) Social roles.
   (c) Procedural roles.
   (d) Individualist roles.

3. **Social facilitation _____ in _____ .**
   (a) Improves performance, complex tasks.
   (b) Reduces performance, complex tasks.
   (c) Improves performance, simple tasks.
   (d) Reduces performance, large groups.

4. **Groupthink can be avoided by using:**
   (a) A 'Beelzebub's lawyer'.
   (b) An 'Evil Genius'.
   (c) A 'Satan's Supporter'.
   (d) A 'Devil's Advocate'.

Content area A
Multiple-choice questions continued

Influences of others on the self

1. **Self-concept is the answer to the question:**
   (a) 'Who are you?'
   (b) 'Where am I?'
   (c) 'Who am I?'
   (d) 'Would you like a drink?'

2. **Our self-esteem is increased by:**
   (a) Comparing ourselves to beautiful people.
   (b) Positive comments from others.
   (c) Thinking about our failures.
   (d) Having roles with social stigma.

3. **A person's confidence in their abilities is:**
   (a) Self-image.
   (b) Self-efficacy.
   (c) Self-esteem.
   (d) Self-concept.

4. **Self-concept is:**
   (a) Vague.
   (b) Well-defined.
   (c) Easy to measure.
   (d) Very precise.

Classical conditioning

1. **In Pavlov's studies, food was the:**
   (a) Unconditioned response.
   (b) Conditioned stimulus.
   (c) Unconditioned stimulus.
   (d) Neutral stimulus.

2. **After conditioning, the neutral stimulus becomes the:**
   (a) Unconditioned stimulus.
   (b) Conditioned stimulus.
   (c) Conditioned response.
   (d) Unconditioned response.

3. **A treatment for gambling addiction is:**
   (a) Immersion therapy.
   (b) Avoidance therapy.
   (c) Aversion therapy.
   (d) Conditioning therapy.

4. **The UCS in Watson and Rayner's study was:**
   (a) A blast of cold air.
   (b) A bright light.
   (c) A loud noise.
   (d) An electric shock.

Operant conditioning

1. **A behaviour followed by a pleasant consequence:**
   (a) Negative punishment.
   (b) Positive punishment.
   (c) Negative reinforcement.
   (d) Positive reinforcement.

2. **Grounding for bad behaviour is an example of:**
   (a) Positive reinforcement.
   (b) Negative punishment.
   (c) Positive punishment.
   (d) Negative reinforcement

3. **Giving someone money for working is:**
   (a) A positive punisher.
   (b) An intrinsic reward.
   (c) A negative reinforcer.
   (d) An extrinsic reward.

4. **Chase *et al*. found:**
   (a) Brain areas associated with reinforcement.
   (b) Operant conditioning cannot explain learning.
   (c) Negative reinforcement does not exist.
   (d) Reinforcement can explain phobias.

Social learning theory

1. **In the context of SLT, a model is:**
   (a) Someone who wears other people's clothes.
   (b) Someone who is observed performing a behaviour.
   (c) A small version of the real thing.
   (d) Made out of plasticine.

2. **Vicarious learning:**
   (a) Occurs without observation.
   (b) Is a direct form of learning.
   (c) Makes imitation more likely.
   (d) Is another term for negative reinforcement.

3. **Imitation is more likely when the:**
   (a) Model is punished.
   (b) Observer and model are different genders.
   (c) Observer identifies with the model.
   (d) Model identifies with the observer.

4. **SLT cannot explain:**
   (a) How phobias are learned.
   (b) Why phobias are more common in identical twins.
   (c) Why children imitate people with high status.
   (d) The findings of the Bobo doll studies.

Influence of biology on behaviour and traits

1. **Neurotransmitters are examples of:**
   (a) Neuroanatomy.
   (b) Evolutionary psychology.
   (c) Neurochemistry.
   (d) Genes.

2. **Extraverts are:**
   (a) Shy.
   (b) Quiet.
   (c) Withdrawn.
   (d) Impulsive.

3. **An introvert's nervous system:**
   (a) Is overactive.
   (b) Is underaroused.
   (c) Responds well to new experiences.
   (d) Is typical of many criminals.

4. **The heritability of E-I is:**
   (a) 57%.
   (b) 100%.
   (c) 0%.
   (d) 28%.

Genetics and inheritance

1. **How genes are expressed in behaviour and characteristics is:**
   (a) Genotype.
   (b) Mainly environmental.
   (c) Entirely genetic.
   (d) Phenotype.

2. **Identical twins have:**
   (a) Same genotype, same phenotype.
   (b) Different genotypes, same phenotype.
   (c) Same genotype, different phenotypes.
   (d) Different genotypes, different phenotypes.

3. **The *SRY* gene plays a role in:**
   (a) The X chromosome.
   (b) Production of female hormones.
   (c) Development of a male embryo.
   (d) Development of ovaries.

4. **The role of genes in a behaviour is:**
   (a) Many genes interact in complex ways.
   (b) Single genes are mostly responsible.
   (c) Genes play no significant role.
   (d) Genes cause behaviours.

Neuroanatomy

1. **Fine movements are controlled by:**
   (a) The motor area.
   (b) The somatosensory area.
   (c) The visual area.
   (d) The spinal cord.

2. **A brain function found in just one hemisphere is called:**
   (a) Functionalised.
   (b) Plasticised.
   (c) Localised.
   (d) Lateralised.

3. **Synapses removed to make room for new ones is:**
   (a) Lateralisation.
   (b) Synaptic pruning.
   (c) Functional recovery.
   (d) Localisation.

4. **Language in the brain is:**
   (a) Distributed very narrowly.
   (b) Partly lateralised and localised.
   (c) Totally lateralised and localised.
   (d) Not lateralised or localised at all.

Organisation of the nervous system

1. **The spinal cord is connected to the:**
   (a) Brain stem.
   (b) Corpus callosum.
   (c) Cerebral cortex.
   (d) Endocrine system.

2. **The brain's control of body movement is:**
   (a) Contradictory.
   (b) Contrafactual.
   (c) Contrarian.
   (d) Contralateral.

3. **The ANS works:**
   (a) Automatically.
   (b) Autonomically.
   (c) Involuntarily.
   (d) All of the above.

4. **The parasympathetic division activates:**
   (a) The fight or flight response.
   (b) The spinal cord.
   (c) The rest and digest response.
   (d) Contralateral control.

Neurochemistry

1. **The gap between nerve cells is a:**
   (a) Gene.
   (b) Neuron.
   (c) Neurotransmitter.
   (d) Synapse.

2. **The main long-term stress hormone is:**
   (a) Testosterone.
   (b) Serotonin.
   (c) Cortisol.
   (d) Adrenaline.

3. **Addison's disease is caused by:**
   (a) High levels of serotonin.
   (b) A lack of cortisol.
   (c) Too much adrenaline.
   (d) Low levels of serotonin.

4. **Which statement is most accurate?**
   (a) Stress is all about physiology.
   (b) Stress is all about neurochemistry.
   (c) People think about stressors differently.
   (d) Stressors affect everyone in the same ways.

Evolutionary psychology

1. **The environment of evolutionary adaptation:**
   (a) Accounts for 10% of our evolutionary history.
   (b) Was more than 10,000 years ago.
   (c) Happened just outside Bolton.
   (d) Has no influence on behaviour.

2. **The peacock's tail is best explained by:**
   (a) Sexual selection.
   (b) Genome lag.
   (c) Survival of the fittest.
   (d) Natural selection.

3. **The fight or flight response also includes:**
   (a) Feed.
   (b) Fail.
   (c) Falter.
   (d) Freeze.

4. **Women's response to stress is:**
   (a) Lend and offend.
   (b) Send and depend.
   (c) Fend and defend.
   (d) Tend and befriend.

MCQ answers

Assumptions of four approaches 1C, 2C, 3A, 4D
Characteristics of three memory stores 1D, 2B, 3A, 4B
Remembering 1C, 2B, 3D, 4D
Reconstructive memory 1B, 2D, 3D, 4A
Cognitive priming 1C, 2D, 3A, 4A
The role of cognitive scripts 1C, 2D, 3C, 4A
Cognitive biases 1A, 2C, 3C, 4C
Conformity 1B, 2B, 3A, 4D
Types of conformity 1D, 2B, 3A, 4D
In-groups and out-groups 1A, 2A, 3C, 4B
Intra-group dynamics 1B, 2A, 3C, 4D
Influences of others on the self 1C, 2B, 3B, 4A
Classical conditioning 1C, 2B, 3C, 4C
Operant conditioning 1D, 2B, 3D, 4A
Social learning theory 1B, 2C, 3C, 4B
Influence of biology on behaviour and traits 1C, 2D, 3A, 4A
Genetics and inheritance 1D, 2C, 3C, 4A
Neuroanatomy 1A, 2D, 3B, 4B
Organisation of the nervous system 1A, 2D, 3D, 4C
Neurochemistry 1D, 2C, 3B, 4C
Evolutionary psychology 1B, 2A, 3D, 4D

Content area A
Assessment guidance

The examination
Unit 1 (Psychological approaches and applications) is externally assessed by one examination. You will be awarded a mark for the whole paper – Distinction (D), Merit (M), Pass (P), Near Pass (N) or Unclassified (U).

The exam is 1 hour 30 minutes. The total number of marks for the paper is 72.

The paper is divided into three Sections (A, B and C), each with 24 marks.

Each Section contains material from both Content areas A and B.

How to answer exam-style questions

Type of question	Example question	Example structure for answer
Short answer questions	State what is meant by 'classical conditioning'. (1)	A type of learning where a neutral stimulus is paired with a UCS so a new stimulus–response association is learned.
	Describe what psychologists mean by 'social categorisation'. (2)	This is when we put people into social groupings based on perceived shared characteristics. For example, someone might think all old people are similar and they have other characteristics such as being slow or grumpy (stereotypes).
Context questions	Merlin was listening to the song *Banana Pancakes* by Jack Johnson. When he went into the kitchen, he immediately noticed the bananas in the fruit bowl. Explain **one** type of priming that he is showing. (2)	Merlin is showing repetition priming. This is because hearing the word 'banana' in the song primed him cognitively so that he noticed the bananas very quickly when he saw them later.
	Sid has been a vegetarian for 20 years. Despite not eating meat, he recently went to a steak restaurant with some friends because he didn't want to appear unfriendly. Explain why compliance is the most appropriate type of conformity to understand Sid's behaviour. (3)	Sid is showing compliance because he publicly agreed to go along with the group. But as he has been a vegetarian for 20 years, he privately would prefer not to go. So he complied just to avoid being rejected by the group. His compliance is temporary because he won't go to steak restaurants without pressure from his friends.
	Evaluate compliance as an explanation of Sid's behaviour. (3)	It might be oversimplifying Sid's behaviour to say he was just complying. There is often more than one type of conformity in situations like this. As Sid and the others are friends, perhaps they have some things in common. So maybe Sid conformed because he identified with the group. This means compliance is only part of the explanation for Sid's behaviour.

Note, an example helps you to get the second mark.

Health warning
The material on assessment advice is not from the exam board. It is our interpretation of the 'rules of the game'. Exams are a kind of 'game' because there are guidelines and rules, and practice is very important to do well. But it is a serious 'game'.

Exams are a gift because they are over and done with in one go. OK, you do have to spend time preparing (see next spread for preparation advice) but at the end of the day it is one exam rather than hours and hours and hours trying to perfect a report.

Command terms
Most questions begin with a *command term*. Each of these terms has a meaning. These are explained in full on page 92.

AO1 Demonstrate psychological knowledge, be able to recall key assumptions and concepts.
- Command words: *describe, give, give a reason why, identify, name, state*.
- Marks: range from 1 to 4 marks.

AO2 Demonstrate understanding by explaining the link between psychological assumptions and concepts to behaviour in society.
- Command words: *describe, explain, interpret, justify*.
- Marks: range from 1 to 4 marks.

AO3 Apply and evaluate psychological assumptions and concepts to explain contemporary issues of relevance to society.
- Command words: *analyse, assess, compare, discuss, evaluate, explain* (only *assess, compare* and *evaluate* require a conclusion).
- Marks: range from 1 to 9 marks.

Timing
Timing is always important in exams because you have a fixed amount of time.

You must spend sufficient time on each answer in relation to the marks but not too much (otherwise you won't give full enough answers to other questions).

You have 90 minutes to gain 72 available marks for the Unit 1 exam. But you also have to read and think (and scenarios can require a fair bit of both).

Taking this into account, a helpful rule of thumb (a guideline) is 'one minute per mark'. So base your timing calculations on this rough figure.

Type of question	Example question	Example structure for answer
Context questions continued	Mia saw her dad drinking a healthy yoghurt drink. When he finished, Mia's mum said to him, 'You really like those drinks, don't you?' Later on, when she was thirsty, Mia took a healthy yoghurt drink from the fridge and drank it. Explain **two** ways that social learning theory could be used to understand Mia's behaviour. (4)	One way is modelling. Mia's dad acted as a model, demonstrating a behaviour for Mia to imitate. She observed him drinking the healthy drink and modelled her actions on his when she had the opportunity. Another way is vicarious learning. Mia's dad probably enjoyed the drink which was confirmed by her mum's comment. Mia observed this and experienced the enjoyment vicariously. She found this rewarding, which made it more likely Mia would imitate her dad's behaviour.
	A woman had her handbag snatched off her in the street. Summer witnessed the attack. She was interviewed by the police and described what she could remember. Using **two** concepts from reconstructive memory, explain why Summer may not have been accurate in her eyewitness description of the attack. (6)	Concept 1 – Rationalisation: Summer's eyewitness memory might be inaccurate because she recalls details in a way that fits her existing schema. For example, if Summer did not get a clear view she might have been uncertain of the attacker's gender or age but described them as a 'young man'. This would fit her schema for a 'street robbery' perhaps based on TV and films. This would make the memory more meaningful to Summer even though it may be wrong. Concept 2 – Shortening: Summer may have left details out altogether because they did not fit her schema. For example, if she expects such robberies to be carried out by a lone individual, she might not recall the suspicious-looking second person acting as a 'lookout'. As a result, her description of the robbery would be shorter than it could be.

The assessment is available in January and May/June each year.

You are allowed to resit any external examination and will get the higher mark of any two attempts. However, it is unlikely you will benefit from this because it merely increases your work burden.

Other mark schemes

A useful guideline is that questions for fewer than 6 marks usually have mark schemes where 1 mark is awarded for each point. Broadly speaking, these are the key criteria for the overall outcome:

Criteria for a pass	Criteria for a distinction
Answer is mostly accurate but with some omissions.	Accurate and thorough with a few minor omissions.
Shows awareness of competing arguments.	Thorough awareness of competing arguments supported by relevant evidence across the unit in well-developed and logical discussion.

...it's how you use it

If you could go into the exam with all of your textbooks, you might not get top marks. How can that be, we hear you ask?

It's because exams are not just about knowing a set of facts – you also need to explain these facts and organise them in a meaningful way. It's not *what* you know, but *how* you use your knowledge that counts.

Effective description

If a description question starts with the word *Identify*, *State* or *Give* and is worth 1 mark, then all you have to do is provide a brief answer. In this case your knowledge is all you need for a good answer – you get 1 mark for accuracy, or zero marks if inaccurate.

Questions that start with *Describe* or *Explain* require more – as explained on the facing page. They need development, they require you to demonstrate you understand, possibly by giving an example.

For example (see what we did there?):

Question: *State what is meant by the term 'schema'.* (1)
Answer: A schema is a mental packet of beliefs and expectations.

Question: *Explain what is meant by the term 'schema'.* (2)
Answer: A schema is a mental packet of beliefs and expectations. For example, you have a schema for trains which consists of what trains look like, what purpose they serve and what happens when you want to get on or off.

Detail is always important. The word 'mental' adds that little bit of extra information – one word can make an important difference.

Effective application

Most questions have a scenario or context. These aim to test your understanding because you have to try to use the information you have learned to explain something new. You can only do that if you understand the concepts.

This means almost every sentence should be related to both the scenario/context and the assumption/context/theory you are using.

Effective evaluation

For effective evaluation you need to do at least two of the following three things (the PET rule):

- **P**oint – state the point you wish to make.
- **E**xplain/**E**laborate/provide **E**vidence – provide some substance to support the claim you are making.
- **T**his suggests that... – end with a mini-conclusion. Sum up the point you have demonstrated.

If you look at every evaluation point in this book you will see this is what we have done.

Effective structure

Examiners are human. Yes, really. You need to help them award you marks. You can do this by organising your answer clearly, just like the ones on this spread.

Less is more

Try to cover fewer points but, with each one, provide detail, explanation, examples, etc.

DON'T write everything you know and hope the sheer volume of facts will impress the examiner. They need to know that you understand it.

Content area A
Revision guidance

Preparing for the exam

You will sit an exam on the topics in this unit. Exams mean revising – but the secret is that revising should happen now. Start revising as you go along.

We have divided this book into spreads. Each spread represents one chunk of the specification as indicated at the bottom right of the spread.

For each topic you should produce a revision card.

For some spreads you might decide to have more than one revision card.

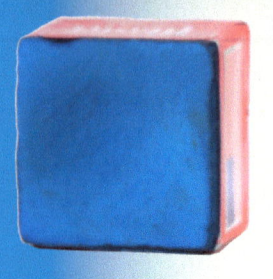

A cue

There are snooker cues and there are other cues – a cue is a thing that serves as a reminder of something else. Actors know they must come in on cue – a reminder or signal.

Psychologists have investigated the value of cues in remembering. They act as a reminder of what else you know.

In the revision card on the right the first column is labelled 'Key point' which can serve as a cue to remember the contents in the second column, labelled 'Description'.

Step 1 See if your cues work

If you just memorise the cues you should be able to produce the information in the second column:

- Once you have produced the revision card, cover the second column and, for each cue, write down what you can recall.
- Check how much you remembered. Maybe you need to add a word to your cue to help you.
- Try again and see if you remember more this time.

Psychological research shows that people often have much more in their heads than they can recall – they just need the right cue.

Step 2 Test your recall

Psychological research has also shown that recall improves dramatically if you TEST your memory. That doesn't mean rereading your notes but CLOSING YOUR BOOK and writing down everything you remember, then checking to see what you left out and testing it again.

Believe in the power of psychology

Revision card

On the facing page is a list of all the topics you need to cover for Content area A.

Below is an example of a revision card for one of these topics.

Description

Topic Reconstructive memory	
Key point (a cue)	**Description**
Reconstructive	Bartlett: store fragments, recall builds it up into meaningful whole.
Not accurate	Bits missing and distorted, e.g. *War of the Ghosts*.
Schema	Mental structures, stored packages of knowledge of world (people, objects, events).
Culture	Born with some basic schema but acquire more through experience. Influences schema, shared expectations e.g. birthday party.
Memory	Reconstructed to fit existing schema, more meaningful, easier to recall.
Shortening	Left out if doesn't fit schema (unexpected).
Rationalisation	Distorted to fit schema because strange or unfamiliar, more sense.
Confabulation	Invented to fill gaps, guided by schema.

Evaluation

Eyewitness testimony	Example of reconstruction leading to inaccurate recall, so convictions not based on this alone.
War of the Ghosts	Bartlett's research, recall affected by schema, inaccurate.
Accurate	Personally important or distinctive memories less affected by schema.

The beauty of this is:

- You reduce what you have to memorise (just memorise the cues). The rest is just engraved in your memory through practice.
- If you do this for every spread as you study it, then you will have all your revision materials ready at the end of the year when you have to prepare for the exam.

This picture is described as a man 'revising' an excavation tyre.

Revise = reconsider or alter.

Revise = reread work previously done. Which means you need to read your notes first and then reread them.

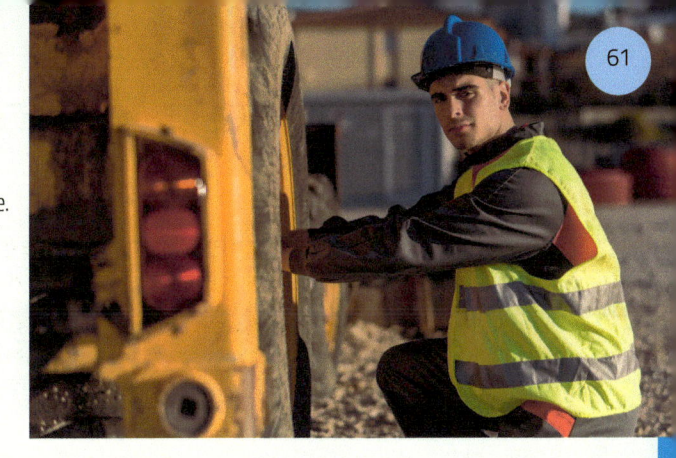

Revision checklist for Content area A

Below are the key topics for Content area A. For each topic you should:
1. Construct a revision card and/or use our summaries (pages 52–53 and 88–89).
2. Test your recall using your cues. Check afterwards to see what you have forgotten.
3. Test your recall again using the cues.
4. Now test your memory of the cue words.

		1. Construct revision card	2. First test of recall	3. Second test of recall	4. Test memory using cues
Cognitive	Cognitive assumptions				
	Characteristics of three memory stores				
	Remembering				
	Reconstructive memory				
	Cognitive priming				
	The role of cognitive scripts				
	Cognitive biases				
Social	Social assumptions				
	Conformity				
	Types of conformity				
	In-groups and out-groups				
	Intra-group dynamics				
	Influences of others on the self				
Behaviourist and social learning	Behaviourist and social learning assumptions				
	Classical conditioning				
	Operant conditioning				
	Social learning theory (SLT)				
Biological	Biological assumptions				
	Influence of biology on behaviour and traits				
	Genetics and inheritance				
	Neuroanatomy				
	Organisation of the nervous system				
	Neurochemistry				
	Evolutionary psychology				

Specification terms are important

We have highlighted 'specification terms' on each spread in a definition box but there are others too. These are examples of specialist psychological knowledge.

Make sure you include these on your revision cards.

The specialist terms turn an impressionist answer ...

... into a detailed one.

Practice

No athlete would dream of running a race without doing many practice runs of the right distance and within a set time. Always write exam answers in the allotted time – taking into account time for reading, thinking and arranging pens on your desk, you've got just over one minute per mark (and you should give yourself a little bit longer for essay questions in Area B, coming up soon). Practise writing answers with the clock ticking. Afterwards, check your revision card and textbook and note any really important things you forgot to mention.

Content area A
Practice questions, answers and feedback

On this spread we look at some typical answers to exam-style questions. The comments provided (in green) from an experienced teacher show what is good and bad in each answer. Learning how to provide effective exam answers is a SKILL. Practise it.

Maneet is a police detective and Marcus is her senior officer. One day, Maneet was out interviewing potential witnesses when one of them had a panic attack and Maneet had to help them. Maneet was late back to the office, and Marcus accused her of being lazy and having a poor attitude.

Question 1 (a): Using the concept of fundamental attribution error, explain why Marcus made his comments about Maneet. (2 marks)

Chen's answer: Marcus accused her of being lazy and having a poor attitude. This is because FAE makes you not consider the situation of earlier, so you are only interested in what happens in the present.

Teacher comments
There's no evidence in this answer that Chen has any knowledge about the FAE. The only link he makes to the scenario is to repeat the information given in the question, so he hasn't explained anything. 0 marks.

Bella's answer: Marcus attributes Maneet's lateness to her personality – laziness and a bad attitude are internal characteristics of a person.

But Marcus has failed to take into account or ignored the situation Maneet was in as a reason why she was late, because she had to help someone.

Bella has identified a correct reason why Marcus made his comments. Then she explains this further using the FAE, with full links to the scenario. Bella includes both individual characteristics and the situation, not just one or the other. There's more than enough here for 2 marks.

Saturn's answer: Marcus did not consider that Maneet was late because of something outside her control in the situation. He was probably quite aggressive towards Maneet, perhaps because he had a hostile attribution bias.

Saturn is correct about the role of the situation, which she partly applies to the scenario. But there's no clear point about Maneet's personality. Instead, Saturn has gone beyond the information given in the scenario (she's making stuff up) and unfortunately written about the wrong cognitive bias. 1 mark.

Question 1 (b): Briefly assess fundamental attribution error as an explanation of Marcus's comments. (3 marks)

Chen's answer: The FAE could give us some practical applications. Marcus made a mistake in his reasons why Maneet was late. He thought it was down to Maneet's personality. This was because of his FAE so he could be helped to realise that he is mistaken. In future Marcus would not make a judgement without all the information about what has happened. So this is a practical application for the FAE.

Teacher comments
Chen's answer is a bit unclear and disorganised. But he has tried to assess the FAE in the context of Marcus and Maneet. Chen firstly identifies a useful strength. He goes on to explain it (unclearly). But Chen's conclusion is weak – he just repeats the opening point about practical applications. A better approach is to explain why this is beneficial for Marcus, e.g. 'This means Marcus would make more accurate judgements about other people's behaviour, which would help a lot in his job as a police officer'. 2 marks.

Bella's answer: A weakness of the FAE is that it only exists in some cultures. You find it in individualist cultures like the UK where people value individual needs more than the community. But in collectivist cultures (China), behaviour is usually thought to be caused by the situation. So the FAE does not exist in all of human behaviour.

Bella seems to have learned a relevant point from the textbook. The point itself is fine, but she hasn't shaped her response to answer the question. Look carefully – there is no link to Marcus and Maneet at all. So this answer does not meet the requirement '… as an explanation of Marcus's comments'. Even though it is quite lengthy it gets 0 marks.

Saturn's answer: A problem with the FAE is that it depends on culture to explain Marcus's comments. If Marcus and Maneet were working in a collectivist culture, Marcus would not attribute Maneet's lateness to her personality but to the situation. This suggests that the FAE is not a universal feature of behaviour, so it is a limited explanation of Marcus's comments.

Saturn has assessed the FAE very well, with a classic PET – Point, Explanation/Evidence, 'This suggests …'. Most importantly, she has used her knowledge properly – this is a fully contextualised answer because Saturn has completely engaged with the scenario (and not just used the names Marcus and Maneet). 3 marks.

Maneet is part of a book club and hated the latest book that was chosen for the group to read. However, at the next meeting everyone else said the author was a great writer, so Maneet said she loved the book.

Question 2: Using the social approach, explain two reasons why Maneet agreed with the rest of the group. (4 marks)

Chen's answer: Maneet conforms with the group because she agrees with them that the book is good.

Maneet might also think that the other people know more than she does, so she goes along with their expertise.

Teacher comments
Chen identifies 'conformity' but this is not enough for a 'reason'. He doesn't explain it any further but he does link to the scenario so this gets 1 mark. For the second point he does identify a reason but doesn't explain it or apply it to the scenario. Chen is making the examiner work very hard to find any credit in this answer. 1 mark.

Bella's answer: Normative social influence – Maneet may have conformed with the rest of the group so she would be accepted. She was afraid the group would reject her, so she decided to go against her true opinions.

Informational social influence – Maneet assumed the others were better informed about the book because they knew more about the author. She agreed because she thought their opinion was correct.

Bella's answer is really well-structured and makes things easy for the examiner to find credit. She identifies two clear reasons, explains them and links them to Maneet. This is a good example of someone using their knowledge to focus on the question. Bella hasn't just written about NSI and ISI but has shaped her knowledge to match the requirements of the question. She makes four key points for 4 marks.

Saturn's answer: Maneet is showing NSI because she didn't want the group to reject her for hating the book.

She is also conforming because she wants to be friends with everyone and be accepted by them.

The first reason Saturn gives is fine – she correctly identifies NSI and explains it in the context of the scenario. Saturn may think she has given a second reason but she hasn't. All she has done is restated NSI, so this is really an extension of the first point. This is a partial answer, so it gets 2 marks.

Maneet has identical twin children, Wanda and Maya. Wanda has always been a 'people person'. She has lots of friends she often goes out with, especially from the local rugby club she plays for. Maya prefers to 'keep herself to herself'. She has always been quiet and shy, spending more time studying and caring for her pet snake than socialising.

Question 3: Identify from this scenario evidence that Wanda and Maya: (a) share the same genotype, (b) have different phenotypes. (2 marks)

Chen's answer: (a) Wanda and Maya are Maneet's children. (b) They are also identical twins.	Teacher comments Chen is very confused. 'Maneet's children' is not enough and 'identical twins' is not a phenotype. But he would have picked up 1 mark if only he had moved his answer to (b) into (a). 0 marks.
Bella's answer: (a) Wanda and Maya are identical twins. (b) They are both quite muscular from exercising.	Bella is right about genotype – a brief answer but correct. Bella is wrong about the phenotype because she is assuming other information that is not in the scenario. What a pity she didn't just use something from the scenario. 1 mark.
Saturn's answer: (a) They are Maneet's identical twin children. (b) Wanda is a 'people person' with lots of friends. But Maya is quiet and shy and doesn't like socialising.	Saturn has both answers correct, contextualised with both individuals in each answer. For questions like these, you can just 'lift' the information from the scenario. There's no need to summarise or even add anything. 2 marks.

Question 4: Explain **one** difference between genotype and phenotype. (2 marks)

Chen's answer: Genotype is just about the genes because it is the whole set of genes you have. Phenotype is more than just genes, it is how they are actually expressed by interacting with the environment.	Teacher comments Chen goes on to show he does know about genotype and phenotype, making his earlier error even more unfortunate. He had the knowledge, but he struggled to apply it in the previous question. You need both skills. 2 marks.
Bella's answer: Genotype refers to the genes but phenotype is about what the genes do.	Bella's understanding of this topic is weak. She has at least attempted to identify a difference but it's incorrect. 0 marks.
Saturn's answer: Genotype means the genes we have got but phenotype means the environment.	Saturn knows more but hasn't expressed it very well. 'The genes we have got' is correct for a mark, but phenotype is not identical to the environment. 1 mark.

Maya became frightened of dogs when she was a child, after a big dog barked very loudly right in her face.

Question 5: Describe, using classical conditioning, why Maya became frightened of dogs. (3 marks)

Chen's answer: Maya has learned to be frightened through classical conditioning, because it is learning through association between dogs and fear.	Teacher comments The only relevant correct material in Chen's answer is the reference to learning through association. As this is linked to the scenario it's worth 1 mark.
Bella's answer: The unconditioned stimulus was a loud noise (barking), which was what originally made Maya frightened (UCR). The dog was a neutral stimulus and produced no fear. But when the dog barked in her face, Maya associated the NS with the scary noise. The dog became a CS and produced the same fear as the UCS, so it is now the CR.	This is another well-structured answer from Bella. There is a logical progression that describes all the stages of classical conditioning – before, during and after. It's clear from her use of terminology that Bella understands how classical conditioning works. 3 marks.
Saturn's answer: When Maya was young, she did not associate dogs with fear, so they were neutral. But she was afraid of loud noises which was not learned. The dog barked in Maya's face so she associated the dog with noise, thinking it might happen again at any time.	Some correct material with some structure. Saturn has described what happens before and during conditioning. But she has left out the 'after'. For another mark, Saturn needed to include the new conditioned response. The answer lacks terminology and the reference to 'thinking' is inappropriate. Saturn doesn't lose marks for this but she can't gain any either. 2 marks.

Jackie is addicted to playing on fruit machines. They get a thrill from all the flashing lights and loud noises and occasionally the money they win. They prefer doing this to being at home with their family.

Question 6: Explain **two** ways operant conditioning can be used to understand Wanda's behaviour. (4 marks)

Chen's answer: Positive reinforcement – Jackie finds that playing fruit machines gives them pleasure from the thrill and the money, which is rewarding so it reinforces them and they play again. Negative reinforcement – by playing fruit machines, Jackie avoids unpleasant consequences of being at home (because they prefer playing the machines), so it is an escape which gives them relief meaning they continue.	Teacher comments Chen has structured his answer to make it very clear to the examiner that he knows about and understands this topic. He has clearly identified two correct ways and clearly explained each one, relating them fully to the scenario. He has also used some technical terms accurately. 4 marks.
Bella's answer: Jackie will continue to use the fruit machines because of the flashing lights that give them a thrill. Another way is to do with how they sometimes win money, which means they will carry on doing it to get a bit better off.	Bella has fallen into the trap of just repackaging the information given in the scenario. There's no evidence in Bella's answer that she understands operant conditioning at all – no technical terms, no clear two ways identified and virtually no explanation. 0 marks.
Saturn's answer: Jackie's behaviour is positively reinforced by the rewarding thrill and flashing lights etc so they carry on playing. But they are negatively punished by being at home, which is why they prefer to spend more time playing the fruit machines.	This is a partially correct answer because the first way is correct. Saturn has identified positive reinforcement and explained it in relation to the scenario. But she hasn't identified a correct second way and appears to be confused about the role of punishment. 2 marks.

Content area B1: Use of psychology to explain contemporary issues of aggression in society

Cognitive approach to explaining aggression in society

Road rage

If you wanted to carry a gun, you wouldn't be able to in the UK because the law prevents you. It's different in the USA. People who are allowed to own guns sometimes keep them in their cars. Does this make them kinder, more considerate drivers? No, it does not.

According to Brad Bushman and his colleagues (2017), people drive more aggressively and are more abusive to other road users when there is a gun in the car (as opposed to a tennis racket). The gun doesn't even have to do anything – it just has to be there.

The weapon primes aggressive thoughts. Or to put it another way, 'the finger pulls the trigger, but the trigger may also be pulling the finger' (Berkowitz and Lepage 1967).

Specification terms

Aggression Behaviour that is intended to cause psychological or physical harm.

Cognitive priming We process a stimulus (word, image, object, etc.) more quickly when we see or hear the stimulus (or a related one) first (the 'prime').

Cognitive scripts Information stored in memory that describes the behaviours typical in a given situation. They are automatically retrieved to guide our behaviour. They are also known as memory scripts.

Hostile aggression Angry and impulsive aggression usually accompanied by physiological arousal.

Hostile attribution bias A tendency to assume that someone else's behaviour has an aggressive or antagonistic motive when it is actually neutral.

Instrumental aggression Goal-directed and planned aggression usually not accompanied by physiological arousal.

Schema Mental frameworks of beliefs and expectations that influence cognitive processing. They are developed from experience.

Verbal aggression Using words to cause psychological damage to another person, e.g. gossip, shouting.

Violent aggression Using physical force to cause physical injury to another person, e.g. punching, kicking.

Instrumental aggression. Not that kind of instrument.

Types of aggression

Hostile aggression This is angry and impulsive ('hot-blooded') *aggression*. It is accompanied by physiological arousal, e.g. increased heart rate and blood pressure. It is often physical but sometimes verbal (see below).

Instrumental aggression Involves using aggression (as an 'instrument') to get what you want. It is planned and usually *not* accompanied by physiological arousal ('cold-blooded', e.g. bullying). It can be physical or verbal and usually intended to provoke a response.

Violent aggression This is using physical force to cause injury to others (e.g. punching, kicking). All violent behaviour is aggressive, but not all aggression is violent.

Verbal aggression Involves using words to psychologically damage another person (e.g. shouting, swearing, 'cutting' remarks). It can be instrumental when used in a campaign to undermine someone, e.g. spreading gossip. But it can also be hostile, e.g. firing off an angry text or social media post in the 'heat of the moment'.

The cognitive approach

Cognitive priming for aggression

As we saw on page 18, if you encounter an aggressive stimulus (the prime), you notice a later related stimulus more quickly (or you may respond more strongly to it). The aggressive stimulus primes aggressive thoughts, so any later stimulus 'triggers' you to behave aggressively (e.g. you think someone is being threatening). This is *cognitive priming*.

Aggressive prime/stimulus This could be watching a violent film, playing a violent game, watching others behaving aggressively (including in sport), or a weapon being present (see left). Priming of aggression can occur over a period of time and is not usually a 'one-off' event (e.g. exposure to many angry posts over time on social media).

Below awareness Priming occurs without us even being aware of it. This is why we can be primed in one social situation and behave aggressively in another situation. For example, you observe a character's aggression in a TV programme and later you are rude to the checkout assistant at the supermarket. You might not have been so rude if you had not seen the TV programme. But you are unaware of the connection – you don't realise you've been influenced.

Hostile attribution bias (HAB)

People with a *hostile attribution bias* (HAB) interpret other people's behaviour as threatening even if it is in fact neutral. This can lead to aggressive behaviour.

Someone with a HAB pays special attention to other people's behaviour, expecting it to be threatening. For instance, if someone accidentally stumbles into them they view this as deliberate. They may feel provoked and become aggressive. If people around them respond aggressively themselves, this confirms to the person with a HAB that their belief was correct and they were justified in being aggressive.

Cognitive scripts and schema

A *cognitive script* is a *schema* (mental framework) which contains our knowledge of how a social situation 'plays out' (page 20). Most people possess cognitive scripts for aggressive situations – what to expect, how to behave, what the consequences might be. These are developed through observing and experiencing aggressive situations.

Aggressive scripts are stored in memory and prepare (prime) us to be 'ready' for aggression. An aggressive script is triggered when we encounter cues in a situation that we perceive to be aggressive (e.g. someone talking too loudly directly at us).

Some people are more aggressive than others. This is because aggressive people have a wider range of aggressive cognitive scripts that are easily retrieved.

GET ACTIVE: Tomos and Sheena

Tomos regularly contributes angry posts on social media often in the evenings. Tomos is a teacher and by the time he gets to school he is usually in a bad mood. He shouts at students and is very 'short' and offhand with other teachers.

Sheena is a firefighter who has a reputation for being 'spiky'. She often misinterprets her colleagues' behaviour. For example, once during training the person she was working with accidentally dropped a hose reel on her foot. He apologised but Sheena squared up to him and they almost came to blows.

1. Identify and explain all the types of aggression in these scenarios.
2. Explain how the cognitive approach accounts for the behaviour of Tomos and Sheena.

Social media can have priming effects by exposing us to angry and aggressive interactions that we may carry over into the face-to-face world.

Evaluation

Practical applications

One strength is that the cognitive approach has created practical real-world benefits.

The cognitive approach has contributed to methods to reduce aggressive behaviours. For example, cognitive therapy aims to change HABs and thoughts that prime aggressive behaviour. Nancy Guerra and Ronald Slaby (1990) helped adolescent prison inmates to replace hostile attributions with positive ones. Compared with a control group, they showed a much-reduced HAB and less aggression (as rated by staff).

This means that using the cognitive approach can help to reduce aggression and the social costs associated with it.

Research support

Another strength is that many studies have found a link between cognitive factors and aggression.

For example, Bram Orobio de Castro et al. (2002) reviewed studies of HAB in children. Most of the studies confirmed there was a significant association between HABs and aggressive behaviour. Peter Fischer and Tobias Greitemeyer (2006) found that after listening to songs with derogatory lyrics about women, men behaved aggressively towards a woman confederate (an example of cognitive priming).

Therefore, there is some research evidence that cognitive factors are centrally involved in aggressive behaviour.

Correlation not causation

One weakness is that cognitive factors may not be causes of aggressive behaviour.

Studies show that aggressive scripts are associated with aggressive behaviour. But this is mostly correlational research, which cannot show that scripts cause aggression. This is because no variables are manipulated or controlled. Instead of people with aggressive scripts being more aggressive, it may be that being more aggressive contributes to a more aggressive script. Or perhaps a third non-cognitive factor is responsible for both the aggressive script and the aggressive behaviour, e.g. learning experiences.

This means the cognitive approach is limited because correlations do not allow us to identify the true causes of aggression.

Exam-style questions

Sami was driving to the shops when another driver almost ran into them. Sami didn't react. But three days later, they saw the other driver's car parked outside a supermarket and used a key to scratch the car's paintwork.

1. Identify the type of aggression shown by Sami. (1 mark)
2. Explain how the cognitive approach might account for Sami's behaviour. (3 marks)
3. Evaluate the view that Sami's behaviour was due to cognitive factors. (3 marks)
4. Explain what is meant by the term 'hostile aggression'. (2 marks)
5. Give **three** concepts from the cognitive approach that can explain aggression. (3 marks)
6. Freida is a big fan of boxing. She was in a crowded pub watching a boxing match on the TV when a man accidentally trod on her foot. Even though he apologised, Freida still got angry and hit him in the face.
   Identify and describe the type of aggression shown by Freida. (3 marks)
7. Discuss cognitive explanations for Freida's behaviour. Your answer should consider **two** of the following:
   - cognitive priming
   - hostile attribution bias
   - cognitive scripts and schema. (9 marks)

Link it

Link aggression to the assumptions and key concepts of the cognitive approach.

One assumption is that the brain can be compared to a computer (computer analogy). In cognitive priming:

- The input is an aggressive stimulus (e.g. watching other people being aggressive).
- The processing is triggering of aggressive cognitive scripts in memory.
- The output is interpreting someone's neutral attitude as aggressive.

What are the links between aggression, hostile attribution bias and the assumption that behaviour is a product of information processing?

In content area B we have changed 'An issue to consider' to 'Link it' because you should be able to link the topics in content area B to the key assumptions and concepts in content area A.

Specification content

B1 Use of psychology to explain contemporary issues of aggression in society

Learners should be able to demonstrate knowledge of different types of aggression.

Learners should understand and apply knowledge of how psychological concepts can be used to explain aggression in society:

- Aggression – behaviours that result in psychological or physical harm to self, others or objects in the environment; hostile, instrumental, violent aggression and verbal/nonphysical aggression.
- Cognitive priming for aggression, hostile attribution bias; cognitive scripts and schema.

Content area B1: Use of psychology to explain contemporary issues of aggression in society

Social approach to explaining aggression in society

Can stereotypes have fatal consequences?

In 2014 Michael Brown, an 18-year-old African American man, was shot 12 times and killed by a white police officer. Brown was unarmed. Other incidents in which young black men are killed by police officers have happened since.

In these cases, it has been argued that the police officers involved hold strong racist stereotypes of young black men and these influence their behaviour. Because the police officers stereotype young black men as aggressive and threatening, they form incorrect beliefs about what the young men might do. Because most police officers do not hold the same stereotypes of young white men, they treat the two groups quite differently.

It was Michael Brown's killing that led to the #BlackLivesMatter movement becoming nationally recognised in the US and around the world.

Specification terms

Conformity When a person changes their opinion/behaviour because they are pressured (or believe they are pressured) by another person or a group.

Desensitisation Reduced sensitivity to a stimulus, either psychological (e.g. less emotional response) or physiological (e.g. lowered heart rate).

Disinhibition A lack of restraint (no longer being inhibited), due to environmental triggers or overexposure to a stimulus.

Institutional aggression Aggressive or violent behaviour that takes place within the social context of a formal organised setting (e.g. a prison).

Media Communication channels (e.g. TV, books, social media sites) through which news, entertainment, education and data are available.

Role modelling Imitating the behaviour of people who have qualities we would like to have or who we admire (alternatively, demonstrating behaviour to be imitated).

Social norm Something that is standard, usual or typical of a social group.

Stereotypes Fixed views of other people based on their perceived membership of a social category.

Influences of others

Conformity to social/group norms

As we saw on page 24, a *norm* is an unstated 'rule' about what behaviours are considered appropriate and inappropriate. Members of a group generally *conform* to shared norms.

Gender norms In many cultures, gender norms dictate that men should use aggression to achieve status, money or other social rewards (Eagly and Wood 1991). Women should be nurturing and gentle rather than aggressive. One exception is that women may be verbally aggressive as long as it releases anger (part of the gender norm that women should be emotionally expressive).

Cultural norms Cultures differ in levels of violent crimes. Cases of 'intentional homicide' (murder) are more than 12 times higher in the USA than in Iceland, accounting for population sizes. This implies these cultures have different norms about aggression.

Stereotypes and aggression

Stereotypes are cognitive 'shortcuts' that allow us to interact in the social world (see page 28). When we meet an individual we fit them into a category and then think we know how they are likely to behave.

Gender stereotypes Physical aggression is strongly associated with stereotyped masculinity. This is dangerous because it can lead to acceptance and tolerance of sexual harassment and violence perpetrated by men against women (i.e. because it is expected).

Ethnic stereotypes Black people (especially men) are often stereotyped as aggressive, more so than any other ethnic group. Again, this is dangerous because it may lead to tolerance of racist opinions and aggressive behaviour towards young black men (e.g. by the police, highlighted by the #BlackLivesMatter movement, see left).

Influence of the media

Role modelling The *media* provides aggressive *role models* for people, especially children, to imitate. Imitation is more likely when the model has characteristics the observer admires, such as fame and wealth.

Desensitisation Normally when we witness aggressive behaviour we experience physiological arousal (e.g. increased heart rate). But repeatedly viewing aggression (e.g. on TV or in computer games) may mean people get used to its effects – they become *desensitised*. They experience less physiological arousal in response to aggression and also feel less empathy for victims (Funk *et al.* 2004).

Disinhibition There are strong social and psychological inhibitions against using aggression. These inhibitions are loosened (*disinhibition*) after we have observed aggressive behaviour in the media. Media depictions can make aggression appear 'normal' (e.g. by showing it being rewarded). Repeated exposure can disinhibit viewers and create new social norms that are more accepting of aggression.

Institutional aggression

Research into *institutional aggression* has mostly focused on prison. Aggression may be caused by the prison environment, which includes other people (inmates, staff). According to James McGuire (2018), two powerful ways in which other people influence prison aggression are:

Gang membership Being a member of a gang is strongly linked to a prison inmate engaging in violence, even if the inmate was not in a gang before prison. This is because gang leaders can exercise control over members in a prison environment. The more involved inmates are with gangs, the more likely they are to behave aggressively.

Staff behaviour Serious violence by inmates is higher in prisons where staff are inconsistent in applying disciplinary measures, e.g. where decisions made by prison officers are regularly overturned by senior managers.

Evaluation

Practical applications

One strength is that understanding of social influences can be applied in prisons.

For example, one effective way to reduce prison aggression is for prison staff to apply rules consistently (McGuire 2018). This helps because it means there has to be communication between staff and with inmates. When communication is good and the rules are clear and applied consistently, inmates are less likely to develop a sense of injustice that can motivate aggression.

Therefore, social influences that affect aggression can be altered to help reduce aggressive behaviour in prisons (and other institutions).

Research support

Another strength is that research confirms the role of social influences on aggression.

For example, people who watched a film depicting aggression as socially acceptable (vengeance) later gave more (fake) electric shocks to a confederate (Berkowitz and Alioto 1973). The violence disinhibited aggressive behaviour because it was presented as vengeance. Other research shows that physiological arousal to aggression gradually reduces in people who habitually experience violent media (Krahé et al. 2011), which is evidence of desensitisation.

This evidence suggests that media such as film and TV are key social influences on aggressive behaviour.

Role of biological factors

One weakness is that biological factors may outweigh social influences on aggression.

Norms, stereotypes and media are important influences on aggression. But some psychologists argue that biological factors are at least equally significant. For example, many studies have shown a link between the male sex hormone *testosterone* and aggression in both men and women. Castrating a male animal (removing its testes) is accompanied by a reduction in both testosterone and aggression (Giammanco et al. 2005).

Therefore, all of the social influences on this spread are only partial explanations of aggression and may have less effect than biological factors such as hormones.

Do you find this image surprising? Is this woman failing to conform to gender-role or cultural norms? Does her behaviour violate commonly-accepted stereotypes about older people, especially women?

GET ACTIVE Images of stereotyping

Go to shutterstock.com or fotolia.com. These websites hold thousands of what are called 'microstock' images that can be used in media as illustrations (there are some in this book). Search for images using terms such as *professional, criminal, terrorist*.

1. Do you think the images are based on stereotypes?
2. Are any of the stereotypes linked to aggression?
3. Do the representations of black and white people in the media reflect the stereotypes we already hold or do they help to form them?

Exam-style questions

Joss was staying with her friend Tami and her family. One day Joss said to Tami, 'Why do you and your mum argue so much? You're always shouting and swearing at each other.' Tami replied, 'We've always resolved our differences like that. My brothers are even worse – they actually physically fight each other. All our friends expect it now.'

1. Explain **two** ways the social approach could be used to understand Tami's family's aggressive behaviour. (4 marks)
2. In the context of aggression, explain what is meant by the term 'social/group norms'. (2 marks)
3. Ryan is one of Tami's brothers. He was sent to prison for assault. In prison, he was beaten up and saw a lot of aggressive behaviour.

   Explain how the social approach can help us understand Ryan's experience of institutional aggression. (3 marks)
4. State what is meant by 'disinhibition' and 'desensitisation' in the context of aggressive behaviour. (2 marks)
5. Rosie is Tami's younger sister who lives in the family home. Rosie sees her family's behaviour every day. She also watches a lot of violent TV and plays aggressive video games.

   Evaluate the extent to which the social approach could be used to explain why Rosie might behave aggressively. (9 marks)

Link it

Link aggression to the assumptions and key concepts of the social approach.

One assumption is that behaviour occurs in a social context (influenced by people around us). As members of social groups, we are pressured to conform to shared norms. One norm may be that aggression is an acceptable way of getting what you want, so you behave aggressively to be accepted by the group.

What are the links between aggression, stereotypes and the assumption that wider culture and society influence people's behaviour?

Specification content

B1 Use of psychology to explain contemporary issues of aggression in society

Learners should understand and apply knowledge of how psychological concepts can be used to explain aggression in society:

- Influences of others, including conformity to social/group norms, stereotypes, role modelling, desensitisation, disinhibition, institutional aggression, influence of the media.

Content area B1: Use of psychology to explain contemporary issues of aggression in society

Behaviourist and social learning approaches to explaining aggression in society

'Mobbing' at work

In some workplaces employees can find themselves the target of something akin to bullying, when workmates gang up together and make life difficult for one person. Ken Westhues (2002) calls this 'mobbing'.

Most workers learn how to mob by observing their 'leader'. They interact with victims by copying the leader's methods. The leader is often in a senior position, so accomplices look up to them because of their status. It also means the leader is in a position to reward his or her accomplices for their support. Because the leader often achieves their goals, accomplices are motivated to imitate him or her.

The conditions for imitation to take place in a workplace are almost perfect and are explained on this spread.

Specification terms

Operant conditioning A form of learning in which behaviour is shaped and maintained by its consequences – reinforcement (positive or negative) or punishment (positive or negative).

Social learning A form of learning in which behaviours are acquired through observation, modelling, imitation and vicarious reinforcement. Cognitive factors play a key role.

Vicarious reinforcement Occurs when a learner observes a model's behaviour being reinforced (also called vicarious learning).

Unplanned, impulsive, uncontrolled. An angry outburst is an example of hostile aggression – not explained well by learning theories.

Operant conditioning

Aggression can be learned directly through *operant conditioning* (see page 36 for a reminder of the basic processes of operant conditioning).

Positive reinforcement

According to Skinner (1932), behaviour is shaped by its consequences. A behaviour that is reinforced is more likely to reoccur; a behaviour that is punished is less likely to reoccur.

Aggressive behaviours are mostly acquired and maintained through positive reinforcement because aggression is an effective way of gaining rewards (you might recognise this as instrumental aggression, see page 64).

Timing of rewards Skinner argued that behaviours become especially strengthened when they are positively reinforced only occasionally (and at irregular intervals). This is how social media notifications work, for instance – because you wait for them and they are unpredictable, it feels more rewarding when they do eventually arrive.

A person who behaves aggressively may be reinforced only some of the time, usually because there is no one else around to approve. If there is no pattern to when the aggression is reinforced (i.e. it is unpredictable), then that is even more powerful.

Types of reward

Aggression brings two main types of reward – tangible and intangible.

Tangible rewards These include money, food and many other physically 'real' rewards. These positively reinforce up to 80% of children's aggressive behaviours (e.g. forcibly taking a toy off another child, Patterson et al. 1967).

Intangible rewards These include pleasurable feelings and social status. Bullying is reinforced by increased status in the school playground (or workplace, etc.) through fear. Other examples include gang members gaining status through fighting, and whole societies that provide social status rewards (e.g. medals, honours) for aggressive behaviour in wartime.

Social learning

Albert Bandura (1973) realised that aggressive behaviour in humans cannot be fully explained by direct forms of learning such as operant conditioning. As we saw on page 38, he argued that most learning of aggression is indirect and occurs through observation, modelling, imitation and vicarious reinforcement. This is *social learning*.

Observational learning and modelling

Children (and to a lesser extent adults) learn specific aggressive behaviours through observing aggressive models (e.g. parents, siblings, peers, media figures). A person observes how an aggressive behaviour is performed, learning how to physically carry it out. However, observation alone does not guarantee that the observer will imitate the aggression – another social learning mechanism is required.

Vicarious reinforcement

As well as observing the aggressive behaviour of models, people also observe the consequences of that behaviour. If the behaviour is rewarded (or at least not punished), then the observer learns it can be a successful means of getting a desired reward.

This is *vicarious reinforcement* or *vicarious learning* – the observer experiences the model's reward 'second-hand', but this is enough to increase the likelihood that the observer will imitate the model's behaviour.

Conversely, if the aggression is punished, the observer learns that it is not effective in gaining a reward and the likelihood of imitation is reduced.

Evaluation

Practical applications
One strength is that there are important applications to social policy.

Aggressive behaviours that underlie some serious crimes are learned through direct reinforcement and exposure to models in the family and in peer networks. Policymakers (e.g. government) could help reduce aggression by developing programmes based on reinforcement of prosocial behaviours and on social learning. One example is mentoring, providing 'at risk' children and young adults with non-aggressive role models to imitate.

This means the behaviourist and social learning approaches could reduce the costs to individuals and societies of human aggression in its various forms.

Research support
Another strength is strong evidence that children do actually learn to be aggressive.

François Poulin and Michel Boivin (2000) found that the most aggressive boys between nine and 12 years old became friends with each other. These relationships were 'training grounds' for antisocial behaviour. The boys gained direct reinforcement through rewards (money, praise, etc.). They experienced vicarious reinforcement through observing the rewarding consequences of each other's aggression.

This study showed that aggressive behaviour readily develops in conditions predicted by the behaviourist and social learning approaches.

Limited explanations
One weakness is that operant conditioning and social learning cannot explain hostile aggression (page 64).

A violent outburst can easily escalate an encounter so that the individual being aggressive receives punishment in return. Operant conditioning and social learning predict that punishment (direct or vicarious) makes future aggressive behaviour less likely. In reality, the opposite is usually true – the punished individual continues to be violently aggressive.

This means that alternative approaches (e.g. biological or social) may be better explanations of hostile aggression.

GET ACTIVE Bullied out of a job

Gregor is a senior manager of a supermarket and has to make cutbacks in his department. He has been making negative comments about one employee, Hadley. More than once he has shouted loudly at Hadley in his office. Adi has frequently seen how Gregor treats Hadley. Adi held a meeting with other employees and didn't invite Hadley, even though it was about her area of work. Adi has also spoken very negatively about Hadley in meetings and around the office. Gregor approved of Adi's behaviour, praised him in front of other staff and privately promised him promotion. The bullying continued for several weeks until Hadley was signed off with stress.

1. Identify and explain **three** types of aggressive behaviour in this scenario.
2. Use the behaviourist and social learning approaches to explain the aggressive behaviour of Gregor and Adi. Using examples in your explanation, refer to the concepts of operant conditioning, social learning and vicarious reinforcement.

Social learning theory explains how TV characters might influence children to behave aggressively.

Exam-style questions

Roland was arrested and put on trial for assaulting a man in the street. During the trial Roland's barrister defended him by stating that Roland had grown up in a violent household and had witnessed many instances of aggression, especially by his father. When he was a teenager, Roland became friends with some boys who would fight each other and get money by threatening others. A psychologist who was called as an expert witness for the defence said that Roland's aggressive behaviour was learned.

1. Give **one** concept from the behaviourist or social learning approach to understanding aggression that could support the view of the expert witness. (1 mark)
2. Using the behaviourist and social learning approaches, explain **two** reasons for Roland's aggressive behaviour. (4 marks)
3. Explain what is meant by the term 'vicarious learning' in the context of aggression. (2 marks)
4. State the meaning of 'social learning' in relation to aggression. (1 mark)
5. Assess the behaviourist and social learning approaches as an explanation of Roland's behaviour. In your answer you should consider:
   - the roles of operant conditioning
   - social learning. (9 marks)

Link it
Link aggression to the assumptions and key concepts of the behaviourist and social learning approaches.

One assumption is that behaviour can be learned from observation and imitation. Children learn to be aggressive by observing aggressive behaviour around them. The sources can be media and adults. These sources are models that demonstrate how aggressive behaviours are performed and that children can learn to imitate.

What are the links between aggression, operant conditioning and the assumption that behaviour is a learned response to environmental stimuli?

Specification content
B1 Use of psychology to explain contemporary issues of aggression in society

Learners should understand and apply knowledge of how psychological concepts can be used to explain aggression in society:
- Operant conditioning.
- Social learning including vicarious learning.

Content area B1: Use of psychology to explain contemporary issues of aggression in society

Biological approach to explaining aggression in society

Violence in the genes?

In 1978, a group of women from the same family attended appointments at a hospital in the Netherlands. They were planning to have children, but there was something about the men of their family that worried them – they were thinking of 14 of their brothers, sons, and nephews.

These 14 had two things in common – they were intellectually impaired and also extremely aggressive. One had attempted to assault his sister, another tried to mow down his boss with his car and two others had set fire to houses. They were all prone to aggressive outbursts, threatening people and constantly getting into fights.

15 years later, a researcher called Han Brunner took blood samples from these 14 men and another 14 of their male relatives. He identified a variation in one gene. All the violent men had it, but the non-violent men did not.

The gene, described on this spread, became known in the media as the 'Warrior Gene'.

Specification terms

Biochemistry See Neurochemistry on page 10.

Brain structures Physical components that make up the neuroanatomy of the brain, including the amygdala.

Cortisol A hormone produced by the adrenal glands as part of the body's longer-term stress response. Cortisol controls how the body uses energy, but it also suppresses the immune system.

Dopamine A neurotransmitter that generally stimulates neural activity throughout the brain.

Limbic system A collection of brain structures, including the amygdala, which are involved in regulating emotional behaviour.

MAOA gene The gene responsible for the activity of the enzyme monoamine oxidase A (MAOA) in the brain. The low-activity variant of the gene is associated with aggression.

Serotonin A neurotransmitter that generally inhibits neural activity throughout the brain.

SRY gene Sex-determining region Y gene which triggers the appearance of testes in an embryo and the development of that individual into a biological male.

Survival of the fittest Natural selection selects the genes that give rise to characteristics promoting survival and reproduction, so they are retained in the population.

Testosterone A hormone produced mainly in testes (and in smaller amounts in ovaries).

A slice through the midline of the brain showing two of the key brain structures related to aggression.
Orbitofrontal cortex (OFC)
Amygdala

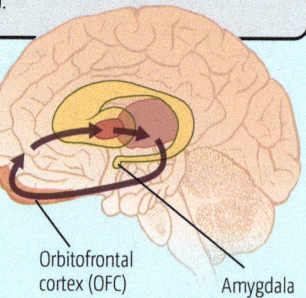

Biological explanations

Evolution and aggression

Individuals in our evolutionary history who were able to survive to adulthood were more likely to reproduce. They would pass on the genes that contributed to the behaviours that made survival possible. One of these behaviours may have been aggression.

For instance, aggressive individuals may have been more successful in competition for limited resources such as food and mates. Men would be more likely to pass on their genes if they were able to 'retain' partners, i.e. prevent them from reproducing with rivals. This was achieved through aggressive *mate retention strategies* such as using physical violence to prevent a partner from meeting other men.

Brain structures and aggression

The *limbic system* is a collection of several structures in the brain that regulate our emotional behaviour. The limbic structure most closely associated with aggression is the amygdala (see diagram below).

Amygdala The sensitivity of the amygdala is an important predictor of aggressive behaviour – the more sensitive the person's amygdala, the more aggressive they are. This is because the amygdala plays a key role in how we assess and respond to threats in the environment. For example, aggressive people tend to have amygdalas that react quickly and strongly to threatening stimuli (Gospic *et al.* 2011).

Biochemistry and aggression

Testosterone The male sex hormone responsible for the development of masculine features. It is linked to aggression mainly because men are generally more aggressive than women and also have much higher *testosterone* levels. For instance, men become more aggressive towards each other at a time in development (after age 20 years) when testosterone levels are highest (Daly and Wilson 1988).

Serotonin A neurotransmitter that affects aggression mainly through its influence on an area of the brain called the orbitofrontal cortex (OFC, see diagram below). Low levels of *serotonin* in the OFC disrupt the activity of neurons, producing emotional instability and reduced behavioural self-control. This leads to an increase in impulsive behaviours, including aggression (Denson *et al.* 2012).

Dopamine A neurotransmitter that influences aggression when people are in competition over resources. This is because *dopamine* is the brain's own 'reward chemical'.

For example, imagine there are two drivers but only one parking space (or two interviewees for one job, etc.). Both people are in conflict with each other and have high dopamine levels because they anticipate winning the competition. This motivates the use of aggression to gain victory. The potential rewards (a parking space and a dopamine boost) encourage risk-taking and impulsive behaviours, including aggression.

Cortisol A stress hormone which also plays a role in aggression in conjunction with testosterone. As we have seen, high levels of testosterone lead to aggressive behaviour. But this is only true when *cortisol* levels are low. When cortisol is high, testosterone's influence on aggression is blocked (Carré and Mehta 2011).

Genetics and aggression

MAOA gene The *MAOA* gene controls the activity of an enzyme called monoamine oxidase A. This enzyme 'mops up' neurotransmitters (e.g. serotonin) in the brain after a nerve impulse has been transmitted across a synapse (see page 48).

The gene comes in two variants, low-activity and high-activity. People who inherit the low-activity variant (*MAO-L*) have low activity of the enzyme, so their neurotransmitter functions are disrupted. They have often been found to be highly aggressive (this was the variant found in the Dutch men studied by Brunner, top left).

SRY gene The *SRY* gene has an indirect influence on aggression through masculinisation of the embryo (see page 42). The *SRY* gene activates testes development that triggers testosterone production in the womb (and at puberty). As we saw above, testosterone may partly explain the common finding that men tend to be more aggressive than women.

Evaluation

Practical applications

One strength is real-world benefits from understanding biological factors in aggression.

Each of the biological factors on this spread offers a target for interventions. For instance, a better understanding of the roles of hormones and neurotransmitters could lead to the development of drugs to control and even reduce aggression. Intervention does not have to be biological. We recognise that genes contribute to aggression, but this influence can be partly counteracted by providing social and psychological support to 'at risk' families.

Therefore, the biological approach provides several potential ways of reducing the costs of aggressive behaviour to individuals and societies.

Research support

Another strength is that research studies support the biological factors on this spread.

Brain scans show high levels of amygdala activity when individuals view images of angry faces (Coccaro et al. 2007). Serotonin-related chemicals are found in lower amounts in violent impulsive offenders compared with non-violent offenders (Virkkunen et al. 1994). Men who use mate retention strategies in heterosexual relationships are more likely to be physically violent towards their partners (Shackelford et al. 2005).

Therefore, there is a lot of research to suggest that biological factors play a key role in aggressive behaviour.

Complex picture

One weakness is that there are many causes of aggression.

Firstly, the biological factors on this spread do not operate in isolation but interact with each other, e.g. brain structures and neurotransmitters. Secondly, there are several other biological factors involved in aggression that are not covered here, such as another neurotransmitter called GABA and other brain structures apart from the limbic system. Finally, these biological factors contribute to aggressive behaviour, but they interact with non-biological factors (e.g. social and psychological) which are equally important.

This shows that the causes of aggression are extremely complex and greater than just any single biological factor.

Sexual jealousy in men can be a powerful cause of aggressive behaviour. What is the evolutionary function of jealousy?

GET ACTIVE A probation officer reflects

Erwin is a probation officer working with high-risk offenders who have been in prison for violent crimes. He has worked in this field for over 20 years and has a lot of experience of criminals and their families.

Erwin has noticed that a high proportion of the people he works with have a medical history that includes brain injury. Others come from families where violent behaviour goes back several generations. Many of the people on his current caseload are addicted to drugs. He has also dealt with many cases of men assaulting their partners.

Erwin wonders if there could be a biological basis to a lot of aggressive behaviour.

Write a brief outline of the biological causes of aggression that would address Erwin's question and that he could share with his probation officer colleagues.

Exam-style questions

Fred grew up in a large extended family. Their dad, uncle and oldest brother all went to prison for assault. Others in the family become aggressive very quickly if they think they are being provoked. Fred is the youngest of the children and the most aggressive. This is because they had to fight for their parents' attention and even to get a fair share of food at mealtimes. So they often physically attacked their brothers and sisters.

1. Explain how Fred's aggressive behaviour can be understood using the concepts of:
   (a) Survival of the fittest. (2 marks)
   (b) Biochemistry. (2 marks)
2. Identify and explain **one** other way in which the biological approach could be used to understand Fred's aggressive behaviour. (3 marks)
3. Evaluate the view that Fred's behaviour is due to biological factors. (3 marks)
4. In the context of aggression, explain what is meant by the term 'limbic system'. (2 marks)
5. Assess biological explanations for Fred's behaviour. Your answer should consider **two** of the following:
   - evolution
   - brain structures
   - biochemistry
   - genetics. (9 marks)

Link it

Link aggression to the assumptions and key concepts of the biological approach.

One assumption is that behaviour is influenced by the CNS, genes and neurochemistry. The amygdala is a structure in the brain, which is part of the CNS. Some people have sensitive amygdalas (may be genetic) which react strongly to threatening stimuli. These people may behave aggressively as a result.

What are the links between aggression, survival of the fittest and the assumption that behaviour is a product of evolution?

Specification content

B1 Use of psychology to explain contemporary issues of aggression in society

Learners should understand and apply knowledge of how psychological concepts can be used to explain aggression in society:

- Biological, including evolution (survival of the fittest), brain structures (limbic system), biochemistry (testosterone, serotonin, dopamine and cortisol), genetics (*MAOA* gene and *SRY* gene).

Content area B2: Use of psychology in business to explain and influence consumer behaviour
Cognitive approach to consumer behaviour

Battle of the laptops

You wander into a big shop vaguely thinking about buying a laptop. They all look mostly identical.

A helpful assistant approaches and, after establishing that you're interested in laptops, asks you a question: 'What do you need from the laptop's memory?' You give the obvious answer: 'I need lots of it.' The assistant thanks you and walks off. That's weird, they didn't try to sell you anything!

Unknown to you, other people are being asked the same question, and others are being asked a different question: 'What do you need from the laptop's processor?' (common answer: 'I need a fast one').

So, what kind of laptop do you eventually buy from the vast range available? Probably the one with lots of memory, and so would most of the people who were asked the same question as you. The people who were asked the processor question would most likely buy laptops with fast processors.

The explanation for this is *cognitive priming* (reported by Jain 2018).

Specification terms

Authority bias A tendency to uncritically accept the views of others we perceive as 'experts'.

Brand loyalty Sticking to a particular company's products over time (e.g. repeated purchases) even when there are better alternatives.

Direct attribute priming In advertising, highlighting the desirable features of a product (e.g. speed), so the consumer recalls the product when they think about the features.

Indirect attribute priming Associating a product with a broader context (e.g. 'natural'), so the consumer recalls the product when they think of the context.

Nice man, but is he really a dentist? He might just be an actor. Why are we always so willing to believe?

Schema and consumer behaviour

We looked at *schema* on page 16. Schema help us to make sense of the world by making it more predictable. But predictability is the enemy of advertising. Schema allow us to say, 'If you've seen one burger advert, you've seen them all', so we are less likely to recall the specific brand being advertised.

Therefore, adverts are more likely to challenge our schema rather than confirm them. This is *schema incongruity*, a deliberate conflict between our schema and an advert's content. For example, by advertising an everyday product in a 'wacky' way, it becomes more memorable.

Cognitive priming and consumer behaviour

We looked at *cognitive priming* on page 18. Priming is highly relevant to advertising – a key purpose of an advert is to prime a product or brand. There are two ways priming is used in advertising.

Direct attribute priming

You can prime the features ('attributes') of a product or brand itself (i.e. directly). This is *direct attribute priming*. So an advert for a phone will highlight the phone's positive features – its size, speed, price, etc. The consumer associates these attributes with the product. Later, when considering the desirable features of a phone, the consumer thinks of the advertised brand.

Indirect attribute priming

A powerful alternative approach is to prime attributes linked with the product or brand, i.e. prime the *context* of a product rather than the product itself (Yi 1990). This is *indirect attribute priming*. Like any prime, context activates schema in the minds of consumers. This makes a product more accessible in memory.

For example, supermarkets invent brands that people associate with desirable attributes. For many people, the name 'Willow Farm' is linked with positive images of farming, the countryside, health, etc. (and the products even have these images on them). The 'Willow Farm' of the brand does not exist. But the consumer associates these indirect attributes with the brand name. Later on, when thinking about the countryside or healthy eating, the consumer is primed to recall 'Willow Farm'.

Cognitive biases and consumer behaviour

Confirmation bias

We looked at *confirmation bias* on page 22. When we buy a product (especially an expensive one), we may look for evidence to confirm we made the right choice. For example, we are overly-impressed by small features of our product and ignore the benefits of alternative brands.

Confirmation bias is self-fulfilling ('I bought this product because it's the best; it must be the best because I bought it'), which helps explain *brand loyalty*.

Brand loyalty

Brand loyalty is important in a market where actual differences between products are quite small and customers upgrade every couple of years. For example, a common perception is that some people buy Apple products purely because they are Apple products. Apple 'fans' recall good things about Apple products, but only bad things about competitor's products (or they ignore them).

Companies exploit the cognitive biases associated with brand loyalty, for example by noting the features their customers like and highlighting these in their advertising.

Authority bias

Consumers tend to assign more credibility to the opinion of an authority figure, who is likely to be an 'expert'. For example, adverts for toothpaste often use 'dentists' to explain the benefits of the product. Consumers are more persuaded by the authority even when they suspect the dentist is actually an actor.

Get Active: A Mars a day...

...helps you work, rest and play. That sentence is part of my schema for Mars bars.

We have schema for countless aspects of the world around us. This includes products that are advertised to us as consumers. To get an idea of how product schema work, think about a product you are familiar with, such as a Mars bar.

1. Make a list of the words you associate with a Mars bar. This list represents your product schema for Mars bars.
2. Compare your schema to those of others. How similar are they? If they are similar, why are they so similar?
3. Outline an advert for Mars bars based on your schema.

Evaluation

Research support

One strength is evidence that cognitive factors affect consumer behaviour.

Adrian North (2012) asked four groups of people to taste and describe wine while background music was being played. Each group heard a piece of music that had different characteristics: one heard a 'powerful and heavy' piece, another heard something that was 'subtle and refined', a third group's music was 'zingy and refreshing' and the fourth's was 'mellow and soft'. The descriptions given by the participants tended to match the characteristics of the music, even though they all tasted the same wine.

This supports priming as a key influence on memory.

Problems of replication

One weakness is that the findings of research are often contradictory.

Some studies support the view that priming and biases affect consumer behaviour, but many other studies do not. This apparent contradiction illustrates the problem of *replication*. For a study to be considered scientific, psychologists must be able to replicate it. That is, they should be able to repeat the study and get the same outcome. But in this area of research, one study often has a surprising outcome that cannot be replicated by other researchers.

This undermines the claims about the value of priming and biases in consumer behaviour.

Ethical issues

Another weakness is that there are ethical issues involved in advertising techniques based on the cognitive approach.

For instance, by definition priming takes place without the individual's awareness. Advertising is obviously intended to influence people. But some adverts may be designed to influence consumers' buying choices and brand loyalties in ways they are not aware of. This could be interpreted as a form of deception, which is unethical.

This means that psychologists should think very carefully about their professional involvement with techniques deliberately designed to manipulate consumers' perceptions of a product.

Exam-style questions

A manufacturer produces a new model of TV. An advertising company wants to run the marketing campaign for the product. The head of the company says they will use direct and indirect attribute priming to market the TV.

1. Explain **one** way the company could use direct attribute priming and **one** way they could use indirect attribute priming to market the TV. (4 marks)
2. Dolly sees an advert for the new TV and immediately buys one from an online retailer. State what is meant by 'schema' in relation to consumer behaviour. (1 mark)
3. Explain how schema could account for why Dolly bought the TV. (2 marks)
4. Yuan uses an online retailer to buy electronic devices. He buys the same company's products every time. Yuan filters out alternative brands so he doesn't have to bother with them. His partner prefers a different brand but Yuan can list all the great features of his products. Yuan likes to read about products he has bought on the company's website.

   Identify **one** cognitive bias and explain how it might influence Yuan's behaviour as a consumer. (3 marks)
5. Identify **one** other cognitive bias that may influence Yuan. (1 mark)
6. Discuss the means used by the cognitive approach to influence consumer behaviour. In your answer you should consider:
   - schema and cognitive priming
   - cognitive biases. (9 marks)

Link it

Link consumer behaviour to the assumptions and key concepts of the cognitive approach.

One assumption is that behaviour is a product of information processing. When we buy products we usually think about (process) our reasons. But processing can be biased, e.g. we justify a purchase (perhaps it was expensive) by processing the good things about the product but ignoring the bad things.

What are the links between consumer behaviour, cognitive priming and the assumption that the brain can be compared to a computer (computer analogy)?

Specification content

B2 Use of psychology in business to explain and influence consumer behaviour.

Learners should be able to demonstrate knowledge of the means used to influence behaviour:
- Schema and cognitive priming, direct and indirect attribute priming.
- Cognitive biases in information processing – authority bias, confirmation bias and brand loyalty.

Content area B2: Use of psychology in business to explain and influence consumer behaviour
Social approach to consumer behaviour

Make it stop, please!

'Baby Shark doo doo da-doo da-doo, Baby Shark doo doo da-doo da-doo, Baby Shark...' repeat until the end of time.

Quite possibly the catchiest song in history, *Baby Shark* has been around for a century and has cropped up occasionally on social media since the mid-2000s. But in 2018 it suddenly became massively popular with over three billion views on YouTube. Why?

Its success is a good illustration of how the concepts on this spread work to influence our behaviour as consumers. It appears to have 'gone viral' after a Twitter hashtag #BabySharkChallenge was created which instantly made the song something that had to be heard by everyone, even though it was originally aimed at toddlers. From there it spawned other hashtags, other videos and spread, until it took over the world...

Specification terms

Bandwagon effect Behaviour change or purchasing decisions can result from the perception that 'everyone else is doing it' (join the bandwagon).

Social proof In situations where we are not sure what to do or believe, we may look to other people for guidance because we think the others are better informed.

A bandwagon – a wagon with a band playing on top. P.T. Barnum (*The Greatest Showman*) invited people to jump on and join in!

Role of others

In Content area A2 we looked at social explanations such as *conformity*, which we will use here to explain certain aspects of *consumer behaviour*.

Conformity to social norms

Social norms are beliefs, expectations and unwritten rules about what any social group considers to be 'proper' behaviour. Most people have a strong desire to conform to these social norms and this is often exploited by advertising.

Behaviours that are publicly visible are ways we signal our group memberships, e.g. the clothes we wear, the music we listen to, the phone we use. Therefore, campaigns and adverts try to influence us by promoting the message that 'if you buy this product, you are like these other people'.

Conformity to social norms is partly explained by *normative social influence* (NSI, first explained on page 24).

Normative social influence and consumer behaviour

Acceptance by other people is a powerful reason for conforming to the norms of a group (Deutsch and Gerard 1955). It appeals to our natural desire to be liked and to avoid being rejected. It leads to *compliance*, i.e. changing our behaviour publicly even if privately we still hold a different view.

Someone subjected to NSI may buy products (or specific brands) in order to 'fit in' with their friends because not doing so might risk ridicule or rejection. We may be willing to change our behaviour (e.g. switch brands, give up smoking, recycle, etc.) if a group's social norms dictate that as the (unspoken) 'price' of membership.

The bandwagon effect

This is a social phenomenon similar to NSI. Most people tend to do something because other people are doing it (a 'herd mentality'). The bandwagon was historically a vehicle used in political rallies in 19th century America. It would carry musicians and dancers and people would jump on it to have fun.

Bandwagon advertising operates on the basis that 'success breeds success'. Once a product or brand is adopted by a 'critical mass' of people, many more join in. This is why companies use 'social media influencers' such as Kylie Jenner to promote their products. The hope is that once a trend is adopted by influencers and their followers, it will 'go viral' and potentially be taken up by millions.

Adverts try to create the illusion that a product (or behaviour) is already popular, perhaps by showing lots of people using it or talking about it. It manipulates consumer behaviour by stimulating demand for a product that was not previously there. For example, the cosmetics company Rimmel uses the slogan 'Live the London Look', implying that huge numbers of people in London are using their products.

Social proof

Social proof is another term for *informational social influence* (ISI, see page 24). We often go along with other people because we believe that they know more than us about the current situation. The more people there are who agree on a course of action or a belief, the more influenced we are.

According to Robert Cialdini (1984), in a situation in which we don't know what to think or do, we look to others for social proof of what is happening and how we should behave. For example, in the context of health, a campaign to change behaviour might imply that lots of people like us are doing something ('72% of people lost weight after following this tip'). This is social proof of what people are doing.

Social proof also explains why rating systems on websites such as Amazon are influential, and why most people are more likely to read Facebook posts with lots of likes than those with very few.

Evaluation

Practical applications

One strength is that conformity to social norms can be used to influence consumer behaviour.

For example, significantly more people use the stairs instead of the lift when they read a notice such as, 'Did you know? More than 90% of the time, people in this building use the stairs instead of the elevator. Why not you?' (Burger and Shelton 2011). This works because most people who read the notice take it as social proof that the norm is to use the stairs.

This demonstrates how social norms and social proof can help change health-related behaviours.

Research support

Another strength is research support for the bandwagon effect.

In one study, teenage students saw an advert for a luxury product (a Ralph Lauren T-shirt) which was associated in the experiment with a famous person (e.g. Beyonce). Compared with a control group of students who saw the advert without the famous person, the experimental group were willing to display a significantly bigger Ralph Lauren logo on their T-shirt (Niesiobędzka 2018).

This shows that the bandwagon effect can explain the sudden popularity of even expensive products in terms of conformity to social norms.

Cultural differences in social proof

One weakness is that the effectiveness of social proof differs between cultures.

Robert Cialdini *et al.* (1999) compared social proof in an *individualist* culture (USA) and a *collectivist* culture (Poland). Participants in both cultures were more willing to agree with a request when told all their peers had agreed than when told none of them had agreed. But the level of agreement was much greater in Poland, suggesting that social proof is more effective in a collectivist culture. This confirms previous findings showing that conformity is more common in collectivist cultures.

This means that campaigners and advertisers who wish to use social proof should take cultural factors into account.

Bandwagon marketing may have potentially dangerous consequences. The same bandwagon techniques that promote the benefits of vaccination can be used for the opposite purpose by so-called anti-vaxxers (see page 115).

Exam-style questions

Ranjana was staying in a hotel for three nights. When she used the bathroom, she noticed a sign saying, 'Please help us save water and protect the environment by reusing your towels. Most guests at the hotel reuse their towels at least once during their stay'. Ranjana watched a video on the hotel company's website showing a famous environmental campaigner reusing a towel. So Ranjana used the same towels through her whole stay.

1. Explain how Ranjana's behaviour might have been influenced by:
   (a) Social proof. (2 marks)
   (b) The bandwagon effect. (2 marks)
2. Explain what is meant by 'conformity to social norms'. (2 marks)
3. Ewan wants to buy a phone. He has seen a positive review of the new iPhone by his favourite social media personality. Lots of the personality's followers have posted photos and reviews of this iPhone on their own accounts. Ewan's friend has one of the new iPhones and she says it's the best phone she's ever had. Ewan was going to get a different phone but he decides to buy the new iPhone instead.

   From this scenario, identify:
   (a) **One** example of the bandwagon effect. (1 mark)
   (b) **One** example of social proof. (1 mark)
4. Discuss how the social approach explains Ewan's behaviour. In your answer you should consider conformity to social norms. (9 marks)

GET ACTIVE Getting students to drink less

The level of drinking on some student university campuses is a cause for concern. Psychologists have tried to use the techniques explained on this spread to reduce alcohol use (i.e. influence behaviour). Some programmes have been more successful than others.

One issue is that most students have completely the wrong idea about how much other students drink. They think others drink a lot more than they really do. Ironically, this means that individual students drink more because they think they need to 'keep pace' with everyone else.

1. *With reference to the concepts on this spread, what strategies could you use to reduce student drinking?*
2. *Are there any potential unintended consequences of trying to change drinking behaviour?*

Link it

Link consumer behaviour to the assumptions and key concepts of the social approach.

One assumption is that behaviour occurs in a social context (influenced by people around us). We are members of social groups that share norms including which products are 'acceptable', e.g. certain clothes. Through normative social influence, members adopt these products in order to fit in with the group and avoid rejection.

What are the links between consumer behaviour, social proof and the assumption that wider culture and society influence people's behaviour?

Specification content

B2 Use of psychology in business to explain and influence consumer behaviour

Learners should be able to demonstrate knowledge of the means used to influence behaviour:

- Social – the role of others, including conformity to social norms ('Bandwagon Effect', social proof).

Content area B2: Use of psychology in business to explain and influence consumer behaviour

Behaviourist and social learning approaches to consumer behaviour

What is Christmas to you?

Is it warmth, comfort, excitement, a welcome break from routine, nostalgia about childhood Christmases?

Or is it annoying relatives, useless presents, the same old same old, too many people forced to have a good time?

For many people (perhaps most?) it's the former – a time associated with good feelings, happiness and enjoyment. Also for many, Christmas is now a time for adverts by big companies such as John Lewis, M&S, McDonalds, Coca-Cola, and not forgetting Lidl.

Why do these companies spend so much money advertising their already well-known brands at this time of year?

The answer is on this spread. They want you to associate their products with the good feelings you have about Christmas. Does it work? Think about a Christmas advert you've seen – how does it make you feel?

Specification terms
See pages 34, 36 and 38.

Before conditioning
The consumer experiences pleasure when they see smiling people (but not when they see the product).

Product (NS) → No response

Smiling people (UCS) → Pleasure (UCR)

During conditioning
The product is presented at the same time as the smiling people, so the consumer experiences pleasure.

Smiling people (UCS) + Product (NS) → Pleasure (UCR)

After conditioning
The consumer now experiences pleasure when they see the product (without the smiling people).

Product (CS) → Pleasure (CR)

Use of reinforcement and association in marketing

Classical conditioning

As we saw on page 34, *classical conditioning* is learning through association.

Emotional associations Classical conditioning is used to associate the focus of an advert (product, brand, etc.) with other stimuli that produce positive feelings (e.g. happiness, warmth). For example, an advert for a burger might show attractive people (or celebrities, see below) enjoying themselves as they visit the burger restaurant.

Advertisers hope this will affect the consumer's behaviour (e.g. buy a product, switch brands, etc.). But even if this doesn't happen, other desirable outcomes are possible, e.g. a more positive attitude towards the product, or greater awareness of it in the marketplace.

Repetition Over time, a *conditioned response* (CR) to a product weakens until it disappears. This process is called extinction. However, extinction can be avoided through repeated pairing of the *unconditioned stimulus* (UCS) and the *conditioned stimulus* (CS). So a product is continually advertised in longer-term campaigns, to restrengthen the association and produce the desired CR.

Operant conditioning

Positive reinforcement Any behaviour that results in a pleasurable consequence is likely to be repeated. For example, you buy a product from a certain brand and have a good experience of it, e.g. the product is good value for money, easy to use, does what you want, etc. You find this rewarding and this makes it more likely you will buy this brand's products again (and less likely if you have a bad experience).

BOGOF and loyalty points Companies use schemes to provide *reinforcement* of buying behaviour. BOGOF (buy one, get one free) is reinforcing because you feel you are getting a bargain. Loyalty schemes offer points for each purchase in a certain store (or of a certain brand). You collect points and exchange them for something tangible, e.g. cinema tickets, free meals, etc. This reinforces your loyalty to the store or brand and means you are more likely to buy again.

Social learning

Modelling and imitation *Modelling* occurs when someone observes the behaviour of another person (the model) and *imitates* it (see page 38). Adverts often show people using products, e.g. vacuum cleaner, car, phone, etc. However, just observing someone else using or buying a product is not usually enough for us to imitate that behaviour. Another *social learning* process is needed.

Vicarious reinforcement We are more likely to imitate a model when we observe them enjoying using the product. We experience *vicarious reinforcement* from the positive emotions of the model, imagining ourselves imitating their behaviour and enjoying the same feelings. This may be enough to motivate us to buy a product.

Use of celebrities in advertising Celebrities are used in advertising because they are potentially powerful models. An observer is more likely to imitate a celebrity if the observer identifies with the celebrity. Identification can happen in two main ways:

- The celebrity may possess something the consumer admires – status, wealth, fame, physical attractiveness, etc. The observer wants to be like the celebrity, so may buy products the celebrity appears to use themselves.

- Identification can also occur when the consumer believes the model is similar to themselves (e.g. gender, age, personality), or they simply like them. This is why some adverts use 'down-to-earth' or friendly celebrities, or place celebrities in everyday situations to 'humanise' them.

Evaluation

Research support

One strength is evidence to support conditioning and social learning.

In one study, a fictitious brand of toothpaste was associated with positive images. Participants expressed more positive attitudes towards the brand, increasing with the number of presentations, which highlighted the role of repetition (Stuart et al. 1987). Also, a review of 46 studies showed that consumers' attitudes towards products were more positive when the products were endorsed by a celebrity than when they were not (Knoll and Matthes 2017).

This shows that conditioning and social learning can influence positive consumer attitudes towards a product.

Ignores key factors

One weakness is that conditioning does not explain the central role of cognitive factors.

When we associate an advertised product or brand with positive emotions, cognitive factors must be involved otherwise everyone would feel the same way. For instance, how positively you feel about a product advertised by Jamie Oliver depends on what you think about Jamie Oliver. We also make rational decisions when we buy products and services, which is why comparison websites exist. But the behaviourist approach ignores the role of such cognitive factors.

This suggests that conditioning is an incomplete explanation of how marketing works.

Real-world effects are unclear

Another weakness is that research into conditioning has been mostly *laboratory* based.

But in the real world of TV viewing and social media use, the influence of advertising is 'messier'. For instance, lab research investigates the short-term effects of advertising on a narrowly-defined behaviour (e.g. choice of snacks 20 minutes after watching an advert for a non-existent brand). Research into the long-term effects of conditioning suggests the effects are much weaker (Schachtman et al. 2011).

Therefore, the research tells us little about the effects of advertising in the real world where conditions are less controlled.

GET ACTIVE The power of Pepsi (not)

In 2017 Pepsi ran an advert in the US that backfired so spectacularly the campaign was ended early.

A major celebrity, Kendall Jenner, was shown walking along a street when she saw a protest and decided to join in. She removed her wig first, as if to imply 'This is the real me', approached a police officer and gave him a can of Pepsi. At this point the protesters realised there was no need to demonstrate for social justice anymore so they stopped. Thanks to Pepsi and the power of Jenner's celebrity, the world was a much happier place.

To make the situation worse, when the backlash took hold, Pepsi apologised... to Kendall Jenner.

1. Using your knowledge of behaviourist and social learning approaches, explain why this advert failed.
2. Explain how you would present the advert to make it effective.

Colourful, fresh and vegetarian. Delicious! What else do you associate with this image? Feeling hungry? Go and buy one!

Exam-style questions

Grace runs a small independent coffee shop. She has a printed menu that includes images of happy people enjoying coffee. She also likes to play music for the customers to relax to.

1. Describe, using classical conditioning, how Grace encourages customers to buy coffee. (3 marks)
2. Grace wants to increase sales and customers so she plans to use a loyalty scheme. Each time a customer buys a coffee, they get a point. After they collect six points, the customer gets a free coffee.

    Describe, using operant conditioning, how Grace's plan could increase sales of coffee. (3 marks)
3. Identify **one** other way Grace could increase sales using operant conditioning. (1 mark)
4. In the context of consumer behaviour, describe what is meant by the term 'social learning'. (2 marks)
5. Grace also plans to create an online advert using a well-known local social media influencer.

    Describe, using social learning, how the influencer might help to sell more coffees. (3 marks)
6. Some time later, Grace is pleased to discover that sales of coffee have almost doubled.

    Discuss how the behaviourist and social learning approaches can help psychologists explain why Grace's sales have increased. In your answer you should consider:
    - conditioning
    - social learning. (9 marks)

Link it

Link consumer behaviour to the assumptions and key concepts of the behaviourist and social learning approaches.

One assumption is that behaviour is a learned response to environmental stimuli. We learn to associate stimuli with a product through classical conditioning. We may buy a product because we associate it with stimuli (e.g. a celebrity) that produce positive emotions within us (e.g. happiness).

What are the links between consumer behaviour, social learning and the assumption that behaviour can be learned from observation and imitation?

Specification content

B2 Use of psychology in business to explain and influence consumer behaviour

Learners should be able to demonstrate knowledge of the means used to influence behaviour.

Use of reinforcement and association in marketing:
- Classical conditioning – emotional association with products, repetition to avoid extinction.
- Operant conditioning – positive reinforcement (buy one get one free, loyalty points).
- Social learning – the use of celebrity/influencers in advertising.

Content area B2: Use of psychology in business to explain and influence consumer behaviour
Biological approach to consumer behaviour

It's a virtual world

Imagine putting on a virtual reality headset and seeing, not a racing car circuit or a battle landscape, but the aisles of a supermarket. Retailers sometimes ask volunteers to do this as part of their neuromarketing, in what is called 'in-store simulation'.

The VR environment allows retailers to see where the virtual shoppers are looking. Which products get most of their attention? Is it something to do with location? It's well-known for instance that the products that become more popular are those placed at eye level because most people ignore the lower shelves. VR is highly interactive, so virtual shoppers can pick products up and put them in a virtual trolley.

VR can also be used in a similar way to assess the impact of adverts and packaging – what do viewers look at most? VR allows researchers to create a 'heat map' showing the most and least viewed areas of a shelf, label or advert (see facing page).

Specification terms

Eye tracking A method of measuring eye movements to study what captures people's attention.

Facial coding A method of measuring facial expressions to study emotional responses.

fMRI A scanning technique used to investigate the brain and other parts of the body. Images are taken of the living brain and sometimes regions of the brain are matched to behaviour by asking participants to engage in particular activities while the scan is done.

Neuromarketing The application of the scientific study of the brain (neuroscience) to marketing (e.g. advertising).

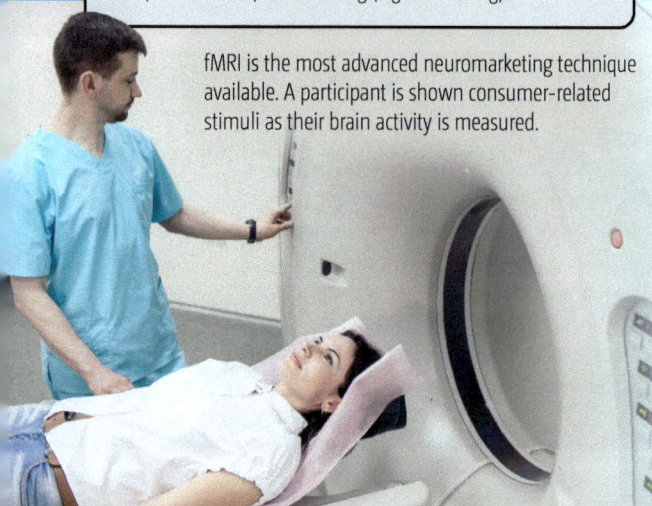

fMRI is the most advanced neuromarketing technique available. A participant is shown consumer-related stimuli as their brain activity is measured.

Neuromarketing

What is neuromarketing?

Neuroscience and marketing *Neuromarketing* applies the study of the brain (neuroscience) to marketing (selling products or services). Neuroscience is based on technologies that measure brain activity (e.g. the three methods below). Neuromarketing uses these technologies to study people's responses to aspects of marketing such as products, brands and adverts.

Brands and products Neuromarketeers look for insights into how consumers feel about brands, what gets their attention and the reasons they do or do not buy a product. The findings of neuroscience are incorporated into campaigns to 'tap into' the brain activity associated with a positive attitude towards a brand or product, for example.

Functional magnetic resonance imaging (fMRI)

Oxygen and blood flow fMRI is a form of brain scanning which measures the activity (function) of the brain when it is 'working'. fMRI detects changes in blood oxygenation and flow in specific parts of the brain. An active brain area requires more oxygen, so blood flow is directed to this area and this can be measured by a scanning machine.

How it works The participant lies in an fMRI scanner and sees an advert or other stimulus as their brain activity is measured continuously in 'real time'. The fMRI scan produces three-dimensional images showing which parts of the brain are active during a mental process (such as deciding whether to buy a product).

Uses In the language of neuromarketing, fMRI helps advertisers understand what features of an advert activate a brain area that 'pushes a consumer's buy button'. So they claim that fMRI can show, for example, whether a person is bored or excited by an advert, or whether they like a product or not. This helps to set pricing – the more people like a product, the higher the price that can be charged for it.

Facial coding

Emotions People's facial expressions are thought to offer a window into their feelings, an idea that goes back scientifically to Charles Darwin (1872).

Because the meanings of facial expressions are to some extent open to interpretation, Paul Ekman and Wallace Friesen (1978) developed a system of coding called FACS, the *facial action coding system*. This is a way of trying to provide some *objectivity* by categorising 'micro' facial expressions from the combined positions of 43 facial muscles.

Uses In neuromarketing, electrodes attached to people's faces detect slight muscle movements as they watch an advert. These movements are correlated with emotional expressions (e.g. smiling) and feelings (e.g. happiness, surprise) to indicate which aspects of an advert the consumer finds appealing.

Eye tracking

Brain activity Many areas of the brain (in the cortex and other regions) are involved in vision and coordinating eye movements. Therefore, eye movements reflect the activities of these brain areas and are associated with cognitive functions of interest to neuromarketeers, such as attention and memory.

Uses Researchers use technology to track a consumer's eye movements as they view a product or advert. This helps neuromarketeers to identify the features of an advert that attract the most attention (i.e. viewers spend the most time gazing at). This can be associated with brain activity to identify the most interesting, exciting or motivating aspects of the stimulus.

Eye tracking can also reveal what consumers find confusing about a product, advert or even packaging (we usually spend longer looking at things that confuse us).

Because the equipment is portable, eye tracking can be used in real-life situations such as restaurants, supermarkets or online. It can also be used in a virtual reality environment (e.g. a virtual supermarket).

GET ACTIVE Design your own

Many companies are known to use adverts based on neuroscientific research. The research has helped advertisers to understand what consumers 'like' even when they do not know themselves. The adverts that have been produced use sound, colour and fonts in creative ways. They 'direct' the viewer to the most important parts of the advert. They try to manipulate emotions (e.g. with a voice-over) so viewers feel more positively about the product.

Think about the neuromarketing techniques described on this spread. Explain how you could use them to design an advert for a mobile phone (you could include virtual reality).

Neuromarketeers can now use virtual reality to track consumers' eye movements in a 'virtual' shop. The red hotspots show where the most attention is focused. Retailers can use this information in designing the arrangement of products.

Evaluation

Practical applications

One strength is that neuromarketing techniques can be used instead of *self-report* methods (e.g. *questionnaires*).

This is because sometimes people are not consciously aware of their responses (or they cannot describe them). For instance in one study using fMRI, activity in a 'reward' area of the brain (the *ventral striatum*) was closely correlated with the popularity of songs three years later (measured by sales figures). But the participants' conscious responses (how much they said they liked the songs) did not correlate with sales figures at all (Berns and Moore 2012).

This suggests that the techniques of neuromarketing can sometimes reveal practically useful information about consumer behaviour.

Relatively ineffective

One weakness is that neuromarketing does not predict consumer behaviour very well.

Vinod Venkatraman *et al.* (2015) asked participants to watch genuine adverts. The researchers used fMRI, eye tracking and facial coding to measure participants' responses. They also used *focus groups*, a well-established non-neuromarketing method in which participants discuss their responses to the adverts. The best technique for predicting advertising success was the focus group. fMRI was the only neuromarketing technique that was at all effective.

This shows that neuromarketing techniques have some usefulness but methods that don't rely on technology (e.g. focus groups) may be better.

Ethics of neuromarketing

Another weakness is that neuromarketing techniques raise ethical concerns.

As an application, neuromarketing aims to predict consumer behaviour and possibly manipulate it. One ethical concern is that neuromarketing may use neuroscientific findings to manipulate responses that people are not aware of and over which they have no control. There is also concern about the unethical use of neuroscientific findings to make inflated claims in order to sell 'expertise' to companies and advertisers.

This unethical manipulation of consumers worries many researchers who believe neuromarketing should be regulated by law.

Exam-style questions

Kenan and Heather volunteered for a research study into advertising. Kenan had to wear goggles which monitored where he was looking. Heather had to lie down in a large scanning machine. Both of them were shown brief adverts.

1. Identify the neuromarketing technologies in this study and explain how they are both used with Kenan and Heather. (6 marks)
2. Identify **one** other neuromarketing technology and explain how the researchers could use it to measure consumer decision-making. (3 marks)
3. Raf has heard about a new eyeliner he plans to buy. He has seen an ad for it and all his friends are raving about it. The manufacturer wants to increase sales so hires a neuromarketing company to market and sell the eyeliner.
   State what is meant by the term 'neuromarketing'. (1 mark)
4. Give **three** techniques used in neuromarketing to measure consumer decision-making. (3 marks)
5. Analyse the company's use of neuromarketing in helping the manufacturer to sell the eyeliner. (9 marks)

Link it

Link consumer behaviour to the assumptions and key concepts of the biological approach.

One assumption is that behaviour is influenced by the central nervous system (CNS), genes and neurochemistry. The brain is part of the CNS. Consumer behaviour is influenced by brain activity, which can be measured with fMRI, e.g. to see which brain areas are active when viewing an advert.

What are the links between consumer behaviour, survival of the fittest and the assumption that behaviour is a product of evolution?

Specification content

B2 Use of psychology in business to explain and influence consumer behaviour

Learners should be able to demonstrate knowledge of the means used to influence behaviour.

Neuromarketing – use of technology to measure consumer decision-making, scanning techniques to detect brain changes in:

- fMRI – measures changes in blood flow that occur with brain activity; reveals level of engagement and emotional responses; used to set pricing and improving branding.
- Facial coding – process of measuring human emotions through facial expressions; reveals emotional responses.
- Eye tracking – measures eye movements, reveals what captures attention, speed of recognition, what grabs attention, what confuses consumers; used to improve adverts and packaging.

Content area B3: Application of psychology to explain gender
Cognitive approach to explaining gender

Livvy James

Livvy was born Samuel and raised as a boy. But for as long as she could remember, she felt strongly that she was really a girl. She preferred dresses to trousers, she liked playing with dolls and she viewed herself as a girl. Livvy's sense of her own gender was being a girl. But when she went to school she did so as a boy.

The conflict between her assigned and expressed gender was causing Livvy distress (which psychologists call *gender dysphoria*).

Gender is usefully seen on a spectrum along which people vary from one another and even throughout their lives ('gender fluid'). It is a spectrum rather than a binary construct in which you are either a boy/man or a girl/woman. Some non-binary people may identify as androgynous (having both masculine and feminine characteristics) rather than as exclusively a man or a woman.

Livvy now identifies and lives as a woman, and works to support transgender people.

Specification terms

Alpha bias The tendency to exaggerate differences between groups, e.g. between women and men, binary and non-binary people, etc.

Androgyny Displaying a balance of masculine and feminine characteristics in one's personality (andro = male, gyny = female).

Beta bias The tendency to minimise or ignore differences between groups, e.g. between women and men, binary and non-binary people, etc.

Binary Describes a choice of two states, for example something can be either on or off, or a person can only be a woman or a man.

Confirmation bias We pay more attention to (and recall more easily) information that supports our existing beliefs. We may seek it out and ignore contradictory information.

Femininity Traits and behaviours considered appropriate for girls/women in a particular culture, distinct from female biological sex.

Gender The psychological, social and cultural differences between boys/men and girls/women including attitudes, behaviours and social roles, as distinct from biological sex. (We use the terms 'man/woman' when discussing gender but 'male/female' for discussions of biological influences.)

Gender dysphoria Describes the discomfort or distress arising from a mismatch between a person's sex assigned at birth and their gender identity. This is also the clinical diagnosis for someone who doesn't feel comfortable with the sex they were assigned at birth.

Gender fluid Having different gender identities at different times, including single-gender and non-binary.

(continued on facing page)

The role of biases

The way we think about ourselves and others is affected by our unconscious *biases*, i.e. our predisposition to think in particular ways. Psychologists have identified two extreme biases that can both lead to inequality, prejudice and discrimination.

- **Alpha bias** is a very *binary* perspective which encourages women and men to identify more closely with one *gender*. It usually devalues women in relation to men (and *non-binary* people in relation to binary, etc.). Alpha bias also creates a sense of abnormality – people who do not conform to traditional gender categories are seen as 'disordered' and needing treatment.
- **Beta bias** misrepresents women's and men's behaviour because it suggests there are no differences even though research shows there are some real differences. This also applies to *transgender* women, who are not men but women, and this difference is denied by beta bias (the same is true of trans men of course). Like alpha bias, beta bias is potentially discriminatory and prejudicial because it fails to acknowledge the different needs of men and women (and of non-binary and *gender-fluid* people). Beta-bias prevents change. This is because it assumes that, as everyone is the same, so everyone should be able to fit into society as it exists (e.g. male-oriented).

Another bias relevant to gender is *confirmation bias* (see definition and discussion on page 22). If a person holds stereotyped views of men, women, *androgynous* and gender-fluid people that are negative then they only notice information that confirms these views. If we ignore contrary information that challenges our stereotypes, then it is much easier to accept the existing inequalities that penalise women and trans people.

The role of schema (gender schema theory)

We looked at the concept of schema on page 16. The *gender schema* contains our knowledge related to gender (e.g. how men and women are expected to behave). Carol Martin and Charles Halverson (1983) suggested that the gender schema has an important effect on memory – information consistent with gender schema is more likely to be stored and recalled than inconsistent information.

For instance, a girl who believes that engineering is 'for men' and nursing is 'for women' will seek out information about nursing, adding it to her gender schema. She will ignore information about engineering and recall more about nursing. Her recall of gender-inconsistent information may be distorted to fit her gender schema (e.g. incorrectly recalling a male nurse as a woman). This misremembering confirms her existing schema.

The role of cognitive priming

How sex-role stereotypes prime gender behaviour

The term *sex-role stereotypes* refers to the fixed views people have of men's and women's roles. Such stereotypes are often based on 'traditional' views of gender behaviour (e.g. women are caring and men are aggressive).

Stereotypes make you more ready to see the world in a way that fits your preconceived views, an example of cognitive priming.

The gender stereotypes that you believe in prime you to expect particular gender-related behaviours. For example, if you are asked to draw a picture of a nurse, you might be more likely to draw a woman than a man because your stereotype of a nurse is a woman. Even names on a job application form can prime a sex-role stereotype, e.g. that an applicant with a 'man's name' will be better at maths.

How gender roles prime gender behaviour

The roles that women and men are seen performing also prime gender-typical behaviour. This can include roles in both the real world and in the media. For example, if a girl sees women/girls portrayed in TV adverts as passive when interacting with adults, this may lead them to take on a similar role when interacting with adults themselves.

Evaluation

Practical applications

One strength is that there are practical uses of the cognitive approach.

For example, in our everyday interactions, we should be neither alpha- nor beta-biased as both are inaccurate ways of understanding gender, which is too complex to be fully explained by focusing on just similarities or differences. Instead, we should acknowledge both forms of bias and accept that there are some important similarities and differences between *gender identities* of all kinds.

Therefore, both forms of bias are equally misleading and we should avoid favouring one over the other.

Research support

Another strength is evidence to support the role of the cognitive approach in understanding gender.

Stephanie Fowler *et al.* (2011) primed gender-related schema in their participants by asking them to write about times when they behaved in stereotypically *masculine*, *feminine* or gender-neutral ways. They all then experienced the cold pressor test, in which the person plunges an arm into freezing water for as long as they can bear it. Men who were primed by writing about feminine-typical behaviours reported less pain and anxiety from the test than other groups.

This finding shows that priming *gender roles* can have some effect on even involuntary behaviours such as the experience of pain.

Neglects key non-cognitive factors

One weakness of the cognitive approach to gender is that it exaggerates the role of cognitive factors and underplays the importance of social context.

It is very likely that social factors are crucial in the early years during which gender develops. For instance, the gender-related behaviour of parents and the rewards and punishments they hand out to children are key influences that are perhaps more important than schema and much better explained by social learning theory (see page 38).

This failure to address how social and cognitive factors interact means the cognitive approach is an incomplete explanation.

A child's gender schema might mislead them into recalling the person in this image as a man.

Specification terms continued

Gender identity A person's sense of their own gender, e.g. man, woman or something else. This may or may not correspond to sex assigned at birth.

Gender priming A form of cognitive priming in which reminding someone of their gender identity triggers gender-related behaviours.

Gender roles Distinct behaviours and attitudes taken on by women and men and usually thought to be 'appropriate' to one gender or another.

Gender schema An organised set of beliefs and expectations related to gender that are derived from experience. Such schema guide a person's understanding of their own gender and gender-typical behaviour in general.

Masculinity Traits and behaviours considered appropriate for boys/men in a particular culture, distinct from male biological sex.

Non-binary A term that suggests gender (or any concept) cannot be divided into two distinct categories, e.g. gender is not a question of being a man or a woman.

Sex Biological differences between males and females including anatomy, hormones and chromosomes, assigned at birth and distinct from gender.

Sex-role stereotypes A set of beliefs and preconceived views about what is expected or appropriate for women and men in a given society or social group.

Transgender Relating to a person whose gender does not correspond with their birth sex.

Exam-style questions

Marvin works for a company that allows employees to take time off to attend to 'childcare issues'. Marvin is a father of two young children and he asks the head of human resources if he could arrive late to work the following day because he needs to take his children to nursery. The head of HR refuses the request and when Marvin asks why she says, 'It's company policy because the owner believes childcare is women's responsibility.'

1. (a) Identify **one** form of bias in this scenario. (1 mark)
   (b) Explain the effects of this bias on equality, discrimination and prejudice in the company. (3 marks)
2. Explain **one** difference between 'sex' and 'gender'. (2 marks)
3. The owner of the company also has two children, Leo and Maria. Some time after watching a TV programme about hospitals, Leo said, 'I liked it when that man did that operation.' Maria pulled a face and said, 'But that wasn't a man, it was a woman.'
   (a) Explain how the cognitive approach to gender might account for Leo's comment. Use the concept of gender schema in your answer. (3 marks)
   (b) Assess the cognitive approach as an explanation of Leo's comment. (3 marks)
4. Discuss the view that gender is mainly due to cognitive factors. In your answer you should consider **two** of the following: the role of biases, gender schema, cognitive priming. (9 marks)

Link it

Link gender to the assumptions and key concepts of the cognitive approach.

One assumption is that behaviour is a product of information processing. We process information about gender according to the sex-role stereotypes we hold in memory. We behave towards women and men in line with these stereotypes.

Specification content

B3 Application of psychology to explain gender

Learners should understand key terms associated with gender, including binary, non-binary, gender fluid, androgyny, transgender, masculinity, femininity, gender dysphoria.

Learners should understand and apply knowledge of how psychological approaches and concepts can be used to understand the typical and atypical gender of individuals in society, including the influence of the following on gender:

- Definition of the terms 'sex' and 'gender'.
- Cognitive – role of biases (alpha, beta and confirmation bias), influence on gender identity, effects on equality, discrimination and prejudice; schema in gender (gender schema theory).
- Cognitive priming – sex-role stereotypes, gender roles, gender priming.

Content area B3: Application of psychology to explain gender
Social approach to explaining gender

Do you still watch Friends?

Even though the last episode of the TV show *Friends* was filmed nearly 20 years ago, it is still incredibly popular amongst five- to 16-year-olds in Britain.

Two of the reasons children give for enjoying it are: 'It teaches me a lot about life' and 'Most people can relate to one of the characters'. It seems that some children perceive the main characters as role models.

Friends' popularity so long after it ended its run is astonishing but the show has been criticised for its rigid portrayal of gender. Most of the characters have gender-stereotyped jobs. Women without a date on Valentine's Day are to be pitied. Weddings mean everything to women but men are commitment-phobic. The supporting characters who do not conform to a conventional gender role are treated as figures of fun – the male nanny, Chandler's drag queen dad, men who carry bags, anyone who might be gay.

Is this one of the reasons why young children like the show, because it reflects the gender stereotypes they are familiar with?

Specification terms

Conformity to gender roles The extent to which a person identifies with a gender-typical (i.e. masculine or feminine) role.

Culture Ideas, customs and social behaviour of a particular group of people or society.

Peer influences Refers to the effect that other people of the same age (and/or those with shared interests) have on how we think and behave.

The hijras of India may constitute a third gender.

Peer influences on gender

Gender identity in childhood

Gender segregation By the age of three years most children can state whether they are a boy or a girl (identification may not be binary but this is an under-researched area). *Gender segregation* also begins at this age, so by the time children reach primary school they spend very little time with other-gender peers (Egan and Perry 2001).

Same-gender peers contribute to gender identity by acting as models for gender-typical behaviour.

NSI and ISI Peers exert *normative social influence* (NSI, see page 24) in the sense that they provide norms of gender-typical behaviour (e.g. 'We don't play with dolls, they're for girls'). This can also be understood as *informational social influence* (ISI) – peers are sources of information about gender-related behaviours (e.g. 'Boys don't cry').

Peers are also a source of sanctions for gender-atypical behaviour (e.g. 'You're a tomboy because you like football').

Gender identity in adolescence

An important element of gender identity in adolescence is *gender typicality*, the extent to which a person feels they are like other members of their gender category (i.e. typical). The individual reflects on their personal qualities and makes a judgement about how closely they fit a gender category.

To judge their typicality, the adolescent compares themselves with their peers ('I am like my friends X and Y, but not like Z, so I am not a typical boy'). In doing so, some adolescents become increasingly aware they are transgender, in that their expressed gender does not match their assigned (birth) sex.

Conformity to gender roles

Felt pressure for gender conformity

An adolescent feels social pressure to conform to the norms associated with a gender role (e.g. how a woman or man is 'meant' to behave), an example of NSI. Pressure comes mainly from parents, teachers and peers (see above), including pressure not to behave in gender-atypical ways (i.e. for boys not to be feminine and for girls not to be masculine).

Gender non-conformity

Felt pressure is a major cause of stress for adolescents who do not conform to gender-role norms. This is because they are trying to cope with a role that many still feel is socially unacceptable. Negative outcomes for non-conforming adolescents include teasing, bullying, and rejection by peers (Jewell and Brown 2014).

The stress associated with a non-conforming identity (not necessarily the identity itself) may explain the incidence of gender dysphoria and accompanying psychological ill-health (Nagoshi *et al.* 2014).

Influence of culture on gender

Culture and third genders

Cultures differ in the extent to which gender is considered binary. Several cultures use the term 'third gender' for people who do not fit the strict classification of woman or man.

For example, some five million people in India, Pakistan and Bangladesh live as transgender. Known as *hijras* in India (see picture, left), they are now recognised as having legal identities in Indian passports (indicated by the letter 'E').

The *fa'afafine* of Samoa are biological males who adopt the traditional gender role of women. They are known for their hard work in a domestic context and dedication to the family. Although fa'afafine may have sexual relations with non-fa'afafine men, they are not considered 'gay' as no such label exists in Samoa.

Evaluation

Research support
One strength is evidence supporting the social approach to gender.

According to Geert Hofstede (2001), women in industrialised cultures have increasingly active roles in the workplace and away from the domestic environment. This has led to a breakdown of traditional stereotypes in industrialised societies, so that the status of women and expectations of their gender role have changed. However, in traditional societies women still occupy the role of homemaker as a result of social, cultural and religious pressures.

This suggests that gender roles are strongly influenced by cultural context.

Gender non-conformity
One weakness is that the social approach does not explain gender non-conformity very well.

Most people, in most cultures, spend their lives with people who conform to gender norms and roles. Social influences such as NSI tend towards gender conformity. If these influences really are powerful, it is hard to explain how some individuals become non-conforming. Perhaps a cognitive element is required, and social influences depend on how we perceive them or think about them.

This suggests that other approaches may be better explanations of the nature of gender.

Peer influences are weak
Another weakness is that some social influences on gender are not very strong.

For example, peer influence may affect gender-related attitudes and beliefs but not actual gender identity. A study by Olga Kornienko et al. (2016) found that adolescent peers significantly influenced felt pressure for gender conformity, as expected. But the researchers were surprised to find that peers were not a significant influence on gender typicality. They concluded that some aspects of gender are influenced by peers but others are not.

Therefore, the social approach does not explain all aspects of gender, such as peer influence.

Boys and girls play together a lot in images like this one. In real life, not so much (see gender segregation, left).

Exam-style questions

Frans has been friends with Erik and Stan since they were boys at primary school. They always played football together and now play in the same Sunday league team. They go out drinking together although all they talk about is football.

1. Explain **two** ways in which Frans' peers may have influenced him to conform to a gender role. (4 marks)
2. In the context of gender, explain what is meant by 'influence of culture'. (2 marks)
3. Explain **one** way in which culture may influence atypical gender. (2 marks)
4. The social approach argues that peer influence has an important effect on gender.

   Give **one** example of the normative influence of peers and **one** example of the informational influence of peers from everyday life. (2 marks)
5. Viola is a nine-year-old girl who loves pink. She is happy but quiet and shy. She enjoys playing with her dolls and looking after her pet cat. Viola has **two** younger brothers. They spend a lot of time wrestling with each other and being loud. They both enjoy racing each other on their bikes.

   (a) Give **three** features of the social approach that can explain Viola's gender. (3 marks)

   (b) Discuss how the social approach helps us understand Viola's gender. In your answer you should consider **two** of the features you gave in your answer to question 5(a). (9 marks)

GET ACTIVE Tatiana

Whilst at primary school, Tatiana spent most of her time with other girls. She had two sisters but no brothers. When given the choice, she always preferred to play with other girls and with girls' toys. But by the time she was 13, Tatiana did not feel she was a 'real' girl and wanted to be a boy. But she felt a lot of pressure to behave like a girl. It made her so unhappy she saw a counsellor who suggested she might have gender dysphoria.

1. *How would you explain the difference between sex and gender in Tatiana's case?*
2. *Explain how gender segregation arose in Tatiana's childhood.*
3. *Using the social approach, explain how Tatiana may have become increasingly aware of her gender identity in adolescence.*
4. *What impact might culture have had on Tatiana's gender identity?*

Link it
Link gender to the assumptions and key concepts of the social approach.

One assumption is that wider culture and society influence people's behaviour. Gender is seen as binary in some cultures but not in others (e.g. the hijras of India). What is considered gender-typical or gender-atypical behaviour is strongly influenced by wider cultural norms.

What are the links between gender, peer influences and the assumption that behaviour occurs in a social context (influenced by people around us)?

Specification content
B3 Application of psychology to explain gender

Learners should understand and apply knowledge of how psychological approaches and concepts can be used to understand the typical and atypical gender of individuals in society.

The influence of the following on gender:

- Social – influence of culture, cultural bias towards gender and roles, peer influences (normative and informational), conformity to gender roles.

Content area B3: Application of psychology to explain gender

Behaviourist and social learning approaches to explaining gender

The 'Beauty Boys' of Instagram

Manny Gutierrez (Manny MUA) is one of several 'beauty boys' who are vloggers/influencers on Instagram and other social media sites. They offer tips about make-up to boys and men (as well as girls and women) and promote an image of masculinity which is, to say the least, at odds with the mainstream binary view.

The most prominent of the beauty boys are ambassadors for big cosmetics corporations such as Maybelline and CoverGirl.

We've been here before. In the 1970s, pop stars like David Bowie, Marc Bolan and Lou Reed presented a gender-fluid approach to the world, sparking outrage and adoration alike.

Specification terms

Operant conditioning A form of learning in which behaviour is shaped and maintained by its consequences – reinforcement (positive or negative) or punishment (positive or negative).

Social learning A form of learning in which behaviours are acquired through observation, modelling, imitation and vicarious reinforcement. Cognitive factors play a key role.

Children observe and imitate masculine and feminine gender behaviours from an early age.

Operant conditioning and gender

We described operant conditioning earlier on pages 36 and 68.

Rewards and punishments

When children behave in ways considered typical of their gender, parents (and teachers, peers, etc.) tend to reward them with praise, encouragement and approval. This reinforces (strengthens) the behaviour. On the other hand, gender-atypical behaviours may be punished (or at least ignored), which weakens those behaviours.

For example, boys are encouraged to play football or with toy cars, to be active and rough in their play and are discouraged from 'girl-type' activities. Girls are encouraged to play with dolls or engage in craft activities, to be passive, gentle and considerate. Tellingly, a girl who is active, who fights and gets into scrapes may well be labelled a 'tomboy' – she isn't seen as being a 'proper' girl.

Differential reinforcement

The kind of reinforcement often given to children is called *differential reinforcement* because boys are reinforced for masculine behaviours and girls are reinforced for different, feminine behaviours.

According to Patricia Kerig *et al.* (1993), the driving force behind differential reinforcement is usually the father. He is most likely to apply differential rewards and punishments for gender-typical behaviours.

Differential reinforcement of gender-typical behaviours is a key process in learning *gender identity*. It continues throughout life and is not confined to childhood (Block 1978).

Social learning and gender

We looked at social learning earlier on page 38.

Modelling

Parents encourage gender-typical behaviours in their children by *modelling* them. For example, a mother may *model* feminine-typical behaviour whenever she tends to her child's needs. Modelling also occurs from the child's perspective – a girl may *observe* her mother's behaviour and *imitate* it.

Vicarious reinforcement

Children also observe the consequences of a model's behaviour, experiencing them indirectly. If the consequence is rewarding, the child is likely to imitate the behaviour (e.g. if a girl observes her older sister being praised for looking after her doll). But if the consequence is punishment, then imitation is less likely (e.g. if a boy observes a classmate being bullied for being 'girly').

Identification

Modelling and vicarious reinforcement are more powerful when the observer identifies with a model. The observer perceives the model as 'like me' and/or 'someone I want to be'. This happens because the model has qualities the observer finds particularly rewarding (e.g. a gender-atypical model who is attractive or interesting).

Influence of the media

Modelling Gender-typical models are available to observers through traditional media (e.g. characters in TV soap operas, talent-show contestants). Online media increasingly provides gender-atypical models, such as influencers who are attractive and have high status.

Vicarious reinforcement The consequences of figures in the media behaving in gender-typical and gender-atypical ways are indirectly experienced by an observer. For example, a gender-atypical pop star being praised on TV may lead to an observer imitating the pop star's behaviour.

Identification An observer is more likely to imitate a gender-atypical model when they identify with them (i.e. they perceive the model as more 'like me' than gender-typical models). As illustrated by beauty vlogger Manny MUA, these high-status figures may provide a more gender fluid kind of role model for observers to identify with.

GET ACTIVE Call the Doctor

Dr Who has been running on and off on British TV since 1963. The programme has always tried to present interesting and exciting characters, especially the Doctor's 'companions' who accompany him on his adventures in space and time.

Over the years, companions have gradually been portrayed as non-binary and gender fluid. In the 1980s, a woman companion called Ace was viewed as quite androgynous for the time (the character was described as 'a fighter, not a screamer'). In 2017, Bill Potts, an openly bisexual woman, was introduced.

And then in 2018 the once-unthinkable finally happened – the Doctor regenerated as a woman!

Children and adolescents make up a sizeable proportion of the Dr Who audience. Explain how the following social learning processes can explain the influence on young people of gender portrayals in Dr Who: (i) modelling and imitation, (ii) vicarious reinforcement, (iii) identification.

Evaluation

Research support

One strength is support from 'Baby X' studies where the same baby is identified either as a 'boy' or a 'girl'.

Caroline Smith and Barbara Lloyd (1978) dressed the same babies half the time in 'girls' clothes' and half the time in 'boys' clothes'. Mothers who believed the babies were boys gave them a hammer-shaped rattle and encouraged them to be active. Dressed as girls, the same babies were given a cuddly doll and reinforced for being passive.

This is evidence of a 'gender curriculum' in the home – gender-typical behaviour is reinforced *differentially* for boys and girls from a young age.

Explains changing norms

Another strength is that the approach offers a convincing explanation of how gender can change over time.

The distinction between what is considered typical behaviour for men and women is much less clear-cut now than it once was. New forms of gender behaviour are increasingly reinforced, whereas in earlier decades they would have been punished or ignored. Portrayals in the media (e.g. advertising, dramas, online) of gender-atypical behaviour are much more common and widely accepted.

Therefore, social learning can explain the growth of fluid and *non-binary* gender identities.

Children are active not passive

A weakness is that children are more active in acquiring gender than the learning approach suggests.

There is more to learning gender than just passively observing models, imitating them and receiving reinforcement. Otherwise children's gender identities would be carbon copies of their parents'. In fact, many children grow up to be much more gender-atypical than their parents, which suggests they actively construct gender rather than passively 'receive' it (e.g. adolescents may deliberately seek out gender-typical models in the media).

This is hard for the learning approach to explain purely on the basis of reinforcement and modelling.

Exam-style questions

When Dora was a child, she often helped her mum with household chores. She enjoyed dancing and singing and looking after her dolls. She once got into a wrestling fight with her brother, and their dad said to Dora, 'Girls like you should know better'. When Dora got older, family and friends often commented on how feminine she was.

1. Describe **two** ways in which Dora's gender can be explained by the learning approach. (4 marks)
2. Dora's younger sibling Diego, 15, told schoolfriends that she identified as a girl. Diego started wearing eye make-up, having seen some online videos. Their parents told her off, but Diego said, 'You don't mind Dora wearing make-up.'
   Explain how the social learning approach accounts for Diego's gender. (3 marks)
3. In the context of gender, explain what is meant by 'operant conditioning'. (2 marks)
4. Briefly discuss the use of the behaviourist and/or social learning approaches to explain Diego's gender. (3 marks)
5. Assess how the behaviourist and social learning approaches can be used to explain Dora's and/or Diego's gender. In your answer you should consider:
   - operant conditioning
   - influence of the media. (9 marks)

Link it

Link gender to the assumptions and key concepts of the behaviourist and social learning approaches.

One assumption is that behaviour can be learned from observation and imitation. This can occur through the media. TV characters provide models of gender-typical behaviour, e.g. in adverts. Children can observe these behaviours and imitate them (this can also explain gender-atypical behaviour).

What are the links between gender, operant conditioning and the assumption that behaviour is a learned response to environmental stimuli?

Specification content

B3 Application of psychology to explain gender

Learners should understand and apply knowledge of how psychological approaches and concepts can be used to understand the typical and atypical gender of individuals in society, including the influence of the following on gender:

- Behaviourist and social learning including – the influence of the media, operant conditioning.

Content area B3: Application of psychology to explain gender
Biological approach to explaining gender

The triumph and tragedy of David Reimer

Bruce and Brian Reimer were twin boys born in Canada in 1965. Bruce was left without a penis when he was six months old after a circumcision operation went wrong.

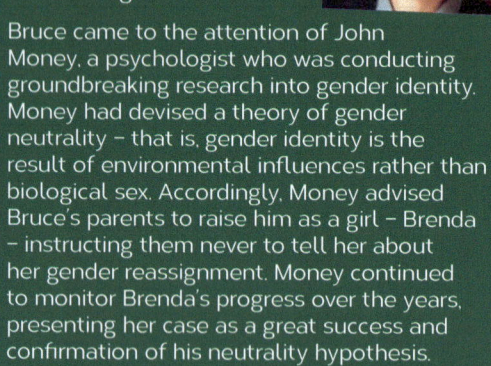

Bruce came to the attention of John Money, a psychologist who was conducting groundbreaking research into gender identity. Money had devised a theory of gender neutrality – that is, gender identity is the result of environmental influences rather than biological sex. Accordingly, Money advised Bruce's parents to raise him as a girl – Brenda – instructing them never to tell her about her gender reassignment. Money continued to monitor Brenda's progress over the years, presenting her case as a great success and confirmation of his neutrality hypothesis.

Brenda was given female hormones when she reached puberty, to counteract the effects of the testosterone surge boys experience at that time. But she never adjusted to life as a female and experienced severe psychological and emotional problems. It may be that her male hormones exerted a strong influence on her gender identity.

Once she learned the truth, Brenda retransitioned to life as a man, David. He swapped female hormones for male ones, married and adopted children, but continued to struggle with the psychological consequences of his upbringing.

Tragically, David Reimer committed suicide in 2004, two years after his twin brother Brian.

Specification terms

Chromosomes Found in the nucleus of living cells and carrying information in the form of genes. The 23rd pair of chromosomes determines biological sex.

Evolution The changes in inherited characteristics in a biological population over successive generations.

Oxytocin Hormone which causes contraction of the uterus during labour, stimulates lactation and contributes to emotional bonding in women and men.

Sex hormones Chemicals circulating in the bloodstream that affect the physical development, sexual development and behaviour of females (oestrogen) and males (testosterone).

The hormone oxytocin is thought to reduce stress and promote feelings of love and intimacy between couples.

Role of sex hormones in gender

Testosterone

Production of *testosterone* in the womb is triggered by the *SRY* gene, a process that initiates development of maleness in the embryo (see page 42). Testosterone levels before and after birth may be responsible for some differences in the brains of men and women (Knickmeyer and Baron-Cohen 2006), e.g. greater relative volume of the amygdala in men (involved in aggression, see page 70).

Congenital adrenal hyperplasia (CAH) Occurs when a genetically female foetus (XX chromosomes) is exposed to unusually high levels of testosterone. The outcome is ambiguous external genitalia resembling a penis and for this reason many are identified as male at birth.

Those who are raised as a girl often show play behaviour and toy preferences that are more typical of boys. Women with CAH mostly express satisfaction with their female-typical identity, but up to 5% say they want to live as a man (Hines 2006).

Oestrogen

Oestrogen determines female sexual characteristics at puberty (e.g. development of breasts, pubic hair and reproductive tissues).

It has a key role in regulating the menstrual cycle. Alongside the physical changes, oestrogen causes some women to experience heightened emotionality and irritability just before menstruation (premenstrual tension or PMT). However, some psychologists argue that PMT is better understood as a social or cultural phenomenon rather than caused by biological factors.

Oestrogen also plays a role in pubertal development in males, e.g. in the growth of bones.

Oxytocin

Women generally produce much more *oxytocin* than men, partly as a consequence of childbirth. Oxytocin is released in massive quantities during and after childbirth. It has an emotional bonding function, making new mothers feel 'in love' with their baby. The hormone also stimulates lactation, making it possible for women to breastfeed their children.

Because it reduces the stress hormone *cortisol*, oxytocin also promotes bonding between adults (oxytocin is the 'love hormone').

Evolutionary explanations for masculinity/femininity

Dominant male theory

Because ancestor males competed for females, the most dominant males mated most often. The genes that contributed to the qualities that made the male dominant survived into succeeding generations. These qualities are masculine-typical traits that were useful in competition with other males for short-term mating partnerships (e.g. risk-taking).

Division of labour

Ancestor men and women adopted different roles to ensure reproductive success. Men were hunters and required masculine-typical characteristics (e.g. aggression) to provide resources for female mates. But if a woman died while hunting, her offspring would be deprived of their food source (reducing her reproductive success). A better strategy was for the woman to gather (pick fruit) and develop feminine-typical characteristics and skills such as nurturing, caring and providing shelter.

Role of chromosomes in gender

As we saw on page 42, the 23rd pair of chromosomes determines a person's biological sex. But the role of chromosomes in gender is much less clear.

Turner's syndrome (TS) This is one example of how an atypical chromosomal pattern can affect gender. About 1 in 5000 biological females inherit just one X chromosome instead of two (see page 42). Adults with TS do not develop a menstrual cycle, ovaries or breasts at puberty. Most identify as women (Bondy 2007), with only a tiny minority experiencing *gender dysphoria*.

GET ACTIVE: Men and women are born different ... so what?

In 2017 James Damore, a software engineer at Google, wrote a memo which he sent to his colleagues. In it, he argued that men and women have different interests, preferences, abilities and identities that are biologically-determined and rooted in evolution. He wrote, 'On average, men and women biologically differ in many ways. These differences aren't just socially constructed because…they're universal across human cultures… they often have clear biological causes and links to prenatal testosterone…they're exactly what we would predict from an evolutionary psychology perspective.' (tinyurl.com/y4skbzma)

Write a memo in response to Damore's message. You can either support or challenge his arguments, but your memo must be firmly based on the evidence.

Obviously there are biological differences between males and females at birth – but how much do they influence our gender, and are they outweighed by social, psychological and cultural influences?

Evaluation

Research support

One strength is that the biological approach can explain masculine-typical gender identity in women.

Donald Baucom *et al.*'s (1985) biologically female participants completed questionnaires measuring masculinity/femininity. High levels of salivary testosterone were correlated with high masculinity and low femininity scores. A feminine identity was associated with low levels of testosterone. Participants with high testosterone saw themselves as independent, active and resourceful (usually considered masculine-typical characteristics).

These findings suggest that sex hormones may play a role in the development of gender.

Neglects social and cultural factors

One weakness is that gender differs across (or even within) *cultures*.

There are important cultural differences in what are considered to be gender-typical behaviours. For example, Amie Ashcraft and Faye Belgrave (2005) argue that African American girls identify closely with masculine-typical and *androgynous* gender roles and link this to the structure of African American families. This points towards *social context* and learning of gender, so is better explained by *social learning theory* (see previous spread).

Therefore, a more useful way of looking at gender is as a combination of biological and social/cultural factors, and research should aim to identify how these interact.

Third gender

Another weakness is that the biological approach tends towards the view that gender is binary.

However, this is contradicted by evidence of a third gender in some cultures. For example, the fa'afafine of Samoa are biologically male but choose to adopt a feminine-typical gender role. They dress as women, perform all domestic tasks and care for the family. A non-fa'afafine man can have sex with a fa'afafine without either of them being considered gay.

This degree of culturally-accepted *gender fluidity* is difficult for the biological approach to explain.

Exam-style questions

Sven describes himself as a 'proper man'. He is extremely competitive and enjoys beating his male friends in various sports and in 'banter'. His approach to work is aggressive and he sees dating as a competition. He believes that women find him very attractive.

1. Explain **two** ways in which sex hormones may influence Sven's behaviour. (4 marks)
2. Describe how the concept of evolution could explain Sven's masculinity. (3 marks)
3. Briefly analyse the biological approach to explaining Sven's gender. (3 marks)
4. Charu and Rhi both identify as women. They have lived together for four years, and plan to have a baby. They have decided that Rhi will give birth, although of course Charu will be fully involved all the way.
   Explain the role oxytocin may play in Rhi's and Charu's relationship. (3 marks)
5. In the context of gender, state what is meant by 'chromosomes'. (1 mark)
6. Kai, Moya and Bill are good friends at university. Kai is very competitive and sees himself as being the 'leader'. Moya is sensitive and considers herself a good listener. Bill identifies as gender fluid, sometimes forceful and independent, and sometimes gentle and shy.
   Discuss how the biological approach could help psychologists explain the genders of the three friends. In your answer you should consider:
   - the role of sex hormones
   - evolutionary explanations for masculinity/femininity. (9 marks)

Link it

Link gender to the assumptions and key concepts of the biological approach.

One assumption is that behaviour is a product of evolution. Masculinity and femininity have evolved over time. Behaviours that benefitted survival, reproduction and offspring differed between genders, e.g. feminine behaviours such as being caring, because this kept offspring out of danger.

What are the links between gender, sex hormones and the assumption that behaviour is influenced by the central nervous system (CNS), genes and neurochemistry?

Specification content

B3 Application of psychology to explain gender

Learners should understand and apply knowledge of how psychological approaches and concepts can be used to understand the typical and atypical gender of individuals in society, including the influence of the following on gender:

- Biological – role of sex hormones (before and after birth: testosterone, oestrogen and oxytocin), evolutionary explanations for masculinity/femininity, role of chromosomes.

Content area B
Revision summary

Use of psychology to explain contemporary issues of aggression in society

Types of aggression
Hostile aggression Hot-blooded, impulsive, physiological arousal.
Instrumental aggression Goal-driven, planned, cold-blooded, little arousal.
Violent aggression Using physical force to cause injury.
Verbal aggression Using words to cause psychological damage.

Cognitive approach
Cognitive priming for aggression Aggressive stimulus primes aggressive thoughts, later stimulus 'triggers' aggressive behaviour.
Aggressive stimulus – e.g. video, game, observing others, not a 'one-off'.
Below awareness – you don't realise the prime influences you, so you're primed in one situation and aggressive in another.
Hostile attribution bias (HAB) HAB means interpreting neutral behaviour as threatening (accident seen as deliberate).
Self-fulfilling because others respond with aggression, confirming the HAB.
Cognitive scripts and schema
Scripts for aggressive situations, developed through observation and experience.
Scripts stored in memory and prime us, triggered when we encounter aggressive cues (aggressive people have wider range of scripts).

Evaluation
Practical applications Therapy used to replace HABs with positive attributions, less aggression (Guerra and Slaby 1990).
Research support HABs linked with aggression in children (de Castro et al. 2002). Song lyrics primed aggressive scripts (Fischer and Greitemeyer 2006).
Correlation not causation Cognitive factors may not cause aggression (third factor?) so limited conclusions.

Social approach
Conformity to social/group norms Group membership depends on accepting group norms, including aggression.
- Gender norms – men 'should' use physical aggression, women verbal aggression to express emotion (Eagly and Wood 1991).
- Cultural norms – norms of aggression differ within countries and between cultures (e.g. homicide in US vs. Iceland).

Stereotypes and aggression We predict behaviour based on social category we fit people into.
- Gender stereotypes – aggression associated with stereotyped masculinity, danger that it can lead to acceptance of violence by men against women.
- Ethnic stereotypes – young black men stereotyped as aggressive, danger that it may lead to tolerance of racist aggression.

Influence of the media
Role modelling – media provide aggressive models to imitate.
Desensitisation – repeated viewing reduces physiological arousal, less empathy.
Disinhibition – aggression is normalised, viewing loosens inhibitions, new social norms more accepting.
Institutional aggression Prison environment is a strong cause of aggression.
Gang membership – strongly predicts violence, leaders exercise control.
Staff behaviour – violence linked to inconsistent use of discipline.

Evaluation
Practical applications Reduce prison aggression by applying rules consistently (McGuire 2018), improves communication.
Research support Viewing violence led to giving more electric shocks (disinhibition, Berkowitz and Alioto 1973), arousal reduced with repeated viewing (desensitisation, Krahé et al. 2011).
Role of biological factors May outweigh social factors, e.g. testosterone in men and women linked to aggression, reduced in animals by castration.

Behaviourist and social learning approaches
Operant conditioning Aggression learned directly.
- Positive reinforcement (Skinner 1932) – real-world aggression only sometimes reinforced and unpredictable, but this has stronger effect and hard to remove.
- Types of reward – tangible (e.g. money, food) and intangible (e.g. social status through bullying, wartime aggression).

Social learning (Bandura 1973) – aggression mostly learned indirectly.
- Observational learning and modelling – observing aggressive model does not guarantee imitation.
- Vicarious reinforcement – observe consequences, model more likely to be imitated if rewarded.

Evaluation
Practical applications Aggression underlying crimes learned through modelling (e.g. family), so provide alternative models (mentors).
Research support Aggressive boys modelled each other's behaviour (Poulin and Boivin 2000).
Limited explanations Weak explanation of hostile aggression because may receive punishment not reward, other explanations better.

Biological approach
Evolution and aggression
Aggression contributed to survival to reproduce, so genes passed on.
Aggression helped in competition for limited resources, men who retained partners through aggressive strategies (violence) passed genes on.
Brain structures and aggression Limbic system regulates emotional behaviour.
- Amygdala – more sensitive in aggressive people, key role in assessing threats (Gospic et al. 2011).

Biochemistry and aggression
- Testosterone – men have higher levels than women and more aggressive, most aggressive when levels highest (Daly and Wilson 1988).
- Serotonin – low levels in OFC disrupt emotional stability leading to impulsive behaviours (Denson et al. 2012).
- Dopamine – brain's 'reward chemical', aggression in winning competition rewarded with dopamine boost.
- Cortisol – low levels = aggression when testosterone high (Carré and Mehta 2011).

Genetics and aggression
- MAOA gene – low activity variant disrupts serotonin (Brunner et al. 1993).
- SRY gene – triggers testosterone, masculinises embryo, indirect influence.

Evaluation
Practical applications Each factor is a target for intervention, e.g. drugs to affect serotonin levels and control aggression.
Research support E.g. brain scans, high amygdala activity viewing angry faces (Coccaro et al. 2007). Retention strategies linked to violence (Shackelford et al. 2005).
Complex picture Biological factors interact, other factors include GABA, non-biological factors equally important.

Use of psychology in business to explain and influence consumer behaviour

Cognitive approach
Schema and consumer behaviour Advertisers don't want adverts to be predictable so challenge schema – schema incongruity (e.g. wacky).
Cognitive priming and consumer behaviour
- Direct attribute priming – prime features of product itself (speed/price of phone, etc.), associate product with desirable features and recall it later.
- Indirect attribute priming – prime features linked to product, i.e. context (Yi 1990), e.g. invented brands associated with wholesome attributes (health, countryside).

Cognitive biases and consumer behaviour
- Confirmation bias – look for evidence we made right choice, self-fulfilling ('It's the best because I bought it').
- Brand loyalty – repeat customers recall good things about brand, bad things about competitors, so highlight the good things.
- Authority bias – we give more credibility to authority figure, e.g. expert endorsing product.

Evaluation
Research support Background music affected experience of tasting wine in direction of music characteristics (North 2012).
Problems of replication Studies are hard to replicate so not scientific and lead to inconsistent findings.
Ethical issues Priming occurs without awareness, some adverts take advantage, possibly deception.

Social approach
Conformity to social norms Adverts suggest a product helps us to be like others.
Normative social influence and consumer behaviour We conform to norms for acceptance (Deutsch and Gerard 1955), leads to compliance, buy products or change behaviour to 'fit in' and avoid rejection.
The bandwagon effect We do something because others are (herd mentality), product bought by enough people means others join in (influencers), adverts create illusion a product is already popular.
Social proof Type of ISI, we are influenced by information that suggests other people are buying something (e.g. ratings), social proof of what others are doing (Cialdini 1984).

Evaluation
Practical applications Signs (social proof) next to lift saying other people use stairs = significant reduction in lift use (Burger and Shelton 2011).
Research support Students willing to display bigger logo of luxury product if it was associated with celebrity (Niesiobędzka 2018).
Cultural differences in social proof Social proof more influential in a collectivist culture (Poland) than individualist (USA) (Cialdini et al. 1999).

Behaviourist and social learning approaches
Classical conditioning
- Emotional associations – associate product/brand with positive feelings to change behaviour (buy, switch) or more positive attitudes.
- Repetition – longer-term campaigns repeat pairing of UCS and CS to avoid extinction of CR.

Operant conditioning
- Positive reinforcement – good experience of product is rewarding, so probably buy again.
- BOGOF and loyalty points – feeling of getting a bargain is reinforcing, so loyal to store/brand.

Social learning
- Modelling and imitation – adverts showing (modelling) a product being used.
- Vicarious reinforcement – observing someone enjoying using product.
- Use of celebrities in advertising – powerful models, imitation likely through identification.

Evaluation
Research support Positive attitudes toward fictitious brand when associated with positive images (Stuart et al. 1987). Attitudes also more positive when brand endorsed by celebrity (Knoll and Matthes 2017).
Ignores key factors Cognitive factors are ignored but must be involved in how we feel about products – we often make rational decisions (e.g. comparison websites).
Real-world effects are unclear Most research lab-based, but real-world effects of conditioning not long-term and weaker (Schachtman et al. 2011).

Biological approach
What is neuromarketing? Using study of brain to market products, advertising. Uses technology for insights into responses, motivation and decisions, e.g. brain activity associated with a product.
Functional magnetic resonance imaging (fMRI) Measures brain activity (blood oxygenation). Watch advert while fMRI builds 3D map of most active areas, which area is the 'buy button'?
Facial coding Facial expressions correlated with advert, facial action coding system (FACS) categorises micro expressions (Ekman and Friesen 1978).
Eye-tracking Monitor eye movements as consumer looks at product or advert, records the aspects that attract attention, use virtual reality (e.g. simulated shop).

Evaluation
Practical applications fMRI predicted success of songs years later but participants' conscious opinions did not, people unaware of 'true' responses (Berns and Moore 2012).
Relatively ineffective Focus groups were most successful technique, then fMRI but other neuro methods ineffective (Venkatraman et al. 2015).
Ethics of neuromarketing Manipulation of behaviour we are not aware of and over which we have no control, use of findings for inflated claims.

Application of psychology to explain gender

Terms associated with gender
Gender = being a girl/woman or a boy/man, different from male/female biological sex.
Gender is a spectrum – non-binary, gender-fluid, gender-neutral or androgynous. Gender-typical matches binary norm, gender-atypical does not. Gender-fluid identity is not abnormal or inferior.

Cognitive approach
Role of biases Can lead to inequality, prejudice and discrimination.
- Alpha bias – binary, encourages identification with one gender, creates sense of abnormality.
- Beta bias – suggests no differences between (trans) men and (trans) women, fails to recognise different needs, prevents change.

Role of schema (gender schema theory) Information consistent with gender schema more likely stored and recalled, recall of gender-inconsistent information is distorted to fit schema.

Role of cognitive priming Sex-role stereotypes and priming – gender stereotypes prime us to expect certain roles and behaviours (i.e. nurse is a woman because they are caring, men better at maths).
Gender roles and priming – e.g. women portrayed as passive on TV may influence girls to behave in same way.

Evaluation
Practical applications Avoid alpha bias and beta bias in everyday life, recognise similarities and differences between all gender identities.

Research support Cold pressor test, men primed with feminine-typical behaviours reported less pain and anxiety (Fowler et al. 2011).

Neglects key non-cognitive factors Social factors crucial in early years of gender development (e.g. rewards from parents), SLT better explanation.

Social approach
Peer influences on gender
- Gender identity in childhood – most children name their gender by three years (Egan and Perry 2001), gender segregation begins, same-gender peers are models for gender identity, peers exert NSI (gender norms) and ISI (sources of gender information).
- Gender identity in adolescence – *gender typicality* involves comparing self with peers, judge how fit into gender categories.

Conformity to gender roles
- Felt pressure for gender conformity – NSI from parents and peers, conform to gender-typical norms and not conform to atypical.
- Gender non-conformity – felt pressure a source of stress for adolescents with gender-atypical identity (bullying, rejection), may lead to gender dysphoria.

Influence of culture on gender
- Culture and third genders – non-binary in some cultures, e.g. fa'afafine in Samoa, biological males but traditional women's role.

Evaluation
Research support Gender roles strongly influenced by cultural context, e.g. women in the workplace vs traditional role of home-maker (Hofstede 2001).

Gender non-conformity Social approach hard to explain non-conformity when NSI tends towards gender conformity, needs cognitive element.

Peer influences are weak Peers affect attitudes and beliefs (felt pressure for conformity) but not identity (gender typicality, Kornienko et al. 2016).

Behaviourist and social learning approaches
Operant conditioning and gender
- Rewards and punishments – children rewarded for gender-typical behaviour (strengthens), punished for atypical (weakens), boys rough and active, girls passive and gentle.
- Differential reinforcement – girls and boys reinforced for different behaviours, driven by fathers (Kerig et al. 1993).

Social learning and gender
- Modelling – parents model gender-typical behaviours for imitation, also media models.
- Vicarious reinforcement – child observes consequences, imitation if reward but not if punishment.
- Identification – observer perceives model as 'like me', so imitation more likely.
- Influence of media – above processes operate through media, both gender-typical and gender-atypical/fluid.

Evaluation
Research support Mothers behaved differently towards baby dressed in boys' clothes or girls' clothes (e.g. toy choice), differential reinforcement (Smith and Lloyd 1978).

Explains changing norms Social norms have shifted, new forms of gender behaviour more often reinforced (through media) than punished, more gender-fluid models.

Children are active not passive Many children more gender-atypical than their parents, so must actively construct gender not passively receive it.

Biological approach
Role of sex hormones in gender
- Testosterone – levels before and after birth linked to brain differences between men and women.
- Congenital adrenal hyperplasia – girls with CAH show male-typical play behaviour, small proportion want to live as men (Hines 2006).
- Oestrogen – female sexual characteristics at puberty, menstrual cycle (PMT).
- Oxytocin – huge amounts during childbirth, emotional bonding, reduces cortisol.

Evolutionary explanations for masculinity/femininity
- Dominant male theory – dominant males mated more often, masculinity-promoting genes survived.
- Division of labour in EEA – hunting men needed masculine traits, domestic women needed caring traits, promoted reproductive success.

Role of chromosomes in gender
- Turner's syndrome – biological females with one X, most identify as women, little gender dysphoria.

Evaluation
Research support High masculinity scores linked to high testosterone, femininity linked with low testosterone (Baucom et al. 1985).

Neglects social and cultural factors African American girls identify with masculine and androgynous traits, SLT better explanation (Ashcraft and Belgrave 2005).

Third gender Some cultures have a third gender, e.g. fa'afafine of Samoa. Biologically male but live as women, culturally-accepted gender fluidity challenges binary view.

Content area B
Multiple-choice questions

Cognitive approach to explaining aggression in society

1. _____ aggression is linked with arousal.
   (a) Hostile.
   (b) Instrumental.
   (c) Cold-blooded.
   (d) Proactive.

2. Cognitive priming for aggression:
   (a) Occurs with our awareness.
   (b) Usually occurs over time.
   (c) Is unrelated to violent media.
   (d) Only needs a stimulus to occur once.

3. Fischer and Greitemeyer found that _____ prime aggression.
   (a) TV programmes.
   (b) Posters.
   (c) Song lyrics.
   (d) Facebook posts.

4. Which is most accurate?
   (a) Cognitive scripts cause aggression.
   (b) Aggression causes aggressive scripts.
   (c) Scripts and aggression are unrelated.
   (d) Scripts are linked to aggression.

Social approach to explaining aggression in society

1. Gender-role norms dictate that women should be:
   (a) Verbally aggressive sometimes.
   (b) Emotionally repressed.
   (c) More aggressive than men.
   (d) The strong but silent type.

2. McGuire showed aggression in prison is linked to:
   (a) Genes.
   (b) Gender-role norms.
   (c) Levels of testosterone.
   (d) Gang membership.

3. 'A reduced level of physiological arousal' is an element of:
   (a) Stereotypes.
   (b) Desensitisation.
   (c) Role modelling.
   (d) Disinhibition.

4. Giammanco et al. argue a biological factor that influences aggression is:
   (a) Gender norms.
   (b) Testosterone.
   (c) Genes.
   (d) Autonomic nervous system.

Behaviourist and social learning approaches to explaining aggression in society

1. Aggression is more likely when it is reinforced:
   (a) Every time it happens.
   (b) Occasionally and predictably.
   (c) Occasionally and unpredictably.
   (d) Negatively.

2. An example of an intangible reward is:
   (a) Money.
   (b) Status.
   (c) Food.
   (d) Toys.

3. Models of aggression:
   (a) Must be real-life only.
   (b) Usually have low status.
   (c) Can exist in the media.
   (d) Are usually unattractive.

4. Operant conditioning and social learning are weak explanations of:
   (a) Relational aggression.
   (b) Hostile aggression.
   (c) Instrumental aggression.
   (d) Aggression generally.

Biological approach to explaining aggression in society

1. The brain's 'reward chemical' is:
   (a) Cortisol.
   (b) Testosterone.
   (c) Serotonin.
   (d) Dopamine.

2. Using mate retention strategies is part of the _____ of aggression.
   (a) Brain structure.
   (b) Neurochemistry.
   (c) Evolution.
   (d) Genetics.

3. The key gene involved in aggression is the _____ gene.
   (a) Low-activity MAOA.
   (b) Dopamine.
   (c) High-activity MAOA.
   (d) 5-HIAA.

4. Which statement is most accurate?
   (a) There are many complex causes of aggression.
   (b) Psychological factors are most important.
   (c) Social factors are most important.
   (d) A single biological factor explains most aggression.

Cognitive approach to consumer behaviour

1. A deliberate conflict between a schema and an advert's content is called:
   (a) Direct attribute priming.
   (b) Schema predictability.
   (c) Schema congruity.
   (d) Schema incongruity.

2. Preferring to accept the word of an expert is an example of:
   (a) Brand loyalty.
   (b) Schema.
   (c) Authority bias.
   (d) Confirmation bias.

3. Which of the following is indirect attribute priming?
   (a) The price of a phone.
   (b) The farm a bottle of milk came from.
   (c) The speed of a car.
   (d) The cleaning power of a dishwasher tablet.

4. Studies into priming:
   (a) Are highly scientific.
   (b) All reach the same conclusions.
   (c) Give contradictory findings.
   (d) Can easily be replicated.

Social approach to consumer behaviour

1. Social proof is another term for:
   (a) Normative social influence.
   (b) The bandwagon effect.
   (c) Informational social influence.
   (d) Compliance.

2. Burger and Shelton studied the effect of social proof on:
   (a) Taking the stairs.
   (b) Buying luxury brands.
   (c) Using non-toxic cleaning products.
   (d) Vaccination programmes.

3. Cialdini et al. found that social proof was more effective in:
   (a) The USA than Poland.
   (b) Group discussions.
   (c) Individualist cultures.
   (d) Collectivist cultures.

4. 'Live the London Look' is an example of:
   (a) Informational social influence.
   (b) Compliance.
   (c) Social proof.
   (d) The bandwagon effect.

Behaviourist and social learning approaches to consumer behaviour

1. **Associating a product with good feelings is an example of:**
   (a) Social learning.
   (b) Classical conditioning.
   (c) Modelling.
   (d) Operant conditioning.

2. **Repetition of a UCS-CS pairing over time avoids:**
   (a) Conditioning of the CR.
   (b) Extinction of the CR.
   (c) Reinforcement of the CR.
   (d) Vicarious learning.

3. **Celebrities are used in adverts because of:**
   (a) Identification.
   (b) Operant conditioning.
   (c) Gamification.
   (d) Negative reinforcement.

4. **Lab-based studies of conditioning show _____ effects.**
   (a) Long-term.
   (b) No.
   (c) Short-term.
   (d) Real-world.

Biological approach to consumer behaviour

1. **fMRI detects:**
   (a) Blood oxygenation.
   (b) Eye movements.
   (c) Muscle movements.
   (d) Facial expressions.

2. **The FACS system applies to:**
   (a) Brain scans.
   (b) fMRI.
   (c) Eye tracking.
   (d) Facial coding.

3. **Venkatraman et al. found the best marketing technique was:**
   (a) fMRI.
   (b) Eye tracking.
   (c) Focus groups.
   (d) Virtual reality.

4. **One solution to ethical problems of neuromarketing is:**
   (a) Conduct more research studies.
   (b) Use more participants.
   (c) Regulate it by law.
   (d) Devise more techniques.

Cognitive approach to explaining gender

1. **_____ bias is a very binary perspective.**
   (a) Schema.
   (b) Alpha.
   (c) Confirmation.
   (d) Beta.

2. **'Men are better at maths' is an example of:**
   (a) Androgyny.
   (b) A gender-inconsistent role.
   (c) Gender schema.
   (d) A sex-role stereotype.

3. **Martin and Halverson's theory is a:**
   (a) Biological theory.
   (b) Non-cognitive theory.
   (c) Social learning theory.
   (d) Gender schema theory.

4. **Fowler et al.'s study used the:**
   (a) Cold pressor test.
   (b) Warm pressing test.
   (c) Cold water test.
   (d) Cold fresher test.

Social approach to explaining gender

1. **Gender segregation usually appears:**
   (a) When the child starts to talk, around age one.
   (b) By three years.
   (c) In adolescence.
   (d) By eight years.

2. **Felt pressure for gender conformity is a type of:**
   (a) Informational social influence.
   (b) Biological factor.
   (c) Normative social influence.
   (d) Cognitive factor.

3. **About _____ people identify as *hijras* in India, Pakistan and Bangladesh.**
   (a) 50 million.
   (b) 5 million.
   (c) 500,000.
   (d) 500.

4. **Kornienko et al. found that peers influence an adolescent's:**
   (a) Felt pressure for gender conformity.
   (b) Gender identity.
   (c) Gender fluidity.
   (d) Gender typicality.

Behaviourist and social learning approaches to explaining gender

1. **A powerful influence on learning of gender identity is _____ reinforcement.**
   (a) Identical.
   (b) Conventional.
   (c) Differential.
   (d) Classical.

2. **Gender-atypical influencers can be powerful role models through:**
   (a) Identification.
   (b) Operant conditioning.
   (c) Differential reinforcement.
   (d) Classical conditioning.

3. **Smith and Lloyd carried out:**
   (a) An animal study.
   (b) A Baby F study.
   (c) A Baby X study.
   (d) A study with adolescents.

4. **Which statement is most accurate?**
   (a) Children have always been reinforced for gender-atypical behaviour.
   (b) Most children have a different gender identity from their parents.
   (c) There are more gender-atypical models in the media nowadays.
   (d) Gender-fluid identities are less common than they used to be.

Biological approach to explaining gender

1. **About _____ of women with CAH want to live as men.**
   (a) 80%.
   (b) 50%.
   (c) 10%.
   (d) 5%.

2. **An evolutionary explanation of gender is:**
   (a) Dominant female theory.
   (b) Dominant male theory.
   (c) Congenital adrenal hyperplasia.
   (d) Turner's syndrome.

3. **Ashcraft and Belgrave studied gender in:**
   (a) African American girls.
   (b) Chinese American boys.
   (c) African American boys.
   (d) Native American girls.

4. **The fa'afafine of Samoa:**
   (a) Are biologically male.
   (b) Are biologically female.
   (c) Identify as men.
   (d) Are androgynous.

MCQ answers

Cognitive approach to explaining aggression in society 1A, 2B, 3C, 4D
Social approach to explaining aggression in society 1A, 2D, 3B, 4B
Biological approach to explaining aggression in society 1C, 2B, 3C, 4B
Behaviourist and social learning approaches to explaining aggression in society 1D, 2C, 3A, 4A
Cognitive approach to consumer behaviour 1D, 2C, 3B, 4C
Social approach to consumer behaviour 1C, 2A, 3D, 4D
Behaviourist and social learning approaches to consumer behaviour 1B, 2B, 3A, 4C
Biological approach to consumer behaviour 1A, 2D, 3C, 4C
Cognitive approach to explaining gender 1B, 2C, 3B, 4A
Social approach to explaining gender 1B, 2C, 3B, 4A
Behaviourist and social learning approaches to explaining gender 1C, 2A, 3C, 4C
Biological approach to explaining gender 1D, 2B, 3A, 4A

Content area B
Assessment guidance

The examination

Earlier in this unit (pages 58–59) we provided information about the examination for Unit 1. You have now studied the entire content on which you will be examined.

Content area B is where you will encounter the 9-mark essay question.

Health warning
Aside from the definitions of command terms, the material on this spread is not from the exam board. It is our interpretation of the 'rules of the game'.

Command terms

On page 58 we introduced the various command terms associated with the three skills (AO1, AO2, AO3) that are assessed in external assessments. We will look at them in more detail here, based on the explanations provided in the specification.

AO1 Demonstrate psychological knowledge, be able to recall key assumptions and concepts.
- *Describe* Psychological knowledge needs to be developed, but justification is not required.
- *Give* Recall a feature or characteristic.
- *Give a reason why* A statement is provided and an explanation required.
- *Identify* Select a correct answer.
- *Name* Recall a feature or characteristic using the correct terminology.
- *State* Recall a feature or characteristic.

AO2 Demonstrate understanding by explaining the link between psychological assumptions and concepts to behaviour in society.
- *Describe* As above.
- *Explain* Requires a justification of a point or an example. Sentences should be linked to provide an element of reasoning.
- *Interpret* Recognise a pattern in a stimulus.
- *Justify* Give reasons/evidence to support a statement.

AO3 Apply and evaluate psychological assumptions and concepts to explain contemporary issues of relevance to society.
- *Analyse* A methodical and detailed examination, breaking down a topic or information.
- *Assess* Give careful consideration of varied factors that apply to a specific situation and identify the most important. Come to a conclusion.
- *Compare* Give careful consideration of varied factors and identify which are the most important or relevant. Come to a conclusion.
- *Discuss* Identify and investigate all aspects of an issue or situation.
- *Evaluate* Consider various aspects of a subject's qualities in relation to its context, such as strengths or weaknesses. Come to a judgement (conclusion), supported by evidence.
- *Explain* See above.

The extended open response question (the '9-mark essay')

Common command words for these questions are *discuss, analyse, evaluate, assess*. BUT your answer needs to be a *balance* of AO1, AO2 and AO3. This is because there are 3 marks for knowledge and understanding (description), 3 marks for application and 3 marks for evaluation.

THIS IS VERY IMPORTANT – do not evaluate for the whole essay; there has to be description and application as well.

You are aiming to write about 320 words for a 9-mark essay. You will help the examiner, and yourself, if you construct an answer which follows a plan.

For example, you could plan to write five paragraphs of about 60–70 words, plus a conclusion if the command word is *assess, compare* or *evaluate*.

Here are some top tips:

For description: show you know and understand the concepts in the question by writing in detail.

For application: use the information given in the scenario throughout your answer, not just at the start or end.

For evaluation: make sure you use PET (see page 59); use evidence (e.g. a research study) to support or criticise a concept; explore a practical application; discuss ethical issues; consider another approach – is it a better explanation of a behaviour and *why*?

How essays are marked

The examiner has a set of criteria to look for. We have created a grid of these criteria below.

Level	Mark	Knowledge and understanding	Gaps or omissions	Points are relevant to the context of the question	Links made to context	Discussion/analysis/ assessment/ evaluation	Considers different aspects and how they interrelate
1	1–3	Isolated elements.	Major.	Few.	Minimal.	Limited.	Generic assertions.
2	4–6	Some accurate.	Minor.	Some.	Not clear.	Partially-developed.	Some, but not always in a sustained way.
3	7–9	Mostly accurate and detailed.	None.	Most.	Clear.	Well-developed.	A range, in a sustained way.

Note
1. Questions that begin *Assess* or *Compare* or *Evaluate* require a conclusion for level 3.
2. Questions that begin *Analyse* require the topic to be broken down into constituent parts.

How to use the levels based mark scheme

You must place a tick in one box in each column that best describes the answer being assessed.

If you are not sure, then place the tick on the line between two boxes.

When you have done this for all six columns decide which row best describes the answer. That determines the level.

To decide on the mark consider whether you are tempted to the level above or the level below, or neither.

Revision guidance

Effective revision
Trust us, we're psychologists.

1. Recall versus recognition
Many students focus on getting the information into their memory but in fact, in an exam, the problem is getting it back out. If I show you your revision card, you say, 'Yes I remember all of that' (this is *recognition memory*), but can you *recall* it in an exam?

Solution Test your recall repeatedly using cues.

2. Processing
Of course you may have difficulty in recalling information – every time you look back at your book or notes you try to push it into your memory, but when you try to recall it with cues later, the details are not there.

The problem is people think rereading and rereading stuff makes it go into your memory. No. Our memories evolved to store important information and not waste time on unimportant information.

Solution You have to do something with it to make it meaningful. Compose a song using the key words and sing them. Have a debate on the topic with friends. Make up a quiz for your friend. Anything more active than just reading notes.

3. Anxiety
Another reason that you forget things in an exam is because of anxiety. You are no doubt familiar with the feeling of being anxious – you start to sweat and maybe your body feels more tense. This is an important biological response (*fight or flight*) to prepare an animal to deal with a dangerous situation – your brain tells your body 'Get ready'. Part of this response shuts down the thinking part of your brain because it might be dangerous if you thought too deeply about what to do next. This is not very helpful in an exam.

Solutions The good news is that things you know well can still be accessed. Therefore, you need to practise, practise, practise your knowledge so it is well-learned.

Also, write answers under timed conditions so you feel slightly stressed when revising.

4. Persistence
Psychologists have shown that one of the key characteristics of students who do well is *delayed gratification*. They can control their impulses – for example, when you see a chocolate bar, do you find it hard to resist eating it straight away? Can you sit there with it on your desk and wait till after you have written that essay?

Solution Research has shown that trying to do just that (practise resisting) can boost your grades.

Preparing for the exam
Revision for external exams is a skill which means you must look for effective strategies and use them.

On page 60, we explained an important technique – the REVISION CARD – which uses cues to trigger your recall of important information.

On the left of this page, we look at a number of other strategies based on what we psychologists know about how the mind works.

Revision checklist for Content area B
Below are the key topics for Content area B. For each topic you should:
1. Construct a revision card and/or use our summaries (pages 52–53 and 88–89).
2. Test your recall using your cues. Check afterwards to see what you had forgotten.
3. Test your recall again using the cues.
4. Now test your memory of the cue words.

		1. Construct a revision card	2. First test of recall	3. Second test of recall	4. Test memory using cues
B1 Use of psychology to explain contemporary issues of aggression in society	Cognitive approach				
	Social approach				
	Behaviourist and social learning approaches				
	Biological approach				
B2 Use of psychology in business to explain and influence consumer behaviour	Cognitive approach				
	Social approach				
	Behaviourist and social learning approaches				
	Biological approach				
B3 Application of psychology to explain gender	Cognitive approach				
	Social approach				
	Behaviourist and social learning approaches				
	Biological approach				

5. Confidence
You learned about *self-efficacy* in this unit (see page 32). If you believe in yourself, it boosts your performance. For example, research shows that girls who have to identify their gender at the start of a maths test tend to do less well than girls who are not reminded of their gender – because it arouses the stereotype 'girls are not as good at Maths as boys'. It lowers their self-efficacy.

Solution Have things above your desk which remind you of your successes. Before the exam, remind yourself how much studying you have done and again think of your successes. Raise your self-efficacy.

Content area B
Practice questions, answers and feedback

On this spread we look at some typical answers to exam-style questions. The comments provided (in green) from an experienced teacher show what is good and bad in each answer. Learning how to provide effective exam answers is a SKILL. Practise it.

Question 1: Grace runs a small independent coffee shop. She wants to increase sales and customers so she plans to use a loyalty scheme. Each time a customer buys a coffee, they get a point. After they collect six points, the customer gets a free coffee.
Describe, using operant conditioning, how Grace's plan could increase sales of coffee. (3 marks)

Chen's answer: The points are positive reinforcement of buying. This is because you get a free coffee so you get something out of it and everyone likes to think they are getting a bargain.

Teacher comments
The only links to the scenario are 'points' and 'free coffee'. Although Chen has identified positive reinforcement correctly, there's little evidence he really understands it, so this gets 1 mark.

Bella's answer: When customers get points and a free coffee they feel good and associate this feeling with the shop so they have a positive view. Later, whenever they think about coffee or the shop, they get this good feeling again which makes them go back for more.

Bella has written about classical conditioning rather than operant. This is a common mistake, so make sure you understand both. There is some use of the scenario but this doesn't matter unfortunately because there's nothing in the answer that's recognisable as operant conditioning. 0 marks.

Saturn's answer: Grace is using positive reinforcement. Each point is a reward for buying a coffee. This is a pleasant consequence for the customer so they are more likely to visit again and buy another coffee. Like any loyalty scheme, the tangible reward of a free cup is reinforcing because the customer has to wait for it and it feels like a bargain.

This is a clear answer because there is a logical progression of Saturn's explanation from one point to the next. This makes it easy for the examiner to credit all the marks. Saturn also makes full use of the scenario without just repeating it. Note how Saturn has broadly made three points for three marks. This is not how answers are marked but it is a useful guideline to keep you on track. 3 marks.

Question 2: Frans has been friends with Erik and Stan since they were boys at primary school. They always played football together, although Frans wasn't very keen to begin with. Now they all play in the same Sunday league team. They go out drinking together although all they talk about is football.
Explain **two** ways in which Frans' peers may have influenced him to conform to a gender role. (4 marks)

Chen's answer: One way is normative social influence. Frans wants to stay friends with the others so conforms to a masculine gender role by playing football and drinking to be accepted by his friends.
Another way is informational social influence. Frans feels the others know better than him about being a man, and being expected to like football and drinking. He conforms to the role because he wants to be right.

Teacher comments
A good answer to this question needs to name two explanations for conformity and explain why they could be reasons for Frans conforming to a gender role. This is exactly what Chen has done in a clear way that uses appropriate terminology and is relevant to Frans' situation. 4 marks.

Bella's answer: Frans wasn't very keen on football at school so playing it was just compliance – he joined in to conform to the gender role so he would be accepted by his friends.
The second way is imitation because Frans observes his friends' gender behaviour and imitates it, mainly because they enjoy it (vicarious).

Bella has gone down a slightly different path with a specific type of conformity. It's perfectly fine to do this and her answer is correct and accurate. But the problem is she has tried to use social learning as a second way. This is not an explanation of conformity and Bella doesn't try to make it relevant anyway, so no marks for this part. 2 marks overall.

Saturn's answer: Frans' friends influenced him because they all play football and go out drinking. Frans did it too in order to fit in.
Frans' friends also influenced him because they had more information about being their gender, e.g. we play football. Frans believed it so he conformed.

Saturn comes up with another way to get 2 marks. She just recycles the scenario rather than uses it and she doesn't name any types or explanations of conformity. But there is some relevant and creditworthy material here. The elements that got the marks were 'in order to fit in' (NSI) and the reference to 'more information' (ISI). A missed opportunity though, because it would have been relatively easy for Saturn to get full marks. 2 marks.

Question 3: Freida was in a pub when a man accidentally trod on her foot. Even though he apologised, Freida still got angry and hit him in the face.
Use **one** aspect of the cognitive approach to aggression to explain Freida's behaviour. (2)

Chen's answer: Priming could explain this because Freida may have been reminded about aggression by something in the room and this made her more ready to be aggressive.

Teacher comments
Chen tries to use priming but it doesn't really work. He could have suggested what the item in the room might be. 1 mark for some relevance.

Bella's answer: Freida may have a hostile attribution bias and therefore interpreted the treading on her foot as intentional, which made her react aggressively.

Bella's choice of hostile attribution bias is more appropriate and well explained, 2 marks.

Saturn's answer: It might be instrumental aggression because Freida wants to get something.

Saturn has selected a third possibility, instrumental aggression. But this is a *type* of aggression not an *explanation*, so 0 marks.

Question 4: Raf has heard about a new eyeliner they plan to buy. They have seen an ad for it and all their friends are raving about it. The manufacturer wants to increase sales so hires a neuromarketing company to market and sell the eyeliner.
Analyse the company's use of neuromarketing in helping the manufacturer sell the eyeliner. (9 marks)

Chen's answer: One neuromarketing method that could be used is a brain scanning method called fMRI. This is because it gives insight into how consumers feel about a product based on the activity in their brains. The company could use a special fMRI machine which scans the consumers' brains so they could find out if a product makes consumers feel good or bad, whether they are interested and excited or just bored. This would be very useful information which they could take and increase the aspects that the consumers feel good about and have more of those. They could also remove or reduce the aspects that people do not feel good about because they do not increase the sales.

Another way the company could increase sales is to use celebrities in an advert. The celebrities would be like role models for consumers to look up to because they would have status, wealth and attractiveness etc. They could get the celebrities to use the product and look like they enjoy doing it. So consumers would copy the celebrities and buy products because they would see the celebrities using them in the advert. Or if not a celebrity then a professional such as a dentist using toothpaste because people will copy experts who are well-informed.

There are many other methods as well but they are not as good.

My conclusion is that fMRI is very good for increasing sales because it would work out what people like and dislike about the product. This would help the company focus on the good things. Using celebrities or professionals is OK but not as good because consumers do not always copy them, so this is not a guaranteed way to increase sales.

285 words

Teacher comments

Chen could set the scene with a brief but relevant explanation of neuromarketing but instead he goes straight into the first method.

His first paragraph gives some accurate description which indicates a basic level of knowledge and understanding, but there isn't much and it certainly isn't detailed. Some of this is quite repetitive. For example, one sentence about 'increase the aspects...' is followed by another sentence that is just the converse, 'reduce the aspects...'. Chen is just using words without adding anything to the explanation.

There is no explanation of how the company could actually use fMRI in relation to the eyeliner. Generally, application to the scenario is very limited. Chen writes about the 'company' and what it might be interested in doing. But he doesn't even mention the eyeliner or how neuromarketing could contribute to an advert to increase sales, which is what the scenario is about. There are also missed opportunities for application. For example, Chen has used 'dentists and toothpaste' as an example rather than refer to the information in the scenario.

Chen has provided just one relevant method so the knowledge and understanding in the answer is 'isolated'. In other words, because there are three methods named on the spec, it is very limiting to write about just one of them – this will always show up major gaps in knowledge (unless of course the question tells you to write about just one thing).

Chen has tried to use the social learning approach as a method. Modelling is not a neuromarketing method so any description and application of it is irrelevant. However, it could be considered an 'alternative explanation' – that is, an explanation of the topic taken from another approach. This could count as evaluation if it is done properly. But Chen's use of the point is again very limited – he probably didn't mean to use the point in this way and it shows. For example, he doesn't explore the nature of the differences between the approaches. Evaluation is therefore almost totally absent.

Finally, Chen has provided a conclusion. The question doesn't require this ('Analyse') and what Chen has written is just repetition of earlier points so it gets no credit.

Everything about the answer says 'level 1' in the levels based mark scheme, but a 'good' level 1, so 3 marks.

Saturn's answer: Neuromarketing is using technology to see how people feel about products and adverts. It is used to increase sales or identify areas to improve in an advert.

One main technique used is brain scanning called fMRI. This shows changes in blood flow that go with brain activity. The company could use this method by getting people to lie in an fMRI scanner and show them an advert for the eyeliner. The measured brain activity would show if they find the advert boring or exciting, do they like the eyeliner or not? From this the company could learn what is appealing about the eyeliner and what price to sell it at (more appealing = higher price).

Another method is eye tracking to see where someone is looking. It is very precise, so the company would find out which parts of an advert or product capture the consumer's attention. This could tell the company that these aspects are most interesting and motivate consumers to buy the eyeliner. Aspects people do not look at could be changed to make them more interesting. This can also be used to improve the packaging because people might look for longer at something that confuses them.

A final method is facial coding. Our facial expressions reflect how we feel so the company could attach electrodes to people's faces. They could use the facial action coding system to measure the expressions and emotional responses to the eyeliner advert. For example, the electrodes would detect tiny muscle movements in smiling, which reflects happiness at certain parts of the advert.

The main strength of neuromarketing is that it can be better than other methods such as people filling in questionnaires. But the main weakness is that it has ethical issues to do with exaggerating what it tells us about adverts. How do they know what brain activity is showing? There is another weakness because it's not as good as focus groups so the company would be better to use these to find out what people think about the eyeliner advert.

341 words

The first thing to notice about Saturn's answer is its structure – it is very well-organised. The methods are clearly indicated and for each one there is description (this is what it is...) and application (this is how it could be used...) and Saturn has made them obvious to the examiner. It's almost as if Saturn imagined headings throughout her essay (but of course she didn't actually use them) – an excellent strategy.

The detail and accuracy of Saturn's descriptions show that she really understands this topic. This is as thorough as you can ask for in the limited time available. You should be aiming for about 320 words in a 9-mark essay. Much longer than this means you might be short of time on other questions.

The weakest part of the answer is the evaluation. Saturn makes an attempt but it is not 'PET-friendly' (see page 59). She has made the common mistake of listing evaluative points without really engaging with any of them. They are not very well-explained. This means her analysis has no depth because it is not well-developed. This is a criterion for level 3 of the levels based mark scheme that examiners use (see page 92). Had she focused on two points with full PET, this answer would probably have gained full marks.

As it is, the knowledge, understanding, application and attempt at some evaluation place the answer in level 3. But the relative weakness of the evaluation puts it at the bottom of that level, so 7 marks.

Unit 2
Conducting psychological research

An armchair psychologist

Oh, I can explain that!
Young people didn't behave like that in my day because their parents were much stricter.
If you just gave them harsher punishment that would stop their bad behaviour.
There should be longer prison sentences for people who break the law.

We are all armchair psychologists. We like to try to explain why people (and animals) behave as they do.

Just listen to people's conversations and you'll hear someone trying to explain behaviour.

➡ Try to think of some of the questions people ask and the explanations they produce.

Contents

Learning aim A: Understand research methods and their importance in psychological inquiry

A1 Principles of research	Introducing research and the scientific process	98
	Informing and improving practice	100
	Types of research process	102
A2 Key terms used in research	Starting research	104
	Hypotheses and a literature review	106
	Sampling techniques	108
	Reliability and validity	110
A3 Research process	Ethical considerations	112
	Conducting research	114
	Assessment guidance	116

Pearson recommended assessment approach

A report discussing the importance of research in informing and improving practice and provision, detailing the way in which research is organised and giving an evaluation of different research methods and their usefulness in answering specific questions.

Learning aim B: Plan research to investigate psychological questions

B1 Research methods	Review of research methods	118
	Experiments	120
	Questionnaires and interviews	122
	Observation	124
	Content and thematic analysis	126
	A few other things	128
B2 Developing research proposals	Planning and managing your pilot study	130
	Assessment guidance	132

A report discussing a proposal for a pilot study that takes account of research questions, methods, participants, procedures, time and organisational management.

Learning aim C: Carry out a pilot study to explore current issues in psychology

C1 Data collection	Data collection	134
C2 Data analysis	Quantitative data analysis techniques	136
	Qualitative data analysis techniques	138
C3 Presenting findings to an audience	Writing up the study and presenting it	140

Learning aim D: Review implications of research into psychological inquiry

D1 Reviewing research process and findings	Review research process and implications of research	142
D2 Implications of research into psychological inquiry		
	Assessment guidance	144

A pilot study, including:
- A report on procedures followed for conducting research and collecting and analysing data.
- A report that discusses the findings and success of the pilot study, the implications of research on practice and provision, and the impact, through self-reflection and feedback from others, on personal and professional development.

Learning aim A1: Principles of research

Introducing research and the scientific process

In plain sight

You can watch the video illustrated here: tinyurl.com/8fuake8

The instructions are: 'Count how many times the players wearing white pass the basketball'.

At the end of the short film people are asked, 'How many passes did you count?'

And then asked, 'But did you see the gorilla?!'

In one study by Daniel Simons and Chris Chabris (1999) almost half the participants (44%) failed to see the gorilla! Can you believe that? The people were staring straight at the gorilla but they actually didn't see it.

Without this evidence you probably wouldn't believe it is true. To be honest, we suspect that some of you don't believe it now – try it out on a few people. Or try a different one made by Simons and Chabris: tinyurl.com/pej6jcl

Simons, D.J., & Chabris, C.F. (1999). Gorillas in our midst: Sustained inattentional blindness for dynamic events. Perception, 28, 1059-1074. Figure provided by Daniel Simons.

Psychological research

Research and gorillas

The simple answer to 'what is research?' is that it means finding out more about the world around you. For example, if you wanted to try a new restaurant, you might research the reviews people have given. Or if you were planning a holiday you might research what offers are available.

In science (and psychology is a science) we aim to be systematic and objective when conducting research to find things out. Take the gorilla example on the left. If we want to find out how people behave when an unexpected object walks past, we can't just ask, 'Do you think you would see the gorilla?'. For a start, people often simply don't know how they would behave. They also wouldn't be very objective – they don't want to look stupid and therefore would say, 'Of course I'd see it'.

For this reason, over many many years, people have worked out objective methods they can use to identify what is 'true'.

Let's be serious

Psychologists are interested in how our minds work and why we do things – but their ultimate goal is to improve people's lives through a better understanding of human thought and behaviour. This is *applied psychology* – applying research to real-life situations.

An interesting application of the gorilla research

Could the 'gorilla' phenomenon be observed elsewhere? Trafton Drew and colleagues (2013) wondered if the same issue happened when radiologists were trying to detect lung tumours and had to peer at a scan (a picture made using X-rays). When they were looking at a scan of a lung did they really see everything that was there? To test this the researchers put together scans taken of peoples' lungs – some had tumours and a few had a gorilla superimposed on the scan (about 4 cm in size). They showed these scans to expert radiologists and found that 83% of radiologists failed to spot the gorilla.

That is a serious failure rate. Drew *et al.* concluded that perhaps radiologists needed to refocus their attention so that they are searching for the unexpected rather than just looking for expected items. This could also be applied to police searching photographs for suspected terrorists.

What is 'science'?

Psychology is often defined as the '*science* of behaviour and experience'.

Science aims to produce explanations so that we can predict and control our world – so we can build bridges that don't collapse or develop safe and effective vaccines to get rid of dangerous diseases.

The use of a scientific approach in psychology is important because people might claim, for example, that a certain drug cures depression. People quite rightly demand evidence to support such claims before they use a new drug for depression.

Empirical evidence

The term 'science' refers to knowledge based on *empirical* evidence. This means knowledge gained through direct experience.

People can make claims about the benefits of a treatment but the only way we know such claims to be true is through empirical evidence. It is not enough to just ask a few people what they think.

- This empirical evidence is called *primary data* because it is collected directly by a researcher.
- It aims to be *objective* evidence rather than personal opinion. This objectivity means that if someone else collected the information it should be the same.
- One way to check this is through *replication* – if the observations are true then you would expect to get the same findings if you repeat the observations.

The scientific process

The human mind does not naturally think in an objective way. We are all biased in the way we think about the world. If we want to discover 'truths' we need a process to follow to ensure that what we are 'seeing' is free from bias.

Scientists aim to record objective information. They then seek to provide an explanation (theory) and then to test their theory by conducting research. You will be learning about this process through the rest of this unit.

Inductive and deductive

Scientists may develop a theory (or general law) based on their observations (called *inductive*) or they may start with a theory and develop expectations from that (*deductive*).

The picture on the left is the burger advertised by a well-known fast-food outlet.

But is that what you actually get?

Where is the evidence?

In order to be certain of facts we need objective, physical evidence – called *empirical evidence*.

Here is the empirical evidence – the actual burger.

Science uses empirical methods to separate unfounded beliefs from real truths. [Thanks to Professor Sergio della Sala for this example of empiricism.]

Assessment practice

At the end of learning aim A you must write:

A report discussing the importance of research in informing and improving practice and provision, detailing the way in which research is organised and giving an evaluation of different research methods and their usefulness in answering specific questions.

This report must be related to a scenario or context, such as the one below:

> When paramedics take patients to a hospital's accident and emergency department, they hand them over to medical staff. At the same time the paramedic also gives the medic relevant information about the patient (vital signs, details of any drugs given, other procedures in the ambulance or at the scene, the patient's response, etc.).
>
> The paramedic relies on their memory – they only have one opportunity to provide accurate and complete information. The consequences of getting it wrong are potentially very severe.
>
> Professor Tim Hodgetts devised a 4-step system called MIST to improve the accuracy of handover information. The paramedic gives details of: Mechanism of injury (how it happened), Injuries (what they are), Signs (e.g. monitoring of pulse), Treatments (e.g. drugs given).
>
> Imagine you have to conduct a piece of scientific research to test the effectiveness of MIST.

You can see the assessment criteria and explanation of command terms on pages 116 and 133.

A1.1 Learning aim A1 – Task 1

The first part of your report for learning aim A will be concerned with a brief introduction to the importance of research and science, topics covered on this spread.

This activity will help you practise the skills required to write the report in response to your scenario/context.

1. Write a paragraph **explaining** what empirical evidence you would need to decide whether MIST works. (A.P1)

   Include the following in your explanation: what empirical evidence is, the scientific process and why it is valuable, primary data, objective evidence and replication. Make sure you refer to the benefits to paramedics doing handovers.

2. **Assess** the value of carrying out research in psychology in this scientific way. (A.M1)

3. **Evaluate** the empirical evidence you explained in your answer to question 1. [HINT: What are the strengths and weaknesses?] (A.D1)

Specification terms

Deductive reasoning Using a general principle to produce particular examples, e.g. developing a theory first and then generating a prediction from this.

Empirical The view that knowledge can only come through direct observation or experiment rather than by reasoned argument or beliefs.

Inductive reasoning Using particular examples to generate a theory.

Objective Free from bias, uninfluenced by personal expectations, emotions or personal opinions.

Primary data Information collected by a researcher specifically for the purpose of the current study (as opposed to secondary data which is data collected by someone else, such as government statistics, and used in a new research study).

Replication Repeating an observation or study to confirm the original finding.

Research To investigate something systematically with the aim of demonstrating facts and producing theories. A disciplined exercise to address questions.

Scientific process A systematic approach to gaining and verifying knowledge.

An issue to consider

Given what you have read so far, try to explain why Cara (who wrote this spread) passionately believes that science is very very important.

Specification content

A1 Purpose and value of research in applied psychology.

- Definitions, to include a disciplined exercise to address questions, the process of inductive and deductive reasoning to solve problems, collection and analysis of primary data to describe, explain, generalise and predict a phenomenon.
- Scientific process, to include objective, empirical evidence, based on data rather than theory alone, controlled variables, replicable, cause and effect, testing theories.

Learning aim A1: Principles of research
Informing and improving practice

A day in the life

Sarah Brothwell is a clinical psychologist, a profession which focuses on diagnosing and treating mental, emotional, and behavioural disorder. Here, she talks about a typical day.

I love working with people.

I work with adults with mental health problems as part of a community team made up of mental health nurses, social workers and psychiatrists. We see people who have been referred by their GPs for a variety of reasons including problems with depression and anxiety, hearing voices, and having a personality disorder.

Today I have a new client to assess. He is a man in his 20s who has been struggling with depression for some years. I ask questions about the problems that have brought him here today, his history and family relationships. We make some links between the difficult things that have happened to him as a child and the self-criticism he now heaps on himself. I will see him again next week.

I see another two clients for ongoing psychological therapy for an hour each and then notes have to be written up on the computer system for each client whom I have seen.

This afternoon I am delivering a training session to other mental health professionals. Teaching others about psychological theory and intervention is an important part of a CP's role. There are always new developments in psychology to keep up to date with and, as well as being a requirement of the British Psychological Society for all applied psychologists to do this, I love the fact that I am always learning new things in this job.

Adapted from *Psychology Review* (2013).

Specification terms

Policy A course of action taken by an organisation or individual.

Practice In this context 'practice' refers to the application of an idea or method.

GET ACTIVE Finding out

At the top of the facing page we discuss the Office for National Statistics (ONS), a vast collection of data about British people and their lives. Go to their website where you will see the A–Z of statistical bulletins. Select a letter and then select a topic of interest.

1. Describe some key statistics from your selected report.
2. Explain **one** way you could use your chosen statistical information to improve provision (e.g. delivery of a public service).

Chicken and egg

It is difficult to say whether theory or practice comes first (like the question of a chicken and egg). In reality they work together. Theory comes from those involved in treating people with mental health problems and this leads to research, which then changes practice which is further assessed by a researcher leading to changes in policy ... you get the process.

Purpose of research: Informing practice

People who work as psychologists are all members of a professional organisation. In the UK this is the *British Psychological Society* (BPS). They may also be members of the *Health and Care Professions Council* (HCPC). Such organisations are concerned with the promotion of excellence and ethical practice.

The ultimate aim of psychological research is to understand and improve lives. This identifies two themes in psychology:

- Understand = research = designing and conducting studies, using these to construct and test theories.
- Improve lives = application = the findings from research are applied to shape practice. There are numerous branches of applied psychology such as health psychology, forensic psychology, child psychology and clinical psychology (which can all be studied in the extended certificate).

Clinical psychology

The branch of psychology that is concerned with mental health is called *clinical psychology* – the term 'clinical' refers to medical practice, so this overlaps with health psychology.

Clinical psychologists like Sarah Brothwell (see *case study* on the left) have to do a degree in psychology and study for a doctorate for a further three years. During that time Sarah learned a lot about theory and research in psychology and also about applying that knowledge in practice. You can see on the left that part of her role is educating other people about psychological theory, though her core job is assisting those with psychological disorders.

Research and practice

Why are research and theory important? Because knowing the causes of psychological disorder can lead to effective treatments. For example, one theory about depression suggests that it is a *cognitive* disorder – it is related to the way you think. Some people focus on negative thoughts ('the glass is half empty rather than half full') and also tend to catastrophise ('my life is always going to be a mess'). Such negative patterns of thinking lead to depression.

Therefore, one therapeutic approach is to challenge such ways of thinking. However, how do we know whether this works? We need to conduct a research study comparing the success rate of two different therapies, for example comparing a cognitive therapy with a drug therapy.

In this way theory leads to practice which is then researched and improved.

Evaluation

Problems with objective research

One weakness with research-based *policy* is that the research itself may be flawed.

One of the most serious problems in research is *researcher bias*. The person who conducts research often has expectations about the outcome. For example, in a study looking at whether younger or older people with depression respond better to a certain treatment, the researcher may expect that older people respond better. Then the researcher may unwittingly communicate this expectation to the participants, subtly discouraging the younger participants and encouraging the older ones – the researcher might just nod their head more often when interviewing some participants.

This means that it is always important to study the methods used in any study (the person *conducting* a study should not be the person who designed the study and therefore should be expectation-free). It also means it is always better to look at more than one piece of research.

Purpose of research: Informing policy

Public organisations such as the NHS decide on a system of principles to guide their decisions and procedures. Such policy decisions are informed by research.

Statistics

Statistics refers to the use of various methods to summarise and detect patterns in a set of data – for example, using the mean or drawing a bar chart. Just looking at a mass of numbers is not helpful, we need averages and graphs. These methods are discussed on pages 136–137 of this unit.

The Office for National Statistics (ONS, www.ons.gov.uk) is the largest independent producer of official statistics in the UK. They are responsible for collecting and publishing statistics at national, regional and local levels.

The ONS publish data, based on their research: on education, childcare, housing, leisure, employment rates, crime and justice, health and social care (including mental health) and other topics related to our social world.

Issues researched in applied psychology

Effectiveness or improvement of practice and provision An example of ONS data on crime and justice are the September 2019 figures in England and Wales which show changes in specific crime rates. For example, there was no change in overall crime rates but a 7% increase in police-recorded offences with sharp knives and a 6% decrease in homicides.

Such crime statistics modify policing strategies in line with new patterns of crime, for example changing provision and practice for dealing with knife crime.

Health trends Statistical information is also published by the government (www.gov.uk). For example, looking at life expectancy in relation to social deprivation. Data from 2020 shows that people living in more deprived areas have a healthy life expectancy of just over 50 years whereas people in the least deprived areas have a healthy life expectancy of 70 years. This is important in deciding about where to direct resources in healthcare.

Strategies for supporting ill health and mental functioning The ONS also publish data on health and social care, including mental health. For example, the percentage of adults diagnosed with mental disorders in the UK in 2017 was 6.6% of the white population, an increase of 2.2% in five years. Whereas amongst the Pakistani-origin population there has been a decrease of almost 1% to 5.2% in 2017.

Such data might be used to inform clinics of likely patient groups who will attend for help or can be used to assess treatment successes. It can also be used to target public awareness campaigns more effectively.

Establishing causes and cures of diseases (and behaviours) Psychopathology is concerned with explaining psychological illnesses. Each of the approaches has an explanation – for example, the biological approach explains depression in terms of faulty *neurotransmitter* levels or *brain structure*.

These explanations have implications for treatment – the biological approach recommends the use of drugs to alter faulty neurotransmitter levels and the use of technologies such as brain scans.

Identifying gaps in provision

All the examples above can be used to work out areas of 'need' – where more resources might improve, for example, the health inequalities in deprived areas.

Evaluation

Problems with crime figures

One weakness with the statistical data is it is only as good as the sample used.

In reality many people do not report the crimes committed against them. This is for a variety of reasons. For example, a victim may not feel the police will take it seriously and therefore don't report it, or a person may wish to avoid the stigma of being a victim. Alison Walker *et al.* (2006) found that only 42% of crimes reported in the British Crime Survey were reported to the police.

This is called the 'dark figure' of unreported crime and means that official statistics only represent a part of criminal activity.

Assessment practice

At the end of learning aim A you must write a report (see previous spread and also page 116). This report must be related to a scenario or context, such as the one below:

Many employees experience stress at work. Stress can lower work performance, decrease job satisfaction and cause absenteeism. Work stress is therefore very costly to individuals, organisations, governments and wider society.

Some employers have consulted psychologists to help them identify and deal with work stress, for example by implementing stress management programmes for employees. A typical programme would first of all identify the level of stress within the organisation. Then employees would be offered training so they can learn techniques to cope with stress.

Imagine you have been asked to set up a stress management programme for a big employer. You would also need to evaluate the success of the programme.

For both of these stages, what empirical evidence would you need and how would you go about getting it?

Finally, you could create a company-wide policy concerning how stress in the organisation should be identified and tackled.

A1.2 Learning aim A1 – Task 2

The second part of your report for learning aim A will be concerned with the importance of research in informing and improving practice, topics covered on this spread.

1. **Explain** how you would use the information you have gathered to improve the company's procedures for tackling work-related stress. (A.P1)
2. **Assess** the value of collecting and using the data on stress in the programme described above. (A.M1)
3. **Evaluate** the processes of collecting and using data on stress in this programme. (A.D1)

An issue to consider

Aside from research, what other factors are likely to influence decisions on practice and policy?

Specification content

A1 Purpose and value of research in applied psychology.

- Purpose of research, to include improving outcomes for individuals, informing policy and practice, extending knowledge and understanding, identifying gaps in provision.
- Issues researched in applied psychology, to include:
  - Effectiveness or improvement of practice and provision.
  - Health trends.
  - Strategies for supporting ill health and mental functioning.
  - Establishing causes and cures of disease, behaviours, advancement in treatments and medication, technologies.
- Organisations involved in research, e.g. Office for National Statistics (ONS), British Medical Association (BMA), British Psychological Society (BPS).

Learning aim A1: Principles of research

Types of research process

Case study

"37 WHO SAW MURDER DIDN'T CALL THE POLICE"
– *The New York Times*
March 27, 1964

In New York City in 1964 there was a brutal murder that attracted considerable interest. The reason for the unusual interest was because there had been many witnesses to the murder but no one helped.

The young woman who was murdered, Kitty Genovese, was coming home from working in a bar at 3am when she was stabbed. Her screams were heard by at least 37 people but no one rang the police. One person leaned out of a window and shouted at the attacker so he disappeared. However, he returned later, fatally stabbing Kitty at the entrance to her apartment. No one rang the police until the final stabbing.

How do we explain this?

So far our 'research' has involved observation of a real-life event. We could use self-report and ask the witnesses or other people how they would explain these events or what they would do if they were in a similar situation. And we could test our explanation in an experiment.

Irving Piliavin *et al.* (1969) did just that. They tried to test whether people become more unhelpful when in a group than when on their own. Piliavin *et al.* did their study on a New York subway train. They arranged for someone to 'collapse' and counted how many people there were on the subway train and how long it took for help to be offered.

In fact the researchers found the size of the group didn't matter but they found people were much more likely to offer help to a person who appeared disabled (he had a cane) than a person who appeared drunk (he carried a paper bag with a bottle and smelled of alcohol). The difference was quite big – 87% versus 17% were helped.

Specification terms
The key terms on this spread are defined in learning aim B, where you can also read about each method in more detail. You may want to do this now.

Doing research

Research involves collecting information. There are a number of different ways to collect information about people's behaviour. On this spread we will very briefly consider the main ones – they will be discussed in greater detail in learning aim B.

Observation
Perhaps the most obvious way to find out about what people do is to observe them. For example, if we want to know what kind of things students do in the canteen at college or how doctors interact with their patients.

Observation can involve watching or listening. It might even involve watching people in a film or reading what people are saying in magazines.

Survey
The other most obvious way to find out about people is to ask them. Asking questions is usually related to what people think or feel about something. If we want to know what people do it is better to watch/listen to them – if you ask 'What do you do in the college canteen?' they may not really know and just tell you what they imagine they do.

A *survey* may involve using a *questionnaire* which is something you could hand out to people or it might be online. Alternatively some researchers *interview* people face-to-face (or on the phone) and may not have a fixed set of questions but adapt the questions as they go along, depending on the answers given.

Experiments
Experiments are special. They usually involve observation or survey as a way of collecting data, as in the study by Piliavin *et al.* on the left – but they have a very important and unique feature. Experiments investigate cause-and-effect relationships. Only experiments can do this.

Consider this: it has been observed (by looking at football match results) that when football teams wear red shirts they are more likely to win – but does the red colour cause them to win? To see if it is a cause we arrange for two teams to play ten football matches.

Week 1: team 1 wears red and team 2 wears blue.
Week 2: team 1 wears blue and team 2 wears red.
Week 3: team 1 wears red and team 2 wears blue.

And so on. At the end we compare the scores whenever a team was in red and whenever a team was in blue.

The only thing that varies is the colour of the shirts. Therefore, we can say this *caused* the team to win. The thing we have varied is called the *independent variable* (IV).

Experiments come in different forms:

Laboratory experiment Not surprisingly this is an experiment that is conducted in a *laboratory*. A laboratory can be any space where it is possible to control variables – makes it easier to control *extraneous variables* and also to control the IV.

Field experiment Unlike a laboratory experiment, a *field experiment* is not literally conducted in a field (though it might be in our football shirt example). A field experiment is one that is conducted in a more everyday environment such as Piliavin *et al.*'s subway experiment on the left.

Natural experiment The title is a bit misleading. *Natural experiments* aren't necessarily natural. What is natural is the IV we are studying. For example, if we wanted to compare the aggressiveness of footballers whose teams play in red versus those who play in blue, we might measure their aggressiveness in a lab. But the IV (wearing red or blue) varied 'naturally'. The experiment makes use of a variable that is naturally changing.

Quasi-experiments The term 'quasi' means 'almost', so 'almost experiments'. Sometimes the thing being varied cannot change, such as gender (we compare boys and girls) or age (we compare younger and older people). So the study isn't quite an experiment because the independent variable isn't really a *variable*.

Research skills

For learning aims C and D you must carry out a *pilot study*, so it is important to consider the skills needed.

Personal skills

To conduct your pilot study you need to be able to work autonomously, i.e. on your own and without someone else's direction. You need to be well-organised and work out a timetable for what needs to be achieved and when. A good researcher will be non-judgemental and unbiased (see *researcher bias* on the previous spread). Finally it is important to behave in a respectful and ethical manner with all participants, which includes discretion and confidentiality (what goes on in the study stays in the study).

Professional skills

Academic research skills and reading techniques are important (for reading past research so you can decide on your aims and procedures). The ability to criticise and analyse will also be important to understand previous research.

When designing the study, health and safety measures and data protection are important. These will also be important in conducting the research, as will be note-taking and record-making to record findings.

A few other methods

Correlational research Studies looking at the degree to which two co-variables are related. For example, if we want to investigate whether there was a relationship between people's self-rating of happiness and their score on an intelligence test.

Case studies A detailed study of one case – one person, one group of people (such as a family or a football team or a school) or an event. This may involve interviewing the individual(s), testing them, observing them, even doing an experiment.

Content analysis An observational study in which behaviour is observed indirectly in written or verbal material such as books or TV programmes. Categories are identified and then instances in each category can be counted. For example, a researcher might analyse the roles women play in TV ads and produce a list of roles (mother, executive, etc.). Then the researcher watches 100 ads, counting the instances.

Desk-based research, primary and secondary research Some studies use data collected by someone else, for example using ONS *statistics* to study the relationship between crime and population density. This is called *secondary research* because the researcher is using someone else's data. It is also called *desk-based research* because the researcher is usually sitting at a desk (!) analysing data and is not required to get out and about collecting it from a lab or the field. Primary research is when the researcher does the messy and time-consuming business of collecting data.

Pilot study This applies to all methods. It is what a researcher does before conducting a full-scale study. The planned procedures are tested on a small group of representative participants. It is vital to do this before spending time and money on a large project.

GET ACTIVE Mr Shambolic

The Department for Transport employs a traffic psychologist, Mr. Shambolic, to investigate driver behaviour. Unfortunately it turns out that Mr Shambolic is…well, pretty shambolic at his job. In fact, he's completely useless as a researcher. He doesn't have the right skills, so the research he does is poor.

Think about the skills a good researcher needs – they are outlined on this spread. Now write a description of Mr Shambolic and all the things he does wrong in his research.

Assessment practice

At the end of learning aim A you must write a report (see pages 99 and 116). This report must be related to a scenario or context such as the one below:

> You now need to think more carefully about how you could carry out the MIST handover project introduced on page 99. Your objective is to find out if MIST improves paramedic handover in A&E departments.
>
> Imagine that your outcome measure (i.e. your measure of effectiveness) is the amount of accurate information that is passed from paramedics to A&E medical staff.

A1.3 Learning aim A1 – Task 3

The third part of your report for learning aim A will be concerned with detailing the way research is organised, a topic covered on this spread and the next five spreads.

For this spread think about your task in relation to the types of research process outlined on this spread.

For each type of research process:

1. Briefly **explain** how you would use it to carry out the project. (A.P1)
   Make sure you also **explain** the relevant key terms. (A.P2)
2. **Assess** the value of using it for this project. (A.M1)
3. **Evaluate** it, in the context of this project, in terms of its strengths and weaknesses. (A.D1)

Finally, choose **one** research process and:

4. **Explain** how you would carry out a pilot study for this project. (A.P1/A.P2)

An issue to consider

Can all research skills be learned? Which ones would be more difficult to learn how to do and why?

Specification content

A1 Purpose and value of research in applied psychology.

- Types of research process, to include a pilot study or an experiment, laboratory and field experiments, natural and quasi-experiments, correlational research, desk-based research, primary and secondary research, self-report techniques, e.g. questionnaires, interviews, case studies, content analysis.
- Professional and personal skills required in order to carry out a pilot research study:
  - Personal skills, to include possessing an enquiring mind, working autonomously, possessing good time-management and organisational skills, using a non-judgemental approach, discretion, confidentiality.
  - Professional skills, to include critical and analytical skills, note-taking, record making, academic research skills, promoting and maintaining health and safety, data protection, reading techniques, e.g. skimming, scanning.

Learning aim A2: Key terms used in research
Starting research

What would you like to know?
- Does eating cheese before you go to bed give you nightmares?
- Who will win the FA cup this year?
- What is the best method for revising?
- Can I jump over a fence?
- What kind of advertising is most effective?
- How do patients rate the treatment they received?
- Does expensive chocolate taste better than cheap chocolate?

As you can see some questions don't really have answers, or at least don't have an objective answer that can be identified without a crystal ball.

Science is interested in questions that potentially have an objective answer – ones where we can work out a method to test a possible answer.

We can simply ask people the questions above – but the answers are not likely to be objective. In some cases we can observe people going about their normal routines. But the most likely route to obtaining a scientific answer is to do some kind of experiment.

In the case of the first question about cheese, we might give some people a fixed amount of cheese before they go to sleep and compare their night-time reports with people who don't eat cheese.

In the case of revising, we could ask groups of people to use different memory methods and compare their recall.

In the case of chocolate we could ... read about our study on the right.

Specification terms
Confounding variable A special class of extraneous variable because it changes systematically with the independent variable (IV). This means that we cannot be sure that any change in the dependent variable was due to the IV. In fact the confounding variable is acting as another IV.

Dependent variable (DV) Measured by the experimenter to assess the effects of the independent variable(s).

Extraneous variable Any variable in an experiment apart from the IV and DV.

Independent variable (IV) A factor that is directly manipulated by the experimenter in order to observe the effect of different conditions on the dependent variable(s).

Operationalisation Defining variables so that they can easily be tested.

Which chocolate is best?
We want to know whether expensive chocolate is worth it – in other words, does it really taste better? We have two ways to try to answer this using an *experiment*.

Method 1. Give one group of people expensive chocolate to taste and one group inexpensive chocolate. Ask all of the people a question (they are actually now our *participants* because they are taking part in the experiment). The question might be, 'On a scale of 1 to 10 how would you rate this chocolate, where 10 is very delicious and 1 is disgusting?'. (This is called an *independent groups* design because there are two separate groups of participants.)

Method 2. Or, ask one group of participants to taste the expensive chocolate and then taste the inexpensive one, and rate each chocolate. (This is called a *repeated measures* design because one person repeats the task).

Identifying some problems
We hope you can see that there are problems with each approach. For example:
- If we used method 1, participants have different tastes in chocolate so the ratings from two groups of participants might not be comparable.
- If we used method 2, participants might always think the first chocolate they eat tastes better than the second chocolate, just because it came first.

These are factors that are getting in the way of our *objective* study. They are called *confounding variables* – because they confound or confuse the study.

Dealing with these confounding variables
We hope you might have some ideas how to cope with the problems. For example, we might deal with bullet 2 by separating the participants into two groups. One group eats chocolate A first and B second, and the other group eats B first and then A.

Or we might give each person eight bits of chocolate, four are chocolate A and four are chocolate B, and hand these out in a mixed-up order, e.g. ABBABAAB. Each time the participant rates the taste and then we can add up the ratings for A and for B, and compare them. In this way there are no effects from order.

Research design
This discussion is all about designing a research study. It is a process which takes a long time – and shortly you are going to have to do this for yourself when you design your *pilot study*. This spread and the spreads that follow are getting you ready to do that ... so practise, practise, practise.

GET ACTIVE Another experiment
Do our beliefs have a profound effect on behaviour? For example, some footballers believe they have to wear lucky socks to ensure they do well in a game, or some students have a lucky charm to take with them into exams. Or some people believe that caffeine in coffee keeps them awake.

But is it simply the belief that is important? Not the socks, lucky charm or caffeine?

1. *How could we test the power of beliefs? Describe what you intend to do as clearly as possible, as if you were writing instructions for someone to follow when cooking a meal. Make sure you carefully operationalise your independent and dependent variables for your proposed study.*

2. *Identify any confounding variables that should be controlled.*

Meet Ivy Deevy.
Many students find it difficult to remember which is the IV and which is the DV.
The name that comes first (Ivy) is the IV which leads to a change in the DV (Deevy).

Which revising method is best?

In our discussion on the facing page we introduced one important term – *confounding variable*.

There are other key terms to learn, but before we introduce them consider this question from the introduction panel on the facing page:

What is the best method for revising?

Think about how you might test this.

_____

One way might be to identify two methods, for example:

Method 1. Spend 15 minutes making notes from your book and rereading the notes.

Method 2. Spend 5 minutes making notes from your book, then put the notes and book to one side and write down everything you can remember. Look at your notes to remind yourself what you forgot, and test yourself again.

One group of participants will do method 1 and one group will do method 2.

Then ... wait for a day ... and finally give everyone a test on the material in the book and see which group remembers the most.

The variables

The word *variables* refers to things that will vary in your experiment, i.e. things that change or become different.

There are two key variables – *independent* (IV) and *dependent* (DV). The experimenter controls the IV and records the effect on the DV.

Here are examples:

	Independent variable (IV)	Dependent variable (DV)
Chocolate	Type of chocolate (A or B)	Rating given for each taste.
Revising	Method of revising (1 or 2)	Score on test at the end.

Operationalisation

A key feature of any variable is *operationalisation* – spelling out exactly what is involved so we can do it. So, in the revising example above we need to operationalise what we mean by 'a test' – it might be a 20-item test with single-word answers.

Extraneous and confounding variables

On the facing page we mentioned confounding variables. Let's explain this a little bit more... At any time there are loads of things that are varying (variables) such as the time of day, the warmth of the room, how much sleep each participant has had and so on. These are all extra variables (extraneous) because they are beyond our key variables – the IV and DV.

Most *extraneous variables* will have no effect on the DV. For example, it shouldn't really matter if it is a spring or summer day when we test the DV (participants' memory) but it might matter if we test all method 1 participants in the morning and all method 2 participants in the evening because many people are more alert in the morning. In this case, time of day is a confounding variable that could affect the DV and must be controlled.

Assessment practice

At the end of learning aim A you must write a report (see pages 99 and 116). This report must be related to a scenario or context such as the one below:

Think again about the stress-at-work project from page 101.

As part of this project, you decide to measure the effectiveness of the stress management programme you devised. You will do this by conducting an experiment.

This may involve comparing two groups of employees – but which groups? And how will you measure effectiveness?

A2.4 Learning aim A2 – Task 4

The next part of your report for learning aim A will be concerned with detailing the way research is organised, which is covered on the previous spread, this spread and the next four spreads.

This activity will help you practise the skills required to write the report in response to your scenario/context.

1. **Explain** examples of extraneous and confounding variables that might be an issue in your experiment. (A.P2)
2. **Explain** the operationalised independent and dependent variables for your experiment. (A.P2)
3. **Assess** whether your choices are the best variables to use in your experiment. [HINT: are there better alternatives?] (A.M1)
4. **Evaluate** your proposed experiment in terms of any confounding and/or extraneous variables that could not be controlled. (A.D1)

An issue to consider

Can you think of your own questions which psychologists might try to answer?

Specification content

A2 Key terms used in research

Meanings and use of research terminology

- Variables and their operationalisation in research, to include independent, dependent, confounding, extraneous.

Learning aim A2: Key terms used in research
Hypotheses and a literature review

That's funny

Here's a question – what makes you smile? Do people smile because they feel happy or do they feel happy because they smiled? Which is cause and which is effect?

A group of psychologists (Strack *et al* 1988) designed a study to test this. If you just tell someone to smile then you have alerted them to what you are about to measure – so Strack *et al* asked participants to put a pencil in their mouth sideways. This made their face muscles tense up as if they were smiling. While still holding the pencil like this, participants were asked to rate a set of cartoons. This was a way of assessing their happiness levels.

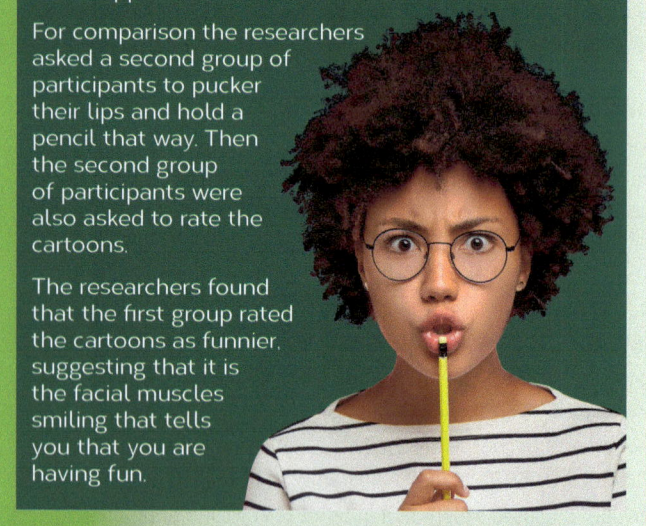

For comparison the researchers asked a second group of participants to pucker their lips and hold a pencil that way. Then the second group of participants were also asked to rate the cartoons.

The researchers found that the first group rated the cartoons as funnier, suggesting that it is the facial muscles smiling that tells you that you are having fun.

Specification terms

Alternative hypothesis The hypothesis in a study is sometimes called the alternative hypothesis because it is the alternative to the null hypothesis. In any study we have an alternative and a null hypothesis.

Directional and non-directional hypothesis A directional hypothesis states the direction of the hypothesis (!) – whether one thing is more than another, for example saying that one group will do better than another group on a task. A non-directional hypothesis just states there is a difference but not the direction of the difference.

Hypothesis A statement of what a researcher believes to be true. In order to test such a statement, it must be clearly operationalised.

Literature review A systematic consideration of what other people have written or said about your chosen research topic. The word 'literature' refers to books, magazines, websites, TV programmes, etc.

Null hypothesis A statement of no difference or no relationship.

Writing a hypothesis

On the previous spread we looked at research questions, such as 'Does expensive chocolate taste better than cheap chocolate?' and 'What is the best method for revising?'.

Research questions are turned into aims, such as 'To investigate whether expensive chocolate tastes better than cheap chocolate'.

And then these aims are formalised as a *hypothesis*. A hypothesis is a statement, not a question. For an *experiment* this statement must contain the *independent variable* (IV) and *dependent variable* (DV) in an *operationalised* form.

Let's consider the experiment on the left.

- The IV is smile or not smile, which has been operationalised so we can measure it – pencil clenched horizontally in mouth or pencil sticking out of mouth.
- The DV is happiness, which has been operationalised as – rating cartoons as funny on a scale of 1 to 5.

We can then express the relationship between the IV and DV:

> Participants who are smiling (pencil clenched horizontally in mouth) rate cartoons as funnier than participants who are not smiling (pencil sticking out).

Other kinds of hypothesis

The hypothesis above is called an *alternative directional hypothesis*.

It is 'alternative' because it is an alternative to the *null hypothesis*. The null hypothesis states that there is no difference between the two conditions whereas the alternative is to state there is a difference. In our case the null hypothesis would be:

> There is no difference in the ratings for funniness given by participants who are smiling (pencil clenched horizontally in mouth) compared to participants who are not smiling (pencil sticking out).

The original hypothesis is *directional* because it states the expected direction of the findings – that one group rates the cartoons as *more* funny. Alternatively we can state the hypothesis with no direction (*non-directional*):

> Participants who are smiling (pencil clenched horizontally in mouth) rate cartoons differently from participants who are not smiling (pencil sticking out).

In a study using a *correlational analysis* there are two variables but the variables aren't IV/DVs so a hypothesis expresses the relationship (not the difference) between the variables. We will look at correlational analysis on page 128.

Studies without hypotheses

Studies that are just *observation* or just *self-report* don't have IVs and DVs and may not have a hypothesis. They may simply have a research question and possibly a set of aims.

Zero, zilch, zip, zippo, goose egg, nought, no, nobody, nothing, not anything, nix, nil ... NULL.

The literature review

On the facing page we started with a research question which led to an aim and then to a hypothesis.

However, researchers usually have another stage somewhere in the middle, which involves reading about what other researchers have discovered.

What is *the literature*?

The term *literature* means 'written work'. In the context of conducting research, *literature* refers to reports written by scientists about their research. An important part of the *scientific process* is that, once a study is completed, researchers publish their study.

Reporting a research study

The academic conventions for reporting research include:

- **Literature review** of previous studies on a similar topic so you know the background and the reason for the current study.
- **Aims** of the current study and the hypothesis.
- **Procedures** described in detail. It is very important that these are described exactly so that anyone else can follow the same steps to check the findings of this study (called *replication*). This section includes details of who the participants were (called the *sample*) and where the study was conducted and how ethical issues were dealt with.
- **Findings** using graphs and other methods of data analysis.
- **Discussion** of what the findings mean. This is likely to include (1) an interpretation of the findings in relation to previous research, (2) a consideration of possible weaknesses in the methods that were used and (3) some thoughts about the implications of the study.
- **Referencing and bibliographies** list specific sources (articles, books, websites, personal communication) and any materials used.

Doing a literature review

The purpose of the literature review is to put together the current knowledge about your selected topic. It also aims to establish the strengths and weaknesses of this previous research.

Start by making notes (e.g. from your textbook, other books, websites) about theories, concepts and studies that are relevant to your research topic. Don't worry about order or relevance but do keep a note of the source.

Put the notes to one side and then construct a logical plan from memory. A literature review is like a funnel – start 'wide' with the general area and narrow down to research that is specifically related to your research question.

At this stage you should just have a list of paragraphs. Look back at your notes and see if you want to add key topics.

Finally, write each paragraph.

GET ACTIVE DIY

Time to try it yourself. Select one of the biological key concepts from Unit 1. Find some studies related to this concept. You can do this by typing some key words into a search engine (e.g. Google). Use Wikipedia as a starting point to understand the topic but never cite Wikipedia as a source – follow the links to other research.

- Just make a pile of notes in no particular order.
- Give yourself a day for the information to settle in your head and then write a list of the key points to cover.
- Finally put these key points in a sensible order, something like:
  - Paragraph 1 – a description of the general concept/theory.
  - Paragraph 2 – describe study 1, include a key strength or weakness.
  - Paragraph 3 – select another study that follows on from the first study.
- And so on. Finish with the aims of your research.

This picture may match your current mood! Understanding research processes takes time. At the beginning you are at the centre of this vortex. But gradually, each time you look at another study or another explanation of an aspect of research, it will become a little clearer. Keep going and you will emerge victorious!

Assessment practice

At the end of learning aim A you must write a report (see pages 99 and 116). This report must be related to a scenario or context:

> Think again about the stress-at-work project which we began on page 101.
> One of the general aims of the project is to assess the effectiveness of a stress management programme for employees. To research this using an experiment, you decide to start with a hypothesis. Also, part of your brief is to write a report on the project for the company's management team.

A2.5 Learning aim A2 – Task 5

The next part of your report for learning aim A will be concerned with detailing the way research is organised, which is covered on the previous two spreads, this spread and the next three spreads.

1. **Explain** what you would include in a literature review for your project report. [Don't write the literature review itself.] (A.P1 and A.P2)
2. **Explain** what your alternative, null and directional hypotheses would be. In doing so you might want to define these research methods terms. (A.P2)
3. **Assess** how your literature review could be used to inform the company's policy regarding stress at work. (A.M1)
4. **Evaluate** the importance of formulating hypotheses and writing a literature review for this project. (A.D1)

An issue to consider

Why is it important for a researcher to read about other studies before developing their own research?

Specification content

A2 Key terms used in research

Meanings and use of research terminology

- Hypotheses, to include directional, non-directional, alternative, null.
- Sources of data and literature, to include primary and secondary sources.

A3 Research process

- Research design: procedures.
- Literature reviews, e.g. internet and library searches, journals, media, statistical information.
- Sources of literature, e.g. primary and secondary, evaluating validity and reliability of literature.
- Academic conventions of reporting research to include presentation conventions, referencing and bibliographies.

Learning aim A2: Key terms used in research
Sampling techniques

Select the numbers 1, 2, 3, 4, 5, 6

Really. In a random draw these 6 numbers are just as likely as any other numbers.

Randomness is not what you may think it is. It means every item has an equal chance of being selected. It is not simply a haphazard selection.

Also, if you replace numbers each time you draw then 1, 1, 1, 1, 1, 1 is just as likely as any other combination.

Try it, on a smaller scale. Put ten slips of paper in a hat, numbered 1–10. Make 20 draws, recording the number and replacing the slip in the hat each time. What do you notice about the numbers you have drawn?

Specification terms

Opportunity sampling A sample of participants produced by selecting people who are most easily available at the time of the study.

Random sampling A sample of participants produced using a random technique so that every member of the target population has an equal chance of being selected.

Sampling techniques A method to obtain a small number of people to represent a target population.

Snowballing Current participants recruit further participants from among people they know.

Stratified sampling Participants are selected from different strata (subgroups) in the target population in proportion to the strata's frequency in that population.

Volunteer sampling A sample of participants produced by asking for people willing to take part.

Participants are drawn from a **target population** (the group of people the researcher is interested in).

This is a **sample** of the target population.

Sampling

When psychologists conduct research they want to be able to draw conclusions about *people* in general – but they can't test everyone in the world or even everyone in their own town. Therefore, psychologists select a small group of participants – called a *sample*. This is drawn from a wider *target population* such as the people in your college or adolescents in your town. The aim is to be able to generalise the findings from the sample to all people. In other words if the participants in the research sample all prefer the expensive chocolate to the cheaper chocolate (experiment on page 104) we assume that is true of all people or at least all people in the target population.

There are five sampling methods that are commonly used.

Opportunity sampling

This is the most frequently used method in psychological research. The sample of participants is obtained by selecting people who are most easily available at the time of the study.

How? Ask people who are walking past you in the street or ask people in your common room at school, i.e. select those who are available.

Volunteer sampling

Probably the next most common method is to ask for volunteers willing to take part. And this is a good way to get a specialised group of participants.

How? If you wanted to study the behaviour of medical students it would make sense to put an ad on the noticeboard of a medical school rather than standing around in a shopping centre.

Random sampling

Every member of the target population has an equal chance of being selected whereas in an opportunity sample, for example, only those who are around at the time have the chance to be selected.

How? Give everyone in the target population a number, put the numbers in a hat and draw out the required number of participants, or use a random number generator on a smartphone.

Stratified sampling

This method is commonly used in polls, for example to find out how people are likely to vote. It is also used in market research, for example to find out what television programmes people watch. For such research it is important to include a good range of different types of people – different ages, different income levels, different towns etc. Therefore, researchers select participants from different subgroups (strata) in the target population and do this in proportion to the subgroup's frequency in that population.

How? Subgroups, such as age groups, are identified and the number in each subgroup in the target population is identified. This is represented as a percentage total of the whole population. For example, 30% of the target population might be 20–29 years old. So, 30% of participants in the study should be in that age group.

The researcher then uses random selection to identify the right number of participants in the age range 20–29 years.

Snowballing

In some research the participants are an unusual group, for example when investigating the effects of diabetes or the experience of being an older mother. One way to get a specific group of participants is by advertising (a volunteer sample), another way is to use *snowballing*.

How? The researcher identifies one participant and then asks that participant to suggest other suitable participants. Thus the sample group appears to grow like a snowball.

Evaluation

Opportunity sampling
+ This is the most convenient technique because it takes little preparation. You just use the first participants you can find. This means it takes less time to locate your sample than if using one of the other techniques.
− However, it is inevitably biased because the sample is drawn from a small part of the target population and therefore is not likely to be representative. For example, shoppers in a city centre on a Monday morning do not represent all people as they are largely not people at work.

Volunteer sampling
+ This provides a good way to find *willing* participants. Researchers need committed participants for time-consuming studies and participants are less likely to drop out because they volunteered.
− However, volunteer participants are probably more willing to be helpful to the researcher. This may mean they try to guess the aims of the study so they can behave in the way the researcher is hoping for. This reduces the meaningfulness of the findings because the behaviour is unlikely to reflect what they really do/think.

Random sampling
+ The main strength is that the sample is unbiased, because all members of the target population have an equal chance of selection.
− However, it takes more time and effort than other techniques because you need to obtain a list of all the members of your target population, then identify the sample and then contact the people identified and ask if they will take part.

Stratified sampling
+ This is the most representative of all the sampling techniques because all subgroups are represented and these subgroups are represented in proportion to the numbers in the target population. This increases control over possible *extraneous variables*.
− However, this method involves a very lengthy process. This means that it is not a technique that is used much in psychological research.

Snowballing
+ This method enables a researcher to locate groups of people who are difficult to access, such as people who go bowling or drug-users (once you have one person you can then ask them to recommend a friend).
− The sample is not likely to be a good cross-section of the population because it is friends of friends.

Note that ... all of the methods end up being volunteer samples – in the end any participant may decline to take part. Therefore, the final sample will share the disadvantage of a volunteer sample.

How many participants should be in a sample?
Questionnaires are relatively easy to distribute by post or online to hundreds if not thousands of people (your sample).

Experiments can use small samples but larger samples are more representative, have less risk of bias and are more likely to identify minor patterns in findings. However, as few as 25 sets of data is acceptable (Coolican 1996).

GET ACTIVE Fun with smarties

Your target population is 300 smarties (or something less edible, such as coloured drawing pins). Count how many of each colour there are in the target population and work out the percentage for each colour.

Try out the various sampling methods with your smarties, selecting a sample of 20 'participants'. Keep a record of each sample.

Do any of the samples you produce offer a true representation of the characteristics of the target population?

(You determine this by comparing, for example, the percentage of yellow smarties in your sample with the percentage in the target population.)

Assessment practice

At the end of learning aim A you must write a report (see pages 99 and 116). This report must be related to a scenario or context such as the one below:

Whichever research process or method you use to assess the effectiveness of MIST (see page 99), an important stage is the selection of your participants. But before you can do this you need to decide what your target population is.

An experiment would compare the accuracy of handover information in two groups – paramedics who use MIST and paramedics who do not. Now you can consider which method is the most appropriate one to use to select a sample.

A2.6 Learning aim A2 – Task 6

The next part of your report for learning aim A will be concerned with detailing the way research is organised, which is covered on the previous three spreads, this spread and the next two spreads.

There are five sampling methods described on this spread. For each one:
1. **Explain** how you would use it to select a sample of paramedics for the project. Make sure your explanations are feasible practically. (A.P1)
2. **Select** the most appropriate method and **assess** the importance of using this method. (A.M1)
3. **Evaluate** the use of the method to select a sample of paramedics. (A.D1)

You can see the assessment criteria and explanation of command terms on pages 116 and 133.

An issue to consider
Can you think of an example of sampling in your everyday life? What sampling method did you use? (Be careful here – it is unlikely to be truly random unless you put all the possibilities in a hat and selected the sample from that).

Specification content
A2 Key terms used in research
Meanings and use of research terminology
- Sampling techniques used to select participants, to include stratified, random, opportunity, volunteer, snowballing.

A3 Research process
- Research design, to include participants, sample size, sampling methods.

B Plan research to investigate psychological questions
- Whether findings can be considered representative of a population.

Learning aim A2: Key terms used in research
Reliability and validity

Meet Mr Reliability and Mr Validity

Mr Reliability is consistent. He's never late. He's in the same mood every time you meet him. He even wears the same suit. Mr Reliability doesn't change.

Mr Validity always tells the truth. He is genuine and honest. People say of Mr Validity 'what you see is what you get' and 'he is exactly what it says on the tin'. Mr Validity never lies.

When planning research, Mr or Ms Psychologist need to make friends with Mr Reliability and Mr Validity.

Reliability

If you measure something, like using a tape measure to record someone's height, you would expect that tape measure to give you the same result tomorrow. Unless, of course the person has grown.

Measuring instruments must give the same result each time otherwise we can't rely on them. If you measure the length of a table or someone's personality, and the measurement is different from the previous time – then we assume the table or person has changed. We rely on the measurement tool to be consistent.

Reliability = consistency.

External reliability

External reliability concerns whether a measure of something varies from one time to another, i.e. is consistent or not consistent over time. If the same *questionnaire* is given to the same person on two occasions the result should be the same. This is called *test-retest reliability* (for obvious reasons).

We use this measure to check the external reliability of a questionnaire. The interval between test and retest must be long enough so that the person can't remember their previous answers but not too long because their thoughts or feelings may have changed and then we would expect their scores/answers to be different.

Inter-observer reliability

In a study where people are being observed, an observer may, for example, count how many times different participants speak. It is easy to make mistakes when counting such things in real time because so much is happening. Therefore, a good system to check on this is to use two or even three observers.

At the end of the observations a comparison is made on the totals recorded by each observer. This is a way of establishing *inter-observer reliability* – how consistent the observers are.

Internal reliability

Internal reliability concerns whether a test or questionnaire is consistent within itself, for example, checking the contents of a psychological test, such as a test to measure your reading ability or intelligence.

We would expect that all items on the test are equally related to the skill/characteristic being tested (reading or intelligence). To check this, *split-half reliability* can be calculated by comparing the scores from two halves of a test. This can be done by randomly selecting half the test items and placing them on form A and placing the other items on form B.

Therefore, you end up with two forms of the same test. Each form should yield very similar scores if the items on the test are consistent, i.e. reliable.

Reliability versus validity

Trust us, it's easy to get the two concepts confused. This example may help you.

It is possible that the circumference of your head could be used as a measure of your intelligence. This would be a reliable measure in the case of an adult (whose head has stopped growing) but not in the case of a child.

However, it is not a valid measure of intelligence as research has shown that brain size is not related to intelligence.

Specification terms

External reliability The extent to which one measure of something (e.g. a person's height or their personality) is consistent over time.

Inter-observer reliability The extent to which there is agreement between two or more observers. This is measured by comparing (correlating) the observations of the observers.

Internal reliability The extent to which something is consistent within itself. For example, all the questions on a personality test should be measuring the same thing.

Reliability Consistency of a measuring tool, including a psychological test.

Specification terms

Concurrent validity The trueness of a psychological test is established by comparing it with an existing, valid psychological test. The new test should produce the same score.

Ecological validity The extent to which a research finding can be applied beyond the research setting. Often research settings are highly controlled and contrived situations and people may not behave in the same way in their everyday lives.

Face validity The extent to which the items on a psychological test look like what the test is claiming to measure.

Temporal validity The extent to which a research finding can be applied to other time periods.

Validity Refers to the 'trueness' or 'legitimacy' of the data collected.

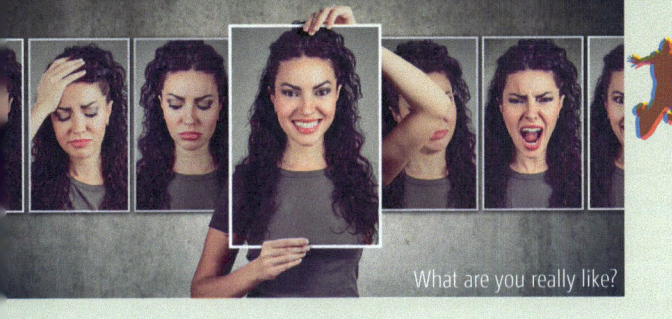

Validity

Validity is probably the most important concept in your psychology course. What psychologists do must represent what is true. If the findings of a research study are not valid then we will act on false information about the world. There are many different kinds of validity but we will look at just four of them.

Ecological validity

In Unit 1 you looked at the study by Ingrid Möller and Barbara Krahé (see page 19) which showed that students who played violent video games interpreted a push as deliberate. The big question is whether people are actually affected in this way in everyday life?

In this study participants didn't watch someone being pushed, they simply read a scenario. Seeing someone being pushed is very different from reading about it. The lack of emotional involvement reduces the ecological validity of this study. *Ecological validity* refers to the extent to which a study represents the world we live in (our surroundings or ecology).

Temporal validity

In Unit 1 you looked at the study on *conformity* by Solomon Asch (see page 24). One of the criticisms that has been made of this study is the date. It was carried out in 1951. Society and *social norms* were different then and such norms are important in determining how conformist people are.

This means that the study may no longer represent how people behave today. The study lacks *temporal validity* – validity over time.

Concurrent validity

Validity is not just important when thinking about research studies. A very important area for psychologists is developing and using psychological tests – tests that reveal information about what people can do. There are intelligence tests, personality tests (see 'Get active' at the top right), tests of mathematical or reading ability, tests of aggression and tests to assess mental health issues.

Psychological tests produce a score and this score may be used to help an employer decide whether you are right for the job or help a clinician decide if you have a serious psychological disorder and need treatment.

One method used to assess the validity of such a test is to compare performance on a new test with a previously validated one on the same topic. To do this participants are given both tests at the same time and then their scores are compared. If the new test produces a similar outcome as the older one then this demonstrates the *concurrent validity* of the new measure. 'Concurrent' means 'doing something at the same time'.

Face validity

Face validity concerns the issue of whether a psychological test looks like it is measuring what the researcher intended to measure. For example, whether the questions are obviously related to the topic. Face validity only requires intuitive measurement.

GET ACTIVE Test your personality

Tests of personality are used, for example, by employers to see if an individual's personality matches job requirements.

A personality test score must be both valid and reliable, i.e. it must accurately reflect the individual and must stay the same over time.

One of the most popular approaches to personality suggests that our personality is a combination of five key traits, called the Big Five Factors. The letters O C E A N stand for:
- Openness to experience, e.g. curious versus cautious.
- Conscientiousness, e.g. organised versus careless.
- Extraversion, e.g. outgoing versus reserved.
- Agreeableness, e.g. friendly versus challenging/detached.
- Neuroticism, e.g. sensitive and nervous versus confident.

1. Write a description of yourself in terms of these five factors.
2. Take a 15-minute test at tinyurl.com/pvnowe4
3. Compare the scores on the test with your description. How valid is the test?
4. Keep a record of your score. In a few weeks take the test again and compare the scores. How reliable is the test?

Assessment practice

At the end of learning aim A you must write a report (see pages 99 and 116). This report must be related to a scenario or context such as the one below:

> To assess the effectiveness of a stress management programme, you need a way to measure employees' stress levels. A common way to do this is to ask employees directly how they feel, think and behave.
>
> So as part of the stress-at-work project (see page 101) you devise a questionnaire to measure employees' experiences of stress. This allows you to compare stress levels before and after the stress management programme or between people who take the programme and those who don't.

A2.7 Learning aim A2 – Task 7

The next part of your report for learning aim A will be concerned with detailing the way research is organised, which is covered on the previous four spreads, this spread and the next spread.

1. **Explain** what is mean by the terms 'reliability' and 'validity'. (A.P2)
2. For each type of reliability, **explain** how you would use it to establish the reliability of your stress questionnaire. (A.P1)
3. **Explain** how you would use concurrent validity to establish the validity of your stress questionnaire. (A.P1)
4. **Assess** how issues of reliability and validity affect the ability of the project to inform company policy on stress at work. (A.M1)
5. **Evaluate** your stress questionnaire in terms of each type of validity. [HINT: would your questionnaire be valid according to each type of validity?] (A.D1)

An issue to consider

Which is correct?
- A measure that is not reliable can be valid.
- A measure that is valid may be unreliable.

Specification content

A2 Key terms used in research
- Reliability and validity, to include internal, external, inter-observer reliability, face, concurrent, ecological, temporal validity.

Learning aim A3: Research process
Ethical considerations

Patient HM

One of the most famous case studies in the history of psychology was Henry Molaison, known to the world as HM until his death.

At the age of 7, Henry was involved in a bicycle accident. As a result of this, he experienced epileptic seizures for many years until these became so severe that he was referred for surgery at the age of 27. A small part of Henry's brain was removed (the *hippocampus*).

The operation was reasonably successful in controlling the seizures but had a terrible side effect – it destroyed parts of Henry's memory. Henry could remember things from the distant past but he was unable to form new memories.

He could no longer remember new facts, faces or places he had been. He read the same magazines with no memory of having read them before. For many years he thought he was 27 but eventually started to guess his own age because he could see that he was older.

His disability provided psychologists with an amazing opportunity to study memory processes and for the next 50 years of his life his abilities were intensively studied.

- The question is this – was he capable of providing his informed consent?
- Do scientists have the right to investigate anyone without such consent?
- Should we continue to protect his identity and only call him HM?

Specification terms

Confidentiality A participant's right to have personal information protected through anonymity and/or by keeping their information safe.

Ethical codes of conduct A set of principles designed to help professionals behave honestly and with integrity.

Ethical considerations Ideas of what is right and wrong.

Gatekeeper consent Permission is provided by a person who stands between the researcher and a potential participant. The gatekeeper provides expert advice and an extra level of protection.

Informed consent Participants are given comprehensive information concerning the nature and purpose of a study and their role in it, so that they can make a decision about taking part.

Informed consent

Informed consent refers to two things:
1. *Giving consent* – any participant in research should have the opportunity to provide their agreement to take part.
2. *Being informed* – in order to give such consent they need information about what participation will involve, e.g. how much time it will take, the kind of things they will be required to do, that they can stop at any time, etc.

Obtaining permission to conduct research

This is achieved by providing prospective participants with any details of the study that may affect their decision to take part and asking them to sign a document indicating their consent.

While this may sound straightforward there are various problems.

Gatekeeper consent

There are some participants who cannot be expected to fully understand the information provided, such as participants under 16 or people who lack mental capacity.

In the case of such participants a parent or other responsible adult should sign on their behalf, though the individual should also be fully informed and have the right to refuse.

In healthcare research it is especially important to appoint a *gatekeeper* because the research may well be of a sensitive nature, for example research with people who have mental health issues or a physical illness. It may require expert insight to truly understand what will be involved in the study and therefore the gatekeeper can appropriately advise prospective participants and their carers.

Deception

In many research studies there is a problem with revealing the true aims at the start of the study because it may affect a participant's behaviour. Consider the study by Albert Bandura *et al.* (see page 38). If the children in this study had been told that the study was looking at their *imitation* of the adult role model's actions, the children may well have behaved 'unnaturally' and the findings of the study would be meaningless. Even informing the parents of the true aims of the study may have led to changed behaviour in the children.

Right to withdraw For this reason some information may be withheld at the start of a study but participants (and their gatekeepers) should be made aware that any participant has the right to withdraw at any time. This offers a limited amount of protection from deception.

Debriefing A further way to deal with the issue of deception is that all research participants should be *debriefed* at the end of the study. They should be informed of any deception and also offered the opportunity to discuss any feelings they had about the procedures of the study.

Ethical behaviour of researchers

Underlying the informed consent procedure is the assumption that researchers design research responsibly.

Protection from harm This would involve full consideration of both physical and psychological health and wellbeing. Psychological health includes doing nothing that embarrasses or reduces a participant's self-esteem. At the end of a study a participant should be in the same physical and psychological condition as at the outset.

Data protection Any information that is collected by a researcher about participants is owned by the participant. Therefore, that data must be protected, i.e. confidential. There are two ways to do this:

- Anonymity – names should not be recorded but instead participant numbers or initials should be used (see the case of HM top left). The location of the research should also be anonymous, such as the identity of a hospital or school.
- Store data in a way that cannot be accessed by anyone else.

Also the data should not be given to other researchers without the consent of the original participants.

Professional guidance

Professionals monitor the standards of their fellow colleagues – both the skills they practise and their ethical behaviour. Doctors in the UK are guided by the *British Medical Association* (BMA), psychologists by the *British Psychological Society* (BPS), healthcare workers by the *Health and Care Professions Council* (HCPC).

Professional groups have the power to suspend members for unprofessional conduct and may prevent them working as a professional in the future.

Research ethics committee (REC)

A REC is a group of people within a research institution who approve a study before it begins. The group may consist of professional and lay people. The committee looks at all ethical issues and at how the researcher(s) plan to deal with these, weighing up the value of the research against ethical costs. In terms of ethics they are concerned with the dignity, rights and welfare of participants, the safety of researcher(s) and the legitimate interests of other stakeholders.

Human and animal rights

Human rights

We believe that people have certain rights. Some of these rights are protected by law, for example the right to privacy is protected in the UK by the Human Rights Act 1998. The United Nations has also defined what rights we should expect, for example the *United Nations Convention on the Rights of the Child* (UNCRC), which includes Article 12: Every child has the right to express their views, feelings and wishes in all matters affecting them.

Animal rights

What rights do animals have? Tom Regan (1984) argues that there are no circumstances under which animal research is acceptable (an absolutist position). All animals are *subjects of a life* – their life matters to them so they should have moral rights.

The 'animal rights' argument can be challenged by examining the concept of rights – having rights is dependent on having responsibilities in society, i.e. as citizens we all have responsibilities. It can therefore be said that, as animals do not have any responsibilities, they do not have any rights.

It may be better to distinguish between rights and obligations. Obligations are owed by humans to animals (e.g. acting humanely).

Can we conduct valuable research without using animals? British law requires that any new drug (e.g. antidepressants) must be tested on at least two different species of live mammal. If we wish to have these treatments available, we must accept the need for such research.

The current approach is to follow the 3Rs with respect to:

- *Replacement* – where possible animals should be replaced with suitable alternatives.
- *Reduction* – if replacement is not possible, then the number of animals used must be reduced to a minimum.
- *Refinement* – the methods used in breeding, accommodation and care must be refined to reduce pain, suffering, distress or lasting harm.

GET ACTIVE Professionals

Psychologists working in hospitals, offices and schools also have to make ethical decisions. The Canadian Psychological Association (2001) publish some dilemmas:

Example 1: A psychologist in human resources interviews a job applicant who has had mental health problems which are now controlled by medication. But if the applicant stops taking the medication this may interfere with their job.

Example 2: A psychologist in the military is asked to design a programme to demoralise the enemy's troops and civilians. The 'enemy' is a country ruled by an immoral regime.

In each case what should the psychologist do?

Assessment practice

At the end of learning aim A you must write a report (see pages 99 and 116). This report must be related to a scenario or context, such as the one below:

> Clinical psychologists such as Sarah Brothwell (see page 100) often become involved in research. For example, the Eating Disorders Research Group at University College London includes clinical psychologists.
>
> You are part of a research team investigating the causes of anorexia nervosa (AN), an eating disorder where a person has a fear of gaining weight, a distorted body image and refuses to eat. Your team uses a volunteer sampling method (see page 108) to recruit 20 women aged 15 to 21 years. The first stage of the project involves the participants completing several questionnaires about themselves and their eating disorder.

A3.8 Learning aim A3 – Task 8

The next part of your report for learning aim A will be concerned with detailing the way research is organised, covered on the previous five spreads and this spread.

1. **Explain two** ethical issues your team would have to consider in their research into anorexia. (A.P1)
2. **Explain** the meaning of the terms 'ethical code of conduct' and 'human rights'. (A.P2)
3. **Assess** the importance of carrying out research into eating disorders in ethical ways. (A.M1)
4. **Evaluate** the research in terms of the ethical issues involved. [HINT: how you could deal with the ethical issues.] (A.D1)

An issue to consider

Should ethical decisions be based on what is best for all?

Specification content

A3 Research process

- Ethical considerations:
  - Use of ethical codes of conduct, e.g. British Psychological Society (BPS), British Medical Association (BMA), own institution's codes of conduct.
  - Ensuring participants have provided informed consent, to include physical and psychological health and wellbeing, mental capacity, understanding of requirements.
  - Obtaining permission to conduct research, to include gatekeeper consent, consent from adults, parents or carers of participants who lack mental capacity or participants under 18.
  - Data protection, to include confidentiality, using research for stated purpose, storage of data, protecting identity of participants and locations when reporting research.
  - Human and animal rights.
  - Professional approach towards conducting research, e.g. ensuring participants are fully informed, duty of care to report health and safety concerns.

Learning aim A3: Research process

Conducting research

A nation of 'morons'*

What is missing from the picture on the right?

Crisco is a: patent medicine, disinfectant, toothpaste, food product?

The number of a Kaffir's legs is: 2, 4, 6, 8?

These were some of the questions on the earliest intelligence tests. If you don't know the answers (a rivet, food product, 2) it tells you something about early psychology. At the beginning of the 20th century psychologists wanted to become respected as scientists and saw an opportunity to do this by developing useful psychological tests. So they devised intelligence tests and piloted them on First World War US army recruits (1.75 million of them).

However, the whole business was a fiasco. First of all, as you can see from the questions above, they struggled to set questions that were culture-free. The questions were based on knowledge that only some people had and therefore were testing knowledge and not intelligence.

In addition, many of the recruits were illiterate. The intention was to test them using pictures but this didn't happen. The outcome was that a vast number of those tested were graded as 'morons'. *The term 'moron' in the title of the article has come to mean 'stupid' but originally was an IQ test classification for someone with a score of 51–70, where 100 points is average.*

The test results were eventually used to inform American immigration law. In the 1920s US immigration authorities started to set quotas for people from certain countries. The Army IQ tests wrongly showed that people from southern, central and eastern Europe were less intelligent than others, and the data was used to support a restriction on immigrants from these areas. It is estimated that up to six million immigrants were prevented from entering the US. This was a disaster for those Jews trying to flee the Holocaust.

Science can have far-reaching social effects.

Source: Gould (1982)

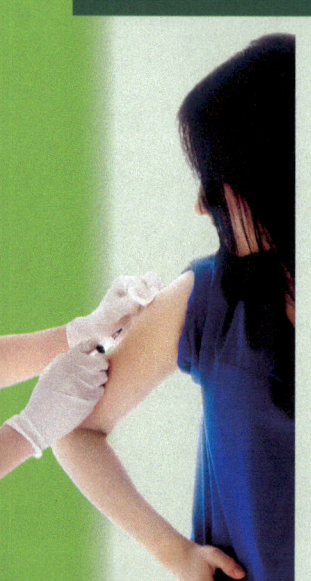

The placebo effect

A 'placebo' pill is one that has no active ingredient (a 'dummy' pill or drug) but giving a person such a pill makes them think they are receiving treatment. Research shows that the belief alone can lead to improvement. In fact research has also shown that if you give a person two placebo pills the effect is even stronger! And if you tell people it's a placebo, it still has benefits.

A placebo doesn't have to be a pill. Some people suggest that massage, for example, may have beneficial effects simply because a person believes it will.

The impact of research

Being a scientist comes with responsibilities. You can't simply produce an IQ test or conduct a study without bearing responsibility for the outcomes.

Socially sensitive research

All psychological research is socially sensitive because it has a direct effect on individual people or on society in general, and if it doesn't, then what's the point? This means that researchers need to think in advance, when planning a study, what the possible effects of their research may be.

One example of the effects of research is discussed on the left. Sloppy science on intelligence led to erroneous conclusions which were used to justify US immigration *policy*.

Research on mental health

Researchers look at explanations for psychological disorders and also assess treatments. Both of these are socially sensitive in the implications for informing *practice* and provision. Let's look at clinical depression, where a person has been experiencing a low mood for more than two weeks and also has other symptoms such as changes in sleep patterns and eating habits (these are some of the criteria used by clinicians to diagnose depression).

In other words we are not talking about 'everyday' depression. Broadly speaking, psychologists have two key explanations for depression – one is biological and one is cognitive. And both explanations lead to different treatments.

A biological approach Research suggests that there may be a *genetic* cause for clinical depression so that in some people levels of the *neurotransmitter serotonin* are abnormally low.

This has clear implications for treatment – drugs that can increase levels of serotonin should be used (antidepressants such as Prozac). There has been extensive research on the effectiveness of such drugs and the jury is still out.

One line of argument is that such research is funded by stakeholders (drug companies) who don't publish negative findings and this leads to an erroneous picture of how effective the drugs actually are.

A second line of argument relates to the placebo effect (see bottom left). However, a study by Andrea Cipriani *et al.* (2018) looked at over 500 trials from both published and unpublished studies. Antidepressants were found to be more effective than placebos. The research continues...

A cognitive approach An alternative suggestion is based on the fact that people have different thinking styles. Some people see the glass as half full whereas others see it as half empty. Cognitive psychologists such as Aaron Beck (1967) have suggested that depression arises when people hold a persistent negative world view as well as having a negative view of themselves and of the future.

The implication for treatment is that therapy needs to deal with the way the person thinks about the world – using an antidepressant pill only temporarily addresses the underlying problem.

What can we conclude?

The research on mental health treatments is sensitive because it affects the decisions made by people with depression, and the professionals looking after them. Believing that the disorder is biological may have a profound effect on the way an individual views themselves and in some cases might even affect a decision to have children who may inherit the disorder.

Other socially sensitive research is even more difficult, for example research on homosexuality. The solution might be not to conduct such research because of the potential effects. Joan Sieber and Barbara Stanley (1988) concluded 'Sensitive research addresses some of society's pressing social issues and policy questions. Although ignoring the ethical issues in sensitive research is not a responsible approach to science, shying away from controversial topics, simply because they are controversial, is also an avoidance of responsibility.'

Examples of socially sensitive research

The Nudge Unit

In 2010 a new government department was set up called the *Behavioural Insights Team* with the aim of using psychological research to help run the country better. It was also known as the 'Nudge Unit' (after a book called *Nudge*) which argued that many human decisions are based on faulty logic.

For example, people often believe certain things (such as junk food is bad for you) but fail to put these beliefs into practice. The authors of *Nudge* argued that people can lead longer and better lives if their decisions are gently 'nudged' in the right direction. For example, junk food might be placed on supermarket shelves which are not at eye level.

The Nudge Unit employs psychologists as part of their team to conduct research and use existing psychological theory to make policy recommendations.

In the case of organ donation the team conducted a randomised controlled trial comparing the effect of different messages on a government website. The message 'If you needed an organ transplant, would you have one? If so help others' was based on reciprocity and fairness and led to an increase in donors.

The MMR myth

In 1998 a UK medical journal published a paper from a research team led by Dr. Andrew Wakefield in which the researchers claimed to have found a link between the MMR vaccine (a three-in-one jab for measles, mumps and rubella) and a syndrome of bowel and brain damage in children. Their research related to the study of 12 children and triggered massive media attention.

The outcome has been an enduring myth that the MMR vaccine causes autism. The consequence over the years has been a decline in children receiving the vaccine and an increase in measles, a dangerous and sometimes fatal childhood disease. In 1980, 2.6 million people worldwide died from measles. By 2014 this had dropped to 74,000 but recently the death rate has been rising due to reduced vaccinations over the last 20 years.

Andrew Wakefield was found guilty of ethical misconduct by the UK General Medical Council (GMC). It was discovered that, before Wakefield conducted his research, he had made an agreement with a solicitor who was looking for evidence to use against drug companies in legal challenges. Wakefield received over half a million pounds from legal aid funds to find that evidence. He had also developed his own alternative vaccines and stood to make a fortune if the MMR vaccine was replaced. Wakefield moved to America and continues to speak against the MMR vaccine.

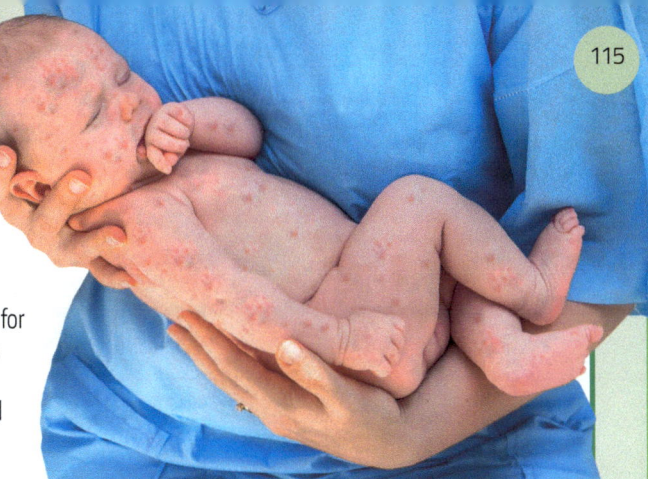

Cases of measles have increased due to some parents' reluctance to use the MMR vaccine. Psychological research plays an important role in changing this decline.

The tearoom trade

Laud Humphreys (1970) wished to demonstrate that certain common prejudices about gay men were mistaken. To do this he pretended to be a 'watchqueen' in a 'tearoom'. A 'tearoom' is a public toilet where men meet for sex with other men. A 'watchqueen' is someone who is allowed to watch the sexual activity and, in exchange, acts as a lookout.

When apparently watching out for danger, Humphreys also made a note of the car registration numbers of the visitors to the tearoom. He later was able to access the addresses of the car owners and interviewed them at home, claiming to be a health services worker. After this he destroyed the record of any individuals' names.

The main finding of this study was that most of the men involved in the tearoom trade led the rest of their lives as heterosexuals often living with their wives.

GET ACTIVE Thinking about psychological research

Several areas of research are described above.

- Justify the research – what benefits does the research offer in comparison to costs (such as invasion of privacy or social control)?
- Assess the potential impact. Who is going to be affected by this research, and how will they be affected?
- Identify the audience. Who is the research aimed at? Who is going to be interested?

You might look back at the research in Unit 1 and try to answer the same questions.

An issue to consider

Students quite often want to conduct their own research studies on topics such as eating disorders and gender identity. Why are people drawn to socially sensitive research?

Assessment practice

At the end of learning aim A you must write a report (see pages 99 and 116). This report must be related to a scenario or context such as the one below:

> On the previous spread you outlined a research study investigating the causes of anorexia nervosa (AN). One member of the team is very concerned about the socially sensitive nature of the research and the effect it could have. Other members offer several arguments to justify the importance of the research project. They all agree that their main objective is to recommend the best treatment approach.

A3.9 Learning aim A3 – Task 9

1. **Explain** the potential impacts the anorexia research project could have. (A.P1)
2. **Assess** the importance of the research into anorexia in terms of improving practice and provision. (A.M1)
3. **Evaluate** the research into anorexia in terms of its potential impacts. [HINT: how would you justify it?] (A.D1)

Specification content
A3 Research process
- Key steps to conducting research, to include justification of research, potential impact and audience.

Learning aim A

Assessment guidance

Learning aim A assessment

You are required to produce a maximum of three reports for Unit 2 which means combining at least two of the four learning aims. It is suggested the report for learning aim A is separate but you can combine it if you wish with learning aim B. No learning aim can be subdivided.

The report can be written or presented as a poster, PowerPoint or in another form.

This report can only be completed after you have studied the content of learning aim A as it is a synoptic assessment – see facing page for an explanation.

Recommended assessment approach

You are required to write a report discussing the importance of research in informing and improving practice and provision, detailing the way in which research is organised and giving an evaluation of different research methods and their usefulness in answering specific questions.

The *Delivery Guide for Unit 2* identifies the three key elements:

- The importance of psychological research.
- How research can help improve practice and provisions in vocational settings.
- Critical evaluation of a number of different research methods.

Assignment briefs

The exam board supplies suggested assessment briefs which you can use – see *Unit 2 Authorised assignment brief for Learning aim A and B Conducting psychological research*.

Your centre can also devise their own assessment brief which should have a vocational scenario/context and a series of tasks to complete.

Vocational scenario	The task (from Unit 2 A Assignment Brief)
The *Delivery Guide for Unit 2* suggests that a scenario could be based around a case study such as a hospital, care centre or other health provider looking to finance research about the link between health and illness. Your report should justify the research, as well as detailing how you would go about answering the research question.	You need to produce a detailed report that **evaluates** the importance of conducting research and the research process involved in psychological inquiries. Your report must also **assess** and **explain** the principles and processes involved when undertaking a psychological inquiry. Your report should include the following: • An **explanation** of the principles involved for conducting psychological research. • An **explanation** of the type of research processes that are conducted. • An **assessment** of the principles and processes and conventions in reporting research. • An **evaluation** of the importance of the scientific inquiry.

Assessment information

Your final report will be awarded a Distinction (D), Merit (M), Pass (P), Near Pass (N) or Unclassified (U).

The specification provides criteria for each level as shown below.

Pass	Merit	Distinction
A.P1 EXPLAIN the principles for conducting psychological research.		
A.P2 EXPLAIN the research process and key terms used when undertaking psychological enquiry.		
	A.M1 ASSESS the principles and processes involved when undertaking psychological inquiry.	
		A.D1 EVALUATE the importance of conducting research and the research process in psychological enquiry.

Marking factors The specification also provides information that an assessor will take into consideration when marking your assignment.

Marking factors	Pass	Merit	Distinction
Reasons for conducting psychological inquiry …	mostly accurate.	detailed.	fully-focused evaluation.
Personal and professional skills required are …	included.	discussed.	justified.
Key terms …	some.	wide range.	comprehensive range.
Understanding of research process is …	included.	clear.	sound.
Learners' reflections on their own research skills …		included.	good evidence.
Examples …	may not be clear.	linked logically.	linked logically.
Report is …	mainly descriptive and focused on personal views.	well-structured and clear.	well-structured and coherent, evidence of original thought.

Self-review checklist

Writing a big report requires organisation and planning.
It is important to set yourself target dates at the outset.
It is also important to write at least two drafts.

First draft of your review of the research process

Remember this is a *draft*. So you can write anything, just get thoughts on the page (see 'Blank page syndrome' on page 133). But do not copy anything, even at this stage (see 'Plagiarism' on the right).

Date to complete first draft: _____

- In the first white column enter the completion dates for each section of your report.
- As you write each section tick when you have explained, assessed and evaluated.

	Date completed	Explain (A.P1)	Explain (A.P2)	Assess (A.M1)	Evaluate (A.D1)
A1 Principles of research					
Introducing research and the scientific process					
Informing and improving practice					
Types of research process					
A2 Key terms used in research					
Starting research					
Hypotheses and a literature review					
Sampling techniques					
Reliability and validity					
A3 Research process					
Ethical considerations					
Conducting research					
References compiled					

Second draft

The next step is to revise your first document. Below is a checklist of things to consider.

Date to complete second draft: _____

	Date completed
I have checked that I have covered each of the seven marking factors (grey column) in the table on the facing page.	
I have gone through and deleted any irrelevant material.	
I have checked that every point has evidence to back it up.	
I have identified long sentences and rephrased them.	
I have checked that each paragraph deals with one idea.	
I have corrected any spelling mistakes.	
I have checked that each paragraph makes reference to the scenario/context.	

Final draft

Read through your completed second draft to polish the report.

Date to complete final draft: _____

Referencing

If you cite any research study or source (such as a website) you need to include this in a list of references at the end of your report.

This list should be in alphabetical order. The conventions for referencing are described on page 144.

Command terms for learning aim A

The assessment criteria for learning aim A (bottom left of facing page) use the command terms EXPLAIN, ASSESS and EVALUATE. These are defined on page 133.

Synoptic assessment

This assessment is synoptic. Synoptic refers to the ability to provide an overview of many different strands of information.

In your assessment you must demonstrate that you can identify and use effectively, in an integrated way, an appropriate selection of skills, techniques, concepts, theories and knowledge from across the whole sector as relevant to this task.

Plagiarism

Plagiarism means to use someone else's work without crediting the source. It means to steal and pass off the words (or ideas) of another as one's own. All the work submitted as your internal assessments must be your own.

We are lucky to have the internet at our fingertips when writing this book and we often cut and paste content into our notes – and it is very easy to forget we have done this. However, we know this can be easily checked and if we were found to have committed plagiarism in our book we would be accused of committing a crime and could be fined or receive a prison sentence for plagiarising someone else's work.

The same is true for you – it is tempting to use something written on a website or in this book and feel 'I can't say it as well as this' and therefore copy it exactly. You cannot do that unless the sentence is in quotes and attributed to the author.

We take great care to ensure that all of our sentences are our own. You must do the same or you will be disqualified from this exam.

Essential advice

Learners may not make repeated submissions of assignment evidence.

You may be offered a single retake opportunity using a new assignment. The retake may only be achieved at a Pass.

Under some conditions, and at your centre's discretion, you may be allowed to resubmit your original work in an improved form and will be given 15 days to do so.

Learning aim B1: Research methods

Review of research methods

As you will probably know, Wikipedia is a free online encyclopedia. Wikipedia is not wicked, but in some academic circles Wikipedia is not regarded very highly because it is written collaboratively by volunteers from all around the world. Anyone with internet access can make changes to Wikipedia articles (read tinyurl.com/ch9q9).

On the other hand there are editors who regularly review all material on Wikipedia to check accuracy. It is also the case that the number of users acts as a kind of review system – anything that is wrong or misleading is quickly spotted and changes are made.

The problem facing you is that it is too good. There is so much information it is hard to know what to include and what to leave out. What you must avoid at all costs is copying material from Wikipedia and you must never cite it as a source.

Use Wikipedia to get an overall picture of the topic but then follow the links to other sources. The task in *Get active* aims to help you do that.

Specification terms

Pilot study A trial run of a research study, involving only a few participants who are representative of the target population. It is conducted to test aspects of the research design, with a view to making improvements before conducting the full research study.

Qualitative research method Any overall design for a study that produces data in the form of descriptions rather than numbers.

Quantitative research method Any overall design for a study that produces data in the form of numbers.

GET ACTIVE Start thinking

Think of a research question you might like to investigate. It might be something related to a topic in Unit 1, or it might be something you have seen in a newspaper or on TV – something to do with human behaviour and vocational psychology (i.e. relating to an occupation or employment).

1. Go online and find a Wikipedia article related to your research question.
2. Write a brief summary of what you have just read. Do this by reading it and then closing the document and writing down what you remember. Go back and check if there are a few other things you would like to add. You don't have to record everything and you must use your own words.
3. Identify one or two research studies from the Wikipedia entry and follow the links which are usually to a short summary (an abstract) of the study. Describe (using the 'close the book method') the key details of the study, especially the findings and conclusions of each study.

It is all about the journey. The point of the pilot study is what you can learn along the way. It is not about the destination – the findings from your study.

So, enjoy your journey.

Your pilot study

It is now time for you to start thinking about your own *pilot study*. The suggested report for learning aim B is described on the facing page. The whole of learning aim B will be concerned with reviewing possible research methods, as well as topics for your study, so you can then decide what your research question will be and what research method(s) you will use. One important thing to note is that the project must relate to the vocational element of this course (i.e. relating to an occupation or employment).

You will then finish the report for learning aim B by writing your proposal.

In learning aims C and D you will conduct your pilot study. The report for learning aims C and D involves detailing the procedures followed in your pilot study, reporting the findings and discussing the findings.

Qualitative and quantitative research methods

One way to classify the different kinds of research methods is QUAL versus QUANT – which refers to the kind of data the research method produces.

Quantitative is about quantities. How much? How long? How many? It basically involves counting and the data is in the form of numbers – how much a person weighs, how long their fingers are, how many times they said 'yes', etc.

Qualitative is anything else. It is about differences between people in terms of qualities rather than quantities, i.e. how you might describe your personality instead of your score on a personality test. Using a list of words to describe yourself is qualitative, your score on a personality test will be a number (so is quantitative).

Different kinds of research method

- *Experiments* tend to be quantitative research methods, though participants may be asked *open questions* to measure the *dependent variable*.
- *Correlations* are quantitative research methods because the two variables being correlated must have numerical values to be plotted on a scattergram.
- *Questionnaires/interviews* may include some questions that produce a numerical answer (quantitative research method) or questions which are open-ended and allow participants to express themselves (qualitative research method).
- *Observational studies* can be qualitative (a researcher simply describes what is observed) but most often behaviours are counted (quantitative).
- *Case studies* involve questionnaires, interviews, psychological tests and observation (i.e. quantitative and qualitative methods).

Next steps

Over the next five spreads we will start to look in detail at the different research methods you might use. These were initially discussed on pages 102–103.

As you work through these methods you can be thinking about a possible topic for your pilot study. Try to keep an open mind so that you end up with something that is both doable (for good marks) and interesting.

Research questions

On page 104 we looked at some research questions, some of which could be investigated with a research study. Others were just questions which could not be *objectively* investigated.

Once you think you have a research question, the next step is a literature review (see page 107). What you want to know is:

- Has anyone else investigated this topic? (If not, then maybe you need to change your question.)
- What has previous research found? Look at a few studies and use them to help narrow your question down. You might even decide to repeat one of the studies.
- The final step for some studies will be to write a specific *hypothesis*. Alternatively you may just have a set of aims.

By the end of this process you should have explored a few research questions.

Painting in the style of *The Kiss* by Gustav Klimt.

You can describe this qualitatively or quantitatively.

Quantitative data	Qualitative data
Painted between 1907 and 1908.	An example of Art Nouveau.
Measures 180 × 180 cm.	Shows how bright, beautiful, and golden everything is when you first kiss someone.
First bought for 25,000 crowns.	
33% of surface covered in gold leaf.	Painted in oil and gold leaf on canvas.

Assessment practice

At the end of learning aim B you must write:

A report discussing a proposal for a pilot study that takes account of research questions, methods, participants, procedures, time and organisational management.

This report must (obviously) be related to your pilot study.

This assessment practice task will help you with the skills required to write a proposal in response to your own aim.

Psychological research has proven to have many useful applications in education.

Imagine you are a teacher who wants to know if students' learning is affected by specific teaching methods. You enlist help from an educational psychologist to conduct an experiment to find out.

Having gained permission and consent, you plan to select two classes from the same school year. One class will be taught using an activity-based method. The other class will experience a lecture-based method. At the end of the experiment the learning of students in each class will be measured.

Your research aim is to find out whether one method leads to better learning performance than the other.

B1.1 Learning aim B1 – Task 1

The first part of your report for learning aim B will be concerned with a proposal for your pilot study, including an explanation of your reasoning for this plan. The next five spreads cover other design aspects that you should consider, explain and evaluate for this plan. We will take you through a hypothetical study.

1. **Plan** a proposal for a pilot study of an experiment to investigate the above research aim on the effect of different teaching methods. (B.P3)
2. This experiment will collect quantitative data. **Explain** the reasoning behind collecting quantitative data to investigate this research aim. (B.P4)
3. **Explain** the reasoning behind the choice of this research question. (B.P4)

An issue to consider

Draw up a list of possible research questions that you might like to study.

Your study should have significance for practice or provision, as you are required to comment on this in your conclusion. It also needs to be practical and ethical – you should avoid socially sensitive issues (such as mental health).

Specification content

B1 Research methods

Advantages, disadvantages and appropriateness of methods to meet the aims and purposes of different psychological investigations, e.g. time, reliability, validity, cost.

- Qualitative research methods.
- Quantitative research methods.

Learning aim B1: Research methods

Review of research methods: Experiments

It's a perfect day

Have you ever asked yourself – what would make a cow produce more milk? Probably not, but you can be sure that many dairy farmers have asked that question.

A group of music psychologists (North et al. unpublished) investigated whether music could make a difference to milk production (that's the research aim).

Procedure

The researchers played fast and slow tempo music to two large herds of Holstein Friesian cattle in the UK. The music was played for 12 hours a day (from 5am to 5pm).

- Slow tempo was operationalised as less than 100 beats per minute, e.g. Aretha Franklin (*What a difference a day makes*), Simon and Garfunkel (*Bridge over troubled water*), Lou Reed (*Perfect day*) and Beethoven's *Pastoral Symphony*.

- Fast tempo was operationalised as more than 120 beats per minute, e.g. Jamiroquai (*Space cowboy*), Supergrass (*Pumping on your stereo*), Mud (*Tiger Feet*), Mousse T vs. Hot 'N' Juicy (*Horny*).

- There was also a no-music condition – a *control* to check that the music actually improved performance (it might be that even though fast music was better than slow music both of them were worse than no music).

Findings

- Slow music = 24.0995 litres of milk per cow per day.

- Fast music = 23.3666 litres of milk per cow per day.

- No music = 23.8907 litres of milk per cow per day.

This represents a 3% increase in milk production for slow tempo.

Experiments

An *experiment* is a specific kind of study where you have an *independent variable* (IV) and a *dependent variable* (DV), as in the study on milk production on the left. In this case the *operationalised* variables are:

- IV = type of music tempo (three levels of the IV = fast or slow or no-music).
- DV = litres of milk per cow per day.

When designing an experiment there are key design decisions:

Repeated measures or independent groups (page 104) In the cow experiment all participants (cows) were exposed to just one of the levels of the IV. This is an *independent groups* design because there was more than one group of participants, one for each level (a level is also called a 'condition').

This study could have been conducted differently. All the cows could have experienced all three levels/conditions. For example, for one week they had no music, for one week fast music and for one week slow music. At the end of each week their milk yield (DV) would be assessed.

In a *repeated measures* design there is one group of participants and all participants experience all levels/conditions of the IV.

Counterbalancing If you use a repeated measures design there is a problem. Participants may do better on one task simply because it always comes first. For example, in the chocolate study on page 104 we suggested that if participants always ate the expensive chocolate first (let's call it condition A) they might rate it higher not because it was better but because they tasted it first.

To deal with this we *counterbalance* – one group of participants do A first and then B (the cheaper chocolate condition), while the other group do B first and then A.

Random allocation In an independent groups design you might happen to end up with all the younger participants in one group. This might act as a *confounding variable* if, for example, younger people prefer sweeter tastes.

To overcome this problem researchers use *random allocation* – they use a random method to determine which participants are placed in which group (you can put all names in a hat and draw out half to be placed in one group).

Controls Counterbalancing and random allocation are methods of controlling confounding variables which we discussed on page 104.

As far as possible researchers must ensure that each participant experiences the same conditions as any other participant. For example, if some but not all participants were in a very cold room during the study this might affect performance and should be controlled.

We also might control temperature even if it affected all participants equally because, if they were very cold or very hungry etc. they wouldn't be behaving 'normally' and this would mean we could not generalise the findings to everyday life. We discussed *ecological validity* on page 111. As far as possible conditions in an experiment should be 'normal' so that we can generalise findings to everyday life.

Ethical issues There are many ethical issues to consider when planning your procedures (see page 112), but here is a special one. Consider the following experiment investigating the question of whether people can actually tell the difference between a drink with caffeine and one without (IV = caffeine/no caffeine, DV = rating taste of the drink).

This study could be done as repeated measures or independent groups – but a key part of design is considering whether you need to tell people any information beforehand that may affect their decision to take part.

In an independent groups design some participants will not receive caffeine, but you can't tell them there is no caffeine beforehand because that will affect their behaviour.

So what researchers do is tell all participants that some participants will have a drink with caffeine and some won't, and they will be informed at the end of the study which condition they were in.

Hypothesis You can write either a *directional* or *non-directional alternative hypothesis* (see page 106).

Specification terms

Causal relationships Situations where one variable makes another variable change.

Dependent variable (DV) Measured by the experimenter to assess the effects of the independent variable(s).

Experiment A research method which demonstrates causal relationships. All experiments have one (or more) independent variable (IV) and one (or more) dependent variable (DV).

Field experiment An experiment conducted in an everyday environment. Usually the researcher goes to where the participants can be found.

Hypothesis A statement of what a researcher believes to be true. In order to test such a statement, it must be clearly operationalised.

Independent variable (IV) A factor that is directly manipulated by the experimenter in order to observe the effect of different conditions on the dependent variable(s).

Laboratory experiment An experiment conducted in a very controlled environment. Usually the participants go to the researcher.

Natural experiment An experiment where the independent variable has varied as a consequence of some other action rather than the researcher's manipulation, such as comparing children who have spent time in hospital with children who haven't.

Quasi-experiment A study where the independent variable is not actually something that varies, such as comparing younger and older people. These are factors that cannot be changed by someone but the effects on a dependent variable can be observed.

GET ACTIVE Was that an experiment?

These studies outlined in Unit 1 are experiments: Tulving and Pearlstone (page 15), Bandura *et al.* (page 38), Fischer and Greitemeyer (page 65), North (page 73) and Fowler *et al.* (page 81). Use your favourite search engine to find out more about them.

For each one identify:
1. The levels of independent variable and how these are operationalised.
2. The dependent variable and explain specifically how it was measured (i.e. operationalised).
3. Whether the data produced is quantitative or qualitative.
4. Explain whether it is a repeated measures or independent groups design.
5. Identify at least **one** control that was used or should have been used.
6. Identify any ethical issues that were important to deal with.
7. Was the experiment a lab, field, natural or quasi-experiment?

Evaluation

Experiments

+ *Causal relationships* can be demonstrated because the researcher has deliberately changed one thing (the independent variable, IV) to observe the effect this has on the dependent variable (DV). No other research method can do this.
− Experiments may not represent everyday life because behaviour is reduced to a very small set of variables – the IV and the DV. In everyday life our behaviour is 'caused' by a mix of many different variables. This leads to low ecological validity.

Laboratory experiments

+ High level of control is possible and therefore *confounding/extraneous variables* can be minimised (increasing validity).
+ Can be easily repeated (*replicated*) to check the findings are the same because most aspects of the environment have been controlled (enhancing validity).
− A contrived situation where participants may not behave naturally (as they would in day-to-day life). This is especially true because participants know their behaviour is being studied and therefore they may act differently from 'normal' to help the researcher. This leads to low ecological validity.

Field experiments

+ Less contrived, the whole experience feels more like everyday life and participants are not *generally* aware they are being observed (though sometimes they are). Therefore, there is usually higher ecological validity.
− There may be ethical issues if participants are not aware of being studied – *informed consent* and *debriefing* may not be possible.
− Less control of extraneous variables (reduces validity).

Natural and quasi-experiments

+ Allows research where the IV can't be manipulated for ethical or practical reasons. This enables psychologists to study 'real' problems, such as the effects of a disaster on health.
− Cannot demonstrate causal relationships because the IV is not directly manipulated.
− May be less control of extraneous variables – though a *natural experiment* can be conducted in a lab.
− Can only be used where conditions vary naturally.

Assessment practice

At the end of learning aim B you must write a report (see previous page). This report must be related to your pilot study.

This assessment practice task will help you with the skills required to write a proposal in response to your own aim.

There are many decisions to be made for a teaching methods experiment (described on the previous spread). Use the contents of this spread to guide you.

B1.2 Learning aim B1 – Task 2

1. Now that you have covered experiments on this spread, refine your proposal for a pilot study by adding details about the method. (B.P3)
2. **Explain** the reasoning behind using an experiment to investigate the research aim. (B.P4)
3. **Assess** the use of an experiment to investigate the research aim. (B.M2)
4. **Evaluate** the use of an experiment to investigate the research aim. (B.D2)

An issue to consider

Look at your list of topics from the previous spread – which of these could be conducted as experiments? Identify an IV and DV for each.

Specification content

B1 Research methods

Advantages, disadvantages and appropriateness of methods to meet the aims and purposes of different psychological investigations, e.g. time, reliability, validity, cost.

- Quantitative research methods.
  - Methods of data collection, including laboratory, field, natural, quasi-experiments.
  - Key features of experimentation, to include dependent and independent variables, hypothesis, causal relationships.

Learning aim B1: Research methods

Review of research methods: Questionnaires and interviews

Patient surveys

In order to provide good medical care it is important to know what both professionals and clients think about the service provided. There are thousands of such survey studies online (look up 'patient survey').

First task – to establish an aim. Magrit Fässler and colleagues (2011) asked whether patients and doctors differed in their attitudes to placebo treatments.

Second task – to construct a questionnaire that can be mailed out to participants. One questionnaire was designed for patients and the other for doctors, each had 13 questions covering similar topics, for example:

- Do you think that physical complaints can get better simply by believing in the effectiveness of the therapy? Yes / Quite often / Rarely / No / I don't know. (closed question)
- For physicians: What would you administer to your patients? (open question)
- For patients: What would you wish your doctor to administer to you? (open question)

Other information was also collected, such as age and gender.

Third task – to pilot the questionnaire with a few patients and doctors and get their feedback.

Fourth task – to select a sample. This study randomly sampled all GPs in a canton of Switzerland. 300 GPs were contacted and asked if they would fill in the questionnaire and all 300 were asked if they would give the questionnaire to the first 20 patients they next saw. Response rates were 87% for patients and 79% for GPs.

Finally, results were analysed. The researchers concluded that GPs rather underestimated how unhappy patients are about being given placebo treatments. The patients felt they have a right to be informed.

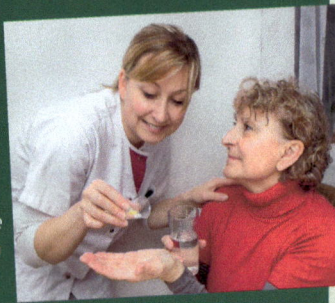

Specification terms

Closed question Has a fixed number of possible answers and provides quantitative data.

Interview A 'live' encounter (face-to-face or on the phone) where one person (interviewer) asks questions to assess an interviewee's thoughts and/or experiences. Questions may be pre-set (structured interview) or may develop during the interview (unstructured interview) or a mixture (semi-structured interview).

Open question Invites respondents to provide their own answers, and tends to produce qualitative data.

Questionnaire Respondents record their own answers. The questions are predetermined (i.e. structured).

Survey (or **self-report**) Any method to gather data by asking people questions.

Surveys

A *survey* is any method used to ask people one or more questions to gain information on a topic of interest. This includes both *questionnaires* and *interviews*.

Questionnaires

Respondents record their own answers. The questions are predetermined (i.e. structured). They are provided in written form which may be online. There is no face-to-face contact with another person.

Writing good questions Questionnaires can be an *objective* and scientific way of conducting research but this involves more than just thinking up some questions.

The questions must be clear. If they are ambiguous then the answer given is likely to be meaningless. Here is an example of ambiguity: 'Did you see the girl with the binoculars?' which could mean 'Did you see the girl who was using the binoculars?' or 'Did you see the girl by looking through binoculars?'.

Questions also must not be *leading*, i.e. the researcher should not state the question in a way that might lead to a particular answer. For example, 'Did you see the umbrella by the door?' suggests that there was an umbrella in the room and it was by the door, whereas 'Did you see an umbrella in the room? If so, where was it located?' is less suggestive. *Leading questions* are an example of how a researcher's expectations may be unintentionally communicated to a participant and affect the *validity* of the answer given. It is most especially a problem in live interviews.

Interviews

When questions are delivered in real time then a survey is called an *interview*. 'Real time' means that the respondent answers each question as it is presented by an interviewer.

Types of interview An interviewer may simply read out a questionnaire (a *structured interview*).

One advantage of the presence of an interviewer is that the respondent can ask the interviewer to explain something, such as asking for an explanation of a question.

However, the great advantage is that questions can be adapted during an interview – and then it is called an *unstructured interview*. In this case an interviewer is no longer just reading out a list of predetermined questions – the questions can be developed based on the answers given.

In a *semi-structured interview* an interviewer may begin with some predetermined questions, and then improvise based on previous answers.

Interviewing methods Typically, an interviewer will take notes throughout an interview, or alternatively, an interview may be recorded (audio or video).

An interviewer needs to be very aware of their effect on the interviewee. Various behaviours such as sitting with arms crossed and frowning communicate disapproval and disinterest, whereas head-nodding and leaning forward may encourage the interviewee to speak.

An interviewer needs to know when and how to speak. For example, they should not interrupt too often and when they do speak they should have a range of encouraging comments such as 'How interesting' to show they are listening.

GET ACTIVE Questionnaires inside an experiment

Find a suitable study mentioned in Unit 1.

1. What was the aim of the experiment?
2. Describe the questionnaires.

Open and closed questions

Both questionnaires and interviews can consist of *closed* and/or *open questions*, though questionnaires may tend to have more closed questions.

Closed questions have a fixed number of possible answers and tend to produce *quantitative data* because the answers can be counted in each category. Most closed questions are fixed-choice, i.e. there is a fixed set of possible answers as in the examples on the right.

Some closed questions have an 'other' category so the range of answers is limited but not fixed – so, strictly speaking, they are not closed because the answers for 'other' can be analysed qualitatively.

+ Closed questions provide data that is easy to analyse.

Open questions invite respondents to provide their own answers. Such questions tend to produce *qualitative data*.

Examples of open questions: 'Describe what being in love feels like' and 'What things make you feel stressed?'

+ Open questions provide a large amount of information, often including unexpected insights into behaviour.

Examples of closed questions

1. Do you find work stressful?   Yes / No / Not sure
2. Which of the following factors at work make you feel stressed? (You may tick as many answers as you like.)
   - ☐ Noise at work
   - ☐ Too much to do
   - ☐ Workmates
   - ☐ Lack of control
   - ☐ Boredom
   - ☐ No job satisfaction
3. How much stress do you feel? (Circle the number that best describes how you feel.)
   At work
   A lot of stress   5 4 3 2 1   No stress at all
   At home
   A lot of stress   5 4 3 2 1   No stress at all
4. Work is stressful. How much do you agree with this statement?

Strongly disagree	Disagree	Neither agree nor disagree	Agree	Strongly Agree
☐	☐	☐	☐	☐

Question 3 is an example of a ranked scale where respondents are asked to give a number to represent their views or feelings. You can have 3-point ranked scales or 7 points or 9 points, etc. Odd numbers are best so there is a mid-point.

There are other kinds of ranked scale. For example, Likert scales allow people to indicate how much they agree or disagree with a statement, see question 4.

Nope, no stress.

Evaluation

Questionnaires

+ People may feel more willing to reveal confidential information on a questionnaire than in an interview because the presence of an interviewer may make them feel they are being judged.
+ Can be easily repeated. Once you have designed a questionnaire (which takes a long time to get right) it can then be handed out to as many people as you want at the same time. Therefore, this is a relatively easy way to collect lots of data.
+ Easier to analyse than an interview because the participants' answers stick to a script.

Interviews

+ People may reveal more information because a skilled interviewer can encourage more thoughtful (and unexpected) responses.
+ Can access information that may not be revealed by predetermined questions.
− Numbers of participants are restricted because of the time it takes to conduct the interview and the expense of training and employing interviewers.
− The interviewer's expectations may influence the answers the interviewee gives (this is called *interviewer bias*).
− Participants may feel reluctant to reveal personal information when face-to-face with an interviewer.

The validity of questionnaires and interviews

− People don't always know what they think about a particular topic or don't know how they would behave in a particular situation. Therefore, their answers may lack *ecological validity*.
− People don't always tell the truth! Or their answers may lack truthfulness because people don't want to look foolish or unlikeable, so they present themselves in a way that makes them 'look better' – this is called a *social desirability bias*.
− The group of people involved (called the *sample*) may be biased because only certain kinds of people fill in questionnaires (literate individuals who are willing to spend time filling them in) or in the case of interviews, only some people are willing to take part in lengthy interviews.

Assessment practice

At the end of learning aim B you must write a report (see pages 119 and 132). This report must be related to your pilot study.

This assessment practice task will help you with the skills required to write a proposal in response to your own aim.

As well as measuring how teaching methods affect learning, you also want to know how the students felt about the experience of taking part in the study.

You and the educational psychologist design a survey (questionnaire or interview) to investigate this research aim: to measure students' subjective perceptions of the two teaching methods, including how they felt about them and their beliefs about effectiveness.

B1.3 Learning aim B1 – Task 3

1. **Plan** a proposal for a pilot study to investigate the above research aim. (B.P3)
2. **Explain** the reasoning behind using a survey to investigate the research aim. (B.P4)
3. **Assess** the use of a survey to investigate the research aim. (B.M2)
4. **Evaluate** the use of a survey to investigate the research aim. (B.D2)

An issue to consider

Look at your initial list of topics – have you thought of some more research questions you might add?

Which ones might involve a questionnaire?

Specification content

B1 Research methods

Advantages, disadvantages and appropriateness of methods to meet the aims and purposes of different psychological investigations, e.g. time, reliability, validity, cost.

- Qualitative research methods.
  - Methods of data collection, to include questionnaires and use of closed and open questions, interviews, surveys.
- Quantitative research methods.
  - Methods of data collection, including questionnaires.

Learning aim B1: Research methods
Review of research methods: Observation

Observing aggression

In Unit 1 (page 38) you studied Albert Bandura's research using a Bobo doll to demonstrate *social learning theory*. This study was a lab experiment but it involved observational methods to measure the *dependent variable* (aggression).

At the end of the study, after the children had watched the model play with the Bobo doll (or not), each child was taken individually to a room with some toys, including a Bobo doll.

The child was observed through a one-way mirror usually by two observers so that *inter-observer reliability* could be calculated (the observations of both observers are compared to see how consistent they are, which reflects reliability – see page 110).

The observers generally did not know which experimental or control condition the child had participated in because this might bias their observations.

The observers recorded what the child was doing every five seconds (providing 240 observations). This is an example of *time sampling*.

Responses were recorded using the *behavioural categories* and provided an 'aggression score' for each child:

1. Imitative aggression responses:
   - Physical aggression – any specific acts which were imitated.
   - Verbal aggression – any phrases imitated, such as 'Pow'.
2. Partially imitative responses:
   - Mallet aggression – uses mallet on toys other than Bobo.
   - Sits on Bobo doll but doesn't behave aggressively.
3. Non-imitative aggressive responses:
   - Punches Bobo doll – strikes, slaps, pushes the doll.
   - Non-imitative physical and verbal aggression – aggressive acts directed at toys other than Bobo, saying hostile things not said by the model.
   - Aggressive gun play.
4. Non-aggressive verbal responses: such as saying 'He keeps coming back for more'.

Specification terms

Controlled observation Watching people (or animals) or listening to them, using techniques which organise (control) the observations, such as using behavioural categories and event/time sampling.

Event sampling Draw up a list of behavioural categories. Then count (tally) every time each of the behaviours occurs during a specified time period (e.g. observing for an hour).

Participant and non-participant observation Whether the observer is also part of the group being observed, or not.

Time sampling Draw up a list of behavioural categories. Then at regular intervals (such as every 5 seconds or 8 minutes), note which of the behaviours are occurring. Or take a sample at different times of day or month.

Observational techniques

Both *surveys* (discussed on the previous spread) and *observations* can be the main method of a study but they are often a technique used to measure the *dependent variable* in an *experiment*, as illustrated in Bandura's study on the left.

Controlled observations

Observing what people do is more difficult than you think. One reason is that, when we watch somebody perform a particular behaviour we see a continuous stream of action rather than a series of separate behavioural components.

In order to conduct systematic observations we need to break up this stream of behaviour into a set of components, called *behavioural categories*. On the left we have listed the behavioural categories used in Bandura's study of *social learning*.

The guidelines for good behavioural categories are:

- *Operationalise* the behaviours. You must actually be able to see (or hear) the behaviour. For example, it is not good to have a category 'person looks/sounds happy' because this means the observer has to make a judgement. It is better to have concrete unambiguous categories, e.g. 'Person is laughing'.
- Cover all possible component behaviours and avoid a 'waste basket' category (i.e. a category where you can include anything that isn't already covered).

In order to develop behavioural categories you can use a method similar to *thematic analysis* (see next spread).

Sampling

There is a second reason why making observations is more difficult than you think – it is difficult to record everything that is happening. Usually continuous observation is not possible because there would be too much to record.

Therefore, observers use a systematic method, such as:

- *Event sampling*, for example, counting how many times a person smiles in a one-hour period. Alternatively a list of behavioural categories may be created and a count is kept of every time any one of the categories occurs within the observation period.
- *Time sampling*, for example, observing a child playing in their garden for an hour and making a note of their behaviours every 30 seconds, or asking students to record what they are doing at 11am and 5pm every day over a period of one month.

Note this is different from the other sampling methods discussed on page 108. When conducting an observation you also have to select a group of participants – and you use the other sampling methods to do this.

Participant and non-participant observation

An observer may be a participant in the behaviour being observed, for example being in a bus stop queue and observing behaviour in the queue. Alternatively the participant watches/listens at a distance from the group and the group may be unaware of being observed.

Overt and covert observation

In an *overt observation*, participants are aware that their behaviour is being recorded. The observer may be a participant in the group or may be a non-participant observer. An overt observation makes it much easier to make observations because the observer doesn't have to hide.

In a *covert observation* the participants are unaware of being observed. The observer may, for example, watch from a window or through a one-way mirror, or listen while sitting next to someone on a train.

Evaluation

Observational research

- **+** What people say they do is often different from what they actually do, so observations give a different take on behaviour than other research methods, such as surveys.
- **+** *Validity/reliability* may be an issue if observers miss some of the things that are happening. One way to check this is using *inter-observer reliability* – two or more observers record the same behaviours and then their observations are compared. If the observations are fairly similar (about 80% should be the same) then this is high inter-observer reliability.
- **–** Observations cannot provide information about what people think.
- **–** Observers may 'see' (or hear) what they expect to see/hear (*observer bias*). This reduces validity.

Behavioural categories

- **+** Behavioural categories enable systematic observations to be made so important information is not overlooked, this enhances validity.
- **–** Categories may not cover all possibilities or may be unclear so that different observers interpret them differently. This means some behaviours are not recorded (low reliability and validity).

Event and time sampling

- **+** Event sampling is useful when behaviour to-be-recorded only happens occasionally. Missing events would reduce validity.
- **+** Time sampling allows for tracking of time-related changes in behaviour.
- **–** In event sampling observations may not be representative if the list of events (behavioural categories) is not comprehensive, this reduces validity.
- **–** In time sampling some behaviours are missed if important behaviour occurs outside the observation interval, reducing validity.

Participant and non-participant observations

- **+** *Participant observation* is likely to provide special insights into behaviour, from the 'inside'. The participant observer has greater familiarity with what is likely to happen and therefore may 'see' greater detail that would be missed by someone new to the situation.
- **–** However, in participant observations *objectivity* is reduced (observer bias). Because the observer is familiar with what is going on, they are looking at the situation more *subjectively*.
- **–** Also it is more difficult to record behaviour unobtrusively if the observer is part of the group being observed, leading to the same problems as overt observation (see below).

The reverse of these points is true for *non-participant observations*.

Overt and covert observations

- **+** Overt observation is more ethically sound – in a covert observation it is difficult to gain *informed consent* and it may be an invasion of privacy to observe people without their prior consent. This is true even in a public place, such as a bus queue.
- **–** However, in an overt observation participants are aware of being observed and therefore may alter their behaviour, for example in a library they might behave how they think they ought to be behaving rather than how they really behave. This reduces *ecological validity*.

The reverse of these points is true for covert observations.

GET ACTIVE Just watch (or listen)

Observing what people do objectively is more difficult than you think.

Work with a partner and take turns observing each other. Perhaps observe one partner working on a difficult task while the other person just reads a magazine.

OR ... you know you want to do this one. Take a seat in a public space such as your college canteen or a shopping centre and watch people go by. Record what people are doing.

1. What behavioural categories might be helpful to record the behaviour?
2. How could you use time or event sampling to make the observations more straightforward and systematic?

Assessment practice

At the end of learning aim B you must write a report (see pages 119 and 132). This report must be related to your pilot study.

This assessment practice task will help you with the skills required to write a proposal in response to your own aim.

Your educational psychologist friend argues that experiments and surveys do not always provide a complete picture of the behaviour you are interested in. The psychologist suggests you conduct a controlled observational study to investigate the learning behaviour of students in each class.

Based on one session of informal observation, the psychologist created some behavioural categories for 'learning behaviours' (e.g. 'student is writing', 'student is talking', etc.).

Now complete the plan for the study, and evaluate your decisions.

B1.4 Learning aim B1 – Task 4

1. **Plan** a proposal for a pilot study to investigate the above research aim. (B.P3)
2. **Explain** the reasoning behind using an observation method to investigate the research aim. (B.P4)
3. **Assess** the use of an observation method to investigate the research aim. (B.M2)
4. **Evaluate** the use of an observation method to investigate the research aim. (B.D2)

An issue to consider

On balance, what kind of observation is best – participant or non-participant, overt or covert, using time or event sampling?

Think of a research question that might use observation and decide which choices you would make.

Specification content

B1 Research methods

Advantages, disadvantages and appropriateness of methods to meet the aims and purposes of different psychological investigations, e.g. time, reliability, validity, cost.

- Qualitative research methods.
  - Methods of data collection, to include participant and non-participant observations, time or event sampling.
- Quantitative research methods.
  - Methods of data collection, including controlled observations.

Learning aim B1: Research methods

Review of research methods: Content and thematic analysis

Latrinalia

There's a word for you – it refers to graffiti in toilets (latrines). What things do people choose to communicate? You probably can give a number of ideas but, if we wish to be scientific, we need a systematic and objective approach.

Enter the process of *thematic analysis* – a set of steps that enables us to summarise observations. James Green (2003) used thematic analysis to compare men's and women's grafitti (a quasi-experiment where the dependent variable was measured with thematic analysis). He called his study *The writing on the stall*.

The final sample was 723 inscriptions from 189 women's toilets and 268 men's toilets and also 266 study booths (to provide a mixed-gender comparison).

The sample was analysed producing several categories including: sex discussions, sex requests, sex descriptions, politics, tax/student fees/debt, personal advice, racism, drinking/drugs, humour, religion, insults, love/romance, music, sport, 'alternative' people, academic courses, graffiti about graffiti, presence (e.g. initials or 'I was here'), sexist remarks, philosophy, exams/study, body image, placations (e.g. 'calm down') and 'other'.

The data was then categorised and a second individual independently coded 25% of the data to check reliability, with 89.7% agreement between coders.

What did Green conclude? Graffiti from the women's toilets tended to be more polite and interactive, whereas those from the men's toilets were more argumentative and negative. The only sexist remarks were found in the mixed-gender context.

Specification terms

Content analysis Kind of observational study in which behaviour is observed indirectly in written or verbal material such as books, diaries or TV programmes.

Thematic analysis (narrative, grounded, discourse and conversation analysis) These are all forms of qualitative analysis where categories ('themes') emerge (are 'grounded') in the data. Basically the same as a content analysis but much more emphasis is placed on developing the themes from the source data.

Content and thematic analysis

These are also forms of *observation* but indirect ones. Instead of observing people directly, people are observed through their conversations or things they produce (interviews, diaries, films, songs, paintings, graffitti). By studying these artefacts (things that people produce) we can learn about what people think and feel and do.

The analysis bit

In both *content* and *thematic analysis*, and also in most observation studies, *behavioural categories* are required. The ultimate aim is to be able to draw some conclusions from the data. In order to do this, the 'observer' needs to find a way to classify and summarise their observations of, for example, children playing in a park or the kinds of conversations people have in a bar.

There is a continuum from:

- Observer decides on categories based on past experience or based on psychological theories (called top-down), to …
- Observer starts with no preconceptions and develops the categories by looking at the data (called bottom-up). This approach is *grounded* in the data itself and is called *thematic analysis* (aka *discourse* or *conversation analysis*).

Looking for themes

In both a content and thematic analysis the issue is about how you decide on the behavioural categories, and the answer is you start by looking for themes – ideas or topics that are evident and may recur in a conversation or book or artwork.

For example, if you were going to conduct a bottom-up analysis of the content of a conversation between a doctor and patient (a conversation analysis):

Step 1 – Collect your data In our case this means recording and then producing a written transcript of the conversation.

Step 2 – Data familiarisation Read and reread the transcript to try to understand the meaning. Make no notes at this time.

Step 3 – Data coding Some categories should have started to occur to you but it is important to keep as open a mind as possible so that you are truly analysing the data and not superimposing your ideas on it (in a top-down analysis you already have the categories). For each sentence or element decide on a meaning (e.g. sadness or pleasure expressed, reassurance, identifying symptoms).

Step 4 – Theme refinement Identify broader themes that consist of the different categories. If there are too many themes it will be difficult to draw conclusions.

Step 5 – Present a report Discuss the various themes, and illustrate these themes with quotations from the doctor/patient. Draw conclusions.

This kind of analysis is discussed again briefly as part of learning aim C (see page 139), where you can read some examples. From the point of view of data collection (which is our concern at this stage), you simply need to collect the data to be analysed.

GET ACTIVE Get practising

Try a thematic analysis of some songs by your favourite artist/band. Follow the steps outlined above.

1. Before you begin, write down the categories/themes you are expecting to find.
2. Now try to open your mind to what else might be there.
3. Discuss your findings with someone else.

Evaluation

Strengths

+ Allows access to both what people think and what they actually do.
+ The data collected represents the true complexities of human behaviour. For example, in conversation analysis people are given a free rein to express themselves in the course of their everyday lives. Therefore, the outcomes are high in *ecological validity*.
+ Very useful for gaining new insights based on what is really happening, such as workers' attitudes towards workplace procedures or how new mothers feel about parenthood. This is important for developing new *practices* and new theories/explanations.

Weaknesses

- Interpreting what people mean is likely to be *subjective* and might be different if another person conducted the analysis. That said, comparisons can be made between coders, demonstrating *inter-observer reliability*.
- It is more difficult to detect patterns and draw conclusions because of the large variety of information collected, and because words cannot easily be reduced to a few simple points.
- Generalisability may be challenged depending on how wide the sample is. If only one doctor-patient conversation is analysed, it cannot be assumed that the same is true of all such conversations.
- The process is very time-consuming and requires experienced researchers to perform the analysis reliably, therefore this kind of research is expensive.
- It is difficult to falsify the findings of *qualitative* analyses because usually no hypothesis is tested and falsification involves rejecting the *null hypothesis*. Falsification is the cornerstone of true scientific research because to demonstrate something is true you must be able to show it is potentially not true (i.e. false). With no hypothesis this is not possible.

Assessment practice

At the end of learning aim B you must write a report (see pages 119 and 132). This report must be related to your pilot study.

This assessment practice task will help you with the skills required to write a proposal in response to your own aim.

After analysing the survey from your teaching methods investigation, you and the educational psychologist agree that there is not enough detail to reach firm conclusions.

You would like to know more about the students' experiences of the two teaching methods, so you decide to conduct a content/thematic analysis.

You ask five students from each class to write a 100-word description of their experiences, feelings, beliefs, etc. Your aim is to compare the two groups and find out if the students consider one teaching method to be more effective than the other.

Key decisions will include selecting the students and identifying your themes/categories.

B1.5 Learning aim B1 – Task 5

1. **Plan** a proposal for a pilot study to investigate the above research aim. (B.P3)
2. **Explain** the reasoning behind using a content/thematic analysis to investigate the research aim. (B.P4)
3. **Assess** the use of a content/thematic analysis to investigate the research aim. (B.M2)
4. **Evaluate** the use of a content/thematic analysis to investigate the research aim. (B.D2)

An issue to consider

If you wanted to find out what leadership style people prefer most, think about how you could research this using the four methods reviewed so far: experiment, survey, observation or thematic analysis.

One technique for identifying categories/themes.

Example 1: Qualitative data collected from three different participants. Colours have been used to identify emergent themes. For example, red identifies the mention of winning or losing.

Participant details	**Question:** How would you describe the behaviour of Aggroville football fans following a match?
Participant 1 Not a sports fan.	Well, put it this way, if they have lost they can get pretty aggro. They are very noisy and when they are in the pubs afterwards, they always seem to be fighting. I wouldn't want to be on a train after a match. They are often really drunk.
Participant 2 Loves football but can't often make it to matches.	Well, Aggroville fans tend to show a lot of camaraderie to each other, they are good lads, they love a bit of a knees-up, you know, obviously it depends on whether we win or not. Sometimes if it's a loss, you know, people just go home and have a quiet night, but yeah if there's a win, it's celebration time. I've never seen any violence or anything.
Participant 3 Identifies as a rugby fan.	My opinion would be that, well I wouldn't want to stereotype but essentially football fans... they don't always go to matches for the love of sport shall we say, it's the pack mentality, they're just there for the booze and to cause trouble a lot of the time.

Example 2: Examples are collected for each theme.

Emergent theme	Not a sports fan	Football fan	Rugby fan
Whether they win or lose	'if they have lost'	'depends on whether we win or not', 'if it's a loss', 'if there's a win'	
Aggressive	'they can get pretty aggro', 'always seem to be fighting'	'I've never seen any violence or anything'	'it's the pack mentality', 'to cause trouble a lot of the time'

[Thanks to Mandy Wood for this example.]

Specification content
B1 Research methods

Advantages, disadvantages and appropriateness of methods to meet the aims and purposes of different psychological investigations, e.g. time, reliability, validity, cost.

- Qualitative research methods.
  - Methods of data analysis, e.g. thematic, narrative, content, grounded, discourse, conversation analysis.
  - Issues in qualitative research, to include generalisability in terms of whether research enriches understanding and generates theory, falsification, validity, reliability.

Learning aim B1: Research methods

Review of research methods: A few other things

Being an only child leads to greater job success

Eating an ice cream every day increases your happiness

More bobbies on the beat reduces crime

Here are some newspaper headlines – all of them *imply* a causal relationship, for example being an only child causes greater job success, or eating an ice cream every day causes you to be happier. In fact they are just correlations. Newspapers are constantly making this error suggesting a *cause* when there is only an observed *relationship* between the variables.

Take the case of increased police officers. What happens is crime figures are noted in the weeks before more police were put on the streets and then compared to crime figures in the weeks after. If there is a decrease in crime it doesn't mean it was because of the increased police. There may have been different weather conditions or local employment rates may have improved (these are alternative variables – *intervening* variables).

The worry is that people believe all these claims – that's why understanding research methods is so important.

Specification terms

Case study The detailed study of one case (such as a family or a football team or a festival). It involves the use of mixed methodologies.

Correlational analysis A method used to assess the degree to which two co-variables are related. The measurement of each co-variable must be quantitative and continuous, such as using rating scales and scores on a psychological test.

Mixed methodology A research study that uses a number of different research methods.

The scattergram below shows a strong negative correlation between global warming and piracy. What could be the explanation? If you don't have an explanation for an apparent correlation then there is likely to be an intervening variable – in this case it might be an increasingly developed world and these are both consequences.

Scattergram showing the global average temperature vs. number of pirates.

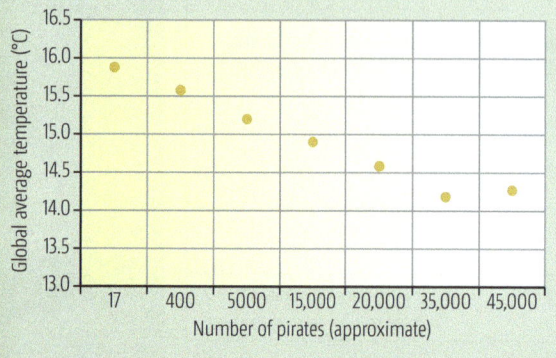

Mixed methodologies

Very few studies use just one research method for data collection. For example, on page 124 we showed you the observation checklist used in Bandura *et al.*'s Bobo doll experiment. The study was a *lab experiment* but *observation* was also used to measure the *dependent variable* (DV). In the study by Möller and Krahé (page 19) a questionnaire was used to measure the DV, with one critical question about how deliberate the push was.

Furthermore some studies don't really have a clear method. For example, Bartlett's study of memory was not an experiment (there is no *independent variable*), participants were questioned about what they recalled but it wasn't really a questionnaire.

The key point is that we can make judgements about validity and reliability without knowing the method – see the facing page. Research methods guide researchers in planning research that is valid and reliable, but knowing the research method doesn't tell us that much about validity or reliability. You need to be thoughtful.

On this spread we are also going to look at case studies and correlational analysis.

Case studies

Case studies are an example of mixed methodologies because inevitably different methods are used.

The defining aspect of a case study is that the focus is on one case (though this could be one institution or one event, in which case many people are involved) – but the data about the case is collected through the use of *questionnaires* and *interviews*, looking at things that have been written (a diary or newspaper report), psychological tests, and so on.

Correlational analysis

Strictly speaking, *correlation* is a technique used to analyse data, it is not a method for collecting data. However, it is the basis of many studies in psychology, especially those analysing health trends or crime trends.

It is often *secondary* or *desk-based research* since the data has been collected by someone else (e.g. government *statistics*). Therefore, the researcher does not have to go out and collect data but just sits at their desk analysing it.

Quantitative data A key requirement is that the data for a correlation (the co-variables) must be numerical and must be *continuous*. This means that it is data that has a fixed and meaningful order. For example, you can't correlate intelligence with 'favourite football team' because football teams don't have one fixed order, as say temperature scales do. We could ask people to rate how much they like football and correlate this with intelligence to see if people who like football are more intelligent.

Scattergrams We will look at these on page 137. Basically, in order to do a correlational analysis you need to be able to plot the data on a scattergram where one co-variable is on the *x*-axis and the other co-variable is on the *y*-axis.

Validity and reliability again

Validity concerns the extent that any research findings truly represent what people do and think and feel. Therefore, the key issues for any study are:

- To what extent are the participants representative of all people? If the sample is just young people, or just Americans, or just people from London, or just men, we cannot generalise the findings to what all people do/think/feel.
- To what extent are participants behaving 'normally'? When people know that their behaviour is being recorded (e.g. in an *overt observation* or in a questionnaire) then they understandably change it to fit in with ideas about what they should be like. This means that psychologists aren't really providing any useful insights. It requires careful research design to conduct valid research while respecting ethical issues.
- To truly understand what people do and think we need to study both aspects – we need to observe them and ask them. Therefore, mixed methodologies have a higher validity. Alternatively a range of studies can each use different methodologies and we can compare the findings – this is called *triangulation*.

Reliability concerns whether our measuring tools are consistent.

- Validity depends on reliability. If a researcher uses a questionnaire to measure the dependent variable in an experiment, that measuring tool must be reliable. We assume that if you gave the same person those same questions a few days later, they ought to be giving the same answers. Otherwise the data is meaningless.

Evaluation

+ Can be used to investigate instances of human behaviour and experience that are rare (for example, mental disorder or a riot).
+ The method produces rich, in-depth data because the focus is on one thing and data can be collected on all aspects of that thing.
+ The complex interaction of many factors can be studied, in contrast with experiments where variables are held constant.
− It is difficult to generalise from individual cases as each one has unique characteristics and/or because we can't make before-and-after comparisons. For example, in the case of Phineas Gage (page 45) we only have anecdotal evidence of what he was like before the accident.
− It is often necessary to use recollection of past events as part of a case study. Such evidence may be unreliable because people's memories are inaccurate.
− There are important ethical issues such as confidentiality and anonymity. Many cases are easily identifiable because of their unique characteristics, even when real names are not given.

Evaluation

+ Correlation is a useful way to spot possible relationships between variables. If a correlation is not strong then we can rule out a *causal relationship*. If the correlation is strong then further investigation is justified because there may be a causal link.
− The big problem is that people mistakenly conclude that a correlation between variables means that one caused the other. For example, if there is a strong correlation between number of violent films watched and levels of aggressiveness, it might be that watching violent films causes that increase but the correlation does not demonstrate this. It might be that having an aggressive personality is an intervening variable – and this causes a person to choose to watch violent films and also causes higher levels of aggression.
− The method used to measure either co-variable may lack reliability or validity. For example, one co-variable may be measured using a questionnaire (such as when measuring aggressiveness). The reliability and validity of the questionnaire would affect the reliability and validity of the study.

GET ACTIVE Valid studies?

Look again at some studies from Unit 1. For each, give one reason why validity might be high and one reason it might be low.

Assessment practice

At the end of learning aim B you must write a report (see pages 119 and 132). This report must be related to your pilot study.

This assessment practice task will help you with the skills required to write a proposal in response to your own aim.

The educational psychologist suggests that personality may be related to preference. Having worked with many students over several years, you know that students differ in their personality type. Some are extraverts (outgoing, sociable, impulsive) and others are introverts (withdrawn, shy, unsociable).

You decide to use a correlational analysis to investigate this research aim: to find out if there is a correlation between personality type and teaching method preference.

B1.6 Learning aim B1 – Task 6

1. **Plan** a proposal for a pilot study to investigate the above research aim. (B.P3)
2. **Explain** the reasoning behind using a correlational analysis to investigate the research aim. (B.P4)
3. **Assess** the use of a correlational analysis to investigate the research aim. (B.M2)
4. **Evaluate** the use of a correlational analysis to investigate the research aim. (B.D2)

An issue to consider
Which is more important – validity or reliability?

Specification content
B1 Research methods

Advantages, disadvantages and appropriateness of methods to meet the aims and purposes of different psychological investigations, e.g. time, reliability, validity, cost.

- Mixed methods:
  ○ Value of using mixed methodologies for conducting research using questionnaires, interviews and observations, e.g. reliability and validity in helping identify underlying causes and perceptions, beliefs, strength of feeling.

Methods of data analysis are also part of learning aim C, where they are covered (see pages 136–139).

Learning aim B2: Developing research proposals

Planning and managing your pilot study

Event planning

All events require management, from the Olympics to a rock festival or a wedding.

Management is required because such events involve a variety of elements that need to be coordinated and they all have a timescale – they all take a set amount of time and everything must be ready for the day of the event.

Event planning is not a trivial activity – you can study for a degree in it. Courses typically involve learning to look after staff, planning the shape of the event itself, bringing in specialist teams, risk management, marketing, sales, accounting, health and safety.

You must consider some of these skills yourself as your project will require very careful planning before the event itself (the data collection bit) and will involve dealing with other people and having to keep an eye on health and safety. You also have your report to manage.

Specification term

Management Organising, planning, controlling and directing an organisation's resources in order to achieve its objectives.

One step at a time. A big project is daunting so, in order to complete it well, just focus on one element at a time. Then move on to the next step. Time management will help you with this.

This is it

The time has now arrived for you to write the proposal for your *pilot study*. Once you have written this report you are committed to this project and this has important implications for your final mark – the assessments for learning aims B, C and D all relate to this pilot study. So take one last look at your decision and start preparing your plan.

1. Your research topic/question

Your study should have significance for *practice* or provision (*policy*), as you are required to comment on this in your conclusion. It also needs to be practical and ethical – you should avoid socially sensitive issues (such as mental health) and research with political implications (you are not conducting cutting edge research). Finally your project should be engaging – if you investigate something that is interesting, you will produce a much better study.

You may want to go back through this unit and Unit 1, listing possibilities.

2. Literature review

You need to conduct a *literature review* (see guidance on page 107). This review should consist of at least three paragraphs – paragraph 1 on the broad topic area/theory, paragraph 2 on one relevant research study, paragraph 3 on evaluation of this research study.

Ideally you will describe and evaluate more than one study as the specification suggests that your pilot study should have a sound *empirical* focus.

Your comments on these studies should lead logically to your aim and/or *hypothesis*. Do not complicate things by having several aims/hypotheses. Keep it simple. There is only credit for good design, not complex design.

3. Research method

What is the best research method to use to investigate your aim/hypothesis? If your overall design is an experiment, you have various design decisions which should all be explained:

- Is it going to be conducted in the *lab* or the *field*?
- How will you *operationalise* the *independent* and *dependent variables*?
- Will you be using a naturally-occurring independent variable?
- Will you choose an *independent groups* or *repeated measures* design?
- What *extraneous/confounding variables* need to be controlled?
- What kind of data will you collect?

If a *survey* is used, you need to explain your choice of, for example, a *questionnaire*, or a *semi-structured interview*. You then need to develop your questions.

If the study involves *observation*, you need to explain your choice of *time/event sampling, participant/non-participant,* and *overt/covert*. You need to develop your *behavioural categories*.

If you are doing a *correlational analysis* or a *content/thematic analysis*, what will the sources of your data be?

> Note: In the *Delivery Guide for Unit 2* it states: Learners also need to formulate a short questionnaire to give to their participants asking about their thoughts on the research. This could include any questions about what should have been changed or what they didn't understand, how the participants thought they performed, whether they understood what they were supposed to do, etc.

4. Other design decisions

Participants and sampling Remember that you are conducting a pilot study and therefore only require a small sample of 10–12 people. However, the sample should represent the kind of participants who would ultimately be involved because you should be testing the procedures on the target audience.

Ethical considerations (see page 112) Identify any ethical issues that may arise and explain how you will deal with them or why they don't require any action. For example, if you are doing an *overt observation* you can explain that privacy is not an issue because you intend to seek *informed consent*.

Procedures The final step is to write down your intended procedures in the same way as someone might write a recipe for making a cake. Every single step needs to be specified in detail so that someone else could repeat the same process exactly. Doing this may inform some of your earlier design decisions and you may wish to make some changes.

5. Organisational management

When working on any project, *management* is crucial, i.e. working out a plan in advance so you know:

- All the individual tasks that need to be completed.
- How you are going to complete them within the specified time.

SMART targets

An important part of managing your research project is setting your own clear and achievable aims and objectives. For every objective you set, confirm it meets the SMART criteria.

- **S**pecific targets – specify what needs to be done for each objective on the facing page and the timescale for completion for each objective.
- **M**easurable targets – goals must be measurable so you can check whether you have achieved them. Focus on observable actions. For example, read three articles, write first draft of the literature review, write final version of the literature review.
- **A**chievable targets – review your plan. Ask yourself whether, with a reasonable amount of effort and application, the objective is achievable. Setting objectives that are too low or unachievable will reduce your motivation.
- **R**eliable targets – your objectives should be realistic. Can you really achieve what you have planned so far? Are the objectives within your capabilities? Can you achieve them within the timescale and the resources that you have? At the same time you don't want to make it too easy – you want to maximise what you do produce.
- **T**ime-bound targets – set clear deadlines and stick to them. One way to manage timing is to use a Gantt chart.

6. Time management – a Gantt chart

A *Gantt chart* is a visual method to use for time management of complex projects. It is named after Henry Gantt, an American engineer and management consultant working about 100 years ago.

A Gantt chart (see below) is a horizontal bar chart that shows the timing of each task. It allows you to see at a glance: what the various activities are, when each activity begins and ends, how long each activity is scheduled to last, where activities overlap with other activities, and by how much, and a start and end date for the whole project.

The bad news is, each time one activity takes longer than you expected, the whole chart has to be redone. The good news is you can use Microsoft Excel to do this automatically, as shown below.

GET ACTIVE Your own Gantt chart

Task	Days since start	Days to complete
Start date	05-Feb-21	
Literature review	0	2
Write literature review	2	2
Record decisions and procedures	4	5
Conduct pilot study	7	5
Analyse data	12	3
Review research process and findings	15	3
Read through and edit	18	4
End date	27-Feb-21	

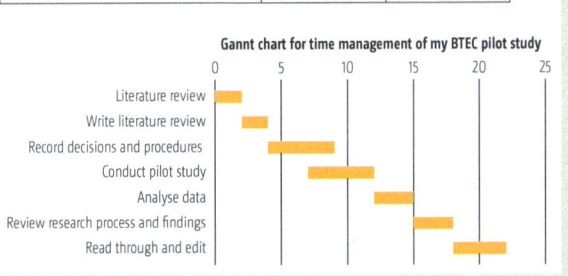

At the top is a table of data to input into the Gantt chart (which is shown below).

In the Gantt chart the first column is a list of the tasks/activities involved in the completion of a project.

Along the top of the chart is a timescale in days.

A bar represents each task/activity. The position and length of the bar reflects the start date, duration and end date of the task/activity.

There are many online sites giving instructions for creating a Gantt chart using Excel, for example tinyurl.com/z428cnz.

Assessment practice

At the end of learning aim B you must write a report (see pages 119 and 132). This report must be related to your pilot study.

This assessment practice task will help you with the skills required to write a proposal in response to your own aim.

Most proposals involve selecting participants. You will need to get their informed consent to take part. A good way to gain consent is to create a consent form for the participants to read and sign.

B2.7 Learning aim B2 – Task 7

1. **Plan** your consent form. (B.P3)
2. **Explain** the information included in your consent form. (B.P4)

An issue to consider

What do you think your greatest challenge will be in this pilot study?

Be aware of the saying 'There are no problems, only solutions'. If you can identify the problem, work out a solution.

Specification content

B2 Developing research proposals

- Identifying and developing a good research topic and questions or hypothesis, to include: identifying sound empirical focus, accessible evidence, significance to practice or provision, ethical, practical, awareness of political implications, relationship to previous research, awareness of implicit values, engaging, answerable.
- Developing research proposals, including research aim, target population and sample, research questions or hypothesis, methodology, procedure, expected outcomes and impact.
- Rationale and content of data collection methods, to include questionnaires, interviews, observations.
- Rationale for research, to include conducting literature review, identifying primary and secondary sources, e.g. journal articles, print and electronic media, assessing reliability and validity of sources.
- Ethical considerations, to include gaining informed consent, gatekeeper and adult consent, mental capacity, age, ensuring physical safety and psychological wellbeing of participants, confidentiality, data protection and safeguarding participants.
- Management strategies including developing specific, measurable, achievable, reliable, time-bound (SMART) targets.

Learning aim B

Assessment guidance

Learning aim B assessment

You are required to produce a maximum of three reports for Unit 2 which means combining at least two of the learning aims. It is suggested the report for learning aim B is separate which makes sense as this is the proposal for your pilot study.

The report can be written or presented as a poster, PowerPoint or in another form.

This report can only be completed after you have studied the content of learning aims A and B as it is a synoptic assessment (see facing page) – see page 117 for an explanation.

Recommended assessment approach

You are required to write a report discussing a proposal for a pilot study that takes account of research questions, methods, participants, procedures, time and organisational management.

The *Delivery Guide for Unit 2* states that your report should:

- Relate to the vocational element of this course.
- Be straightforward.
- Be ethically sound.

Assignment briefs

The board supplies suggested assessment briefs which you can use – see *Unit 2 Authorised assignment brief for Learning aim A and B Conducting psychological research*.

Your centre can also devise their own assessment brief which should have a vocational scenario/context and a series of tasks to complete.

Vocational scenario	The task (from Unit 2 B Assignment Brief)
The *Delivery Guide for Unit 2* suggests that your pilot study should take the form of an experiment, observation, questionnaire or an interview. Caution should be taken not to use topics such as mental health or any procedures that could possibly cause harm or distress.	Produce a detailed report that evaluates and assesses the methods utilised when planning research proposals in psychological enquiry. Your proposal for a pilot study must include the following: • A proposal **plan** for a pilot study using the appropriate methods. • An **explanation** of the proposal for your particular study. • An **assessment** and **evaluation** of the different research methods when planning research proposals in psychological inquiry.

Assessment information

Your final report will be awarded a Distinction (D), Merit (M), Pass (P), Near Pass (N) or Unclassified (U).

The specification provides criteria for each level as shown below.

Pass	Merit	Distinction
B.P3 PLAN for a pilot study using appropriate methods.		
B.P4 EXPLAIN proposal for own pilot study.		
	B.M2 ASSESS different research methods when planning research proposals in psychological inquiry.	
		B.D2 EVALUATE different research methods when planning research proposals in psychological inquiry.

Marking factors The specification also provides information that an assessor will take into consideration when marking your assignment.

Marking factors	Pass	Merit	Distinction
Different research methods will be …	given a basic outline.	analysed.	critically evaluated.
Advantages and disadvantages will be given …	for some examples.	clear consideration of a range of methods, may be examples in different contexts.	detailed consideration of a range of methods in different contexts.
Examples …	not always appropriate.	well-structured and show good understanding.	fully focused, structured and show sound understanding.
The research proposal will contain information about the participants, procedures, research questions or hypothesis and the methodology to be used, as well as ethical considerations and a timeline for completing the pilot project.			detailed and justified.
Research proposal linked to literature, methodologies and references …	some attempt, using academic conventions.	generally accurate.	highly focused.
Discussions …	weak in structure and may contain inconsistencies.	some use of critical evaluation.	demonstrate originality of thought and critical thinking.

Self-review checklist

This research proposal is especially important because it sets the scene for the remaining assessment for Unit 2. If you don't get this right then your report for learning aims C and D will be affected.

That said, if the design of your pilot study is flawed, you will have a lot to analyse in the final report!

First draft of the proposal for your pilot study

Remember this is a draft. So you can write anything, just get thoughts on the page (see 'Blank page syndrome' on the right).

But do not copy anything, even at this stage, because you will later forget it was copied.

Date to complete first draft:

- In the first white column enter the completion dates for each section of your report.
- As you write each section tick when you have planned, explained, assessed and evaluated.

	Date completed	Plan (B.P3)	Explain (B.P4)	Assess (B.M2)	Evaluate (B.D2)
B1 Research methods					
Literature review					
Research aims/hypothesis					
Research method to be used					
Other design decisions					
B2 Organisational management					
SMART targets					
Time management					
References compiled					

Second draft

The next step is to revise your first document. Below is a checklist of things to consider.

Date to complete second draft:

	Date completed
I have checked that I have covered each of the six marking factors (grey column) in the table on the facing page.	
I have gone through and deleted any irrelevant material.	
I have checked that every point has evidence to back it up.	
I have identified long sentences and rephrased them.	
I have checked that each paragraph deals with one idea.	
I have corrected any spelling mistakes.	
I have checked that each paragraph makes reference to the scenario/context.	

Final draft

Read through your completed second draft to polish the report.

Date to complete final draft:

Referencing

If you cite any research study or source (such as a website) you need to include this in a list of references at the end of your report.

This list should be in alphabetical order. The conventions for referencing are described on page 144.

Command terms used in this unit

The assessment criteria for learning aims A, B, C and D are:

Analyse = A methodical and detailed examination, breaking down a topic or information.

Assess = Consider factors that apply to a specific situation, come to a conclusion.

Evaluate = Consider strengths/weaknesses, come to a conclusion.

Explain = State and then justify or give an example.

Perform = Carry out what needs to be done to complete a given activity.

Plan = Create a way of doing a task to achieve specific objectives showing progress from start to finish.

Blank page syndrome*

We all experience it – when you try to start writing something you end up staring at that blank page and can't think where to begin.

It doesn't matter where you begin! That's what a first draft is about. Just write anything – but do write in your own words not chunks copied from the internet or this textbook, otherwise you will forget and they will end up in your final version (see 'Plagiarism' on page 117).

*It's more likely of course to be a blank screen syndrome.

Learning aim C1: Data collection
Data collection

Even experts do it

We asked Professor Fiona Gabbert, Professor of Applied Psychology at Goldsmith's University London, to describe her own experiences of things not going to plan when conducting a research study. She decided to ask members of her department and found that pretty much everyone had a story to share!

Some of these problems are thankfully picked up in the piloting stage. For example, sending participants off on an adventure across campus (that they would later be interviewed about) only to find out they didn't have access to the buildings they were told to visit.

Or finding out that the video snippets that needed to be rated weren't compatible with most smartphone devices. Luckily, these glitches were immediately evident, and fixes were put in place before the full study commenced.

Other times things have gone wrong due to an oversight, such as the time one of us ran a study where participants were only meant to be able to view a video once, but the link remained accessible meaning they could have watched it multiple times before the second phase of the study a week later. Fortunately, it was possible to check if anyone had revisited the videos, and none had – disaster averted!

Last, a few of us meticulously planned a study that enabled us to examine reluctant witnesses in a controlled lab-based setting. We predicted that we'd have some participants who would refuse to be interviewed, some that were only partially cooperative, and so on. What we didn't expect was that every single participant used the same tactic – appearing pleasant and fully cooperative on the face of it, while actually lying to protect their partner! This was incredibly interesting, but the study had to be stopped halfway through so that we could refine the procedure to introduce more variability in tactics used.

GET ACTIVE Problems and solutions

There are no problems, only solutions.

As you are conducting a pilot study remember that problems are expected to arise – so don't feel bad. It is very important that you make notes to use later when writing your report.

On the other hand – it is as well to be prepared.

1. Identify **three** problems which you think might occur.
2. Now think of **three** solutions to your problems, and amend your plan.

Conducting your pilot study

Learning aim B was concerned with planning your *pilot study* and now learning aim C is carrying it out. Therefore, much of your time at this stage will be spent collecting your data rather than reading this textbook and doing activities.

The *Delivery Guide for Unit 2* advises: 'For this assignment it is critical that learners are given enough time and guidance within lessons in order to carry out the study successfully'.

The specification (at bottom right of facing page) lists the tasks involved in planning your pilot study, collecting data and writing the report of your pilot study. In brief this is what you should have in front of you in order to start collecting your data:

- A *literature review*.
- Your research question, aim and/or *hypothesis*.
- The method to be used – a record of your design decisions.
- A detailed description of your intended procedure.
- A time management plan.

Materials

You will now need to assemble any materials required for the study. Some of these are things you need to develop yourself, such as an *informed consent form* and a *debrief*, as well as any *questionnaire* that is required or list of *behavioural categories* for an *observation*.

You may need certain equipment such as a timer or somewhere for participants to sit and write.

Data collection

How will you collect and record your data? You may need to devise a table to record data collected (see facing page). You may need a recording device to record what participants say or do.

You should also consider your 'venue' – where are you going to conduct the study?

Permissions

You need to think of permission from participants (the informed consent form) but also from any other stakeholders, such as the venue where you will conduct your study and also approval from your teacher.

Conducting research is a very responsible activity and you are representing all psychologists when doing your own study, and therefore must behave as a professional.

Participants

Finally you need to recruit your participants based on the design decisions you have made. What *sampling* method? What *target population* are you going to obtain the sample from? How many participants?

Once participants have arrived you must brief them on the aims of the study and the procedures which will be involved. Also inform them of all ethical issues (such as *confidentiality*) and how you will be dealing with these issues.

Afterwards

Debrief participants by thanking them for their time and also telling them more about the study. For example, you may not have told them the aims of the study at the start because it would affect their behaviour.

You can also offer to send them a copy of your final report if they are interested.

Collating and analysing your data

And now you must decide how to represent and analyse your *quantitative* and/or *qualitative data*. The facing page and next few spreads are focused on doing this.

Collating and recording raw data

The term 'raw data' refers to the data you have collected before you have organised it in any way. For example, if you used questionnaires you will have many sheets of paper with participants' answers. Transfer this data to a record sheet or table – this is where you begin to organise data and start to see patterns. 'Playing' with the data will help you to understand it.

The size and shape of the table depends on your data but here is one example that illustrates several issues.

Questionnaire on stress
Q1. What is your age?
Q2. Circle the number that best describes how stressed you generally feel: (Very stressed) 1 2 3 4 5 (Not very stressed)
Q3. On a separate piece of paper, describe what makes you feel most stressed.
Q4. How are you most likely to deal with stress? Circle one answer.
- Going out with friends.
- Physical exercise.
- Drinking, smoking or similar.
- Other _____.

Table to summarise the raw data

The data you collect directly from participants is the 'raw' data – data that has been through no processing. Below is a summary of the answers from four participants.

Participant	Answers to each question				
	Q1	Q2	Q3	Q4	etc.
AD	17	4	Studying	F	
GF	22	1	Family arguments	PE	
TM	35	2	Travelling to work	PE	
KW	28	2	Work	O	
etc.					

The answers have been coded.

Things to note

You can identify your participants using initials or you can number them.

Q1 and 2 produce quantitative data which means we can analyse them using, for example, *measures of central tendency* and graphs (see next spread). We could also correlate the answers to questions 1 and 2.

We might later be interested in exploring the kind of answers given to Q2, for example participants may be avoiding the extreme values so a wider rating scale might help avoid this.

Q3 is an open-ended question, collecting qualitative data, so we can identify themes/categories.

Q4 is an alternative way to collect qualitative data where the categories are pre-decided (makes analysis easier) so we can immediately count the number of each answer given.

In addition there is an 'Other' category which requires *thematic analysis* and could be useful to help refine the questionnaire because new categories might emerge.

It might be useful in your debrief to ask participants if they found any questions difficult to answer, or to get any other feedback.

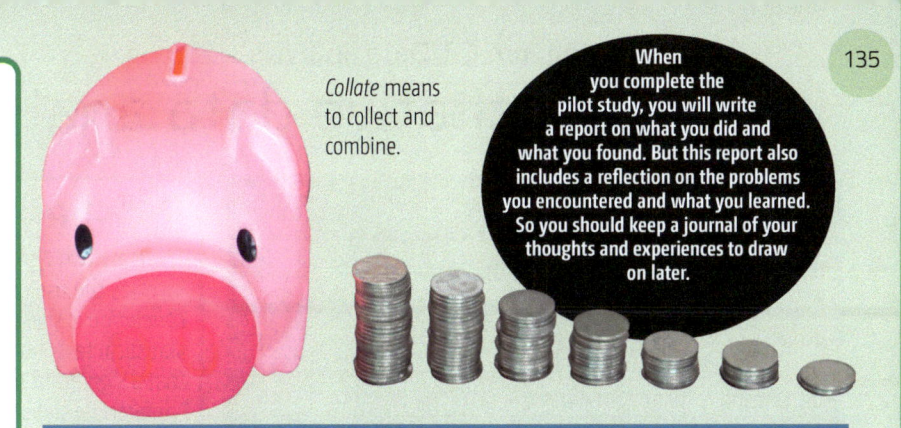

Collate means to collect and combine.

When you complete the pilot study, you will write a report on what you did and what you found. But this report also includes a reflection on the problems you encountered and what you learned. So you should keep a journal of your thoughts and experiences to draw on later.

Assessment practice

At the end of learning aims C and D you must write:
- **A report on procedures followed for conducting research and collecting and analysing data.**
- **A report that discusses the findings and success of the pilot study, the implications of research on practice and provision, and the impact, through self-reflection and feedback from others, on personal and professional development.**

This report must (obviously) be related to your pilot study. The full assessment criteria for learning aims C and D are on page 144.

Having spent a lot of time planning your pilot study, you must now carry it out and collect your data. So, for the rest of this unit you will be working on your pilot study as the context.

C1.1 Learning aim C1 – Task 1

Answering the question below should help you in terms of writing up your report of the process.

1. **Explain** in detail the procedures you used to collect your data. (C.P6)

   Make sure you address the requirements highlighted on this spread (e.g. include information about materials used, design decisions taken, methods used to recruit participants, how you recorded the data, etc.).

An issue to consider

It is said that the difference between *data* and *information* is that data refers to the figures whereas information is when the data has been processed (organised, structured) to make it meaningful. Information provides context for the data.

What is data and what is information on this spread? How does the 'information' help us understand our data?

Specification content

C1 Data collection
- Developing and refining questions or hypotheses, e.g. through identification of literature.
- Recruitment of participants, to include sample size and features.
- Gaining permission and consents.
- Data collection using qualitative and quantitative methods.
- Data collation, e.g. organisation of numerical data, coding, defining themes and trends, interpreting qualitative and quantitative data.

C2 Data analysis
- Quantitative data analysis techniques.
- Qualitative data analysis techniques, e.g. thematic and narrative analysis, coding.

Learning aim C2: Data analysis

Quantitative data analysis techniques

Lies, damned lies and statistics

The American writer, Mark Twain, said there are three kinds of lies – lies, damned lies and statistics. Why have people got it in for *statistics*?

The term 'statistics' simply refers to organising, analysing and interpreting data. It's not the statistics themselves that are the problem, it's the spin that's put on them.

Here are three statistics for you from cracked.com. Read the explanations below the graph to see how the statistics are misleading.

- Hand sanitisers kill 99.9% of germs *
- 90% of dentists recommend a particular brand of toothpaste **
- Autism is increasing. ***

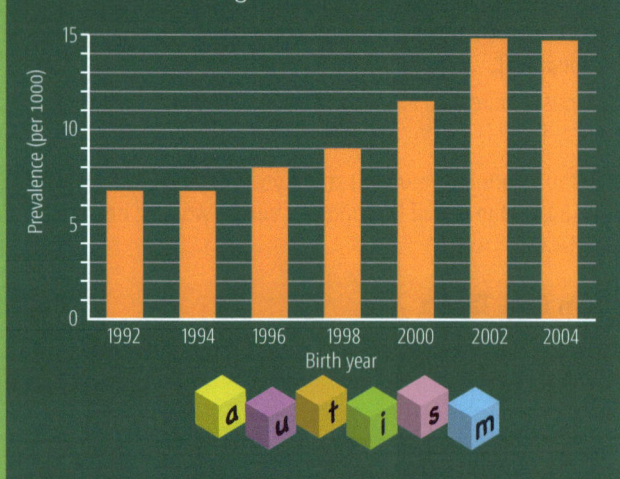

* This only applies in lab conditions (a point not mentioned). In real-world settings the figure drops to under 50%.

** Information not mentioned is that dentists could select more than one brand of toothpaste so all toothpastes came out well.

*** The increase is probably because the criteria used to diagnose autism have become broader.

GET ACTIVE Play with numbers

The descriptive statistics on this spread should be familiar to you from studying GCSE Maths. You can have great fun (really) playing with the numbers – change individual values and see what effect this has. There is also an educational value because such play helps you understand the concepts.

For example:

- Standard deviation and mean (tinyurl.com/z446c9m) – type in numbers and watch how each extra number causes the SD and mean to change.
- Plot a graph (tinyurl.com/y2l87v9j) or scattergram (tinyurl.com/yyfgna7p) and press 'GRAPH IT'. Change values and press 'GRAPH IT' again to see how the plot changes.

Descriptive statistics

There are two types of *statistics: descriptive* and *inferential*. Inferential statistics involves the use of inferential statistical tests to determine if a *difference* or *correlation* is significant. You are not required to study or understand these statistical tests but be aware that most research does use them in order to claim that a significant result has been demonstrated.

Inferential statistical tests are supported by descriptive statistics – numbers or graphs that *describe* the data and allow us to detect patterns which might be important (significant).

Measures of central tendency

Measures of central tendency tell us about typical or average values for a data set.

Mean Add up all numbers and divide by the number of numbers. It is a 'sensitive' measure because it reflects the values of all the data in the final calculation. Only the mean uses all the values in the final calculation. However, it can be unrepresentative of the data set if there are extreme values. For example, you can see here how a few numbers have a large effect on the mean:

Set A: 5, 7, 8, 11, 12, 16, 18   Mean = 11.0
Set B: 5, 7, 10, 11, 14, 17, 41   Mean = 15.0

Median Place all values in order and select the middle value. If there are two middle values calculate the mean of these two values. A positive is that this method is not affected by extreme scores. For example, in the data sets A and B above, the median in both cases would be 11. However, the median is not as sensitive as the mean.

Mode Identify the group or groups which is/are most frequent or common. Useful when the data is in categories. For example, asking people to vote for their favourite colour. The mode would be the colour that was most often chosen. It is not a useful way of describing data when there are several modes.

Measures of dispersion

Measures of dispersion tell us about the spread of a set of data – are the items closely bunched together or spread out?

Range Arrange data in order from lowest to highest and subtract the lowest number from the highest number. This is easy to calculate but affected by extreme values. It also fails to take account of the distribution of the data.

Standard deviation (SD) is usually worked out with a calculator. It is basically the mean distance of all values from the mean – so it takes both the range and distribution into account. However, it may hide some of the characteristics of the data set (e.g. extreme values).

Percentages

It is always better to represent findings as percentages so different data sets can be compared.

For example, you might compare the memories of students using two different revision strategies and find that 8 students using method 1 got better than half marks and 12 students using method 2 got better than half marks. In order to draw any conclusions we need to know the total number of students in each group.

Method 1: 8 out of 20 got better than half marks.
Method 2: 12 out of 32 got better than half marks.

We can't compare them directly because the total number is different.

Method 1: 40% got better than half marks [8/20 × 100].
Method 2: 37.5% got better than half marks [12/32 × 100].

Specification terms
They're all defined on the spread.

Graphs

We looked at using tables on the previous spread. Below we look at more descriptive statistics – graphs and distributions. All graphs must have a title and the *x* and *y* axis must be labelled.

Bar chart The height of each bar represents the frequency of each item. Bar charts are especially suitable for data that has no particular order such as Graph A on the right which represents categorical data. In a bar chart a space is left between each bar to indicate the lack of continuity.

Histogram is the official name of a bar chart which represents continuous data. Again the height of each bar represents the frequency of each item. The area within the bars must be proportional to the frequencies represented (see Graph B). This means that the vertical axis (frequency) must start at zero. In addition the horizontal axis must be continuous. Finally there should be no gaps between the bars.

Scattergrams are used to illustrate a correlation between two co-variables by plotting dots to represent each pair of scores. One co-variable is on the *y*-axis (in our case a rating for beauty) and the other is on the *x*-axis (age in years). For each individual we obtain a score for each co-variable.

- *Positive correlation* = both variables increase together (Graph C).
- *Negative correlation* = age increases as beauty decreases (Graph D).
- *No correlation* = no pattern (Graph E).
- *Curvilinear correlation* = the co-variables increase together up to a point and then one co-variable starts decreasing while the other continues to rise.

The extent of a correlation is described using a *correlation coefficient*. This is a number between +1 (perfect positive correlation) and −1 (perfect negative correlation). The correlation coefficients for the graphs on the right are +.76, −.76 and +.002. The plus or minus sign shows whether it is a positive or negative correlation. The coefficient (number) tells us how closely the co-variables are correlated. −.76 is just as closely correlated as +.76.

Distributions Histograms show how a data set is spread out (i.e. 'distributed') – it shows where most people scored, and what we mean by 'most' is the mean, median or mode.

Normal distribution (Graph F) has a characteristic symmetrical bell-shape. The mean, median and mode are at the same point and values are more or less evenly distributed on either side. The dotted red lines show standard deviations from the mean, 68.26% of the scores should lie within one standard deviation of the mean. Many human characteristics, such as shoe size and intelligence, form this distribution.

Skewed distribution The mean, median and mode do not all share the same value.

In a positive skew (Graph G) most of the scores are bunched towards the left. The mode is to the left of the mean because the mean is dragged to the right by the extreme scores tailing in a *positive* direction (tail to the right). If we plotted scores on a psychological test measuring symptoms of depression this would be the likely distribution – most people would get a low score.

In a negative skew (Graph H) most of the scores are bunched to the right and some tail off in a *negative* direction (to the left).

Graph A: Bar chart to show favourite colour.

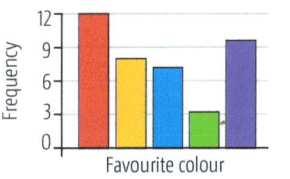

Graph B: Histogram with line graph superimposed to show the ages of people who attended a concert.

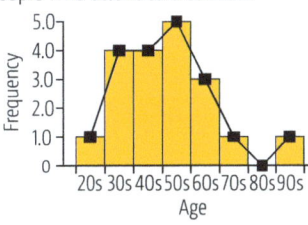

Graphs C, D and E: Scattergrams of the possible relationship between age and beauty.

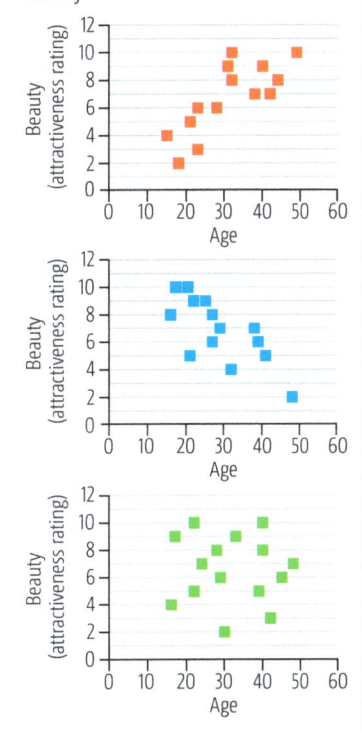

Graph F: Normal distribution.

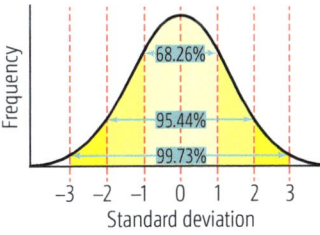

Graph G: Positive skew.

Graph H: Negative skew.

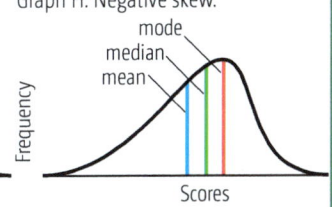

Tables and graphs allow us to 'eyeball' our data and see any pattern in the results at a glance – as the saying goes, 'a picture is worth a thousand words'.

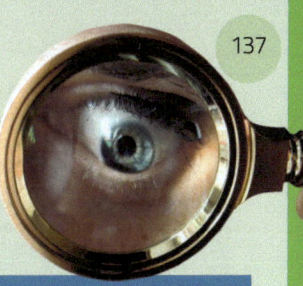

Assessment practice

At the end of learning aims C and D you must write a report (see page 144). This report must be related to your pilot study.

You should now analyse, summarise and present your data using the appropriate methods on this spread. The purpose of analysing data is to help understand what your findings mean.
If you have collected quantitative data, you may need to calculate the appropriate measures of central tendency/dispersion as well as percentages, and to plot a suitable graph (or graphs).

C2.2 Learning aim C2 – Task 2

Answering the questions below should help you in terms of reporting the findings of your pilot study.

1. **Explain** the findings of your pilot study using appropriate formats. (C.P6) [i.e. use descriptive statistics.]
2. **Analyse** the findings of your pilot study. (C.M3) [i.e. draw conclusions from the descriptive statistics.]

An issue to consider

Explain why descriptive statistics are so useful.

Specification content

C2 Data analysis

- Quantitative data analysis techniques:
  - Descriptive statistics, to include measures of central tendency, mean, mode, median, range, standard deviation.
  - Correlations and distributions, to include correlation, correlation coefficient, normal and skewed distributions.

Partly covered here:

C3 Presenting findings to an audience

- Summarising data using different formats, to include tables, graphs, pie charts, bar charts, histograms, scattergrams.

Learning aim C2: Data analysis

Qualitative data analysis techniques

Apprenticeships

The Institute for Public Policy Research (IPPR) conducted qualitative research on the experience of apprenticeships in the UK (Lawton and Norris 2010). The IPPR describe themselves as the 'UK's leading progressive think tank, producing cutting-edge research and innovative policy ideas for a just, democratic and sustainable world'.

The research primarily involved the use of focus groups with female apprentices aged between 16 and 24. A *focus group* is a small group of people selected to represent the target population. The members worked in hairdressing, retail, early years childcare, hospitality and social care. Male engineering apprentices were included as they tended to have higher pay. Finally career advisors and employers were also interviewed.

In addition to the focus groups there was a questionnaire – it is worth having a look as it is a good example of how to do a questionnaire (see tinyurl.com/y68nx8v5). The conversations of the focus groups are interesting to read as well.

One of the key conclusions was there is some evidence that a minimum wage for apprentices could increase completion rate but low pay was not the primary reason why young people left – more important was low job satisfaction and poor-quality training.

The IPPR has continued to research apprenticeships – have a look at their website.

Specification terms
See page 126.

Triangulation
In mathematics the term *triangulation* refers to a method of determining the exact location of a point (such as on a map) by taking measurements from various positions.

In research we use multiple and diverse perspectives to provide a fuller picture of a phenomenon by comparing the findings from different kinds of research.

For example, when investigating successful management strategies at work, we might conduct an observation of people in a work environment, conduct interviews (and use a qualitative analysis) and do a case study.

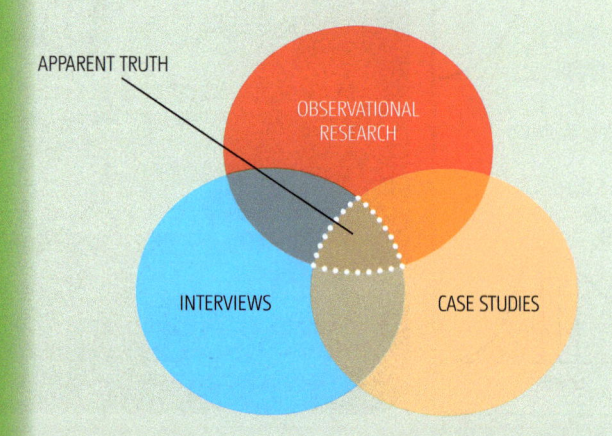

APPARENT TRUTH

OBSERVATIONAL RESEARCH

INTERVIEWS   CASE STUDIES

Analysing qualitative data

This spread is important if you have conducted an *interview*, *questionnaire*, *observation* or *content/thematic analysis*. It is also important if you have used observational or *survey* techniques as part of an *experiment*.

We have already discussed the process of thematic analysis on page 126. Thematic analysis may be used during the planning part of your study or you may be using it now to analyse the data you have collected.

Questionnaire or interview
Perhaps one question in your questionnaire produced *qualitative data*. This means you need a method to summarise the answers you were given. You can apply thematic analysis.

- Step 1 – list all the answers you were given to a particular question or group of questions.
- Step 2 – read and reread the answers to understand the meaning. Take no notes.
- Step 3 – start listing some categories/themes (coding the data). Try to keep an open mind. One way to do this is illustrated on the facing page.
- Step 4 – group items together into broader themes to help focus your analysis.
- Step 5 – in your final discussion list your themes with quotes from the original answers.

Observation
If you conducted an observation without any *behavioural categories*, you now need to conduct a thematic analysis. It might be that you have videoed the behaviour and need to identify themes in this visual record.

You should follow the same steps outlined above. In the case of a video you may first want to transcribe the contents of the recording.

Subjectivity
One of the issues with qualitative analysis is the bias of the person doing the coding. Qualitative analysis is a *subjective* process and scientific research aims to be *objective*. There are a number of ways to deal with this issue.

Reliability The data can be coded by a second person and categories compared. Individuals might discuss the categories – in a similar way to the *nominal group process* described on the facing page.

Furthermore, once categories/themes have been identified then two people can use them to code the data and *inter-observer reliability* can be considered.

Reflexivity One of the strengths of qualitative research is that it is subjective. It seeks to investigate behaviour from the perspective of those who experience it. The term *reflexivity* is used to describe the extent to which the process of research reflects a researcher's values and thoughts. In order to enhance the scientific nature of qualitative research this inevitable subjective bias must be recognised. Instead of trying to minimise or remove subjectivity, this is dealt with by acknowledging that the subjective nature is part of the research itself. Therefore, the researcher enhances the *validity* of the research by including comments on how their influence has affected the research process.

Triangulation This is the process of looking at a number of different research studies (quantitative and qualitative) to see to what extent they all point in a similar direction. If they do 'triangulate' this is good support because they each bring a different perspective to the data collected.

Studying what stresses students

We asked 20 students 'What are the things that make you feel stressed?'. Below are a few answers.

We have analysed the data by identifying the themes in the answers and categorising (or coding) everything in terms of one of these themes.

Answers	Themes
School and exams make me feel stressed because the amount of work is hard to complete and can make me feel overwhelmed. I don't like to feel things are out of my control. Approaching exams is stressful as I begin to second guess if I am prepared or not.	Pressure of work and meeting deadlines. Exams and revision. Feelings that arise from stress, e.g. being out of control, procrastinating. Coping strategy, being prepared. Other worries outside of school, e.g. losing things and money worries.
I don't find many things stressful as I realise most minor inconveniences will not ruin my life. I feel I am able to cope with most stressors, however some things such as exams and some school work stress me sometimes. Also when I lose things at home such as keys it makes me feel slightly stressed.	
I have exams and deadlines and problems that I would imagine would stress other people, yet I feel prepared and relaxed. I'm not very financially stable at the moment which does occasionally cause stress but not for long.	
Being disorganised in the face of multiple deadlines makes me feel stress as you don't know what you need to do. The stress makes me want to avoid acknowledging what I need to do and procrastinate.	
I feel stressed by exams and revision because I feel under pressure to go to university. Other elements of school such as coursework and deadlines also make me feel stressed. I work with children who make me feel stressed when they misbehave and don't do as they are told.	

Stress analysis using nominal group process

Helen Bland *et al.* (2010) conducted a qualitative study of sources of stress, types of stressors, and coping mechanisms employed among undergraduate American college students. They used a slightly different process of qualitative analysis – called *nominal group process*.

You can read the report of this study here: tinyurl.com/yywd5uc4. It is an excellent example of the way research is reported (including a *literature review*, details of the method used and the findings, followed by a conclusion and evaluation).

Procedure First they asked 200 students 'What are the things that cause you stress?' Next they asked the students 'Please take 5 to 10 minutes to list all the things that have personally caused you stress during your college years. These can be big events that you experienced or minor hassles. There is no right or wrong answer.'

When that task was completed, participants then joined a small group of about ten students and each reported their answers to the group. A facilitator recorded the key points on flipcharts until all items were listed. Clarification of each item, if necessary, was then made. Participants were asked to evaluate the group's input, and then individually ranked the top five items on a note card. The group discussed the rankings and reached a consensus. The whole process took about half an hour.

Findings The top five stressors were schoolwork, money, time management, parents/family and tests (content/time). In fact relationships and boyfriend/girlfriend were also listed and, jointly with parents/family, constituted the largest category.

GET ACTIVE TV analysis

TV programmes are a good source of data for analysis. Record a few programmes – you might record multiple episodes of one of your favourite programmes (*EastEnders*, *Britain's Got Talent*, *Pointless*) or a range of programmes aimed at a similar audience.

Set yourself a research aim such as, 'How are women represented?' or 'What emotions are dealt with in the programme(s)?' or 'What makes the audience laugh?'.

Pudsey, winner of *Britain's Got Talent* 2012 (along with his owner Ashleigh). What is the winning formula for *BGT*?

Assessment practice

At the end of learning aims C and D you must write a report (see page 144). This report must be related to your pilot study.

If you have collected qualitative data, you are still able to analyse, summarise and present your data using the appropriate methods on this spread. The purpose of analysing data is to help understand what your findings mean.

Whether you have used a questionnaire, interview or observation method, this spread will help you to conduct a thematic analysis of your data.

C2.3 Learning aim C2 – Task 3

Answering the questions below should help you in terms of reporting the findings of your pilot study.

1. **Explain** the findings of your pilot study using appropriate formats. (C.P6) [i.e. use descriptive statistics.]
2. **Analyse** the findings of your pilot study. (C.M3) [i.e. draw conclusions from the descriptive statistics.]

An issue to consider

Which is better – quantitative or qualitative data? Can you think of situations where one is better than the other?

Specification content

C2 Data analysis

- Qualitative data analysis techniques, e.g. thematic and narrative analysis, coding.

Learning aim C3: Presenting findings to an audience
Writing up the study and presenting it

Feeling nervous?

You may feel nervous about doing a presentation. All speakers feel nervous, but there is a good way to overcome this.

Instead of worrying about what people might think, focus instead on what a lovely opportunity this is. You have worked hard at crafting your pilot study and (hopefully) chosen a topic you feel is interesting. When you feel your nerves coming back, think about yourself and your enjoyment in telling others about your work.

Yes, they may think you could have done it better – but it's not about them, it's about you and this opportunity to develop yourself.

Anyway, why should they judge you harshly? You are a novice, not an experienced researcher. You're a student, learning a craft.

Also remember that they will all still be your friends afterwards, whatever you do. They will all be impressed that you stood up and described your own research study.

GET ACTIVE What is an academic journal?

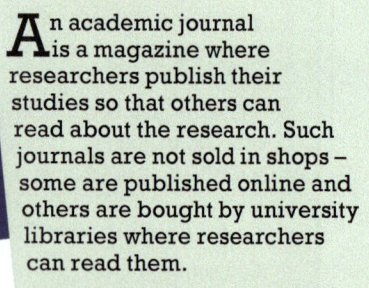

An academic journal is a magazine where researchers publish their studies so that others can read about the research. Such journals are not sold in shops – some are published online and others are bought by university libraries where researchers can read them.

The format for your report (abstract, literature review, method, findings, discussion) follows the format used in such journals.

Look at some articles online and identify the key elements, for example:

- Bahrick *et al.*'s (1975) study was outlined on page 12. You can read the abstract here tinyurl.com/4kn7a4dd
- Fischer and Greitemeyer's (2006) study is mentioned on page 65. Look at the journal article at tinyurl.com/4e9f7uc9
- North's (2012) study is on page 73, see tinyurl.com/42yffzmm
- Fowler *et al.*'s (2011) study is on page 81, look at tinyurl.com/ypt872xn

Writing your report

The specification requires that you know the appropriate format of how to write up a research project (below) and also how to present your findings to an audience (facing page).

Psychologists aim to be scientific in their research and part of the *scientific process* is recording your research study in detail and making that available to other scientists and end users, so they can assess the *validity* of the findings. Other researchers may wish to *replicate* the study to check the validity of the findings or they may wish to make small changes to, for example, the procedure or sample to see if that alters the outcome.

A report should contain the following sections:

Abstract A summary of the study covering the aims, hypothesis, the method (procedures), findings and conclusions (including implications of the current study). You are not required to include this.

Literature review A review of previous research (theories and studies), so the reader knows what other research has been done and understands the reasons for the current study. The researcher states their aims, research prediction and/or hypothesis.

Note – you should have already written the literature review (see page 130).

Method and procedure (data collection) In this section of a report researchers aim to provide sufficient detail so that someone else could exactly repeat the study conducted. The details that need to be included are:

- Design, e.g. *repeated measures* or *covert observation*. Design decisions should be explained (why did you choose that design?).
- Participants – how many? Demographic details (e.g. age, gender, job).
- Sampling technique – how were the participants selected? Were any participants rejected?
- Apparatus/materials – descriptions of any materials used such as a *questionnaire*, photographs or a stopwatch. Examples should be included in the report but full details of e.g. a questionnaire should appear in an appendix to the report.
- Location – details of where the research was conducted.
- Procedures, including standardised instructions (what were the participants told about the study?), the order of events. What the researcher(s) actually did, a step-by-step set of instructions (so they could be repeated).
- Ethical considerations – Mention any procedures related to dealing with ethical issues, such as a *debrief*.

Findings (data analysis) Details are given about what the researcher found. Do not include raw data such as the answers from every participant. This section contains summaries of the data – tables, *measures of central tendency* and *dispersion*, and graphs so a person can see at a glance what you found.

In the case of *qualitative research*, categories and themes are described along with examples within these categories.

Conclusions can be drawn about the findings – what does the data mean?

Discussion See next spread.

References The full details of any journal articles or books that are mentioned in the research report are given. The format for the references is shown on page 144. The references should be listed in alphabetical order.

Presenting your pilot study

It is suggested in the specification that you present your findings to an audience so you can get feedback on your *pilot study*, which is required for your final report. (You should also have feedback from participants – see page 135.)

The presentation
This is a great opportunity to develop the skill of talking to a group of people. Here are some things you could consider.

PowerPoint Using PowerPoint slides means you can show your audience information, such as the questionnaire you used or graphs of the findings. Good slides should have very limited information – a few bullet points to remind you what to say. If you have too much content you end up reading it out instead of talking to your audience.

An alternative is to create a poster display though again too much information is overwhelming, and text/images must be large enough for your audience.

Divide your talk into sections You can follow the same structure as given on the facing page – start with a brief summary of the whole project. Then describe the background and your aims, and so on.

Rehearse Do several practice runs so you can remember what to say for each bullet point (a bit like the technique we describe for remembering information for exams using cue words/phrases, see page 93).

For each practice run stand up in a room and deliver your presentation to the walls. It is no good just reading through the slides, you need to practise out loud and in a situation that makes you feel slightly anxious.

Rehearse in front of a friend and ask them to be honest about whether you have any off-putting mannerisms or phrases. For example, do you overuse a phrase such as 'OK', 'like' or 'err'?

Or video yourself to see what your talk actually looks like from the point of view of the audience.

Delivery Probably your biggest worry is anxiety. One way to cope with this is to try to slow yourself down. Take a breath. A little bit of silence doesn't matter, everyone will be happy to have a break to think about what you just said.

Another strategy is to begin the talk with something familiar such as why you decided to study psychology! This allows you to relax a bit.

Engaging with your audience
The aim of this presentation is for you to get feedback which will help you assess your pilot study. Decide on suitable points in the talk when you could invite the audience to ask questions, for example:

- After hearing the literature review, could they suggest other research questions/aims?
- Did they fully understand the method you used and the rationale for it?
- Do they have any questions about the findings?

If they do ask questions that you can't answer, it is better to admit that you don't know rather than trying to bluff or make something up.

Remember to record the session so you can later listen to their comments.

What have Emma Stone and Ariana Grande got in common?

They both experience anxiety, as do most actors and singers. You are not alone.

Assessment practice

At the end of learning aims C and D you must write a report (see page 144). This report must be related to your pilot study.

You could write the report of your pilot study using the format explained on this spread.

It is important that you also present your pilot study to an audience, and devise of way of getting feedback from them.

C3.4 Learning aim C3 – Task 4
Answering the questions below should help you in terms of organising your report and considering how to evaluate your study including the feedback from an audience.

1. Write up your pilot study and present it in a suitable format in order to **explain** your findings. (C.P6)
2. **Evaluate** your findings and the effectiveness of your pilot study using feedback from your audience. (CD.D3)

An issue to consider
Why do you think the people who designed this course decided it was a good idea to require students to present their findings to an audience?

Specification content
C3 Presenting findings to an audience.
- Summarising data using different formats, to include tables, graphs, pie charts, bar charts, histograms, scattergrams, other pictorial representations, video, narratives.
- Feedback from others, e.g. opinions on approaches taken, findings, outcomes and possible future developments.

Learning aim D: Review implications of research into psychological inquiry

Review research process and implications of research

That's all folks!

Remember that it is all about the journey.

Your pilot study was not focused on producing cutting-edge research in psychology, but on learning about the process of research and developing your skills. It was about deciding on an aim and then being able to design procedures to investigate your aims.

Therefore, your review should not just focus on small details but should look at the bigger picture. Don't just trot out a list of small adjustments that could be made to any study (e.g. 'there could have been more open-ended questions') but think about the things that really struck you about the data that was collected and how you could have changed the design to produce more useful information.

Also focus on you – what have you learned in this process?

Healthy psychological wellbeing

The specification suggests that you should consider how your findings could promote 'healthy psychological wellbeing'. This is defined as experiencing a sense of contentment and satisfaction with all elements of life. This is certainly one of the aims of psychological research – to help people and society lead more satisfying lives.

Here's an interesting question – how can you *operationalise* healthy psychological wellbeing? Doing that may help you consider how your pilot study might promote such wellbeing.

Reflect and review – your discussion

One of the most important aspects of your *pilot study* is what you can learn from it. This part of your report is an essential component of the mark you will be given for learning aim D (see next spread for the assessment information, especially the **marking factors**).

In the discussion section of your report you must consider the research process and findings (below) and also the wider applications and implications (facing page). You might use the subheadings provided below when writing this section.

Review research process and findings

Review the research question This is where you consider your answer to the original research question and state whether the *hypothesis* has been confirmed. You should state your conclusions. This is different from describing findings. Findings are facts, conclusions are generalisations.

For example: In a research study one group of participants were given a treatment for depression (therapy A) and a second group were given therapy B for depression. After two months both groups were assessed for symptoms of depression.

The findings are shown in the table on the right. You can see that mean improvement for therapy A is better than therapy B – that is a fact. What it *means* is that therapy A is a better treatment …

Therapy	Mean improvement	Standard deviation
A	5.8	5.9
B	4.2	1.4

… But the standard deviation is quite large which *means* that therapy A worked well for some participants but less well for others (scores were widely spread out). Therefore, overall, therapy B might be better to use because it was more consistent.

Link to previous research In your initial *literature review* you presented findings/conclusions from previous theory and research. Now you should reflect on how your findings support or challenge previous research.

For example, if a previous study found that therapy A was the best you might now challenge this (if your findings were like the table above), and suggest that the previous study might have ignored the spread of the findings or may have used a different type of participant or some other reason.

Evaluation of the research Look at strengths and weaknesses of your study. You might consider:

- The research design, e.g. how might it be improved?
- The participants, e.g. would it have been better to use a different kind of sample or sampling method?
- Implementation, e.g. were the instructions for participants clear enough, was the environment suitable for testing participants, were some *ethical considerations* overlooked?
- Findings, e.g. were there different *descriptive statistics* that might have been more useful?

There are three things to bear in mind when doing this.

First, draw on the feedback given to you in your presentation.

Second, do not feel you should list every problem you encountered. All studies can be criticised for the kind of participants, the location, ethical problems and so on. Select four or five important issues that are relevant to your pilot study and make sure you explain them well. Also suggest how you would deal with them.

Finally, your evaluation should consider how the design of the research might be improved in order to help promote change or healthy psychological wellbeing.

Implications of your research

The discussion section of a report also considers the future. What might be the next steps for your research question?

> Do check the marking factors on the next spread because the implications (and self-reflection) are specifically mentioned.

Identifying key elements for future research
Perhaps one of your findings stands out as being a topic that could lead to a new research question. Describe this potential new research question.

You might also discuss how your project could be adapted for a larger scale project.

The specification furthermore suggests that you might consider how the research *subject* can be developed for future research. So you might also consider how the general topic area could be further researched.

(Remember it is better to develop a few points in depth rather than write one superficial sentence for each.)

Impact on practice and provision Again, select one or two of your findings and consider how these might be used in the 'real-world'. This might include considering how your findings could be used to provide better childcare or better *practices* in school. Your findings might be relevant to relationships between doctors and patients, or police and criminals or witnesses, and so on.

The specification in particular mentions 'impact on improving life chances, advancements in technologies, treatments, understanding of phenomenon'.

Self-reflection

The final part of your pilot study is to consider what you have gained from this project. This might include:

- New knowledge. Consider the studies and theories you have researched.
- New expertise/skills. You are likely to have acquired some transferable skills that will assist you in the future, such as working to deadlines, analysis of the reliability of sources, presentation skills, writing in an analytical way, and time management skills.
- Your own professional development. This project might relate to your chosen career path and have given you ideas on how to proceed.
- A review of whether your targets were realistic. You can be positive ('I managed to keep to the deadlines in my Gantt chart') as well as negative.

GET ACTIVE What advice would you give?

Your supervisor is teaching this course next year and would like your advice for the next group of students.

1. Identify **three** key pieces of advice that you would give to your supervisor's students about how to complete the pilot study successfully.
2. Write a list of dos and don'ts.

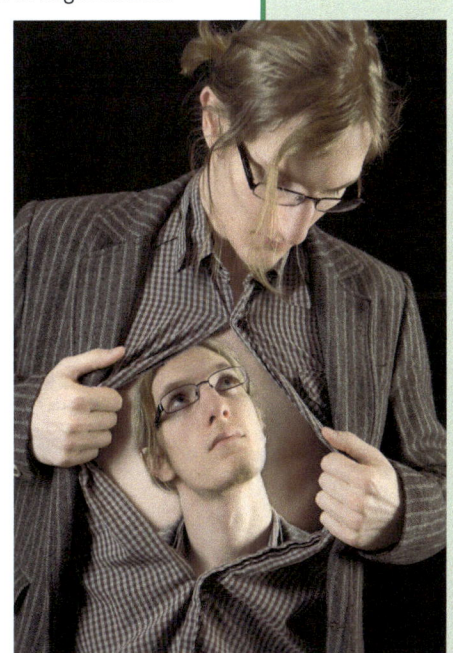

Assessment practice

At the end of learning aims C and D you must write a report (see next spread). This report must be related to your pilot study.

> Right at the start of this process we recommended that your pilot study should be on a topic that relates to wider issues such as provision of services, professional development and future practice. This is one of the things you need to reflect on, also considering feedback from your audience (see previous spread).

D.5 Learning aim D – Task 5
Answering the questions below should help you in terms of organising your report and considering how to write the discussion of your pilot study.

1. **Discuss** how successful your pilot study was using self-reflection and feedback from others. (D.P7)
2. **Explain** what the implications of your findings are for future practice, provision and professional development. (D.P8)
3. Using self-reflection and feedback, **analyse** the findings of your pilot study in terms of their implications for future practice, provision and professional development. (D.M4)
4. Use self-reflection and feedback from others to **evaluate** your findings in terms of implications for future practice, provision and professional development. (CD.D3)

An issue to consider

How is your self-reflection likely to be different from the feedback given by others? How is it likely to be similar?

Specification content

D1 Reviewing research process and findings
- Review success of research on answering research questions, confirming hypothesis.
- Factors relating to the interpretation, discussion and presentation of research findings and the evaluation of the success and usefulness of the research.
- Issues encountered during the research process, e.g. research design, participants, implementation, findings.
- Review research process in identifying and promoting change, and promoting healthy psychological well-being.

D2 Implications of research into psychological inquiry
- Identifying key elements for future research.
- Impact on practice and provision.
- Impact on improving life chances, advancements in technologies, treatments, understanding of phenomenon.
- How research subject can be developed for future research.
- Self-reflection on research process and future personal professional development.

Learning aims C and D
Assessment guidance

Learning aims C and D assessment

You are required to produce a maximum of three reports for Unit 2 which means combining at least two of the learning aims. It makes sense to combine learning aims C and D as we have done here. This is your report of the pilot study proposed in learning aim B.

The report can be written or presented as a poster, PowerPoint or other form.

This report can only be completed after you have studied the content of learning aims C and D as it is a synoptic assessment (see page 117 for an explanation).

Recommended assessment approach

You are required to write a report:
- On the procedures followed for conducting research and collecting and analysing data.
- Discussing the findings and success of the pilot study, the implications of research on practice and provision, and the impact, through self-reflection and feedback from others, on personal and professional development.

Assignment briefs

The board supplies suggested assessment briefs which you can use – see *Unit 2 Authorised assignment brief for Learning aim C and D Conducting psychological research.*

Vocational scenario	The task (from Unit 2 C/D Assignment Brief)
The scenario was decided in learning aim B.	The *Delivery Guide for Unit 2* states that the report for learning aim C concerns three areas: 1. Preparing for the practical research. 2. Carrying out the practical research (data collection and analysis). 3. Writing up the findings effectively and in the appropriate format. The report for learning aim D is a review of the pilot study, to include positives and negatives based on: • Self-reflection. • Feedback from others.

Referencing conventions

You must include the details of all references cited in your report. These go at the end of the report.

Names are given in alphabetical order with last name followed by initial. When multi-authored works have been quoted, it is important to include the names of all the authors, even when the text reference used was *'et al'*.

Book references, e.g.

Offer, D., Ostrov, E. and Howard, K. (1981) *The Adolescent – a psychological self-portrait*. New York: Basic Books.

Note, the title of the book is in italics.

Journal references, e.g.

MacKay, G. (2002) The disappearance of disability? Thoughts on a changing culture. *British Journal of Special Education, 29*(4), 159–163.

Note, the journal name and volume number are italicised.

Internet references, e.g.

Roller, E. (2016) Your facts or mine? *The New York Times*, 25 October 2016, retrieved from https://www.nytimes.com/2016/10/25/opinion/campaign-stops/your-facts-or-mine.html [Accessed March 2019].

Personal communication

Robertson, M. (2012) personal communication.

Command terms for learning aim C

The assessment criteria on the right are defined on page 133.

Assessment information

Your final report will be awarded a Distinction (D), Merit (M), Pass (P), Near Pass (N) or Unclassified (U).

The specification provides criteria for each level as shown below.

Pass	Merit	Distinction	
C.P5 PERFORM a pilot study in one area of psychology.			Identify and analyse findings.
C.P6 EXPLAIN findings using appropriate formats.			
	C.M3 ANALYSE findings from conducting own research using appropriate formats.		

Pass	Merit	Distinction	
D.P7 DISCUSS success of own research using self-reflection and feedback from others.			Explain strengths/weaknesses of design and ideas for improvement.
D.P8 EXPLAIN implications of own research on future practice, provision and professional development.			
	D.M4 ANALYSE own research findings using self-reflection and feedback from others for future practice, provision and professional development.		
		CD.D3 EVALUATE findings, and the effectiveness of own research, using appropriate formats, self-reflection and feedback from others, and the implication for future practice, provision and professional development.	Evaluation

Self-review checklist

First draft

The list in the table below reflects the headings we have suggested for your report but there is another list which is important – the marking factors in the table at the bottom of the page. You must make sure you cover these at your target level.

Remember this is a *draft*. So you can write anything, just get thoughts on the page. But do not copy anything, even at this stage.

Date to complete first draft:

	Date completed	Explain (C.P6)	Analyse (C.M3)	Discuss (D.P7)	Explain (D.P8)	Analyse (D.M4)	Evaluate (CD.D3)
• In the first white column enter the completion dates for each section of your report. • As you write each section tick when you have explained, analysed, discussed and evaluated.							
C Findings							
Procedures for data collection							
Data analysis							
Presenting to audience							
D Discussion							
Review research question							
Link to previous research							
Evaluation of the research							
Future research							
Impact on practice/provision							
Self-reflection							
Further references compiled							

Second draft

The next step is to revise your first document. Below is a checklist of things to consider.

Date to complete second draft:

	Date completed
I have checked that I have covered each of the eight marking factors (grey column) in the table below.	
I have gone through and deleted any irrelevant material.	
I have checked that every point has evidence to back it up.	
I have identified long sentences and rephrased them.	
I have checked that each paragraph deals with one idea.	
I have corrected any spelling mistakes.	
I have checked that each paragraph makes reference to the scenario/context.	

Final draft

Read through your completed second draft to polish the report.

Date to complete final draft:

Marking factors The specification also provides information that an assessor will take into consideration when marking your assignment.

Marking factors	Pass	Merit	Distinction
Rationale for research, research questions, methodologies and procedure …	basic information.	logical.	logical and accurate.
Discussion of data analysis tools …	brief details.	well-structured.	analytical.
Findings displayed …	at least two different formats.		variety of formats.
Structured according to academic conventions and referencing …	an attempt.	well-structured.	accurately structured.
Success of the research project, using feedback from others and self-reflection …	a few reflections.	an argument.	critical evaluation.
Impact of research on areas of practice and provision in supporting the development of strategies, treatments and understanding of their chosen area of research …	an identification, although examples may not always link well to the research project.	critical analysis.	excellent understanding.
The impact of research in supporting personal and professional development …	some consideration.	considered examples and some original thought.	well-considered examples and originality of thought.
How the pilot study could be adapted for a larger-scale research project …	brief overview.	a discussion.	a logical and well-reasoned discussion.

Index with glossary

Adrenaline A hormone produced by the adrenal glands as part of the body's immediate stress response (fight or flight). Adrenaline strongly stimulates heart rate and contracts blood vessels. 46, 48

Aggression Behaviour that is intended to cause psychological or physical harm. 64–71, 86, 124

Allele Some genes have more than one form, in which case each form is called an 'allele'. 42

Alpha bias The tendency to exaggerate differences between groups, e.g. between women and men, binary and non-binary people, etc. 80

Alternative hypothesis The hypothesis in a study is sometimes called the alternative hypothesis because it is the alternative to the null hypothesis. In any study we have an alternative and a null hypothesis. 106, 120

Androgyny Displaying a balance of masculine and feminine characteristics in one's personality (andro = male, gyny = female). 80

Associative priming We process a stimulus more quickly (or recall it more easily) because we earlier encountered a stimulus that is often paired with it. 18

Attribution The process of explaining the causes of your own or someone else's behaviour. 22

Authority bias A tendency to uncritically accept the views of others we perceive as 'experts'. 72

Autonomic nervous system (ANS) Communicates signals between the spinal cord and internal body organs. It is 'autonomic' as the system operates involuntarily (i.e. automatically). It has two main divisions: sympathetic and parasympathetic. 46

Aversion therapy A behavioural treatment based on classical conditioning. A maladaptive behaviour is paired with an unpleasant stimulus such as a painful electric shock. Eventually, the behaviour is associated with pain without the shock being used. In covert sensitisation the aversive stimulus is not real but imagined. 35

Bandwagon effect Behaviour change or purchasing decisions can result from the perception that 'everyone else is doing it' (join the bandwagon). 74–75

Behavioural categories Objective methods to separate a continuous stream of action into components. Behaviours are counted. 124

Beta bias The tendency to minimise or ignore differences between groups, e.g. between women and men, binary and non-binary people, etc. 80

Binary Describes a choice of two states, for example something can be either on or off, or a person can only be a woman or a man. 80, 82

Biochemistry See Neurochemistry

Brain structures Physical components that make up the neuroanatomy of the brain, including the amygdala. 70–71

Brand loyalty Sticking to a particular company's products over time (e.g. repeated purchases) even when there are better alternatives. 72

British Medical Association (BMA) The British Medical Association is the professional association and registered trade union for doctors and medical students in the United Kingdom. 113

British Psychological Society (BPS) The representative body for psychologists and psychology in the UK, which aims to promote excellence in psychology, raise standards of training and practice in psychology, and increase public awareness of psychology. 113

Capacity Amount of material that can be kept in a memory store. 12–13

Case study The detailed study of one case (such as a family or a football team or a festival). It involves the use of mixed methodologies. 128, 138

Causal relationships Situations where one variable makes another variable change. 121

Central nervous system (CNS) Consists of the brain and the spinal cord and is the origin of all complex commands and decisions. 10, 40, 46

Chromosomes Found in the nucleus of living cells and carrying information in the form of genes. The 23rd pair of chromosomes determines biological sex. 42, 86

Classical conditioning A form of learning where a neutral stimulus (NS) is paired with an unconditioned stimulus (UCS), taking on its properties so that a new stimulus–response association is learned. 34, 76

Closed question Has a fixed number of possible answers and provides quantitative data. 122–23

Cognitive Refers to 'mental processes' (e.g. thoughts, perceptions, attention) and how they affect behaviour. 10

Cognitive biases Errors in how we process information, which affect our attention, memory and decision-making. 22–23

Cognitive priming We process a stimulus (word, image, object, etc.) more quickly when we see or hear the stimulus (or a related one) first (the 'prime'). 18, 64

Cognitive scripts Information stored in memory that describes the behaviours typical in a given situation. They are automatically retrieved to guide our behaviour. They are also known as memory scripts. 18, 20, 64

Collectivist People who place more value on the 'collective' (i.e. the other group members) rather than each individual being most focused on themselves. Collectivist cultures also value interdependence rather than independence. 10

Common goals The outcomes of group activity that all members share and work towards. 30

Compliance The individual privately disagrees with the group but goes along with it anyway, usually because they do not want to be rejected. 26, 58, 74

Computer analogy The human brain can be compared to a computer with input, processing and output stages. 10, 12, 18

Concurrent validity The trueness of a psychological test is established by comparing it with an existing, valid psychological test. The new test should produce the same score. 110–11

Conditioned response (CR) The response produced by the conditioned stimulus (CS) on its own. A new association has been formed so that the neutral stimulus (NS) now produces the unconditioned response (UCR) (which is now called the conditioned response, CR). 34

Conditioned stimulus (CS) A stimulus that only produces the desired response after pairing with the unconditioned stimulus (UCS). 34, 76

Conditioning Means 'learning'. Operant conditioning is a form of learning in which behaviour is shaped and maintained by its consequences, which include positive reinforcement, negative reinforcement and punishment. 11

Confabulation When details are added to a memory to fill in the 'gaps', to make recall meaningful. 16–17

Confederate An individual in a research study who is not a real participant and has been instructed how to behave by the researcher. 24

Confidentiality A participant's right to have personal information protected through anonymity and/or by keeping their information safe. 103, 112

Confirmation bias We pay more attention to (and recall more easily) information that supports our existing beliefs. We may seek it out and ignore contradictory information. 22, 80

Conformity When a person changes their opinion/behaviour because they are pressured (or believe they are pressured) by another person or a group. 24, 66

Conformity to gender roles The extent to which a person identifies with a gender-typical (i.e. masculine or feminine) role. 82

Confounding variable A special class of extraneous variable because it changes systematically with the independent variable (IV). This means that we cannot be sure that any change in the dependent variable was due to the IV. In fact the confounding variable is acting as another IV. 104–05, 120

Congenital adrenal hyperplasia (CAH) An inherited disorder causing low levels of cortisol and high levels of male hormones. This leads to the development of male characteristics in females, and early puberty in both boys and girls. 86

Consumer behaviour The study of all the activities associated with the purchase and use of goods and services. 72

Content analysis Kind of observational study in which behaviour is observed indirectly in written or verbal material such as books, diaries or TV programmes. 103, 126

Controlled observation Watching people (or animals) or listening to them, using techniques which organise (control) the observations, such as using behavioural categories and event/time sampling. 124

Conversation analysis See thematic analysis.

Correlation coefficient A number between −1.0 and +1.0 that represents the direction and strength of a relationship between co-variables. 137

Correlational analysis A method used to assess the degree to which two co-variables are related. The measurement of each co-variable must be quantitative and continuous, such as using rating scales and scores on a psychological test. 106, 128

Cortex The outer part of an organ. The cerebral cortex is the surface layer of the forebrain. 44

Cortisol A hormone produced by the adrenal glands as part of the body's longer-term stress response. Cortisol controls how the body uses energy, but it also suppresses the immune system. 48, 70

Counterbalance An attempt to control for the effects of order in a repeated measures design: half the participants experience the conditions in one order, and the other half in the opposite order. 120

Covert observation Participants' behaviour is watched and recorded without their knowledge or consent. 124, 140

Cue A 'trigger' that allows us to access material in memory. Cues can be meaningfully linked to the material (e.g. mnemonics) or can be indirectly linked by being encoded at the time of learning (e.g. external context and internal state). 14–15

Culture Ideas, customs and social behaviour of a particular group of people or society. 10, 82

Debrief A post-research interview designed to inform the participants of the true nature of the study and to restore them to the state they were in at the start of the study. 112, 134

Deductive reasoning Using a general principle to produce particular examples, e.g. developing a theory first and then generating a prediction from this. 99

Dependent variable (DV) Measured by the experimenter to assess the effects of the independent variable(s). 104, 121

Descriptive statistics The use of graphs, tables and summary statistics (measures of central tendency and dispersion) to identify trends and analyse sets of data. 136

Desensitisation Reduced sensitivity to a stimulus, either psychological (e.g. less emotional response) or physiological (e.g. lowered heart rate). 66–67

Desk-based research Research conducted at a desk rather than face-to-face with participants, collecting data directly. It is another name for secondary research. 103

Differential reinforcement Rewarding some behaviours in preference to others; a form of selective reinforcement. 84

Direct attribute priming In advertising, highlighting the desirable features of a product (e.g. speed), so the consumer recalls the product when they think about the features. 72

Directional and non-directional hypothesis A directional hypothesis states the direction of the hypothesis (!) – whether one thing is more than another, for example saying that one group will do better than another group on a task. A non-directional hypothesis just states there is a difference but not the direction of the difference. 106

Discourse analysis See thematic analysis.

Discrimination Harmful behaviour directed at groups or individuals because they share characteristics (e.g. ethnicity). 28–29

Disinhibition A lack of restraint (no longer being inhibited), due to environmental triggers or overexposure to a stimulus. 66

Dopamine A neurotransmitter that generally stimulates neural activity throughout the brain. 49, 70

Duration Length of time material can be kept in a memory store. 12–13

Ecological validity The extent to which a research finding can be applied beyond the research setting. Often research settings are highly controlled and contrived situations and people may not behave in the same way in their everyday lives. 110–11, 121

Empirical The view that knowledge can only come through direct observation or experiment rather than by reasoned argument or beliefs. 98–99, 130

Encoding The process of converting information from one form ('code') to another so it can be stored in the various memory stores and passed between them. 12–13

Environment of evolutionary adaptation (EEA) The habitat in which a species evolved its most recent adaptations. In humans this ended about 10,000 years ago. 50

Ethical codes of conduct A set of principles designed to help professionals behave honestly and with integrity. 112

Ethical considerations Ideas of what is right and wrong. 112, 130

Event sampling Draw up a list of behavioural categories. Then count (tally) every time each of the behaviours occurs during a specified time period (e.g. observing for an hour). 124–25

Evolution The changes in inherited characteristics in a biological population over successive generations. 10, 86

Experiment A research method which demonstrates causal relationships. All experiments have one (or more) independent variable (IV) and one (or more) dependent variable (DV). 102, 104–05, 120–21

External reliability The extent to which one measure of something (e.g. a person's height or their personality) is consistent over time. 110

Extraneous variable Any variable in an experiment apart from the IV and DV. 104, 121

Extraversion One end of a personality dimension with introversion at the other end. Extraversion includes such traits as being outgoing, sociable, sensation-seeking. 40–41

Extrinsic rewards Pleasurable consequences of a behaviour that come from the external environment, e.g. praise, money. 36–37

Eye tracking A method of measuring eye movements to study what captures people's attention. 78–79

Face validity The extent to which the items on a psychological test look like what the test is claiming to measure. 110–11

Facial action coding system (FACS) A set of characteristic facial expressions that can be used to record facial behaviour. 78

Facial coding A method of measuring facial expressions to study emotional responses. 78

Femininity Traits and behaviours considered appropriate for girls/women in a particular culture, distinct from female biological sex. 80, 86–87

Field Conducting research in 'the field' usually means working with participants in an environment that is more familiar to them than a lab. Field research can happen in many locations, such as shopping centres, trains, hospitals, etc. Such environments may be new to participants, i.e. they are not the participants' natural environments but, in general, the setting is more natural. 102

Field experiment An experiment conducted in an everyday environment. Usually the researcher goes to where the participants can be found. 102, 121

Fight, flight, freeze response The body is physiologically aroused to either confront a threat, flee from it, or stay still to avoid it. 50

fMRI A scanning technique used to investigate the brain and other parts of the body. Images are taken of the living brain and sometimes regions of the brain are matched to behaviour by asking participants to engage in particular activities while the scan is done. 78

Focus group Groups of people used in research to discuss their feelings/thoughts on a topic. The group of people may have an interest or expertise in a particular area, for example a group of people with an addiction or a group of health professionals dealing with people with an addiction. 79

Fundamental attribution error In explaining the reasons for other people's behaviour, we focus on their personal characteristics and overlook the role of the situation. 22–23

Gantt chart A type of bar chart that illustrates a project schedule. The width of the horizontal bars in the graph shows the duration of each activity, and these are linked to each other. 131

Gatekeeper consent Permission is provided by a person who stands between the researcher and a potential participant. The gatekeeper provides expert advice and an extra level of protection. 112

Gender The psychological, social and cultural differences between boys/men and girls/women including attitudes, behaviours and social roles, as distinct from biological sex. (We use the terms 'man/woman' when discussing gender but 'male/female' for discussions of biological influences.) 51, 80–87

Gender dysphoria Describes the discomfort or distress arising from a mismatch between a person's sex assigned at birth and their gender identity. This is also the clinical diagnosis for someone who doesn't feel comfortable with the sex they were assigned at birth. 80

Gender fluid Having different gender identities at different times, including single-gender and non-binary. 80, 84, 87

Gender identity A person's sense of their own gender, e.g. man, woman or something else. This may or may not correspond to sex assigned at birth. 81–83

Gender priming A form of cognitive priming in which reminding someone of their gender identity triggers gender-related behaviours. 81

Gender roles Distinct behaviours and attitudes taken on by women and men and usually thought to be 'appropriate' to one gender or another. 81–83

Gender schema An organised set of beliefs and expectations related to gender that are derived from experience. Such schema guide a person's understanding of their own gender and gender-typical behaviour in general. 80–81

Gender typicality The perception that a person is behaving/thinking in a manner representative of their gender group, e.g. a girl behaving/thinking in a feminine manner. 82

Genes Inherited DNA with instructions for building physical and psychological characteristics that influence behaviour. 10, 42

Genome lag Changes to the environment occur much more rapidly than changes to our genes. 50–51

Genotype An individual's total set of genes. 42–43

Group cohesion The extent to which group members are psychologically bonded and 'pull in the same direction'. 30

Grounded analysis See thematic analysis.

Groupthink The tendency of cohesive groups to strive for agreement, which overrides the need to analyse decisions realistically and to consider criticisms and alternatives. 30–31

Health and Care Professions Council (HCPC) An independent, UK-wide regulatory body that sets and maintains standards of professional conduct for health professions. Its main purpose is to protect the public. 100, 113

Hemispheres The forebrain (largest part of the brain) is divided into two halves or hemispheres. 44, 46

Hippocampus A structure in the subcortical area of each hemisphere of the forebrain, associated with memory. It is part of the limbic system, and is therefore also involved in motivation, emotion and learning. 112

Hormones Chemical substances that circulate in the bloodstream and affect target organs. They are produced in large quantities, disappear quickly but have powerful effects. 46–48

Hostile aggression Angry and impulsive aggression usually accompanied by physiological arousal. 64, 69

Hostile attribution bias A tendency to assume that someone else's behaviour has an aggressive or antagonistic motive when it is actually neutral. 22, 64

Hypothesis A statement of what a researcher believes to be true. In order to test such a statement, it must be clearly operationalised. 106, 121

Identification The individual temporarily goes along with the norms and roles of the group because they see membership as part of their identity. 26, 76, 84

Imitation Occurs when a learner copies the behaviour they observed being carried out by a model. It is more likely to occur when the observer identifies with the model. 10, 38

Independent groups Different participants are allocated to two (or more) experimental groups representing different levels of the independent variable. 104, 120

Independent variable (IV) A factor that is directly manipulated by the experimenter in order to observe the effect of different conditions on the dependent variable(s). 104, 121

Indirect attribute priming Associating a product with a broader context (e.g. 'natural'), so the consumer recalls the product when they think of the context. 72

Individualist People who value the rights and interests of the individual. This results in a concern for independence and self-assertiveness. People tend to live in small families unlike collectivist societies. Individualism is typical of countries like the USA, in contrast to countries such as China that tend to be collectivist. 10, 23

Inductive reasoning Using particular examples to generate a theory. 99

Inferential statistics Mathematical procedures for drawing logical conclusions (inferences) about the target population from which samples are drawn. 136

Informational social influence (ISI) We agree with the behaviour of others because we believe it is correct. We accept it because we want to be correct. 24–26

Information processing Behaviour can be understood in terms of information flowing through the cognitive (mental) system in a series of stages. 10, 16, 18

Informed consent Participants are given comprehensive information concerning the nature and purpose of a study and their role in it, so that they can make a decision about taking part. 112

In-groups and out-groups Social groups we perceive ourselves to be members of (in-groups) and not members of (out-groups). 28

Institutional aggression Aggressive or violent behaviour that takes place within the social context of a formal organised setting (e.g. a prison). 66

Instrumental aggression Goal-directed and planned aggression usually not accompanied by physiological arousal. 64, 68

Internalisation The individual goes along with the group opinion because they genuinely believe it is correct, so private views are changed. 26–27

Internal reliability The extent to which something is consistent within itself. For example, all the questions on a personality test should be measuring the same thing. 110

Inter-observer reliability The extent to which there is agreement between two or more observers. This is measured by comparing (correlating) the observations of the observers. 110, 125

Interview A 'live' encounter (face-to-face or on the phone) where one person (interviewer) asks questions to assess an interviewee's thoughts and/or experiences. Questions may be pre-set (structured interview) or may develop during the interview (unstructured interview) or a mixture (semi-structured interview). 102, 122–23, 138

Interviewer bias A form of researcher bias, in this case the researcher is an interviewer. 123

Intra-group dynamics The psychological processes that take place in any group. 30–31

Intrinsic rewards Pleasurable consequences of a behaviour that come from within the individual, e.g. feeling of achievement, interest. 36–37

Introversion One end of a personality dimension with extraversion at the other end. Introversion includes such traits as shyness, being withdrawn, avoiding new experiences. 40–41

Laboratory (lab) Any setting (room or other environment) specially fitted out for conducting research. A lab is not the only place where scientific experiments can be conducted. It is, however, the ideal place for scientific experiments because it permits maximum control. Labs are not used exclusively for experimental research – for example, controlled observations are also conducted in labs. 77, 102, 121

Laboratory experiment An experiment conducted in a very controlled environment. Usually the participants go to the researcher. 121

Lateralisation of function The two brain hemispheres are specialised to perform different functions. Some functions are mainly controlled by one hemisphere rather than the other (e.g. language). 44

Leading question A question (or statement) which, because of the way it is phrased, suggests a certain answer. For example: 'Did you see the knife in the man's hand?' (when there was no knife). 122

Learned response A behaviour acquired through conditioning, either association (classical) or rewards/punishments (operant). 10, 76

Limbic system A collection of brain structures, including the amygdala, which are involved in regulating emotional behaviour. 70–71

Literature review A systematic consideration of what other people have written or said about your chosen research topic. The word 'literature' refers to books, magazines, websites, TV programmes, etc. 106–07, 130–31

Localisation of function Specific brain areas control and regulate specific physical and psychological activities. 44

Long-term memory (LTM) Permanent memory store with practically unlimited capacity, storing memories for up to a lifetime. Encoding is mainly semantic (meaning). 12–13

Management Organising, planning, controlling and directing an organisation's resources in order to achieve its objectives. 130

MAOA **gene** The gene responsible for the activity of the enzyme monoamine oxidase A (MAOA) in the brain. The low-activity variant of the gene is associated with aggression. 70

Masculinity Traits and behaviours considered appropriate for boys/men in a particular culture, distinct from male biological sex. 81, 86–87

Mate retention strategy Methods used by one person in a sexual relationship to keep their partner. 70

Measures of central tendency The general term for any calculation of the average value in a set of data. 136

Measures of dispersion The general term for any calculation of the spread or variation in a set of scores. 136

Media Communication channels (e.g. TV, books, social media sites) through which news, entertainment, education and data are available. 66

Memory scripts See cognitive scripts

Mixed methodology A research study that uses a number of different research methods. 128

Model A person who is modelling behaviour. 11, 38

Modelling Either an observer imitates the behaviour of a model, or a model demonstrates a behaviour that may be imitated by an observer. 38, 68

Motivation The drive to behave in a way that achieves a goal or satisfies a need. 36–37

Narrative analysis See thematic analysis.

Natural experiment An experiment where the independent variable has varied as a consequence of some other action rather than the researcher's manipulation, such as comparing children who have spent time in hospital with children who haven't. 121

Natural selection The major process that explains evolution whereby inherited traits that enhance an animal's reproductive success are passed on to the next generation and thus 'selected'. Animals without such traits are less successful at reproduction and their traits are not selected. 50

Negative reinforcement In operant conditioning, the process of learning in which a behaviour is more likely to be repeated because an unpleasant stimulus is removed – the removal is rewarding. 36

Neuroanatomy Structure of the brain and other parts of the nervous system. 40, 44–45

Neurochemistry Relating to substances in the nervous system that regulate psychological functioning. 10, 48

Neuromarketing The application of the scientific study of the brain (neuroscience) to marketing (e.g. advertising). 78–79

Neuron The basic building block of the nervous system. Neurons are nerve cells that process and transmit messages through electrical and chemical signals. 40

Neurotransmitters Chemicals (e.g. serotonin) in the nervous system that transmit signals from one neuron to another across synapses. 40, 48–49

Neutral stimulus (NS) Any stimulus that does not produce the desired response. It becomes a conditioned stimulus (CS) after being paired with the unconditioned stimulus (UCS). 34–35

Nominal group process A structured method for group brainstorming that encourages contributions from everyone. 138

Non-binary A term that suggests gender (or any concept) cannot be divided into two distinct categories, e.g. gender is not a question of being a man or a woman. 80–81

Noradrenaline A hormone and a neurotransmitter that generally has an excitatory effect, similar to adrenaline. The hormone is produced by the adrenal gland. Americans use the term norepinephrine. 49

Norm Something that is standard, usual or typical of a group. 24

Normative social influence (NSI) We agree with the behaviour of others because we want to be accepted and liked, and to avoid rejection. 24, 82

Null hypothesis A statement of no difference or no relationship. 106

Objective Free from bias, uninfluenced by personal expectations, emotions or personal opinions. 98–99

Observation Actively attending to and watching (or listening to) the behaviour of others (models). 10, 38

Observer bias In observational studies there is a danger that observers' expectations affect what they see or hear. This reduces the validity of the observations. 125

Oestrogen The primary female hormone, playing an important role in the menstrual cycle and reproductive system. 86

Open question Invites respondents to provide their own answers, and tends to produce qualitative data. 122

Operant conditioning A form of learning in which behaviour is learned and maintained by its consequences – reinforcement (positive or negative) or punishment. 36, 68, 84

Operationalisation Defining variables so that they can easily be tested. 104, 122–23

Opportunity sampling A sample of participants produced by selecting people who are most easily available at the time of the study. 108

Overt observation Participant is aware of being observed. 124

Oxytocin Hormone which causes contraction of the uterus during labour, stimulates lactation and contributes to emotional bonding in women and men. 86

Parasympathetic division The part of the ANS responsible for reducing physiological (body) arousal, e.g. the rest and digest response. 46–47

Participant and non-participant observation Whether the observer is also part of the group being observed, or not. 124–25

Peer influences Refers to the effect that other people of the same age (and/or those with shared interests) have on how we think and behave. 82–83

Person perception Information stored in memory about which personality characteristics often go together, which guides our impressions of other people. 20–21

Phenotype The observable characteristics which result from the interaction between an individual's genotype and environmental factors. 42–43

Pilot study A trial run of a research study, involving only a few participants who are representative of the target population. It is conducted to test aspects of the research design, with a view to making improvements before conducting the full research study. 103, 118

Plasticity The brain is 'flexible' enough to change and adapt as a result of experience and new learning. This generally involves the growth of new connections (synapses). 44–45

Policy A course of action taken by an organisation or individual. 100–01

Positive reinforcement In operant conditioning, the process of learning in which a behaviour is more likely to be repeated because it is pleasurable – the pleasure is rewarding. 36, 68

Practice The application of an idea or method. 100–01

Prejudice A negative attitude towards a group or an individual because they are a member of that group. 28–29

Primary data Information collected by a researcher specifically for the purpose of the current study (as opposed to secondary data which is data collected by someone else, such as government statistics, and used in a new research study). 99

Priming We notice a stimulus (word, image, object, etc.) more quickly when we see or hear a related stimulus first (the 'prime'). 18, 72

Punishment The consequence of a behaviour is unpleasant, making the behaviour less likely to be repeated. 36–37

Qualitative data Information in words or pictures, non-numerical. It can be turned into quantitative data by placing the data in categories and then counting frequency. 138

Qualitative research method Any overall design for a study that produces data in the form of descriptions rather than numbers. 118

Quantitative data Information in numbers, i.e. quantities. 136

Quantitative research method Any overall design for a study that produces data in the form of numbers. 118

Quasi-experiment A study where the independent variable is not actually something that varies, such as comparing younger and older people. These are factors that cannot be changed by someone but the effects on a dependent variable can be observed. 121

Questionnaire Respondents record their own answers. The questions are predetermined (i.e. structured). 122–23, 128–29

Random allocation An attempt to control for participant variables in an independent groups design which ensures that each participant has the same chance of being in one condition as any other. 120

Random sampling A sample of participants produced using a random technique so that every member of the target population has an equal chance of being selected. 108

Rationalisation When parts of a memory are distorted to fit your schema, to make the memory meaningful. 16

Recall In free recall the individual generates information without a cue. In cued recall, a cue assists retrieval of information. 14, 80

Recognition A form of memory retrieval where you identify something based on previous experience. 14–15

Reconstructive memory Pieces of stored information are reassembled during recall. The process is guided by our schema so that we produce a 'memory' that makes sense (even if it is inaccurate). 16–17

Reinforcement A behaviour is followed by a consequence that increases the probability of the behaviour being repeated. 36–39, 68–69

Reliability Consistency of a measuring tool, including a psychological test. 110–11

Remembering The activity of retrieving information from a memory store. 14–15

Repeated measures Each participant takes part in every condition being tested. Each condition represents one level of the independent variable. 120

Repetition priming We process a stimulus more quickly (or recall it more easily) because we encountered it earlier. 18

Replication Repeating an observation or study to confirm the original finding. 18, 99

Research To investigate something systematically with the aim of demonstrating facts and producing theories. A disciplined exercise to address questions. 99

Researcher bias A researcher's expectations or beliefs which may encourage certain behaviours in participants. Leads to a researcher effect. 100

Role modelling Imitating the behaviour of people who have qualities we would like to have or who we admire (alternatively, demonstrating behaviour to be imitated). 66

Roles The functions that individuals perform within a group – task, social, procedural or individualist roles. 30–31

Sample A group of people who take part in a research investigation. The sample is drawn from a (target) population and is presumed to be representative of that population, i.e. it stands 'fairly' for the population being studied. 108

Sampling techniques A method to obtain a small number of people to represent a target population. 108

Schema Mental frameworks of beliefs and expectations that influence cognitive processing. They are developed from experience. 16, 64

Scientific process A systematic approach to gaining and verifying knowledge. 98–99

Secondary research Research using information that has already been collected by someone else and so pre-dates the current research project. In psychology, such data might include the work of other psychologists, or government statistics. 103

Self-concept How a person perceives and thinks about themselves (self-image) and values themselves and their attributes (self-esteem). 32–33

Self-efficacy A person's confidence in their ability to achieve success. 32

Self-esteem How a person values themselves and the extent to which they accept and like themselves. 32–33, 112

Self-image A person's awareness of their mental and physical characteristics, based on positive and negative beliefs about themselves. 32–33

Self-report Any method to gather data by asking people questions. 79

Semantic priming We process a stimulus more quickly (or recall it more easily) because we earlier encountered a stimulus related to it in meaning (semantics = meaning). 18

Semi-structured interview An interview where some questions are predetermined but also new questions are developed as the interview proceeds. 122

Sensory memory (SM) Memory stores for each of our five senses, e.g. vision (iconic store) and hearing (echoic store). Encoding in the iconic store is visual and in the echoic store is acoustic. Capacity is huge but duration is very brief. 12

Serotonin A neurotransmitter that generally inhibits neural activity throughout the brain. 48, 70

Sex Biological differences between males and females including anatomy, hormones and chromosomes, assigned at birth and distinct from gender. 80–81

Sex hormones Chemicals circulating in the bloodstream that affect the physical development, sexual development and behaviour of females (oestrogen) and males (testosterone). 86–87

Sex-role stereotypes A set of beliefs and preconceived views about what is expected or appropriate for women and men in a given society or social group. 81

Sexual selection Attributes or behaviours that increase reproductive success are more likely to be passed on and may become exaggerated over succeeding generations of offspring. 50–51

Shortening When part of a memory is left out, so what remains is shorter. 16–17

Short-term memory (STM) Limited-capacity memory store. Encoding is mainly acoustic (sounds), capacity is between 5 and 9 items, duration is up to 30 seconds without rehearsal. 12

Snowballing Current participants recruit further participants from among people they know. 108

Social categorisation Putting people into social groupings based on their shared characteristics (e.g. ethnicity). 28–29

Social context Influences from other people, either individually or in groups. 10, 81, 87

Social desirability bias A tendency for respondents to answer questions in such a way so as to present themselves in a 'better light'. 123

Social facilitation The tendency for individuals to perform better on a task when other people are present. 30–31

Social learning A form of learning in which behaviours are acquired through observation, modelling, imitation and vicarious reinforcement. Cognitive factors play a key role. 38, 68, 84

Social learning theory (SLT) A way of explaining behaviour that includes both direct and indirect reinforcement, combining learning theory with the role of cognitive factors. 38

Social norm Something that is standard, usual or typical of a social group. 66

Social proof In situations where we are not sure what to do or believe, we may look to other people for guidance because we think the others are better informed. 74–75

Split-half reliability A method of determining the internal reliability of a questionnaire or psychological test. Test items are split into two halves and the scores on both halves compared. Scores should be similar if the test is reliable. 110

SRY gene Sex-determining region Y gene which triggers the appearance of testes in an embryo and the development of that individual into a biological male. 42, 70

Statistics A method of collecting, summarising and analysing data for the purpose of drawing some conclusions about the data. 136

Stereotypes Fixed views of other people based on their perceived membership of a social category. 28, 66

Stratified sampling Participants are selected from different strata (subgroups) in the target population in proportion to the strata's frequency in that population. 108

Stress response Physiological changes in the body when a stressor occurs. There is an immediate response (fight or flight) regulated by adrenaline, and a longer-term response involving cortisol. 48–49

Subjectivity The tendency for a researcher to perceive or interpret information from a personal perspective, resulting in bias. The opposite of objectivity. 138

Survey (or self-report) Any method to gather data by asking people questions. 122

Survival of the fittest Natural selection selects the genes giving rise to characteristics that promote survival and reproduction so they are retained in the population. 50, 70

Sympathetic division The part of the ANS responsible for increasing physiological (body) arousal, e.g. the fight or flight response. 46, 48

Synapse The junction between two neurons. This includes the presynaptic terminal, the synaptic cleft and the postsynaptic receptor site. 44, 48

Target population The entire group a researcher is interested in, the group about which the researcher wishes to draw conclusions. For example, if a sample is taken from a group of men aged 30–60 living in London then the target population is London men in this age group and conclusions should only be applied to this target population. Usually researchers apply the conclusions to a wider population and then questions are asked about generalisability. 108, 109

Temporal validity The extent to which a research finding can be applied to other time periods. 110–11

Test-retest reliability A measure of whether something varies from one time to another, i.e. is consistent over time. A questionnaire or interview is repeated a second time to see if the same answers/score is produced. 110

Testosterone A hormone produced mainly in testes (and in smaller amounts in ovaries). 67, 70

Thematic analysis (narrative, grounded, discourse and conversation analysis) These are all forms of qualitative analysis where categories ('themes') emerge (are 'grounded') in the data. Basically the same as a content analysis but much more emphasis is placed on developing the themes from the source data. 126

Time sampling Draw up a list of behavioural categories. Then at regular intervals (such as every 5 seconds or 8 minutes), note which of the behaviours are occurring. Or take a sample at different times of day or month. 124

Traits Distinct characteristics that make up personality, e.g. friendliness, warmth, sociability, shyness, moodiness, etc. 40–41, 86

Transgender Relating to a person whose gender does not correspond with their birth sex. 81

Triangulation Comparing the results from a number of studies, some of which are highly controlled (but more 'artificial') and some with low control (but more like everyday life). If the studies have similar findings this increases the likelihood that the conclusion represents something genuine (i.e. is valid). 129, 138

Unconditioned response (UCR) An unlearned response to an unconditioned stimulus (UCS). 34–35

Unconditioned stimulus (UCS) Any stimulus that produces a response without learning taking place. 34, 76

Unstructured interview An interview where no questions are decided in advance. 122

Validity Refers to the 'trueness' or 'legitimacy' of the data collected. 110–11, 120–21

Ventral striatum Major portion of the basal ganglia and functions as part of the reward system. It includes the nucleus accumbens. 79 Verbal aggression Using words to cause psychological damage to another person, e.g. gossip, shouting. 64, 124

Vicarious learning/reinforcement Occurs when a learner observes a model's behaviour being reinforced (hence also vicarious reinforcement). 38, 68

Violent aggression Using physical force to cause physical injury to another person, e.g. punching, kicking. 64

Volunteer sampling A sample of participants produced by asking for people willing to take part. 108

Acknowledgements

p13 Photograph from Cara Flanagan's yearbook, reproduced with permission; p16 Folk tale *The War of the Ghosts* from Bartlett (1932) *Remembering: A study in experimental and social psychology*, reproduced with permission of Cambridge University Press through PLSclear; p44 Illustration of Dr Wilder Penfield, reproduced with the kind permission of Canadian Medical Hall of Fame (CMHF) and Irma Council; p45 Phineas Gage artist impression, courtesy of Barking Dog Art; p80 Photograph of Livvy James, reproduced with the kind permission of John Anyon/Worcester News; p86 Photograph of David Reimer, reproduced with the kind permission of Sipa/Shutterstock; p98 © Figure provided by Daniel Simons, www.dansimons.com, Simons, D. J., & Chabris, C. F. (1999). Gorillas in our midst: Sustained inattentional blindness for dynamic events. *Perception*, 28, 1059–1074; p112 Photograph of HM from PERMANENT PRESENT TENSE by Suzanne Corkin. Copyright © Suzanne Corkin, 2013, used by permission of The Wylie Agency (UK) Limited; p134 Photograph of Fiona Gabbert, reproduced with kind permission of Fiona Gabbert.

Picture credits

Cover © PremiumVector / Shutterstock

Shutterstock ©: p3 Rosapompelmo; p6 Mind Pixell, Subbotina Anna, Rocketclips, Inc., Bits And Splits, Tatyana Dzemileva, Kddesignphoto; p7 Simone van den Berg, Carla Francesca Castagno, studiostoks, Suwin; p8–9 Mauricio Graiki; p10 ArtFamily; p11 Eric Isselee; p12 life_infiniti; p14 Maxx-Studio; p15 Bulgn, Sarah Holmlund; p16 Ammit Jack; p17 Lisa-S; p18 Ljupco Smokovski, TheLiftCreativeServices; p19 StockImageFactory.com, Milleflore Images; p20 Sergey Mironov, Roman Samborskyi; p21 Monkey Business Images; p22 Twin Design, Dean Drobot; p23 YAKOBCHUK VIACHESLAV; p24 Cory Thoman; p25 Andrey Pavlov; p26 Timea Jager, BearFotos; p27 fizkes; p28 Carlo Toffolo, ASDF_MEDIA; p30 A. Solomennikov; p31 NDAB Creativity; p32 file404, Dean Drobot; p33 Haelen Haagen; p34 chrisdorney; p35 Maxx-Studio; p36 klee048; p37 studiostoks; p38 Royyan Wijaya; p39 OSTILL is Franck Camhi, valeriya_sh; p40 Dinendra Haria, Salienko Evgenii; p41 Gorodenkoff; p42 Kenneth Sponsler, Nathan Devery; p43 nobeastsofierce, Julien Tromeur; p45 Alex Mit p46 Tatiana Popova; p47 SciePro; p48 faizan joiya; p49 Alex Mit, Cast Of Thousands; p50 Stepan Kapl; p50–51 Dualororua; p51 Yuri Schmidt; p53 StockImageFactory.com, nobeastsofierce, Andrey Pavlov; p54 Eric Isselee; p55 ASDF_MEDIA; p56 Salienko Evgenii; p57 Cast Of Thousands; p58 Sarawut Aiemsinsuk, matkub2499; p59 iQoncept, Platova Lera; p60 indigolotos, Olga Danylenko; p61 FotoAndalucia, mammoz, oksana2010, OSTILL is Franck Camhi; p64 Ezume Images, ShotPrime Studio; p65 963 Creation; p66 John Gomez; p67 giorgiomtb; p68 lightwavemedia, Ollyy; p69 greenland; p70 Jolygon; p71 View Apart; p72 Mizkit, LightField Studios; p73 Roman Samokhin; p74 Azindianlany; p75 didesign021; p76 Sergey Kohl; p77 Frannyanne; p78 Cast Of Thousands, Garnet Photo; p79 MONOPOLY919; p81 BigPixel Photo; p82 Christian Bertrand, AJP; p83 Monkey Business Images; p84 Dfree, fotofeel; p85 Shelby Allison; p86 Gustavo Frazao; p87 Katrina Elena; p89 ShotPrime Studio, fotofeel, Katrina Elena; p93 Ermolaev Alexander, Rtstudio, Ewa Studio; p96 Ozgur Coskun; p99 MaraZe, Vladimir Gjorgiev, chrisdorney; p100 BlurryMe, Eloine Chapman; p101 Dennis Owusu-Ansah; p102 Rtimages; p103 Marcos Mesa Sam Wordley, chrisdorney; p104 Asier Romero, VectorsMarket, Ixepop; p105 glenda, Dennis Owusu-Ansah; p106 Vgstockstudio, Cast Of Thousands, Cookie Studio; p107 HobbitArt, Chanakarn Tanjun, Dennis Owusu-Ansah; p108 Aigul Elkundieva, jan kranendonk; p109 gcpics, chrisdorney; p110 Sudowoodo, DeiMosz, Bankrx, Iulian Valentin; p111 pathdoc, Dennis Owusu-Ansah; p112 Image of Henry Molaison by Suzanne Corkin. Copyright © Suzanne Corkin, 2013, used by permission of The Wylie Agency (UK) Limited, pathdoc; p113 Straight 8 Photography; p114 Elena Kharichkina; p115 andriano.cz; p117 Bits And Splits; p118 Casimiro PT, Creaturart Images; p119 Liliya Kulianionak, Elnur; p120 Burry van den Brink, Valentyn Volkov; p121 Elnur; p122 Tibanna79; p123 Elnur (both); p124 dima shiper; p125 Elnur; p126 Miro Kovacevic, Everett Collection; p127 Elnur; p128 Lenscap Photography, Denis---S; p129 Elnur; p130 Adha Ghazali, kramynina; p131 Elnur; p133 I'm Friday, Nicoleta Ionescu; p134 emka74; p135 Supreme photographer; p136 lestyan; p137 I.Dr; p138 LightField Studios; p139 Jaguar PS; p140 Jeff Baumgart, Iulia Ghimisli; p141 studiostoks, Kathy Hutchins, lev radin; p142 Giorgio1978, Rido; p143 Ken Tannenbaumgart, Iulia Ghimisli; p125 studiostoks, Kathy Hutchins, lev radin; p126 Giorgio1978, Rido; p127 Ken Tannenbaum

Alamy ©

p74 Danita Delimont / Alamy Stock Photo; p102 Everett Collection Inc / Alamy Stock Photo

Creative Commons

p34 Photograph of Ivan Petrovitch Pavlov. Photogravure after Lafayette Ltd. Wellcome Collection, London. Public Domain Mark. CC BY 4.0 (https://creativecommons.org/licenses/by/4.0)

Other illustrations © Illuminate Publishing